Christianity Mediaeval and Modern

D0528095

Christianity
Mediaeval and Modern

A Study in Religious Change

Dennis Nineham

SCM PRESS LTD

© Dennis Nineham 1993

All rights reserved. No part of this publication may be
reproduced, stored in a retrieval system, or transmitted, in
any form or by any means, electronic, mechanical
photocopying, recording or otherwise, without the prior
written permission of the publishers,
SCM Press Ltd.

334 00182 X

BATH COLLEGE OF
HIGHER EDUCATION
NEWTON PARK LIBRARY

CLASS No.
270.3 NIN

SUPPLIER
DAW

DISCARD

First published 1993
by SCM Press Ltd
26–30 Tottenham Road, London N1 4BZ

Typeset by Regent Typesetting, London
and printed in Great Britain by
Mackays of Chatham, Kent

To the Warden and Fellows of Keble College, Oxford,
in grateful recognition
of the continued kindness they have shown me
over a period of nearly a quarter of a century

Contents

Preface

In a letter to Dame Laurentia McLachlan, Edmund Bishop wrote: 'Study carefully the original documents *first* and try to see what one makes of them oneself on paper; and *then* go to modern authoritative writers. What have I not had to suffer ... by listening to "authoritative writers" and correcting myself by them? Don't mistake me: I don't say don't read 'em, one *must, it's a dereliction of duty not to do so*: BUT don't think that just by reading 'em and then going to the documents just to furbish up one's pages with correct references, one has come to *knowledge*. No: "try the Spirits", examine, verify, *try* 'em ... and one not so infrequently finds one has to "try" them by a *renewed* careful study of the original documents oneself. Amen.'[1]

He was, as usual, absolutely right, and for one who has spent most of his working life in the field of New Testament studies to have undertaken a work such as this needs something of an apology in both senses of the word. In particular, a relative newcomer to early mediaeval history is bound to some extent to plead guilty to what Bishop deprecated. I have tried, needless to say, to read the original sources as extensively as I could, and I can at least plead that I have not taken over references to those sources without going to the original myself in each case to see what it meant in context. Where secondary sources are concerned, there is one I should like to single out for special mention, namely the Thèse d'État of J. Chélini, *La Vie Religieuse des Laïcs dans l'Europe Carolingienne*, which for some reason seems not to have been published. I recall the pleasure, not to say profit, with which I spent many days in Duke Humfrey's Library reading the four large volumes of it in typescript.

As for apology in the sense of self-explanation, I have tried to provide that in the introductory chapter. Having written this book fully persuades me that the best way of discovering whether and in what ways a religion changes is by examining various phases of it, each in the appropriate historical and cultural context. I shall feel I have succeeded if the book – even perhaps by its very defects – persuades others to make a similar approach to the period covered here and to other phases of the history of Christianity. I fancy a background in sociology would be of great assistance.

Writing a book of this sort requires that one should have many of the

key texts and secondary authorities at one's elbow, and I should like to
thank a number of librarians who have made that possible for me by giving
me special concessions and showing exemplary patience with a borrower
who must at times have seemed unlikely ever to return his loans. Gratitude
is particularly due to the librarians of Keble and Manchester Colleges,
Oxford; Bristol University Library; Ripon College, Cuddesdon; St
Stephen's House Theological College; and the Oxford History and Theology Faculty Libraries. The staff of Bodley's Library work nowadays under
difficult conditions, as a consequence of inadequate funding, but within
the severe constraints that imposes, they have been very helpful, especially
Miss Jackie Dean of the Lower Reading Room desk, and Mr Richard Bell,
the Head of Reader Services. I should also like to offer warm thanks to
Miss Jennifer Ellis for typing a considerable portion of a difficult manuscript with cheerfulness and great efficiency.

A word is perhaps in place about the Bibliography. After some thought I
decided to give no list of original sources. Specialists will in any case know
where to look, while for other readers the references in the notes will
probably suffice. Professional historians may be surprised that these
references are normally to Migne's *Patrologia Graeca* and *Patrologia
Latina*. This is deliberate: the book is intended for theologians and
theological students as much as for historians, and I guess that many such
students will have access to the volumes of Migne, but not to better and
later editions. Where anything seemed to hang on the differences between
these editions and Migne, the critical text in MGH or some more modern
edition has been cited. The secondary literature is vast, and I have confined
the Bibliography to books and articles I found particularly useful in
writing the book. It may be worth pointing out that where the word
Religious is spelt with a capital R, it refers, as in the Middle Ages, to the
monastic life and the men and women engaged in it. Paragraphs in smaller
type draw out general points in greater detail, or provide illustrative and
justificatory material, without affecting the general drift of the book.

I have been grateful for the continued support and encouragement of
friends, especially John Bowden, the publisher of the book, who has been
unfailingly helpful since the project was first broached with him some
ten years ago, my old friend Tom Baker, who read through an almost
indecipherable manuscript and made many helpful suggestions, and that
best of all friends, my wife, who has done the same for me, and a thousand
other things as well. Tom Baker and Christopher Evans also gave me
invaluable help with proof correcting and index preparation.

Abbreviations

AA SS	*Acta Sanctorum*, Antwerp 1643ff.
AA SS OSB	*Acta Sanctorum Ordinis S.Benedicti* (9 vols), Paris 1688–1701
Aelfric	*The Homilies of Aelfric*, ed. B. Thorpe (2 vols), London 1844, 1846 (first part of *The Homilies of the Anglo-Saxon Church*)
Anal Boll	*Analecta Bollandiana*, Paris and Brussels 1882ff.
CCcm	*Corpus Christianorum: continuatio medievalis*
CCL	Corpus Christianorum (Series Latina), Turnhout 1953ff.
CMH	*Cambridge Medieval History*, ed. J.B. Bury et al. (8 vols), Cambridge 1911ff.
CSEL	*Corpus Scriptorum Ecclesiasticorum Latinorum*
EH	*English Hymnal*, London 1906
EHR	*English Historical Review*, London 1886ff.
ERE	*Encyclopaedia of Religion and Ethics*, ed. J. Hastings (13 vols), Edinburgh 1908ff.
Homélies	*XIV Homélies du IXe Siècle*, ed. P. Mercier, Paris 1970
MGH	Monumenta Germaniae Historica
Neale	J.M. Neale, *Mediaeval Preachers and Mediaeval Preaching*, London 1856
PG	Patrologia Graeca, ed. J.P. Migne, 162 vols., Paris 1857ff.
PL	Patrologia Latina. ed. J.P. Migne, 221 vols., Paris 1844ff.
RS	Rolls Series, London 1858ff.
SCH	*Studies in Church History*, London 1964ff.
ST	St Thomas Aquinas, *Summa Theologica* (there are many editions)
Vulg	Vulgate

(The Bible was read in the tenth century in a variety of Latin versions, but principally in Jerome's version, known as the Vulgate. These versions included what is known today as the Apocrypha as a full part of scripture. Chapter and verse divisions hardly existed, but when these were added later they often differed from those in the standard English translations. In such cases both references are given: e.g. Ps. 31.24 [30.25] means that what is verse 24 of Psalm 31 in the English versions is verse 25 of Psalm 30 in the Latin.)

1

Introduction

The origins of this study lie in a long-standing preoccupation with the question of the relation between religion and cultural change. The book makes no claim to be a piece of disinterested historical research, even were such a thing possible, nor does it claim to uncover hitherto unknown truth about the past. The focus of attention is on the question: does, and should, religion change in response to alterations in the cultural situation? That is a question of considerable interest to Christians, not least at a time when the church is being encouraged in some quarters to allow its stance to be controlled by a tradition of teaching which arose in cultural contexts very different from any in the modern West.

Debate on the matter has been inconclusive, partly, it may be suspected, because it has generally been conducted at a high level of generality. It therefore seemed worth exploring whether an appeal to a specific period in the past might be illuminating. If it were possible to show in some detail what it meant to be a religious believer at a particular time and place in the past, it might also be possible to discover how far it meant just that, as the result of identifiable historical, economic, social and other conditioning factors.

Readers might then be able to judge for themselves how far being a believer then was different from being a believer now (or at any other time in history); how important the differences are; and how far they are the result of cultural conditioning, both past and present.

When it came to choosing a time and place to study, the limitations of the author's knowledge dictated that the believers studied should have been Christians; and considerations of practicability suggested that the time and place should be ones about which there was evidence enough, but where the enquiry was not rendered unmanageable either by superabundance of available material or by the existence of a very wide belief-range among the people to be studied. It also seemed wise to avoid periods, such as that of the New Testament or the Reformation, to which many modern readers might be expected to have strong emotional reactions. At the same time, the period needed to be sufficiently remote from our own for significant differences, if any, to be likely to show up clearly.

The choice eventually fell on northern France in the period just before and after 1000 CE. Mediaevalists will recognize this as something of an end of an era, from a religious point of view; but they may express surprise at the choice on the grounds that few writings of any religious significance were produced at the time, and that it is notoriously difficult to discover what the feelings of tenth-century people were, including their feelings about religion. It is also true that Frankish society at the time was sharply divided into a number of separate groupings, and that people's outlook will have varied considerably according to the group to which they belonged. What is more, literacy was confined to the upper classes – in fact mainly to one of them – and the mass of the people have left us no direct evidence of their feelings and beliefs.

'The proof of the pudding is in the eating,' and readers will judge for themselves how far these difficulties have been overcome in what follows, based, as it is, on printed sources and secondary authorities. One thing, however, may be said at once. The culture of the early Middle Ages was a relatively static one, so that it is sometimes (though by no means always) possible to use texts from earlier periods, and occasionally even from later periods, as evidence for the tenth century.

Something needs to be said about the spirit in which this study has been undertaken. When dealing with the beliefs and outlooks of earlier periods, ecclesiastical historians often adopt one of two approaches. Some tend to emphasize certain elements in past expressions of the faith which they isolate from their contexts and treat as timeless truths. For example, in the period we shall be studying the idea of transubstantiation as an explanation of what happens in the mass was explicitly formulated for the first time, and increasingly accepted. Roman Catholic historians have sometimes treated it in the way described, regarding it as a doctrine true for all subsequent ages which just happened to receive explicit recognition for the first time in this period. Such a way of looking at things, however, seems to underestimate the interconnectedness of ideas in a particular cultural context. There certainly are truths which achieve recognition for the first time at a particular date, in the sort of way envisaged. For example, the heliocentric character of the solar system was discovered – or, strictly speaking, re-discovered – at the time of the Renaissance; but the logic of religious belief-statements is different from that of astronomical hypotheses. Statements about the supernatural have to be made in the terms of ordinary language, used in a non-literal sense. For that reason, if no other, religious discourse is very closely bound up with the contemporary use of language in general. It is therefore questionable how far one element of a religious system can be isolated from its linguistic context and treated as valid for all later formulations of the religion in question. For example, the doctrine of transubstantiation uses 'substance' as a philosophical concept in a way that few philosophers today feel able to accept.

Other church historians adopt what may appear to be an exactly opposite approach. They tend to absolutize *our* understanding of

Christianity, and use it as a yardstick for evaluating earlier understandings, rather as a schoolmaster marks the work of his pupils, judging it by the criterion of his own understanding of the subject, taken as an absolute.

In fact both approaches share the assumption that we now know what Christianity is and can evaluate earlier expressions of it in the light of that knowledge. No doubt there is an element of truth here – it would be strange if religion were the only area in which new insights had not been granted or achieved. Nevertheless, *our* perception of what Christianity is is presumably as culturally conditioned as any previous perceptions have been; and while our circumstances may enable us to appreciate things to which earlier periods were blind, they may also blind us to things which they appreciated. The danger is that if you begin to study the outlook of some bygone group with the inbuilt assumption that their outlook was only an imperfect approximation to your own, you will find difficulty in taking them and their outlook seriously. You will emphasize elements which contained the seeds of what you regard as legitimate later developments, and overlook, or soft-pedal, those that did not. You will find it hard really to understand their outlook, for in their eyes their faith was not just an imperfect adumbration of what was to come later, but *the* way of salvation, the means of communion between God and man, the truth according to which they were content to live and in which they hoped to die.

In the process you rob history of a good deal of its interest. In 1854 the German historian Leopold von Ranke discussed this matter. He spoke scathingly of an understanding of progress according to which the life of mankind raises itself higher in every generation in such a way that each generation completely transcends the one before, with the result that the latest generation has the advantage, earlier generations being only the bearer of what was to come after. This, he says, 'would be an injustice on the part of God. Such a "mediatized" generation would not have any significance in and for itself. It would have significance only as a step up to the following generation, and it would not stand in any direct relationship to God.' Against this he states his clear opposition: 'I maintain that every epoch is in unmediated relationship with God (*ist unmittelbar zu Gott*) and that its worth rests not on what arises from it but on its own existence, its own peculiar characteristics.' He adds: 'The study of history and of the individual life in history gains its unique attraction only as the result of the fact that every epoch must be viewed as something valuable in itself, the study of which appears worthwhile in the highest degree.'[1]

On such a showing, the aim must be, in another phrase of von Ranke's, to uncover the past 'as it actually happened' (*wie es eigentlich gewesen*). What that means in this case may be made clearer if we look at the work of an anthropologist. When Branislow Malinowski studied the religion of the Trobriand Islanders, he did not assume that religion is a homogeneous transcultural phenomenon of which the elements, such as magic or witchcraft, for example, can be provided with a general definition, and then attempt to fit the religion he was studying into the procrustean bed of that conceptual framework. He realized, or at any rate went a long way towards realizing, that religion can only usefully be discussed with reference to a specific case where what count as the divine, as belief, and as criteria of right belief, have had assigned to them the definite value proper to them in a particular community.[2] What he attempted to do was to describe the various elements in the religion of the Trobriand Islanders, and the manner of their articulation, and then to explore why just those elements and that articulation seemed to the Islanders the obviously right and natural ones.

To do that involved him in a careful exploration of the history of the Islanders and of their cultural and economic situation. Only so was there any hope of even beginning to see the matter as they themselves saw it. Malinowski had to spend a long time among the Islanders, long enough for them to stop thinking of him as an alien intruder and to trust him enough to be prepared to confide in him the inwardness of their religion as they experienced it, and for him to be able to understand what they were saying. There was no question of his attempting to 'mark' their beliefs and practices against some supposedly objective scale, or trying to show that it was right here and wrong there, or even that it was nearer the truth in some places than in others. Apart from anything else, the cultural gap between the Trobriand Islanders and the Western world was too great for that to be practicable.

So far as that supplies a model for such a study as this, it also highlights the difficulties. Malinowski had personal contact with the subjects of his study and could ask them questions. From the tenth century we have only inanimate remains, particularly books, and the trouble with books, as Plato said,[3] is that you cannot ask them questions; and the books are in any case silent on many matters about which we should like information. For this study is not simply an essay in the history of doctrine, as that term is usually understood. We shall be concerned with the attitudes and factors which gave rise to the doctrine and with the attitudes and outlook to which it in turn gave rise.

In the light of the anthropological model, we shall not expect to find a single coherent pattern of either belief or practice. Every group of human beings has a story, that is, a symbolic or pictorial account of the total environment in which it finds itself. The situation is never tidy, however. No group has ever produced or inherited a story and then deduced from it a set of attitudes and patterns of behaviour, as by a logical process. The reasons for the untidiness vary according to the situation. In a pluralist society such as ours, there are various groups and sub-groups, each with its own story; and the very fact that people are aware of this makes them the more unwilling to have their lives entirely conditioned by *any* story: they become sceptical of the claims of stories. Also they are in a position to know something of the content of stories other than that of their own group, and they sometimes allow certain aspects of their lives to be moulded by those other stories in a way which is not strictly consistent with the tenor of their own group's story.

Even in a society such as we shall be studying, which was much more nearly a society of a single story, we must not expect too much tidiness. The religious story, at any rate where the 'higher' religions are concerned, usually exists in two forms, or on two levels, the mythological and the doctrinal. The mythological form consists of a number of myths, legends and 'historical' narratives which have grown up in various periods and circumstances, and exhibit at most a limited unity and coherence. Precisely for that reason, there also exists a doctrinal form of the story. This results from an attempt to combine the contents of the various myths and narratives into a single, intellectually consistent, whole. Such an attempt requires considerable sophistication, and as a result, the full doctrinal system of a religion will normally be beyond the comprehension of the majority of the adherents, and many of them will be largely ignorant of it. The story as it affects them will for the most part be the mythological story, and some of them will be more impressed by some elements of it, others by others, with consequent differences in its overall impact on their attitudes and behaviour.

What is more, the story is far from being all there is to a religion. There are also the patterns of behaviour, private and corporate, and the rites and devotional practices, as well as many other elements. Most of the behaviour patterns and ritual practices will owe their authority to their customary status. They will often have derived from much earlier times, which were governed by a different form of the story, or even by a quite different religious story altogether. Consequently they will sometimes mesh in very imperfectly with the story in its current form. In that case either the story may be augmented or modified to take account of these practices ('aetiological myths') or, very often, the practices may have come in the course of time to seem so obviously appropriate, and indeed necessary, that their incompatibility with the current form of the story will either escape notice or not be deemed important enough to deserve any action.

Every religious system is thus in an uneasy, and often unstable, state of equilibrium. The way the various elements are articulated, and the degree of emphasis placed on each, may vary a good deal; and if a religion lasts, and finds expression in a number of cultural settings, not only is the balance of emphasis as between the elements likely to vary from one situation to another, but some elements are likely to be dropped, to all intents and purposes, and others to be added.

On one matter the anthropological parallel offers a warning: we must make no *a priori* assumption about whether Christianity is basically always and everywhere the same, or approach the tenth-century Franks with an implicit definition of it, into which we try to fit their belief and practice.

Lastly, if Malinowski's need for prolonged personal contact with the subjects of his study suggests that an enquiry such as this should be undertaken, if at all, only by a lifelong professional mediaevalist, there may be truth in that. The most that can be done is to quote Chesterton's dictum that 'if a thing is worth doing it is worth doing badly', and to express the hope that the very inadequacies of what is presented here may provoke some competent mediaevalist to give a more adequate account.

2

The Franks

Who were the inhabitants of tenth-century France whose cultural situation and religious outlook we shall be studying? They were known as Franks, a name originally used for a group of composite tribes who by the third century CE were dwelling on the east bank of the middle and lower Rhine. In the fourth century they crossed into northern Brabant as confederates (*foederati*) of the Romans, and then, under a series of able military leaders, expanded westwards, until in the later fifth century, led by the warlike Clovis (a Germanic form of Louis), they were in control of all parts of what is now France, except for Brittany, Burgundy and Provence, and of considerable areas of modern western Germany. By this time many of them, and some of their leaders, had been converted to Christianity, and the process reached completion at the end of the century (the precise date is uncertain) when Clovis himself accepted baptism and, after the manner of the time, brought the remainder of his people with him, at least formally.

Although comparatively little is known about the Franks' customs and ways of life before their conversion, some of these proved influential later. Frankish institutions were designed for an agricultural civilization based on single estates or small villages, each one being more or less coterminous with a clan, whose members claimed common ancestry. The villagers divided the available arable land among them in strips while enjoying communal rights over the adjacent forestland, pastureland and sources of water. The basic unit was the tribe, whose members were divided fairly rigidly into three groups: the nobility, whose members claimed descent from the gods and wielded the effective power, both in peace and war; the freemen – the great majority – who were expected to bear arms and had the right to attend the assembly, though not to initiate business; and a group comprising the semi-free *liberti* (freedmen) and the *laeti* (subject members of other tribes), slaves and certain others. The women seem to have had very few rights.

Frankish law was customary law, and according to it the clan had a very large part to play, being expected to provide protection and justice for its members. If the person or honour of one of them was injured, the exaction of an appropriate restitution was the duty of the clan, which had to prosecute a feud, or vendetta, against the guilty party if he or she could be discovered. In the course of time virtually every crime came to have an accepted price assigned to it, and guilty parties could expiate their wrongdoing by paying the appropriate *Wergild*, or man-price. The size of this depended not only on the nature of the injury but on the rank and status of the victim. Injuring a member of a noble family, or one of its animals, for example, attracted a much higher payment than a comparable injury to a freeman.

So far as it is possible to reconstruct early Frankish customs, it seems that, at any rate in time of war, the nobles chose an overall chieftain from among their ranks, the main criterion being natural capacity, though once appointed, a chieftain usually tried to hand on his position to members of his family, a process that could lead to a great deal of rivalry, since primogeniture was not part of Frankish custom. Like other nobles, a chieftain had a right to a 'following' and was expected to take counsel with his *comites*, or comrades.

Literacy, though not unknown, was rare, and in general the Franks of this period were culturally primitive. Focillon wrote of them that 'by their mentality (*statut moral*), their political organization, their instincts and their art, they belong to pre-history, or, if you like, to proto-history'.[1]

He had in mind that 'the moral life of the princes is without any restraint; their annals are a long succession of acts of violence, assassinations, spoliations, perjuries and cruelties inflicted on the weak'. No one who has read the accounts of them, even after their nominal conversion to Christianity, in the pages of Gregory of Tours, will hesitate to agree with that.

War was virtually a way of life with these people; every able-bodied free male was trained for it from youth, and courage was the supreme virtue, for which murder, rapine and rape could be forgiven. Franks of all classes were people of very strong emotions and urges, with very little inclination or ability to avoid giving them instant expression. They treated one another ferociously and inflicted savage punishments on alleged criminals, whose guilt had been established by very insecure methods. In scattered and ill-lit communities, with slow means of communication, it was difficult to establish the facts, and trials were often decided on the evidence of compurgators, men of good standing who testified to their belief in the innocence of the accused,[2] or by subjecting both parties to the ordeal, which consisted of a test such as walking through a fire or standing for a long time with arms outstretched, the one who emerged the more unscathed being presumed innocent. The assumption was that the supernatural powers were involved and would not countenance an inequitable outcome.

Just how these supernatural power were conceived or worshipped it is hard to say in detail.[3] The early Franks were certainly polytheists, and honoured their gods with sacrificial offerings and sacred meals, usually held in sacred groves, on mountains or in the proximity of sacred trees, stones or springs. They seem to have shared the general Germanic belief in an after-life and in the close relations between the dead and their successors. The will of the gods was discovered through oracles, and innumerable rites were practised to ensure health, prosperity, the fertility of the crops and herds, and success in war.

There appears to have been no professional priesthood, political and religious functions being the responsibility of the same leaders, especially the chieftains. Religion was essentially a practical matter; like most peoples at a comparable stage of development, the Franks expected tangible practical help from the gods they worshipped. It is characteristic that, according to Gregory of Tours,[4] when Clovis accepted Christianity, it was because of what he took to be evidence that Christ was a more effective help in battle than the Germanic gods.

Whatever the motives for it may have been, Clovis's conversion had some important consequences for his people. Whether he realized it or not, his decision to opt for the Catholic version of Christianity, in contrast to the Arian version adopted by most other Germanic leaders, was a sound one politically. His being a Catholic endeared him to his Gallo-Roman subjects, who were Catholics, thus making the unification of the population much easier. It also ensured him the support of the Gallo-Roman inhabitants in the territories of any other Germanic tribes he might decide to invade; and it made him *persona grata* with the popes, who came to regard the Franks as their favourite sons and to look to them for defence and protection.

With all this behind them, Clovis's sons extended the Frankish territory to include Burgundy, Provence and further areas of Germany; but the dynasty – known as the Merovingians, after Meroveus, their (semi-) legendary founder – became effete, and in 751, with the support of the papacy, it was superseded by another line in the person of Pepin the Short, who was anointed king by Boniface, and later, with his family, by the pope himself, on the model of the anointing of David and Solomon in the Old Testament. This line, known as the Carolingian, ruled the part of France with which we shall be concerned more or less continuously until 987, when Hugh Capet was appointed king and began the Capetian line.

The most outstanding member of the Carolingian line – from whom in fact it gets its name – was Charles the Great (Charlemagne, ruled 768–814), who may have been something of an old ruffian, but was also something of a genius, a man of outstanding energy and political and military ability. Under him the Frankish territories were extended to include parts of northern Italy and northern Spain and further areas of what is now western Germany, the inhabitants of the newly conquered Saxon lands being forcibly converted to Christianity.

As we have seen, pre-Christian Frankish chieftains fulfilled religious functions, and Charlemagne believed that he, like his Old Testament counterparts, was responsible for the spiritual as well as the temporal well-being of his subjects.

At the time of Clovis's conversion, Christian clergy in Gaul had been few, so that the Franks had had to be baptized thousands at a time, with a minimum of preliminary instruction. Consequently their Christianity was only skin-deep, and that continued to be the case throughout the Merovingian period. Charlemagne decided on a programme of religious education and consolidation. He gathered at his court at Aachen a group of outstanding scholars from all over Europe and caused accurate copies of the Latin classics to be made and studied. The idea was to deepen knowledge of the Latin language, so that the Bible – known to the Franks only in Latin versions – could be more accurately understood and expounded. He sent to Rome for copies of the services and canon law in use there, with a view to ensuring that the practice of Christianity in his territories should conform exactly with the authoritative Roman model. He ordered the founding of schools, and encouraged his bishops to meet and promulgate instructions on faith and morals; he backed their directives with secular sanctions, and supplemented them, where necessary, with religious legislation of his own.

Although he enjoyed the titles 'king of the Franks' and, after 800, 'emperor of the Romans', it was not primarily in these terms that Charlemagne conceived his position. He thought of himself, rather, as a tribal leader, what in England would have been called a *Bretwealda*, that is, a warrior who had inherited, or established, authority over other warriors and their followers, and kept it by force of personality and arms. There was no fisc; Charlemagne relied on the spoils of war, and sometimes on property purloined from the church, for the largesses needed to keep his *comites* (by this stage perhaps best translated 'counts') satisfied and loyal. The sheer size of his domains meant that he had to appoint members of his *comitatus* (which now included many bishops) as semi-independent rulers of various parts, though at the same time he inaugurated a system whereby personal representatives (*missi*) chosen by him perambulated the kingdom and reported to him on the loyalty, competence and fair dealing of the counts.

Basically, he regarded his realm, just as his forebears had done, as his private possession, to be divided among the members of his family at his death. It so happened that in 814, when he died, there was only one son, Louis the Pious, to succeed him; but when Louis died in 840, he had arranged for the kingdom to be divided between his sons. Predictably – especially as a second marriage and family had caused him to alter his original dispositions – this led to rivalry and armed confrontation between the heirs, with the result that central authority was gravely weakened. All this happened at a particularly critical time, for between the middle of the

ninth and the middle of the tenth century Francia was subjected to a
further, and very savage, wave of barbarian invasion, this time from the
Vikings, or Norsemen, of Scandinavia.

These skilled and intrepid seamen attacked the coastal areas, often
penetrating far inland up the major waterways. At first they concentrated
on sudden and brief incursions, pillaging monasteries, palaces and castles,
or exacting Danegeld before they withdrew, and causing widespread
devastation if they were unsuccessful.

> The scale of their attacks was considerable. They are said to have mounted
> forty-seven major invasions of Frankish territory, sacking, among other places,
> Rouen, Nantes, Toulouse, Paris (which they spared on one occasion for seven
> thousand pounds of silver), Reims, Dordrecht, Limoges, Bordeaux (where they
> massacred the population), Beauvais, Bayeux, St Lo, Meaux, Evreux and
> Tours, which was pillaged at least seven times.

In the tenth century the situation changed and the raiders became more
interested in settling, being willing to do at least nominal homage to the
king in return for the grant of lands.[5] When the first rumblings of the
Viking incursions made themselves heard, even Charlemagne was hard
put to it to deal with them; the weakened central authority after the time of
Louis was quite incompetent to do so, though some of the kings were more
successful than might have been expected. The result was that, so far as
defence was possible, it had to be provided piecemeal by the nobles in
charge of individual areas. The king's peculiar status as the Lord's
anointed was still recognized, but what were virtually separate territorial
states began to crystallize, and, so far as the great majority of the people
were concerned, their *effective* sovereign was the local lord, supported by
his vassals. The period was one of dispersion of power, and of social
disintegration, throughout western Francia.

The effect was the more significant because advances in military technique had greatly altered the balance of power between the classes. As we
have seen, in early Frankish society the mass of men were expected to bear
arms, and as recently as 732, when Charles Martel, a forebear of the
Carolingians, had defeated Muslim forces at the battle of Tours and
Poitiers, foot-soldiers had played their part. After that, however, the use of
infantry had become unnecessary, and the freeman class had become what
was called an *inerme vulgus,* a crowd without arms, forced to rely for their
defence on those who could afford horses and cavalry equipment. Those
who were not equipped to fight were bound to be at the mercy of those
who were, and in conditions such as those of the Viking invasions,
Frankish farmers and their families had no alternative but to put themselves under the protection of local members of the ruling class. These
latter imposed contractual obligations in return for such protection as they
afforded; and although for a time their protégés enjoyed a variety of

statuses, which carried greater or less degrees of freedom and independence, in practice they developed into a single class which comprised
the overwhelming majority of the people, and was almost totally under the
domination of the various local lords. Conditions varied somewhat, but
broadly these people were expected to contribute a specified proportion of
their produce to the lord's support, to work for a specified number of days
each year on his private land, to carry out the building and carting work he
needed done, to pay for the grinding of their corn at his mill and to fulfil
certain other obligations; and the contract always specified that these
conditions applied also to their descendants. Their status thus became
hereditary.

Arrangements regarding their smallholdings and the management of
communal land followed broadly those which had obtained in early
Frankish times. Immemorial custom largely controlled relations between
villagers, and those of villagers with their lord; but although evidence
might be given by the older men as to what the custom was, in the last
resort matters of dispute had to be decided in the lord's court, and in
practice there was little right of appeal. Consequently the will of the lord
normally prevailed, and the peasants – for this is what they had in fact
become – had little alternative but to accept it.

To return briefly to the early days of Frankish settlement in the West, it is
important to emphasize that though the invaders were often violent and
cruel, they were in general content to settle alongside the Gallo-Roman
and other inhabitants of the country, allowing them to keep a considerable
portion of their land and, what is more, to live in accordance with their
own codes of law. For all its violence, their conquest may be described as a
sort of symbiosis with the existing inhabitants. The Franks had a high
regard for Roman culture – what they called *Romanitas* – and they were
content to be permeated and deeply influenced by the culture of the much
larger Gallo-Roman population among whom they had settled. The
cultural significance of that must not be overestimated, however. Although Gaul had once been a highly civilized part of the Roman empire,
Roman civilization had degenerated drastically by the time the last Roman
emperor in the West, Romulus Augustulus, was removed from power in
476. The cities, and the excellent system of communications between
them, on which Roman civilization had rested, had largely disappeared in
the West, and the economy had become a scattered rural one presided over
by local magistrates, bishops and landlords, many of the people being
reduced to a more or less serf-like status.

The result was that culturally, the Gallo-Romans by whom the Frankish
invaders were confronted on arrival were not dissimilar from themselves;
this made intermarriage and cultural assimilation relatively easy, though
they did not take place on any large scale for some time. By the tenth
century, however, the Franks of our area were quite largely of mixed,

mainly Gallo-Roman and Frankish, descent, but that did not mean that they were any less bellicose than their Frankish forebears had been. Although the old Frankish tongue was still understood as late as the ninth century, by the tenth century the Franks of the north-west were generally Romance-speakers, something which had begun to divide them from their German-speaking fellows further east; this also meant that, despite the relatively recent development of their language, they could no longer understand Latin or the services of the church which were conducted in it.

Frankish life in the tenth century was thus comparatively primitive. The great majority of the people lived in small, scattered and isolated settlements, such towns as there were being very small – by modern standards little more than villages – each one clustering round a palace, castle or monastery on which its economy depended. Life was accordingly extremely isolated.[6]

The houses of the peasants were no more than small huts, into which whole families were crowded; and even the castles and palaces were cold, damp and uncomfortable, and provided little more opportunity for privacy than the peasants had. There has been considerable disagreement about the extent and depth of the suffering caused to ordinary people by the Viking invasions. Contemporary sources paint a very dark picture, but it must be remembered that these were all the work of ecclesiastics, and churches and monasteries, with their treasures, are likely to have been the worst sufferers.[7]

Whatever the truth of that may have been, this was an age when war, including war between rival Frankish lords, was the normal condition, rather than peace, and the peasants could suffer terribly from the hostilities, being driven from their homes and having their houses and lands devastated and their crops burnt; Wood speaks of 'the Dark Age equivalent of modern saturation bombing or chemical warfare'.[8] Food was in chronically short supply and most of the people were undernourished, at any rate by modern standards. Famine and disease were rife.[9]

Here the lack of technology was important. Crop yields were low and farming methods, although labour-intensive – and the labour was the hardest of hard labour at that – were highly inefficient. At first wooden ploughs, suitable only for light Mediterranean soils, were in use; and even when heavier metal-shod ploughs, and harnesses suitable for horses, instead of the slow oxen, became available, lack of money and peasant hostility to change prevented their introduction until well into our period. Exact figures are hard to arrive at, but the rate of yield seems often to have been less than 1.6:1, and rarely more than 2:1; and it has to be remembered that of what they produced the peasants had to give a substantial proportion to their lords; so, when provision of seed-corn is taken into account, the amount of food available for them and their families and animals must have been very small.

Such was the situation when conditions were favourable. Pierre Riché has drawn from contemporary sources a list of the natural disasters that could interfere with these conditions, and gives a harrowing account of the situations that resulted.[10] The lack of communications-technology prevented the large-scale movement of food from one area to another to deal with such situations.

The widespread and often chronic malnutrition which resulted from shortage of food lowered resistance to the variety of diseases which were always present and often reached epidemic proportions.[11] The overcrowding, lack of ventilation, sharing of accommodation with animals, insanitary and pest-ridden conditions, and absence of even elementary hygiene rendered the poorer people in particular highly vulnerable to infection.

The rate of infant mortality was high, even in the noblest families. In one set of graves which has been excavated, child skeletons formed forty per cent of the total. Even in the twelfth century there was a life expectancy of only forty or fifty years, and in the ninth century Einhard, the friend and biographer of Charlemagne, was reckoned to be at an advanced age when he died at sixty-five. Charlemagne himself, who lived to be seventy-two, was regarded as a positive prodigy of longevity. In his day only thirty-nine per cent of women reached the age of forty, and of the men less than a third got to fifty. Death was a constant feature of life.

Whatever the precise effects of the Viking attacks, it seems safe to borrow a phrase from Thomas Hobbes and describe the life of these Franks as 'solitary, poor, nasty, brutish and short'.[12] Only the first word in that quotation calls for further comment. We have seen that the great majority of people lived in small rural communities. These were often in isolated locations surrounded by dense forest or undrained swamp, into which villagers were afraid to penetrate. In many cases, therefore, there was little communication between one settlement and another. On a larger scale, too, the Frankish community as a whole was isolated. Poor communications meant that even the rulers knew very little about what was happening outside their own territories. The world of the Eastern empire, and of the increasingly separate Eastern church, was visited by few; the world of Islam by even fewer. Consequently, even the affairs and policies of the Byzantine world were little understood, to say nothing of the movements of tribes and nations further east, although these often impinged indirectly on the West, for instance in their influence on the Magyar invasions which coincided with those of the Vikings. As a result, events which could in principle have been understood in ordinary terms, and prepared for in advance, could only be understood as direct acts of God.

By contrast, if solitariness is taken to mean individual privacy, that, as we have seen, is something in which the early mediaeval world was almost wholly lacking. Whether at court or in the monastery, in the castle or the peasant's hovel, the mediaeval man or woman lived cheek by jowl with others, both by day and night. This, as we shall see, had its importance for religion.

3

The Cultural Background

We have looked at ways in which the outlook of the northern Franks in the tenth century was influenced by their Frankish origins and early history. It was also influenced, however, by the culture of the Gallo-Roman world in which, by the tenth century, they had been living for some five hundred years. Gallo-Roman culture derived mainly from that of the ancient Romans, and ultimately from Greek civilization; but the situation had deteriorated throughout the western Roman empire, and by the tenth century little was known directly of classical, or indeed more recent, Greek thought.[1] The secular schools were closed in the fifth and sixth centuries; after that virtually no one in the West could read Greek, and the Greek classics were a closed book, except for a few works such as Aristotle's *Categories* and *de Interpretatione*, which had been translated into Latin by Boethius (c.480 to c.524). Even these could not be properly understood, because it is impossible to understand answers without understanding the questions they were intended to settle, and the early Middle Ages had no comprehension of the problems which had preoccupied the classical Greek philosophers. Nor had they any understanding of the dialectical method which the works of Plato and others presuppose. It is significant that in his *Etymologies* Isidore of Seville (c.560 to 636), one of the chief purveyors of classical learning to our period, treated *philosophia* as little more than a container in which minor subjects are arranged in a comprehensive plan.[2]

So far as classical thought percolated to the early Middle Ages, it was mainly through the medium of ecclesiastical writers, but the influence was no less powerful for that. Most of the Fathers, as the Christian writers of the early centuries were called, had been steeped in ancient philosophical thought and deeply influenced by it, even if they had not always understood it fully; and through Augustine in particular, many Platonic ways of thinking reached the mediaeval West, though they were often employed rather simplistically.

Plato taught that only what is unchanging is fully real and worthy of study; in fact it alone can be known. *Epistēmē*, knowledge in the full sense, is possible only in dealing with the lasting and immutable, that is, the divine,[3] the unchanging principles of logic and mathematical relations, musical intervals and their relation to the length of the string, or the behaviour of the heavenly bodies, which, although they move, do so according to a changelessly recurring pattern. Acquaintance with the changing physical objects and relationships which make up the empirical world can never be more than *doxa*, usually translated 'opinion' (the stress being on the vagueness and uncertainty), and is no part of the liberal sciences, that is, those appropriate to the *liber*, or free man.[4] The world of nature is the province of artisans and slaves, who may be able to cope with it satisfactorily at the practical level (*technē*), but have neither the education nor the leisure to theorize about it. The result was that the Greeks, who excelled so in art and philosophical speculation, were comparatively speaking weak in science, and particularly technology. If these were not despised, they were certainly not regarded as a subject for the attention of a free man.

> If Aristotle's empirical investigations seem at first sight to belie this, a closer reading will serve only to confirm it. A revealing example of the late classical outlook on the matter is provided by the fifth-century pagan writer Martianus Capella, who defended the absence of medicine and architecture from the seven 'liberal' arts on the ground that 'their attention is given to mortal and earthly things, and they have nothing in common with the ether and the gods; so it is not unseemly to reject them with loathing'.[5] No doubt the plentiful supply of slaves in classical antiquity had something to do with this attitude; the leisured classes were not directly subjected to the hardships lack of technology occasions.

Even such advances as had been made in these fields were largely lost under the Roman empire. The Romans found the more abstract parts of Greek science hard to assimilate, and tended simply to accumulate the opinions of Greek authorities without any critical investigation or attempt at verification, with the result that a great deal of superstition and folklore crept into the works of even leading writers such as Pliny the Elder. W. Durant says tersely: 'The indifference of the Romans cooperated with that of the Christians to almost dry up the stream of science long before the barbarian invasions.'[5]

Such disregard of, and contempt for, the natural world could only be deepened with the coming of Christianity, which regarded the world as fallen and therefore as not revealing the truth of God in the way the unfallen world had no doubt done. The Bible, the other main source of Gallo-Roman culture, strongly reinforced the classical attitude. It had nothing to offer with regard to technology, nor did it encourage empirical investigation of nature. The writers of the New Testament had expected the end of the world at any moment and therefore showed little interest in what was so soon to disappear.

With such a background as this, it is small wonder that the early Middle Ages paid scant attention to the natural world. Just as Plato had concentrated on the eternal Forms rather than the earthly things which were patterned on them, so for the tenth century it was the supernatural world, not the world of nature, which was authentic reality. Since everything it was necessary or salutary to know about the natural world had already been revealed in Scripture, to seek for more could only betoken lack of faith or overweening pride, and distract attention from the supernatural.

Thus in the fifth century Paulinus of Nola wrote, with reference to 'the whole sensible appearance of things' (*omnes rerum temporalium species*), that it is 'the lotus flower; so men forget their own land which is God, the country of us all'.[7] The defensive tone of Isidore's introduction to his *De Natura Rerum* is very instructive in this connexion. He will, he says, 'explain something of the nature and causes of things ... and describe ... the system of days and months ... the changes of the seasons ... the nature of the elements, the courses of the sun and moon' and the like, but he hastens to make clear that he will not go beyond 'the writings of the ancients, especially the works of Catholic writers', and feels the need to insist that 'to know the nature of things is not the wisdom of superstition, if the knowledge is put to proper use; otherwise Solomon would never have claimed to have had such things revealed to him' (the reference is to Wisdom 7, 17–19). The contents of the work make clear how little Isidore took such knowledge to matter; he did not greatly mind what the world was like. Thus he sometimes uses language which implies a spherical earth, and at other times language which implies that the earth is flat, without ever explaining, or even discussing, the contradiction; he clearly did not regard the matter as important. In one place he says the earth is at the centre of the universe, surrounded by a single sphere of fire, elsewhere that it is surrounded by seven concentric spheres, which create a harmony by the sound of their varied revolutions; and he adds: 'let no human being have the temerity to claim to know how many are involved'. Elsewhere he states it as his own view that the sun is much bigger than the earth, and only appears smaller because of its distance from us, while the moon is smaller than the earth. Yet in other places he takes it to be 'in no way established (*nulla ratione firma videtur*) whether the sun is only as large as it seems' and 'whether the moon is spherical or concave'. He offers no attempt at a resolution, and clearly, although he was the most learned writer on such subjects in the whole of the early Middle Ages, and the principal authority on them for the following centuries, such matters were of only peripheral interest to him. In this he was entirely typical; but on the basis of such cursory and superficial treatment no worthwhile technology could be built.[8]

If both the classical and the biblical inheritance prompted a lack of interest in the workings of the natural world, some passages in the Bible encouraged a positive hostility towards it. 'Friendship towards the world is enmity with God', said James (4.4), while John wrote that 'the world lieth in the evil one' (I John 5.19).[9] Taken, as they were, to refer to the world of nature, such passages gave rise to a deep suspicion and even, as we shall see, hatred, of it in some quarters. As understood at the time, the New Testament was also hostile to the body and the flesh (cf e.g. Matt. 10.28; Gal. 5.19 or Rom. 8.7–8). According to mediaeval belief, a human being is a combination of soul and body in which the soul is the dominant partner, whose efforts after union with God the body is simply meant to subserve. In a fallen world, however, as Augustine had insisted, the body is the source of irrational and well-nigh uncontrollable lusts which lure the soul away from its search for God; and it must therefore not only be despised but severely repressed and reduced to slavery (I Cor. 9.27, *castigo ... et in servitutem redigo*; Rom. 8.13, 'put its deeds to death'; or Rom. 12.1, 'offer as a sacrifice').[10]

Inevitably, such an outlook affected the study and practice of medicine. There was virtually no empirical study of medical matters. Despite Galen's skill as a physiologist and dissector of animals, even such limited advances as the empirical Greek physicians had been able to make, in the absence of a developed technology, were largely lost in the earlier centuries of the Roman empire. From the time of Pliny the Elder (died 79 CE) medical writers increasingly based their accounts on earlier written authorities – often rather dubious authorities at that – rather than on observation; and by our period medicine, like other subjects, was largely a matter of book-learning. The ancient ideas of the four elements of which the universe is made up, and of the four humours in the body, were taken over uncontested, and it was believed, for example, that 'the mind is placed in the citadel of the head, like God in the heavens, to look upon and govern all from a high place'. The liver was said to be 'the seat of fire which flies thence up to the head, as to the heavens of our body. From this fire the rays of the eyes flash.'[11]

L.C. MacKinney, a recognized expert on early mediaeval medicine, gives a terse verdict on treatments based on such wholly unscientific ideas. They 'did no harm', he says in effect, 'but normally no good either'.[12] Many of them were based on the supposed affinities of things: for example, pain in the eyes was treated by removing the eye of a dog and applying it to the affected organ; toothache by sprinkling the ashes of a dog's tooth into a cup of mulled wine and drinking the potion.[13] The efficacy of such remedies was often supposed to depend partly on their being accompanied by magical formulas or appropriate prayers. For example, when herbs were being gathered for medicinal use, certain prayers over them were prescribed by the church authorities, and certain days in the church calendar were regarded as specially propitious for the purpose.[14]

Mediaeval medical practice involved an appeal to both natural and supernatural agencies, and in so doing it followed the Bible. For example, in Ecclus. 38.11–13 (then a full part of the Bible) a sick person is advised to make appropriate offerings to God and then to 'leave the physician to do his work. His task is of divine appointment.' (The whole section deserves to be consulted.) For the mediaeval church, as for the author of Ecclesiasticus, this was a delicate matter. Illness was clearly an evil, often the work of the devil; and the example of Jesus in the Gospels suggested that it should be relieved. Had not God endowed various plants with the necessary medicinal properties? On the other hand, despite John 9.2–3, illness was regularly interpreted as a divine punishment for sin, and in that case attempts to interfere with its course would run counter to God's will. It was for this sort of reason that many mediaeval *hospitia* provided only sketchy medical attention, as distinct from nursing care, thus being hospices rather than hospitals. Also, in a society where the spiritual was taken to be so much more important than the bodily, illness was often taken to be salutary. 'It is advantageous (*utile*),' says Isidore, 'for those who are well and strong to become infirm ... lest through the vigour of their health they should be defiled by illicit passions and the desire for luxury.'[15]

Such an ambiguous stance was bound to leave people somewhat confused. It was clearly difficult to put much confidence in the activities of contemporary doctors; and as they observed the same treatment applied to apparently identical cases, with widely varying results, people could only conclude either that life was mysteriously arbitrary, or that it was the moral condition of the patient and God's consequent attitude towards him or her that counted, rather than anything that medical science could do. With regard to health, as to so much else, relations with God mattered more than any human activities.

The influence of the heritage from the Bible and the ancient world was in some ways reinforced, and in some ways modified, by a specifically Christian factor, the doctrine of creation. According to it, God had created the world some six thousand years previously, only days before he created human beings. He had created it exactly as it is now, with the same seas, landmasses, mountains, rivers, flora and fauna, and he had created it solely with a view to the well-being and salvation of its human inhabitants; in that sense mediaeval thought was entirely anthropocentric.[16]

Being supremely rational, God would not have created anything, or given it the form it has, without a purpose, and that purpose must in every case have been concerned with human well-being. To seek knowledge of a thing in order to discover God's purpose for it, and for human beings through it, was entirely legitimate, and a good deal of energy was expended on the project. This explains Isidore's meaning when he wrote that knowledge of the nature of things could be justified if it 'was sought for proper purposes' (see p. 18 above). Augustine likewise taught that study of this world is legitimate if the purpose is that 'by means of the corporeal and temporal we may comprehend the eternal and spiritual'. Even so, he insists that it must be a matter of 'using', not 'enjoying', the world.[17]

Along one line of application, this led to great interest in a work known as the *Physiologist*, which appears to have been put together in Greek in the second century CE, on the basis of accounts current at the time in Alexandria. During the Middle Ages it went through various, ever expanded, editions and translations, and it was second only to the Bible in popularity. As its title ('The Naturalist') indicates, it claimed to give an account of the animal kingdom, but it was far from being a scientific work. Many of the animals it described were fabulous – the unicorn and the phoenix, for instance – and those which were not had characteristics attributed to them which a minimum of fieldwork would have shown they did not possess. These characteristics were believed to convey some moral or spiritual lesson. What the *Physiologus* in fact offered was a quasi-allegorical treatment of the animal kingdom.

Books which dealt with animals along these lines were known as bestiaries, and there were others which dealt similarly with plants and stones (*herbaria* and *lapidarii*). It is difficult to be sure just how literally educated people took these accounts, but the description of animals by Isidore, for example, even when he is not concerned to draw any moral, suggests that scholarly knowledge of the natural world was not at a much higher level. The significance of the bestiaries and similar works is the greater because they were the source of many of the sculptures and pictorial representations in churches by which popular ideas were influenced.

The doctrine of creation had wider implications. If the universe, more or less as it stood, was the direct product of infinite intelligence, not only must each creature have a significance for mankind, but all parts of the whole must be related in a rational and in principle intelligible way. The world was seen as an integrated unity, about the past of which universal histories could be written, and about each characteristic of which a monograph could be produced. The Middle Ages produced innumerable books with titles such as *de aeternitate mundi* or *de vanitate mundi*. Within that unity each part bore a relationship, which must in principle be intelligible, both to the whole and to every other part. Each part was believed to bear the impress of the whole, so that the human being, for example, could be understood as a microcosm of the universe. The four humours of the human body, for instance, were related to the four elements of creation, and we have seen how the human mind in the head could be likened to God in the heavens, or the liver to fire, with its upward movement. These were not seen simply as arbitrary comparisons.

As that suggests, the relation of each part of the universe to the others meant that one thing could be used as a natural symbol of another, and symbolization was a prominent feature of the culture. Symbols were not seen as something arbitrary or artificial. It was not simply that things *could* be used as symbols, or be invested with symbolic meaning by human beings. They *were* symbols, and the task was to discover their intrinsic significance as such. 'Every created being,' said Honorius of Autun, 'shadows forth truth and life.'

By the same token, words bore a real relationship to the things they denoted. To understand the meaning of a word was to understand the nature of what the word stood for. Etymology was thus an important path of entry to truth. As Isidore said, 'the explanation (*expositio*) of words sufficiently indicates what they mean'.[18] From the point of view of modern linguistic science, mediaeval etymologies, like those of the ancients, are entirely fanciful, but for the people of that time they were a source of important truth. For example, Isidore says that *homo* (mankind or human being) comes from *humus* (earth) because God created us from the dust of the earth, and we are to remember that it is to dust we must return. *Decorus* (proper, beautiful) was derived from *de(cus) cor(dis)*, meaning 'beauty of heart', or 'spiritual beauty', reminding us that bodily, purely earthly, beauty, if it is lacking a firm moral basis, is evil and the work of the devil.[19]

The names of things were thus not simply given them by human caprice; the conjunction of certain names with certain things was part of the nature of reality, and was no doubt known to Adam when he named things (Gen. 2.19). Such an attitude to names implies a comparable attitude to things, which were taken to have some sort of ultimate, or metaphysical, existence.

In the light of the doctrine of creation, mediaeval people felt the solidarity of the universe quite as strongly as its multiplicity. Phenomena which for us are quite unconnected were for them closely interrelated, so that analogies could be perceived between them, and analogous behaviour attributed to them. Conceptions established in one sphere seemed applicable to others, and in particular it was deemed possible to move from the natural to the supernatural, and vice versa. Thus the behaviour expected of kings could be expected of God, while motives such as characterize human actions were ascribed to the behaviour of things. The sun, Isidore said, 'goes further to the south (thus making winter) in order that the land may be enriched by winter rain and frosts; and then goes north again in order that fruits may mature and what is green in the damp weather may ripen in the heat'. Or 'night occurs so that the light may be sufficiently tempered for certain creatures that cannot endure the light of the sun'.[20]

A different sort of example of this sense of the analogous interrelation of things explains why it was thought no accident that God produced twenty-two works in the beginning, that there were twenty-two *sextarii* to a bushel, twenty-two letters in the Hebrew alphabet, 'from which the divine law is composed', twenty-two generations from Adam to Jacob and 'twenty-two books of the Old Testament as far as Esther'.[21]

The divine ordering of reality was believed to be hierarchical through and through. Since God, who is the highest good, was at the apex of the hierarchy, and the regulating principle of the whole, everything was seen from a moral and axiological standpoint. From God downwards all beings descended in an order of being which was also an order of value. Near the bottom were a group of creatures which exist but do not live (e.g. stones); higher up were those that exist and live but have no sensation (e.g. plants), and higher still those that exist, live and have sensation but have no reason (animals). The characteristics which determined the position of the various types of being in the Great Chain of Being (as it was later called) had been specifically assigned to them by God from the beginning. Each type of being thus had a given nature, and its excellence consisted in its exhibiting fully the characteristics proper to that nature. Human beings, while sharing with lower creatures existence, life and sensation, also shared with the angels the power to reason and understand; yet for them, too, excellence consisted in conforming to the God-given nature of their group.

Such a view of virtue had important consequences. Not only were human beings in general expected to behave in conformity with their essence as human, willingly accepting, for example, the limitations involved in the status accorded them in the Great Chain of Being;[22] the particular social role allotted to any given human being was seen as his or her vocation and he or she was expected to conform faithfully to it, and indeed show identity with it.[23] The way of affirming oneself in the mediaeval world was by way of self-abasement and self-denial, which included the denial of all that was particular or ab-normal. Mediaeval man was corporate man, and the good human being conformed to the pattern divinely ordained for his or her type of humanity. The saint of the typical saint's *Life*, for example, is not depicted as an individual, with his or her peculiar spiritual odyssey and way of developing toward sanctity; the process is commonly represented as a sudden conversion, usually of a stereotyped sort; and once sanctity has been achieved, the saint is depicted as behaving in the sort of ways, and performing the sort of miracles standard for that type of saint.[24] Similarly, the figures who appear in the chronicles are seldom portrayed in their individuality. The actions and motives ascribed to them are those appropriate to members of the royal or knightly or clerical class to which they respectively belong. As Philip Aries shows, the point applies even to children, who were seen simply as human beings – small adults – without there being any great sense of the growth of human personality, or the education necessary for it. All this helps to explain how, as we shall see, sins could be classified externally, without much regard for the individual motives or circumstances that led to their commission.

Of individuality in the modern sense of arriving independently at one's own view and remaining true to it the tenth century had little conception. Correctness mattered more than integrity; the rightness of one's view more than its being one's own. When Boethius defined human personality, he defined it as *rationalis naturae individua substantia* (a particular instance of rational nature).[25] *Individuum est ineffabile*, the tag ran: 'what is individual is inexpressible'; mediaeval thinkers almost always put *universitas* rather than individuality in the foreground. To conform to the appropriate type, that was excellence.

If God had created the world with the express intention that it should form the *mis-en-scène* of human life, it ill behoved human beings to attempt to change it in any significant way. Lack of tools and technology prevented early mediaeval people from adopting the modern attitude which treats nature simply as an object, to be mastered, exploited and transformed. They saw it rather as a God-given environment with which they had to align and identify themselves; and they therefore had little urge to alter it, even had they been able to do so. Who were they to alter the environment which God had devised for them?[26]

Mediaeval people thus saw themselves as part of nature; and the nature to which they belonged had been endowed by God with a regular and rhythmical character: the days, the seasons, seedtime and harvest, came round with unbroken regularity, and human beings could only fall in with the pattern. This had a profound effect on the outlook of people for whom nature loomed as large as it did for them. For them, as Gurevich says, 'the unique and the unprecedented had no independent value; the only truly real acts were those sanctified by tradition and regularly recurrent'.[27] Human life, like the life of circumambient nature, should consist of repeated actions which earlier generations had performed in the same way. Innovatory behaviour was at a discount, and in the religious sphere in particular, people's repetition of acts which could be traced back to a divine prototype connected them with the divinity and conferred reality on them and their lives. For the tenth century, virtue resided in the regularly repeated and the well established; the novel and unheard-of were deeply suspect.

A further aspect of the tenth-century attitude to creation requires some imagination to envisage. For us (apart from superficial worries about the number thirteen and such things), numbers are value-neutral, and space and time simply neutral coordinates. For the tenth century, by contrast, all these were divine creatures, just as concrete and tangible, and having as much 'materiality' as material objects. Therefore different numbers, times and places could possess different qualities.[28] The divine wisdom was reflected in the numbers impressed on all things. Augustine taught that 'the number system is the thoughts of God', and that a knowledge of numbers was a key to the meaning of the universe. Three, for example, the number of the Trinity, symbolized all that was spiritual, while four, the number of the world-elements and the bodily humours, stood for the physical world. The products of these, by addition or multiplication, seven and twelve, symbolized respectively the union of two natures and the penetration of matter by spirit. It was thought no accident that there were four corners of the earth, four evangelists or four major prophets, seven modes in Gregorian music, seven days of creation and so of the week, seven words from the cross, seven gifts of the Holy Spirit, seven chief virtues, seven deadly sins and, later, seven clerical orders and seven sacraments; or that there were twelve tribes of Israel, twelve apostles and twelve items in the Apostles' Creed. In a similar way different times and places were believed to have been endowed with different characters, so that different kinds of behaviour were appropriate to them. Night, for example, was an evil time, and specially heavy penalties were imposed for misdeeds committed at night. By contrast, certain times were specially propitious for the gathering of medicinal herbs, and extra success was thought to attend the use of herbs collected at them, just as weddings solemnized on Fridays were most likely to be happy. Some times owed their character to supernatural connexions, for example, Sunday to its being the day of Christ's resurrection, Lent to its being the forty days when Christ fasted and was tempted, or the feast of a saint to its being the day when the saint died and was translated to heaven. 'The better the day, the better the deed', we sometimes say; the Middle Ages really believed it.

In the same sort of way, different places were believed to have been assigned different characters. Jerusalem, for example, which was widely believed to be the geographical centre of the world, was thought to have been the divinely prepared site for the events of the first Easter and Whitsun, which in turn hallowed it. By contrast, places outside the Christian world were a sort of religious wasteland in which, as the Crusades would show, behaviour that would have been wrong at home was fully permissible. The presence of a saint's remains could confer a sacred status on a place, and so could the power of God brought to bear through rites of consecration. Prayers said, and pious actions performed, on such holy ground could be expected to have greater efficacy.

Given its classical and biblical background, this was naturally a text-based culture. People sought knowledge through books, not through observation or experiment. What is more, the age was one acutely conscious of its cultural inferiority to previous ages, whose achievements it greatly admired, even if it did not fully understand them.[29] Scholars would therefore have felt it presumptuous to suppose that they could discover what their greater and wiser predecessors had not known. In general, as we shall see, this was a culture for which the ideal state was in the past.

Education, like scholarship, was text-based, and concentrated almost exclusively on the seven liberal arts. From the time of Martianus Capella these were divided into the more elementary *trivium* (literally, place where three roads meet), namely grammar, rhetoric and dialectic, and the *quadrivium* (crossroads): music, arithmetic, geometry and astronomy. If that sounds a fairly comprehensive and advanced educational programme, appearances are deceptive. As we have seen, the Latin in which all scholarly work was done, and all ecclesiastical and legal documents were written, was no longer the spoken tongue of any Frank, and the *trivium* amounted to no more than a training in how to speak and write Latin correctly, and to marshal one's ideas cogently and persuasively. Education was mainly confined to would-be clerics, and the main aim of the *quadrivium* was essentially practical. Students were taught basic definitions and the essentials of calculation to a sufficient level to enable them to read and sing church music and to calculate the occurrence of the feasts and fasts of the church calendar.[30]

In order to learn Latin, students needed not only texts of Donatus and other handbooks of grammar, but acquaintance with the writings of authors who wrote the language correctly. It was recognized that the best models of Latinity were to be found in pre-Christian writers, but these tended to expose students to lascivious scenes or passages which communicated non-Christian ideas, or both, and many teachers were not prepared to take the risk. They taught Latin from the Bible, especially the Psalms (in many circles *discere psalmos* became the term for 'learning Latin'), and the best Christian writers they could find, such as Lactantius and Prudentius. However, as we have seen, Charlemagne encouraged the copying and reading of pagan classics, and it is to Frankish copyists that we owe the preservation of a number of classical texts. Charlemagne and his circle used classical names as nicknames for one another, and they were not the only ones to be attracted by classical Latin literature. A fierce debate went on for centuries about the propriety of reading, or at any rate enjoying, classical authors, those in favour of the practice arguing that it could be justified if the aim was a legitimate one, that is, principally, the better understanding of the language, and hence of the Latin Bible and the Latin Fathers. From Augustine onwards the text in Exodus (3.22) about spoiling the Egyptians was prayed in aid, and so was Deut. 21.10ff. as interpreted by Jerome.[31] An interesting tenth-century example of this attitude is to be found in Ermenrich of Ellwangen who quoted Virgil constantly in his grammatical treatise, but hastened to make clear his firm conviction that the poet was in hell, and added: 'just as dung spread on the field enriches it to good harvest, so the filthy writings of the pagan poets are a mighty aid to divine eloquence'.[32] Others, however, admitted to being genuinely attracted by the writings of the ancients, especially the poets. In Charlemagne's court these writings were studied and appreciated, and quite a classical culture grew up, one manifestation of which was a flowering of charming, if rather derivative and artificial, nature, and even love, poetry.[33]

This trenches on the vexed question of the extent to which people in the early Middle Ages appreciated the beauty of the natural world. The case of Bernard of Clairvaux, who is said to have travelled all day along the shore of Lake Leman so deep in inner contemplation that he failed even to notice the presence of the water, can hardly be taken as typical; and there is some evidence for real awareness of natural beauty. The sites of monasteries, for example, seem sometimes to have been chosen on account of their beauty as well as their remoteness (see plate 11), and there is a story of some villagers in the eleventh century who made great efforts to prevent the cutting down of a spruce tree on account of its beauty.[34] Nevertheless, people were certainly worried lest concern with nature should deflect their attention from the supernatural, and depictions of nature, both visual and literary, tended to be derivative and conventional, based less on observation than on traditional models. Probably people were too close to nature, too aware of its intransigence and messiness, and the hard work it necessitated, to be passionately drawn towards it in the way later urban dwellers have been. It tended to be seen through traditional categories as a source of edification.[35]

In addition to what it tells us directly about religious attitudes and beliefs in tenth-century Francia, the content of this chapter has an important indirect bearing on the religion of the period. For it helps us to understand why there was so little interest in, or success with, technological development. The point must not be exaggerated. Lynn White and others have shown that the age was not as backward, technologically, as used to be supposed. We have already referred to some of the improvements in agricultural technology; and the watermill and the stirrup, for example, though not Frankish inventions, were exploited by the Franks and others in the tenth century.[36]

The fact remains, however, that the tenth century was a relatively primitive period, without the resources to master the environment or maintain life at more than a low level. Not only did this lead inevitably to an attitude of passive acceptance of the way things were; it meant that people had to look to religion for ways of coping with many situations with which subsequent generations have coped by means of technology. In seeking to understand many of the directions religious activity took in the tenth century, the relative lack of technology is something to be kept constantly in mind.

4

The Impact of Religion

Perhaps the first thing that needs to be emphasized about Frankish Christianity is the unquestioning way in which it was accepted and the sheer actuality of it. As we have seen, pluralism is a great solvent of the conviction that one's own outlook is totally true; of pluralism in that sense tenth-century Francia was almost totally innocent. When Clovis was converted, he brought his whole people with him, and Charlemagne insisted that all his subjects must be Catholic Christians. Failure to be baptized meant disfranchisement and virtual outlawry. Citizenship and being a Christian were synonymous. Everyone one knew was a Christian like oneself.

As far as the Jews were concerned, in the ninth century they had enjoyed quite a high reputation in court circles. Legislation had been passed to help them in the practice of their religion and they had made a certain number of converts from among the upper class and also from among their slaves; but very few people now knew enough about Judaism even to consider embracing it, and in general the Jews were suspect as deicides.[1] Still fewer people had ever had contact with a Muslim, or even knew of the existence of Islam. The Qur'an was not translated into Latin until the twelfth century, and before that, as Southern says, the Muslim world seemed to those who knew of it 'a kind of parody of the Christian world where a strange trinity of gods, Tervagan, Mahomet and Apollo, were worshipped in "synagogues and mahumeries" filled with idols and images'.[2] There was no question of any rivalry to Christianity from that quarter in the tenth century. Ancient Graeco-Roman polytheism was known only to a very small minority, and the philosophical systems which had taken the place of religion for most educated Greeks and Romans were not, as we have seen, sufficiently known or understood to present themselves as world-views alternative to Christianity. As will become clear later, pre-Christian Frankish religion was not without its influence, but it was too primitive and incoherent to be presented as an integrated system which had any prospect of rivalling the Christian faith.

'For atheism,' as Henry Adams wrote, 'the world was not ready.'[3] We hear of individuals having difficulty with particular items of the faith, and even occasionally of a loss of faith in God altogether; but such doubts were rare, and never more than passing. There could be no question of a coherent and articulate atheist position.[4]

Alasdair MacIntyre makes an important point in this connexion. Mediaeval thinkers were well aware that the faith involved incoherences, inconsistencies and apparently insoluble difficulties (some examples of which will be discussed later); but unlike many modern thinkers, for whom such difficulties lead to scepticism about the truth of Christianity as a whole, they saw them 'as difficulties, but no more, an incentive to enquiry, but not a ground for disbelief', and as 'tolerable, to be treated as apparent and not real'.[5] The explanation is that the concepts with which mediaeval theologians worked 'were part of a set of concepts which were indispensable to the forms of description used in social and intellectual life at the time'.[6] In other words, the concepts of religion were integral to the only way people had of making sense of the world and ordering their lives. It was, for example, impossible to think of the universe except as the product of supernatural agency which had produced it and now maintained it in existence. Alternative conceptualizations were simply not available. T.E. Hulme wrote: 'There are certain doctrines which for a particular period seem not doctrines, but inevitable categories of the human mind ... a denial of which is looked on by the men of that period just as we might look on the assertion that two and two make five.'[7] These things, which are simply taken for granted, he designates 'doctrines felt as facts', and in tenth-century Francia one of them was the general Christian account of reality.

If there were thus no alternatives to weaken faith in the Christian account of things, there were strong factors, conscious and unconscious, making for acceptance of it. So far as conscious socialization was concerned, secular, as well as ecclesiastical, government was firmly predicated on the truth of Christianity, and committed to promoting it. We have already seen how failure to accept and practise the Catholic faith laid one open to both secular and ecclesiastical sanctions (in the last resort the dreaded excommunication, which carried loss of all civil rights as well as exclusion from heaven); and the general organization of society, with the king as the Lord's anointed and the bishops as his trusted advisors, presupposed the truth of the Christian faith. What is more, every child grew up in a community where baptism was universal; where everyone accepted the status of the priest and paid him his tithes; where the church building, small and insignificant though it usually was by later standards (see plate 6), was the largest in the village, and impressive to the peasants, with its wealth of candles and the precious stones and metals which adorned its reliquaries. In the tenth century, every significant personal occasion, from the cradle to the grave, was accompanied by appropriate Christian rites, and so were public occasions such as sowing, harvest or grape-gathering. The divisions of the year were determined by the feasts and fasts of the church calendar, and the feeling-tone associated with each season was given by the church – the feeling-tone of Christmas was quite different from that of Lent, for example, and the feelings in question were the opposite of what the natural rhythm might have suggested. Even the times for legal and financial settlements were geared to the ecclesiastical seasons. No one doubted that, if accompanied by appropriate conduct, the various ceremonies were effective, and kept life going; so to have questioned the truth of the faith on which they rested would have meant putting a question-mark against the entire life and fabric of society. It would in fact have meant staring into the abyss of chaos, and it was something unimaginable by even the most imaginative tenth-century mind.

The result of all this was that reality was actually *experienced* more or less exactly as it was pictured in the church's teaching.[8] Unseen supernatural beings and powers were accepted as real, rather in the way that we to-day accept the existence of beings such as bacteria and viruses, which, though most of us have never seen them, we recognize as having the power to affect our lives drastically, and sometimes irretrievably.

To express the matter in a rough and ready, and very preliminary, way, we may say that reality was experienced as existing in two sections, rather like an iceberg. The visible world was the lesser, and less significant, part and rested at every point on an altogether vaster, invisible world, without the support of which it could not have continued to exist. Communication was possible between the two worlds. By prayer, and by appropriate ritual and conduct, the inhabitants of this world could exert influence on the other, while, by a mysterious mode of operation, the other world was constantly controlling the course of things in this, often through the agency of supernatural beings who came over into it.

The inhabitants of the invisible world were by no means all friendly. In addition to God and his angels, there were the devil and his myrmidons; and no difficulty was felt in supposing that any of these might influence and alter the course of events at any moment. So, in all planning and decision-making, their likely reactions had to be taken into account as fully as those of natural agents and agencies.

It would be an exaggeration to say that there was no recognition of secondary causes. Obviously, for example, dampness caused rust and melting snow caused floods; and it could not fail to be observed that things normally proceeded according to a regular pattern: night invariably followed day, for instance, and winter invariably gave place to summer. Yet some summers were good and produced bumper harvests, others were late and led to shortages or famine; and according to the Bible, even the sequence of night and day had more than once been suspended (e.g. Josh. 10.13; Isa. 28.21; Ecclus. 46.5; Mark 15.33). There was no sense of a universally interlocking causal system. For the most part, it was believed, God causes, or allows, events to proceed in an orderly and predictable way, rather as a helmsman on a calm and empty stretch of water keeps his craft on a straight course at a steady speed. However, if the presence of rocks or other craft requires it, he alters course appropriately; in either case he is always in control. In the same way, it was thought, God was always free to alter course and steer events in any direction his purposes required.

> Something like that was the view of Augustine in his later years, as expressed in Letter 137, for example, or in *de Trinitate* (e.g. III.4 (9); III.5.11 or III.6.11). Augustine had also recognized, however, that certain natural events happen through physical necessity, and Boethius (from whose *Consolation*, Book 3, the analogy of the helmsman is derived) seems to have thought that the natural world is governed by regular rules with which God does not interfere. In a commentary on the *Consolation* written at the end of the ninth century, however, Remigius of Auxerre implicitly returns to a position more like that outlined above.
>
> The fact is that tenth-century Christians, like their New Testament predecessors, had not really thought the matter through. They had no doubt that both the main movements of history and some individual moments in it were more or less directly controlled by God, without attributing every minor event directly to his will. In practice they attributed to God's action events which seemed to them particularly significant.[9]

Mediaeval people thus lived in a personalized environment, and it was therefore easy to interpret what happened as reward or punishment for good or bad conduct, whether individual or corporate. Uncommon natural phenomena, such as eclipses, meteors, comets, or even prolonged thunder and lightning, were frequently interpreted as having been sent as punishment or, more commonly, as warnings of punishment to come.

By the same token, in such a personalized universe it was easily supposed that human beings could solicit or deflect interventions from the supernatural world. We have ample evidence, for example, of attempts by peasants to ward off by more or less magical means eclipses and other phenomena which terrified or threatened them (see further p. 119 below). Such efforts were usually viewed with suspicion by the church authorities, but at a more sophisticated level they, too, encouraged attempts to secure the good will of the supernatural world and to stop the devil in his tracks. There were ways of achieving such ends acceptable to the church; for God was believed to have revealed the kinds of behaviour and types of ritual in response to which his favour and forgiveness might be won, and the devil defeated.

Such a view of reality made it easily possible to see religion as a substitute for technology. What a very undeveloped technology could not do to mitigate disease and famine, or to increase the fertility of the fields or bring success in war, might be achieved through God's power, if the appropriate ways of winning his favour were deployed. As we shall see, this aspect of religion was an extremely important one in the tenth century; for, as Southern writes in this connection, 'as human beings men were powerless. They could only survive through their dependence on the supernatural.'[10]

One element in the situation as it was understood made an especial impact. According to the church's teaching, no one ceased to exist at the moment of physical death. Whether they liked it or not (and the proviso should be noted), all human beings were destined to exist for ever.[11] Moreover, apart from the possibility of a limited period in purgatory (on which see pp. 134–5 below), they would do so, it was believed, either in conditions of perfect fulfilment and happiness, or in a state of subjection to an eternity of indescribable torture and wretchedness. Once a person was dead, there was no possibility of transition from one state to the other. Detailed descriptions of the two states were common in sermons, and they were also frequently portrayed in painting and sculpture, the second state being pictured in gruesome detail. Probably no item of the church's teaching was more vividly impressed on people's imagination, and this obviously added a further dimension to their response to their environment.

People in the modern West, recognizing the increasing probability of their having a long period after retirement, take out insurance of some sort during their working lives to ensure that their retirement is as happy and carefree as possible. In the same sort of way, people in the tenth century did what they could in this life to ensure that they would spend eternity in heaven. As we shall see later, on a strict interpretation of official theology, an individual's fate after death did not depend wholly on his or her freely-willed conduct in this life. Nevertheless, the burden of preaching and teaching was that if you wanted to avoid damnation, you must behave appropriately in the here and now. What counted as appropriate behaviour was by no means confined to virtuous living. There were rites and ceremonies to be carried out, and the fact that the provision of these was beyond the means of many, gave rise to a good deal of anxiety.

In the light of all this, it will be evident that much religious practice tended to take on a somewhat utilitarian aspect. Needless to say, tenth-century Christians did not always live up to their beliefs. Indeed they did so less than we might perhaps have expected, for they were still in some ways semi-barbaric, with strong passions which they found as difficult to bridle as their pre-Christian ancestors had done. That, however, in no way contradicts the claim that the supernatural world and its powers had overwhelming reality for them. People to-day who smoke or over-eat do not seriously question the medical verdict that such activities are highly injurious. They accept it but choose to ignore it in the interest of short-term satisfaction. Similarly, whatever the conduct of tenth-century Franks may have been, to an extent we can scarcely imagine, the supernatural world and its powers, both good and evil, were as real to them as this world and the people with whom it brought them into contact. In all their doings the supernatural had to be reckoned with no less than the natural; and when they failed to embody this recognition in their conduct, the result, as we shall see, was a state of unease and deep anxiety.

5

The Christian Story

The outlook of the Franks in the tenth century was thus largely dominated by a single religious story. A good deal of the available evidence might suggest that this story was simply the account of things contained in the Bible. Certainly the Bible, which then included what we call the Apocrypha, was accorded the highest possible status, since it was believed to have been directly inspired by God throughout, and so to be the ultimate source of truth on matters of all sorts.

> For the extent to which God was believed to have been the author of the Bible in an almost literal sense, we may consider a characteristic passage of Gregory the Great, who declares that it is pointless to discuss the identity of the human author of any biblical book, because 'its author is known to have been the Holy Spirit'. 'If we were reading the words of some great man whose letters we had received,' he says, 'it would certainly be silly ... to investigate the sort of pen used. Since we hold the author (of the Bible) to be the Holy Spirit, what are we doing when we search for the human writer but making enquiry about the pen?' In the same passage he, like many others, describes the Bible as written *dictante spiritu sancto* (at the dictation of the Holy Spirit).[1]

Even on questions not strictly religious, when the Bible pronounced unequivocally, that settled the matter. For example, since Ps. 93.1 (92.2) said that God 'founded the world to abide immovable', any suggestion that it travels round the sun was ruled out. Or since Genesis declared that the universe, in exactly its present form, was created in a period of six consecutive days, that was believed to be the case, even though the question could be raised whether these were normal twenty-four hour days. Again, the tree of life as described in Genesis 2 and 3 might be allegorized, but the fact that such a botanical specimen stood in the Garden of Eden was not to be questioned. From such biblical data further facts were deduced, so that it was believed possible, for example, to determine that creation took place in the sixth millennium BCE and even that the date on which it began was 18 March.[2] In ways such as this the Bible largely controlled people's conception of the nature and history of the universe, independent investigations such as might eventually have led to doubts about the biblical data being discouraged as the result of the conviction that any knowledge not available from the Bible could not be important and might be dangerous to possess.[3]

The inspired character of the Bible meant that a lot of the behaviour and practices it describes became binding precedents for subsequent ages. Individual morality was determined by such texts as the Ten Commandments and the Sermon on the Mount, while at the corporate level the fact, for example, that a monarchical form of government was to be found in both Testaments, and that there was no mention in the Bible of republics, presidents or popular assemblies, made any but monarchical government virtually inconceivable. Indeed, the Carolingian Franks came to see themselves as the successors of the Israelites: Charlemagne was saluted as *novus David*,[4] and the royal throne at Aachen (Charlemagne's capital) was modelled, like much of the palace itself, on Solomon's building as described in the books of Kings and Chronicles. We have already seen how Pepin and his sons were anointed as the successors of the last Merovingian king, on the model of the anointing of David and Solomon as the successors of Saul, and Charlemagne explicitly cited the precedent of Josiah in support of his claim to be responsible for the spiritual, as well as temporal, well-being, of his people.[5]

That the Bible was able to control the lives and institutions of the Franks in this manner was partly due to the fact that the Jews of the monarchical period were in many ways on the same cultural level as the early Middle Ages, and also to the fact that the Frankish outlook was largely unhistorical. Being the products of a static culture, they were not aware how much things had in fact changed, and so could believe themselves to be following biblical precedents far more exactly than was in fact the case: correspondences which were in fact only verbal could seem much more.

> For the reason just given, the biblical precedents in question came largely from the Old Testament. It is perhaps significant that in one of the four mosaics of the time to have been preserved, that at Germigny-des-Prés, God is represented under the form of the Ark of the Covenant; and some scholars have pictured the religion of our period as so dominated by the Old Testament as to be a 'Mosaic Christianity' or a 'Christianity of Law'.[6]
>
> Writing in the ninth century, Dhuoda, who regularly relies on Old Testament precedents in her advice to her son, reveals a conception of God hardly distinguishable from that of the terrible God of the Old Testament.[7] There was no doubt an element of propaganda in all this. In an imperfectly Christianized empire, which the rulers were trying to unify with the aid of the clergy, the Jerusalem of the kings and high priests was bound to appear an attractive precedent.

When, towards the the end of our period, dialectic began to be used as a means of discovering truth, biblical texts were quoted as the unassailable premises of arguments, and in general there can be no question about the authority ascribed to the Bible and the extent to which it controlled both the way people behaved and their picture of reality.

Nevertheless, the ascription of inerrancy to the Bible has raised problems in every period of the church's history, for the Bible is in fact a collection of very disparate works, deriving from a variety of places and cultures over a period of nearly a thousand years; naturally, therefore, it contains many irreconcilable narratives and a considerable amount of mutually incompatible teaching. If such a collection was to be made the basis of a coherent story, or system, it needed very sophisticated handling. At first this was not explicitly acknowledged, but it became increasingly clear as alternative, and often incompatible, interpretations of biblical material began to emerge in connection with particular questions. To what extent did God the Son share his Father's divinity? Was Jesus as fully human as he was divine? To such questions the Bible appeared to suggest conflicting answers, but, given its divinely inspired character, that appearance, it was felt, must be delusive. What was needed was a way of interpreting the Bible which would do justice to the entire contents without raising any suggestion of inconsistency.

Accordingly, Christian scholars borrowed from pagan and Jewish authors the interpretative method known as allegorization. This was a complex procedure which took many forms, but in essence it rested on a conviction that every passage had a range of spiritual meanings in addition to its literal meaning. Indeed in some cases, it was claimed, God had intended no literal meaning at all.

> At first it was usual to distinguish only a literal and a spiritual sense, but at least from the time of John Cassian (360–435) the spiritual sense came to be divided into three: the allegorical sense proper, which communicated theological meaning; the moral, or tropological, which applied the text to the individual's conduct; and the anagogical, by which eschatological truth was conveyed. According to the doctrine of 'multiple senses', a single text might yield each of the four senses. A mediaeval reader came looking for such meanings, which were not regarded as arbitrary or subjective products of the interpreter's fancy. They were believed to be objectively present, intended by the divine author quite as much as the literal meaning. The search for these meanings was a search for something actually there.

> The unit of interpretation was normally a short section of text, often less than what we should think of as a single verse. God, it was felt, had been capable of making a single phrase the vehicle of spiritual truth, more or less in isolation from its context. New interpreters could always approach the text expectantly because the treasures God had hidden in it could never be exhausted.

> Since Jesus' life, death and resurrection formed the decisive moment in God's dealing with the world, everything in the Bible was believed to relate to it, the Christian church being seen as continuous with the people God had chosen for himself in the Old Testament. The problem of ostensible divergences between the Old Testament and the New was mainly dealt with through another interpretative method which at the time was not sharply distinguished from allegorization. This was typology, and it rested on the belief that every person and event in the New Testament had, by God's will, been prefigured by one or

more persons or events in the Old, known as 'types' (*typos*). For example, Eve, the woman through whom sin entered the world, was the type of Mary, through whom salvation from sin came. The Israelites' being saved by passing through the waters of the Red Sea was a type of baptism; and what happened to Jonah was a type of Christ's death and resurrection. Innumerable type-antitype relationships were established, and the idea was that what was said about the type in the Old Testament would help to illuminate the New Testament reality to which it pointed and, conversely, that the Old Testament type could be more fully understood in the light of its New Testament fulfilment. In this way many of the apparent contradictions between the two Testaments could be explained.

Interpreters frequently passed over the literal meaning without comment and, as we have seen, from the third century, biblical statements which, taken literally, appeared to contradict current doctrinal or moral teaching were taken not to have been intended by God to have any literal meaning at all. Their inclusion in the Bible had been entirely for the sake of their spiritual application.[8] The typological method, which had its roots in the New Testament itself,[9] continued in constant use down to and after our period, and on the basis of it it was possible to discover in the Bible a single coherent system, or rather story.

This story, in the form it assumed over the years, rested in part on non-biblical material. It began with God's first creative act by which he brought the angels into existence to share his blessedness. Some of the angels fell from grace, however, and with a view to replacing them, God created this world and the human beings for whom it was to be the setting. The fallen angels had not been annihilated, however, and under their malign influence the first two human beings also fell from grace in a way that involved all their descendants with them. The rest of the story told how God had intervened in history over the years in order to save from among fallen humanity enough men, women and children to make up the number of fallen angels and eventually to become his companions in heaven. Any single divine intervention only made sense if interpreted in the light of the others – as would be true of the individual items of a government's foreign policy – but taken together they formed a *Heilsgeschichte*, or salvation history. This history could be used as a leading-thread or *Leitmotiv* with which all the elements in the Bible could be associated in such a way as to give them unity and coherence.

Although some adumbrations of this idea could be found in the Bible itself, the developed form of the story was very much an interpretative construct, the product of theologians with presuppositions very different from those of the Jewish authors of the Bible. These early Christian theologians were known as the Fathers, and the great majority of them were not only familiar with Greek philosophy but were themselves the educational products of it, mainly in its Platonic and Neoplatonic forms. It seemed clear to them that Christian truth had to be expressed in the categories of this philosophy which they largely accepted, and a great deal of their effort went into transposing the originally Jewish form of the faith into these new terms. Such transposition had important consequences; for example it meant identifying the biblical God with the supreme principle of Hellenistic philosophy, and that principle, as we have seen, was impassible, that is, incapable of changing or being changed or influenced in any way. It will be apparent that all this involved reinterpretation on a considerable scale, not least, as we shall see, in regard to the doctrines of the Incarnation and of redemption.

The Fathers did not profess to give a fully comprehensive and systematic account of the Christian position; but as one disputed question after another was settled to the satisfaction of the majority, something emerged which could be presented to educated Christians and pagans alike as a coherent statement of at least large areas of Christian belief.

> Some questions were settled as the result of a gradually growing consensus; more significant, or highly controversial, matters were formally discussed by bishops meeting in conferences known as councils, and settled by majority voting, after which a creed, or collection of canons, was issued defining what had been decided. Especially in the case of large and widely representative (ecumenical) councils which discussed important issues, acceptance of these conclusions eventually became obligatory on all orthodox believers.

By the tenth century it was this doctrinal account which had come to be regarded by the authorities as the Christian story. Acceptance of it was the badge of orthodoxy and without belief in it no one could expect to be saved. Although it was thought of as no more than a distillation of biblical truth, it in fact went considerably beyond the biblical data, which it combined in new ways and understood along new lines. In the process violence was sometimes unconsciously done to the meaning of the original (as recovered by modern critical study).

> An example of the way the tradition could go beyond the biblical data is provided by the figure of Anne, the mother of the Virgin Mary. She and her husband Joachim were becoming very much part of the Christan story by our period, and the question was beginning to be raised whether the Virgin's birth had been such as to exempt her from the original sin which afflicted all other human beings. The Bible contains no reference to the Virgin's parents or her birth;[10] the source was a second-century work, known as the *Protevangelium of James*, one of a number of apocryphal works quoted as authoritative by early mediaeval writers. Anyone who reads, for example, the tenth-century *Homilies of Aelfric*, will realize that congregations can have been in no position to know whether the stories told them from the pulpit had any biblical basis or not.[11] It is true that such stories were not an essential part of the doctrinal tradition, but they played their part in forming the outlook of the time, and in the case of such a doctrine as that of the Immaculate Conception were a decisive factor.

All this was the more important because the ecclesiastical story, once established, came to exercise a controlling influence over the way the Bible was understood. For example, once it had been decided that the Virgin

Mary retained her virginity intact throughout her life (itself something for which the Bible provided no warrant), the biblical description of Jesus as her oldest son (Luke 2.7) or the references to his brothers and sisters (e.g. Mark 3.31; 6.3) had to be explained, or explained away, accordingly. Or when the complete equality of God the Father and God the Son had become an article of faith, a text such as John 14.28, 'the Father is greater than I', had to be interpreted in conformity with it. In general no one was at liberty to interpret any biblical text in a way which conflicted with the doctrinal tradition. So far from the Bible's exercising a critique of the tradition, something very like the opposite occurred. The tradition defined what the Bible *must have* said and meant. A striking, if not particularly significant, case is to be found in the Vulgate, where Jerome, or one of his predecessors, actually added to the text of the Book of Tobit words designed to bring it into line with current church teaching on sexual morality.[12] Such tinkering with the text was exceptional, but the dominance of the tradition over biblical interpretation remains a fact. Obviously, it was made easier by the allegorical method, which always enabled an interpreter to find the meaning for the biblical text which fitted in with the doctrinal system. As the Roman Catholic scholar R.E. McNally puts it, 'almost all the Bible exegesis of the years 650–1000 is marked by a rigid adherence to the interpretations of the ... Fathers of the Church'.[13]

It was thus the Fathers who were the real arbiters of tenth-century Christianity. They were regarded as scarcely, if at all, less inspired than the biblical text they expounded,[14] and if a hitherto undecided theological question was raised, it was to them that appeal was made.

> In our period the only such questions to be raised were mostly of a rather peripheral kind; perhaps the only ones of any significance were the question of predestination raised by Gottschalk of Orbais (*c.* 804–*c.* 869) and the question of the precise status of the consecrated host in the mass, which centred on the celebrated controversy between Ratramnus and Paschasius Radbert and others in the mid-ninth century.

Such appeal was often problematic because the tradition remained elusive, in the sense that there was no comprehensive collection or catalogue of the decisions and definitions which made it up. They were to be found in a variety of documents, of varying degrees of authority, from the creeds and canons of the great ecumenical councils, down through the acts of lesser synods, and the decretals and rescripts of popes and other church leaders, to the writings of individual Fathers. To aid in the process of defining the tradition, collections of official documents were drawn up; catenas of the writings of the Fathers, and especially of their biblical interpretations, were produced; and lists were prepared to make clear which of them might safely be treated as orthodox and authoritative.

Jerome's *de viris illustribus* and the *Institutes* of Cassiodorus served in this way, and the so-called *Decretum Gelasianum* was particularly influential because of its supposed authorship by a pope, though in fact it probably dates from the early sixth century. In the field of canon law and Christian morals, a collection of decisions was made by Dionysius Exiguus in the mid-sixth century, and formed the basis of the collection sent by Pope Hadrian I to Charlemagne in 774.

Although the allegorical method continued to be used, writers after about 650 seldom produced interpretations of their own, but contented themselves with reproducing those of the Fathers. At the most, they claimed to see just a little further because, though dwarfs, they were sitting on the shoulders of giants. By the tenth century the tradition, so far as it had developed, was so set in concrete that any creative theological thinking would have been regarded as unnecessary and presumptuous, even had the age been capable of it. The appeal was simply to authority. Already in the third century Pope Stephen I had warned that there should be no innovation in connection with the tradition (*nihil innovetur nisi quod traditum*), and in the sixth century Pope Hormisdas wrote: 'Our safety lies principally in (*prima salus est*) guarding the rule of right faith and not deviating in any way from the ordinances of the Fathers.'[15]

We saw in the Introduction that the doctrinal form of a religious story is seldom understood by the unsophisticated majority, and that was certainly the case in the early Middle Ages. Even for many of the clerics and other educated people, a good deal in the doctrinal tradition was hard going. Since knowledge of ancient philosophy had largely disappeared, many of the problems with which the Fathers had wrestled in their attempts to clarify the faith were no longer understood, with the result that the full inwardness of their writings was often lost. The theologians who most influenced the age were Gregory the Great (540–604) and Isidore of Seville (*c.*560–636), and their grasp of the work of the earlier Fathers on whom they relied, particularly Augustine, was distinctly limited. The subtleties largely eluded them, and it was in a rather rough and ready form that they passed the tradition on.

Naturally, too, tenth-century theologians were influenced by the cultural situation of their own day. For example, in an increasingly feudal society the word 'lord' carried very definite connotations, and these, as we shall see, coloured the way in which the word and others associated with it were understood when they were encountered in the Bible and the Fathers. Such unconscious reinterpretation was made all the easier by the unhistorical character of the culture. This, as we have seen, fostered the idea that the way words had been used in earlier times was the same as the way in which they were used in the present.

The upshot was that, for all the determination to be true to the tradition, it tended to be understood in an imperfect and simplified form.

For the great majority it was too rarefied to be understood at all. What then was their understanding of the religious story by which they were expected to live? As we saw, the impact of religion on such people tends to be mainly through the myths, legends and quasi-historical narratives contained in sacred books, and tenth-century peasants will have been familiar with some biblical stories. Yet it would be easy to exaggerate the extent to which that was the case. Two things need to be borne in mind. First the extreme rarity of Bibles. It took the skins of some 350 calves and innumerable hours of scribal labour to produce a whole Bible of moderate size, with the result that Bibles were prohibitively expensive.[16] Even a working copy cost almost twice as much as most parish priests earned in a year. Consequently copies of the Bible, especially complete copies (*tota*), were extremely rare. Few churches or priests' houses would contain a copy, and we hear of one newly consecrated bishop who found that his palace did not contain a copy of the New Testament.[17]

The result was that few priests knew more of the Bible than was contained in their service books, and even that they often failed to understand. This brings us to the second thing we must remember, which is the low level of clerical culture at the time.

As we shall see, the church in most parishes had been built by the lord of the manor and was regarded by him as effectively part of his property, to be served by a priest of his choice. Not wanting anyone who might provide rival leadership, or cause trouble, he frequently chose one of his own serfs for the post. Usually, though not always, the man selected was given his freedom, and then underwent a very sketchy education before returning as parish priest. Once installed, he was expected to stay for life, and the parishioners were forbidden to accept any other ministrations than his. Whatever his status in theory, he was usually treated by the lord exactly like the rest of his servants; he was in fact no more than a peasant among peasants. He found difficulty enough with the Latin of the fixed part of the mass; his ability to translate the variable biblical readings set for Sundays and feast-days was usually very limited. He would know, and pass on, certain key stories from the Bible, the story of Adam and Eve, probably, and a few stories from the Gospels; but neither he nor his people would have anything that could be called a real knowledge of the Bible.[18]

Especially since the publication of A.N. Didron's *Iconographie Chrétienne* in 1843, it has been customary to claim that ordinary people were familiarized with the contents of the Bible through works of art, particularly the sculptures and wall-paintings in the churches. The remark of Gregory the Great that 'what scripture is to the educated, images are to the ignorant' has frequently been quoted, and so have similar statements in such writings as those of Paulinus of Nola and John of Damascus, or in the Acts of the Synod of Arras in 1025.[19] There is certainly some truth in this. Members of a congregation who had been exposed, week after week, to a representation of some biblical scene were bound to ask about it, and their parish priest, however ignorant, could hardly have failed to equip himself to answer their questions, and no doubt very often make it a theme of his sermons.

Nevertheless, it is now generally agreed that the point has been considerably exaggerated. As Emile Mâle pointed out, most church art was not primarily didactic in intention, but was intended to glorify God; and pictures were therefore often located in parts of the church where they were visible to the divine eye, but indecipherable by human eyes, especially as tenth-century churches had no large windows and were lit only by candles; and as Hrabanus Maurus pointed out, such paintings tended to fade.[20] The art of stained glass was only in its very early infancy in the tenth century, and church art was governed by a conventional symbolism as impenetrable by ordinary people then as it is for modern visitors to old churches. The best example of church painting to survive from our period is that at Müstair in eastern Switzerland. It consists of numerous small panels, arranged in five bands, each panel depicting a gospel scene. The pictures in the upper bands must have been difficult to make out, and the general effect is one' of great complication, especially as the original painters seem to have got the order wrong in places. It is difficult to be sure how far the worshippers even in such a church as this would have learned the gospel story from the decorations; and few parish churches would have had paintings anything like this, if indeed they had any paintings at all. When we take into account that such representations as there were, were as likely to have been of individual saints as of biblical scenes, it will be clear that church art contributed to a general knowledge of the Bible only to a very limited extent.[21]

The question of the influence of the Bible on the faith and culture of our period is thus a complicated one. That the Bible had very great influence is beyond doubt. In part that influence was direct, but, especially where theological matters were concerned, it tended to be mediated through a tradition which was to some extent a distorting prism, so far as the original meaning was concerned, but which by the tenth century was so unquestioningly accepted that it was invulnerable to any critique from the side of the Bible itself. The great majority of people, even among the upper classes, knew nothing of the Bible directly. Even had they been able to read, and had the opportunities or privacy to do so, no texts would have been available for them. Universal Bible study of the sort introduced, or at least desiderated, after the Reformation and the invention of printing, was out of the question on purely practical grounds. Private Bible study was a prerogative of the extremely small minority, though no doubt the fruits of it were passed on through lessons and sermons. As we shall see, however, the effect of such study was largely confined to the stimulation and reinvigoration of traditional piety.

As for the great majority, their hold on the Christian story, either in its biblical or its doctrinal form, was both tenuous and patchy; and, as we shall see, their religious centre of gravity lay elsewhere, in areas which many modern readers would think peripheral to the faith, as indeed many of the Fathers would have done.

6

God the Lord

(i)

As soon as we turn to the detailed contents of the story, and the impact it had on the Franks, we see the importance of the fact, already emphasized, that different groups in this culturally diverse society appropriated it in very different forms.

Most of the Fathers had conceived God primarily as the *summum bonum*, the sum of all possible perfections, and as such supremely desirable. In our period such a philosophical approach was confined to a minority, and it will be considered later, in connection with monastic spirituality. However, one consequence of it may be mentioned now. If God alone was the sum of all perfections, then his creatures must be less than perfect. This recognition led to what we may call a metaphysical humility, a sense that, quite apart from anything they do or fail to do, human beings always 'come short of the glory of God' (Rom. 3.23). To be a human being was in itself to be less than what it is possible to be; and in a period which failed to distinguish very clearly between metaphysical and moral categories, the result was that being human tended to be felt as a ground not only for humility but for guilt.[1]

Much commoner was a conception of God which took its cue from the opening words of the Creed: 'I believe in God the Father Almighty, maker of heaven and earth', the emphasis being taken to lie on 'almighty' and on 'maker of heaven and earth'. The opening chapters of Genesis were interpreted as meaning that God created the world *ex nihilo*, and it was thus entirely his property or domain. Augustine had written that 'God is called creator in relation to his creatures just as the master is called master in relation to his slaves', and the *Libri Carolini* quoted the statement, giving the words the full meaning they will have carried in the context of eighth-century social conditions.

In the Bible God was constantly referred to as *dominus*, or lord. Today the word 'lord' is almost entirely confined to religious contexts, but in the tenth century it enjoyed widespread currency in secular contexts, and its meaning there undoubtedly affected the way it was understood in relation to God.[2] Your earthly lord – and everyone except the king, or even perhaps the emperor, had one – was the wielder of power and authority who exercised control over you, and to whom you owed due service and obedience. God, the ultimate ruler, was naturally seen as *the* lord, who wielded supreme power and authority, and controlled all. The idea was developed in the *libri Carolini* (end of the eighth century), for example; and in Anselm's writing in the late eleventh century it largely controls the vocabulary. God is a feudal lord with control over three groups of vassals, angels, monks and laity, all of whom owe him vassal service. In Helgaldus's Life of King Robert God is described as 'the *dominator* of all things', before whom even Cherubim and Seraphim must 'bow the neck'.[3]

If God was a lord writ large, he was also a king writ large, and this was another biblical conception interpreted in the light of contemporary conditions. Earthly kings and emperors, for all the awe, reverence and mystery that surrounded them, were seen as no more than pale reflections of the heavenly majesty, and owing abject submission to it. In an ivory of the period, for example, which is typical of many similar works of art, the emperor and empress are shown doing obeisance to God above, in the same sort of way that their subjects did obeisance to them (see plate 4). In the early sixth century Pope Gelasius had described God as 'the highest and true emperor',[4] and in the East the emperor as *cosmocrator* (world-ruler) was often pictured confronting God the *pantocrator* (ruler of all). In a poem by Dungal, an Irishman at Charlemagne's court, we read that 'there is only one who is enthroned in the realm of the air, the *altitonans* (one who thunders on high)';[5] and in poetry, as well as pictorial art, God is pictured as a great warrior who lived in a fortress 'after the manner of an earthly king',[6] the fortress closely resembling Charlemagne's palace at Aachen, and seen as the prototype of it. In it there were places for the saints and for the magnates of the empire.[7] In an age which took a very concrete, realistic view of the supernatural, all this was symbolized in the gold and precious stones which bedecked representations of God and of the halls where he was envisaged as living, just as they enriched the persons and halls of kings and emperors.

What was stressed about God was his *honor*. As his subjects, human beings owed him *servitium debitum* (service due). What he wanted from them was recognition of his lordly power; it was to the *honorem dei* that Christ had to offer his sacrifice, and it is *ad honorem dei* that God wills the punishment of the sinner. 'To you,' wrote Dhuoda, in an address to God, 'belong royalty and power; the fulness of the earth is yours throughout the world. Everything is in servitude to you.' As '*dominator* of all things' God exercises a never-ending sway, 'a kingdom and empire (*regnum et imperium*) that abide for ever and ever'.[8]

Such a view of God would not naturally lead people to expect a very warm or intimate communion with him. Earthly kings and lords often behaved, or at any rate seemed to their subjects to behave, in an arbitrary and high-handed way; a subject did not expect to understand all that his sovereign did, still less to enjoy intimate relations with him. Even in the eighteenth century, Dr Johnson, after meeting George III, could protest that 'it was not for me to bandy civilities with my sovereign; when the King had said it, it was to be so'.[9]

The evidence of other periods of Christian history might lead us to expect that in such circumstances there would be a compensating emphasis on the figure of Christ as a merciful intermediary; he, after all, had been human and shared human feelings, pain, grief and terror. In our period, however, a number of countervailing factors were at work.

The view of Christ's manhood put forward by the dominant orthodoxy was a sophisticated and rather artificial one. According to it, Jesus Christ was God the Son, creator of the universe, made flesh, the second person of the Trinity, co-equal with the Father, existing in human form. Jesus was not an independent human being, but the Word of God existing under the conditions of human life. Even while on earth he never ceased to be with the Father; even when born into this world, he continued, as divine, to control it.[10] Consequently, his humanity and human experience had not been simply like ours. St Athanasius, one of the most trusted and revered of the Fathers, could speak of his apparent ignorance in the days of his flesh as 'usefully pretending not to know', while another highly-regarded Father, St Cyril of Alexandria, could describe his passion as 'a suffering that was no suffering' (*apathōs epathen*).

Whether or not such language was correctly interpreted, it led to a reluctance in the early church to portray the earthly Jesus pictorially as a man among men. He was represented under such forms as those of a sheep or a shepherd, which may seem unimperious ways of picturing the heavenly ruler, but which were used to avoid the need for direct pictorial representations of him as a human being, in the same way that some artists were led by motives of awe and respect to symbolize God the Father simply by a commanding hand stretching down from heaven at the top of the picture.

Representations of the crucifixion did not come till later. The first unquestionable reference to a crucifix is to be found in Venantius Fortunatus in 560 CE. At the end of the seventh century the Trullan Synod enacted that Christ could be – indeed must be – 'shown hereafter in his human form ... so that without forgetting the height from which the divine Word stooped to us, we shall be led to remember his mortal life, his passion and his death'.[11]

Although the disciplinary canons of the Council were not formally accepted in the West, they were not without effect; but in many of the resultant representations of the crucifixion there was such a determination not to forget the divine status of the crucified figure that his head was shown on a larger scale than the rest of his body and in a more impressive form, partly because of the completely literal way Paul's words in I Cor.

11.3, 'the head of Christ is God', were understood at the time. His eyes were shown open, his arms stretched straight out and his legs side by side. Normally he wore a robe (*colobium*, see plate 1) and a crown. Even the wound in his side was portrayed as a token of victory. There was little or no emphasis on the human agony. Southern describes such crucifixes as 'expressing the sense of that remote and majestic act of divine power which ... filled ... men's minds'.[12] This was *Christus Victor*, 'God reigning from the tree', as Venantius Fortunatus expressed it in a hymn familiar at the time.[13] As Fichtenau says, 'Christ's human and friendly traits were pushed into the background', and the suffering was minimized, though the effects of it were stressed strongly enough.

> In fact it was the effect of what Christ had done, rather than the doing of it, that was emphasized; the salvation rather than the suffering. Christ was physician and fountain of life, the *salvator mundi*, and even in that capacity he was portrayed as an essentially lordly, and rather terrifying, figure, for example on the Aaby crucifix, which dates from just after our period (see plate 1).

If the patristic story already had a somewhat tenuous hold on the manhood of Christ, the tendency to play it down was reinforced in the tenth century by experience of Arianism in the comparatively recent past. Visigothic Arianism had pictured the Trinity as a sort of divine clan in which the king's son was strictly subordinate to his father. In reaction, the orthodox – including the Visigoths when they changed to Catholicism – emphasized the identity of Father and Son almost to a fault, especially as they had to fight an adoptianist theology in Spain at the end of the eighth century. Father and Son thus became almost indistinguishable.

If there was comparatively little emphasis on Jesus the man, there was strong emphasis on Christ the governor. After his victory on the cross, he had gone down to break the iron gates of hell and then returned to heaven like a victorious king returning from a successful campaign, acclaimed by the heavenly hosts and the 'magnates' of heaven, as a returning warrior would have been on earth.[14] Now, as world-governor, he demands the submission of all nations and rulers. There are many representations of him in this capacity, some of them juxtaposed with a portrayal of him on the cross. He is often pictured in a mandorla which creates an ideal sphere for him, and has the effect of cutting him off from us below. In many of these illustrations he inhabits a heavenly sphere and has a foot on a sphere representing the world below, in token of his dominion over it. Here he is the *pantocrator*, the ruler of all, portrayed with crown, throne, sun, moon, the alpha and omega, symbols of universal power, and worshipped by hosts of angels and the adoring elders of the New Testament.[15]

We may perhaps sum up the three functions of Christ as perceived at the time like this. First, as priest, he continually celebrates the rite of his sacrifice, in intercession and supplication for us. More will be said about this later. Secondly, there is his royal function. It is by his example and the delegation of his authority that earthly rulers rule, and those responsible for administering law distinguish right from wrong. He controls the two provinces, celestial and terrestrial, of a single kingdom, and leads the various orders in a sort of militia in the battle against evil. Thirdly, as judge he presides over the supreme *curia*, which meant both a court and the household of a noble, and distributes to his subjects according to their need. On the last day he will light the fire and burn the wicked.[16]

In the light of all that it is easy to see what Fichtenau meant when he said that 'Christ was thus made almost the sole representative of the Holy Trinity'. Even when the Father was more strongly emphasized, as he was by some Carolingian writers, a Christ conceived in this way was clearly not a figure with whom warm or intimate relations were likely to be envisaged or attempted,[17] the more so as the remote and awful deity of whom the Father and the Son were equally representative was also a God of wrath.

The wrath of God figures more prominently in the New Testament than is commonly recognized, and in the tenth century the Old Testament was taken to be as fully inspired as the New. The Old Testament God was confessedly a jealous God who frequently broke out in anger, and showed no mercy to his enemies, often punishing even those who had not been aware of offending him.

In an age which, as we have seen, had little understanding of secondary causes, the evils that befell society were assumed to be punishment from God; he must indeed be angry with his people, it was felt, if he visited so much suffering upon them. At the personal level also, the deaths and illnesses of individuals were interpreted as divine punishment for what they had done, even if in many cases no one could be sure what this had been. God was believed capable of bringing about the slaughter of countless enemy troops – mostly conscripts at that – to ensure the victory of an army which had won his favour; and it must be remembered that orthodox doctrine had no doubt or qualms about his intention to damn the great majority of the world's population, including all babies who died unbaptized. Small wonder if such a heavenly lord seemed quite as arbitrary and high-handed as any earthly lord.

As we shall see, the need was recognized to reconcile all this with God's justice. Yet, whatever might be said on that score, a God such as this was clearly not one to be trifled with; and it must be remembered that his likely reaction had to be taken into account in everything that was planned.

(ii)

According to the Christian story as it reached the Franks, God had a quite specific reason for being angry with the human race, and once again the story was interpreted in contemporary terms. By an act known as *diffidatio* a man might reject the authority of his feudal overlord and submit himself to another. The practice was greatly discouraged, and might lead to fighting between two overlords, but if the rules of *diffidatio* had been observed, the rules of war also had to be observed. It was believed that Adam and Eve, both conceived of as historical figures, had done something of just this sort, rejecting the lordship of God and submitting to that of the Devil instead. As we have seen, when a man submitted to a lord, all his family and his descendants were involved with him. In the same way all Adam and Eve's descendants, that is the entire human race, were committed to the Devil and owed service to him. Except for those who responded to God's countervailing action, they formed, as Agobard of Lyons put it, a sort of *corpus diaboli*, 'one body, composed of lost angels and men, destined for a common doom'.[18]

The Christian story had received its form in this matter at the hands of Augustine, and though the church did not accept his account in its entirety, it was deeply influenced by it. As a result of the sin of Adam and Eve in the garden of Eden, the entire human race became a *massa perditionis* (literally, 'a mass of perdition'), the members of which shared in their ancestors' guilt, and deserved the pains of eternal damnation from the moment of conception, which, in a fallen world, always involved lust, and was the means by which the inherited taint of guilt was passed on. So from the moment of conception, not to say birth, every human being deserved damnation. As Gregory the Great put it, 'every living being is conceived in the guilt of our first parent. We are born condemned sinners ... and we come into the world deserving to die' (*cum merito mortis nostrae*).[19]

This meant that simply to be born was to be hell-worthy, that the eternal damnation of even the youngest unbaptized baby was fully justified, and that if the entire human race had ended up in the unending tortures of hell, God's justice would in no way have been called into question. Any outcome better than that was simply a result of his unmerited mercy.

In fact, through the saving events chronicled in the Bible he had made possible for us a return to our true allegiance by means which observed the rules of war, as it were, and avoided any injustice to the devil, or breach of his rights. Central to this divine action was Christ's death on the cross, and accordingly it stood, interpreted along these lines, at the centre of religious faith and practice. As we have seen, there was not a great deal of emphasis on the human suffering of Christ in the tenth century, but the cross itself, often described as the tree, or the wood (*lignum*), was seen as the instrument of redemption, just as the tree in the garden of Eden had been the instrument of sin. The two trees were often treated as a typological pair, and it was generally agreed that adoration could properly be addressed to the cross, as in Anselm's famous prayer.[20] Such adoration was encouraged, and it was expressed in such hymns as the *Pange Lingua* ('Sing, my tongue, the glorious battle') and *Vexilla regis* ('The royal banners forward go') of Venantius Fortunatus. Through them and other works of art, as well as through the mass, the church expressed its gratitude to God for having made available, if only to some, a way of escape from the eternal damnation which would otherwise have been the fate of all.

The way to avail oneself of this divine action was first through baptism, but before that can be understood, we must note that, in addition to inheriting their guilt, all human beings inherited from Adam and Eve a strong, indeed virtually irresistible, tendency to sin, on their own account – what Augustine called *non posse non peccare* (an inability to avoid sin).

What baptism was believed to do for those who received it was, first, to wash away original sin (as participation in Adam's sin was called) and clear them from the eternal penalty that involved; secondly, to wash away all actual pre-baptismal sins of which they might have been guilty; and thirdly, to incorporate them into Christ and admit them to the church, where they could find the means for resisting sin thereafter.

Though baptism was thus a necessary condition of salvation,[21] it was by no means a sufficient condition. We have seen that post-baptismal sin was virtually unavoidable, so being baptized and becoming a member of the church was no guarantee of salvation. The *externa communio*, the outward and visible church, was a *corpus permixtum*, a body made up of good and bad Christians, and to be clearly distinguished from the *communio sanctorum*, that is, the church in the true sense, composed of the elect, all those who were destined for salvation (even if at the moment, some of them were not yet members of the *externa communio*). While it was true that 'outside of the church there is no salvation', membership of the visible church carried no guarantee of belonging to the communion of saints. There was, therefore, plenty of room for anxiety about one's own standing and salvation.

If baptism did not obviate post-baptismal sin, how was such sin to be coped with? As we have seen, a sin was regarded as an injury to God's honour; as such, it aroused his wrath, and could not be dealt with without punishment and suffering. Gregory wrote, 'God never spares one who offends; he never leaves a sin without taking vengeance on it. For either man himself punishes it in himself by doing penance, or God in dealing with man in vengeance for it, visits it with his rod. Thus there is never any sparing of sin; it is never loosed without vengeance.'[22] There was no doctrine of radical forgiveness. It was universally agreed that there could be no forgiveness without appropriate punishment. God's *honor*, like that of any feudal lord, had to be 'satisfied'; to have forgiven sin without satisfaction, it was felt, would have been a breach of justice and the rightness of things on God's part. Hence the constantly recurring refrain in Gregory and later theologians, with regard to the forgiveness of post-baptismal sin: *sive per nos, sive per deum* – either we make satisfaction ourselves or God does it for us, that is, by inflicting suffering on us.[23] Either way, the penalty had to be paid.

However vital, the effects of baptism were thus limited. Though the baptized were freed from the *guilt* of original sin, they were still subject to the misery the heavenly lord had inflicted on mankind as punishment for it, in particular the certainty of death, and in the meantime, the hard struggle to get sufficient food, and the pains and dangers of childbirth. It was largely in terms of such a literal acceptance of Gen. 3.16ff. that the early mediaeval church sought to reconcile the goodness of the creator and the wretchedness of the situation in which mankind found itself.

If baptism was a sign of the merciful disposition of God, certain aspects of it must have suggested a rather different picture to the reflective. It was effective only if correctly administered in the threefold name. When an ignorant Bavarian priest got the Latin formula wrong, there was considerable disagreement about whether the baptism had been acceptable to God; and a midwife was severely censured for letting a dying baby go to hell as a result of using the wrong words in baptizing it. Priests were expected to teach the correct formula to the midwives in their area; and if they themselves delayed baptizing the newly-born babies in the parish, they were punished, on the grounds that they were running the risk of letting some of them die unbaptized, and so, it was unquestioningly assumed, go to hell. The God presupposed in all this was one who would not take the intention for the deed, even in relation to young children; and although it was justified in official theology, God's willingness to countenance the eternal damnation of the overwhelming majority of the human race must have had its effect on people's conception of his character.

Rather similar feelings may have been aroused in connection with the teaching that salvation depended on the the holding of a very precise set of beliefs. As Burchard of Worms put it at the beginning of the eleventh century, 'anyone who does not have the correct faith does not belong to God'. The assumption that orthodox belief was essential to salvation lay behind the obligation rulers were believed to have to ensure that such belief was held by all their subjects – to see to it, as Ratramnus put it, that 'in accordance with the apostles' teaching, all should think the same and say the same'.[24] Of an unorthodox notion the same writer wrote, 'it is a sin not only to express it, but even to think it'.[25] Prohibiting the expression of certain types of view is something with which we are familiar today, for example, in connection with racial discrimination, but it always rests on the conviction that their expression could have undesirable consequences.

In the tenth century the belief was that the holding or expressing of unorthodox belief would lead to damnation, and that rested on a particular view of God.

> In practice the impact of this insistence on correct belief fell almost entirely on the clergy and the Religious; others were assumed to believe what the church believed, by what was called *fides implicita*, unless there were grounds for thinking otherwise. As there had been little heresy for some time,[26] the matter was not as important as it became later. Nevertheless the orthodox faith was complex and involved many fine points;[27] the belief that God insisted on it as a condition of salvation must have coloured feelings towards him, even if subconsciously.

Taking all this into account, we can hardly help concluding that God must have appeared to many in the tenth century in what would seem to us an arbitrary, and indeed tyrannical, light. We must bear in mind that everything which happened was taken to be more or less directly attributable to him. To recognize something of the confusion about him that this must have caused it is only necessary to imagine what confusion would arise today if everything that happened to nations (the earthquakes, the epidemics, the military vicissitudes) and to individuals (the illnesses, the bereavements, the unemployment) were viewed as direct divine visitations.

Calamities were seen as God's punishments, but people were often at a loss to know what had merited them. In Helgaldus's *Life of King Robert*, for example, we hear of an eclipse which was taken to presage some divine punishment, but no one could discover what it was for. Sometimes the offence was identified *post eventum*, but in a case reported in the Life of St Anskar, it took a soothsayer to make clear what the fault had been, and it is worth noting that it was Christ who was said to have inflicted the punitive damage, which consisted in the death of numerous (entirely innocent) children, grandchildren and other relatives of the offender ('Christ has ruined you').[28] This was by no means the only case where punishment was visited by God on people totally unconnected with an offence, of which even the perpetrator was sometimes unaware.[29] Signs of divine approval could also be difficult to interpret. In the life of the saintly Gerald of Aurillac, for instance, we are told of an annually expanding circle of green grass round his tomb. No one could discover the meaning of it, yet a meaning it was bound to have, for 'it is certain that nothing happens on this earth without a (supernatural) cause'.[30]

God's good will was of the utmost practical importance, but it was not secured once-for-all at baptism; it had to be kept, or won, thereafter. In face of the uncertainties just described, it was difficult to know how to win it or whether it had been won. The result was often profound insecurity and uneasiness. Wallace-Hadrill writes that 'the Gallo-Frankish God ...

1. Aaby crucifix

2. Trumeau, Souillac

3. Charlemagne's throne, Aachen

4. Ivory of Otto II

5. Carolingian manuscript

6. St Peter, Mistail, Switzerland

7. Otto II enthroned

8. A late tenth-century crown

presided over a society ever on the look-out for evidence of his pleasure or displeasure. It can hardly be surprising that he was greatly feared.'[31] In the ninth century Louis the Pious seems to have felt that appeasing an angry God was part of his role as emperor, and with that in mind he prayed, fasted and gave alms, almost feverishly, until the bishops told him that propitiation was their business.

The situation was not made any easier by the heteronomous character of the mediaeval moral outlook. Modern believers may feel justified in using their own moral insights and experience in order to arrive at a general understanding of what is right. So far as they act in accordance with it, they will not feel in any danger of incurring God's severe displeasure. No such option was available in the tenth century. Who were fallen human beings that their moral sense should provide a window on to the principles by which God worked and judged? Had not Solomon written: 'With difficulty we guess even at things on earth, and only with labour find out what lies before us. Who has ever traced out what is in heaven? Who shall know thy thought?' (Wisdom 9.16–17a). God's will for his subjects could be discovered only as he had chosen to declare it in the Bible and the various canons and ecclesiastical decisions authoritatively based upon it. When learned bishops such as Hincmar of Reims or Fulbert of Chartres were consulted on moral questions, as they often were, they invariably relied on texts in the Bible and the Fathers and on official ecclesiastical decisions for an answer. Yet, as we have seen, it was difficult to find one's way about in this mass of often conflicting authorities. How could one be sure one had not overlooked or misinterpreted some divine pronouncement, and that it was for that reason that one had incurred God's displeasure?

How far was the understanding of the supernatural world revealed so far modified by beliefs about the lesser beings supposed to inhabit it alongside God?

7

The Lesser Inhabitants of the
Supernatural Realm

(i)

As we have seen, the supernatural world of the tenth-century imagination contained many beings other than God. The most prominent, or certainly one of the most prominent, in the popular mind was the devil. Although, as we saw, his rights over mankind as a whole had been bought out, he still existed and was constantly active everywhere. It would be difficult to exaggerate the actuality of the devil and his agents for people of this period, or the vivid and unquestioning realism with which they were pictured. Jerome had written that 'the entire human population of the world is as nothing compared with the entire population of spirits',[1] and Cassian had said that 'the air between heaven and earth is so crammed with spirits, never quiet or finding rest, that men are fortunate not to be permitted to see them'.[2] Evil spirits could be in the air you breathed, the water you drank or the meat you ate. The learned, as we have seen, believed that these evil spirits were fallen angels.

> Though widespread, this view was not held by all theologians. It went back originally to some words in the Septuagint version of Deut. 32.8, not found in the Hebrew or Latin texts: 'he fixed the bounds of the peoples according to the number of the angels of God'. According to Anselm and others, since the 'proper nature' of the creation had from the beginning involved the existence of a finite number of sentient beings, the fallen angels had to be replaced. Attempts were sometimes made to discover what the finite number was, but Isidore was more typical when he wrote: 'The number of the good angels, which was diminished after the fall of the evil angels, will be completed by the number of elect human beings, a number that is known only to God.'[3] Even so, there remained the rather threatening fact that the number of those who would be saved was a limited and predetermined one.

Most people, however, just accepted the existence of all these spirits, without asking how they had come into existence or why God had not annihilated them. They simply felt that God had an opponent ranged against him, as earthly lords often did, and they saw themselves caught up in the resultant struggle, just as they were when some hostile lord invaded their lord's domains.

It was accepted that these demonic forces would be active right to the end of time; and though after the final judgment the elect would be exempt from the devil's influence, hell, where he and his minions presided, would be eternal, and so, presumably, would they. Meanwhile they were tirelessly at work attempting to detach everyone from God. They employed two strategies, working either by guile or by terror. In the former case, they normally appeared in disguise. For example, a young man to whom a demon appeared in the form of a beautiful maiden had been lured into grievous sin before realizing what was happening or who was behind it.[4] When it was a question of terrorizing people, demons tended to appear as themselves, but in hideous and terrifying forms. A passage describing such an appearance is so revealing of the complete reality of the demonic world to early mediaeval people that it deserves to be quoted *in extenso*, especially as the victim was, by the standards of the day, a scholarly and sophisticated man. At the beginning of the eleventh century, the devil appeared to the monk Ralph Glaber before the office of Matins in the monastery of St Léger de Champeaux. 'I saw a mannikin-like being, horrible to look at, rise up at the foot of my bed. As far as I could judge, he was of medium height, with a skinny neck, a thin face, jet-black eyes, a lined and wrinkled forehead, pinched nostrils, a prominent mouth, thick lips, a receding, very narrow chin, a goatee beard, hairy tapering ears, bristly, shaggy hair, teeth like those of a dog, a pointed skull, a swollen chest, a humped back, shaking thighs and dirty clothes.'[5]

Innumerable saints' Lives represented their subjects as constantly subject to satanic attack and temptation; indeed one of the purposes of these Lives was to reveal to the faithful how such attacks were best dealt with. Yet lesser mortals must have asked themselves anxiously how they could expect to fare, if the heroes of the faith had only just succeeded in emerging victorious.

Le Goff speaks of 'the terrible anxiety which gripped everyone almost the whole time: to see the devil appear'.[6] That fear was closely connected with the monstrous and terrifying forms with which the popular imagination peopled both land and sea. Lonely and uninhabited places, in particular, were believed to be full of hideous and malign creatures. No doubt much of this came down from pre-Christian times, but by the tenth century it was associated with Christian beliefs about the devil. Many a village, surrounded by the thick forest land which separated it from its nearest neighbours, must in some ways have resembled a village in a jungle clearing, the environment all around hostile and threatening. It was here, and in desolate undrained marshland, that many terrifying monsters were believed to hide, ready at any time to pounce. Modern visitors to early mediaeval churches will have noticed the monsters and horribly grimacing faces carved in wood and stone. Many of these are illustrated and discussed in George Henderson's *Early Medieval*. To cite only two instances, he writes of how 'in the horrid confrontation at Moissac the ancient theme of man versus monster reaches its climax', the demon being 'muscular yet insect-like, obese yet emaciated, human in outline, yet with the clawed feet of a wolf or bear, and with a cruel, distorted, bestial head'.[7] He also describes the famous trumeau at Souillac, on which the lions and griffins, interpreted by Marbodus Bishop of Rennes as the enemies of the human soul, tear and rend one another, as well as the naked man at the top, caught between two monsters. 'This energetic visual fantasy,' Henderson writes, 'sums up many centuries of European art', and expresses 'that dark undercurrent of vehemence and tension most often expressed in the representation of the destructive teeth and talons of ferocious beasts'.[8] It was in this monster-ridden environment, sometimes (see plate 14) almost reminiscent of Hieronymus Bosch, that most tenth-century Franks felt themselves to be living.

Not only did the devil tempt people into deserting God; he and his agents constantly brought material disaster upon them, for example, to quote a later mediaeval source, 'starting wars, and tempests at sea in which they caused men to drown, arousing sometimes mortal enmity between neighbours,[9] starting fires and dangerous gales, making mothers overlie their babies and leading both men and women to commit suicide'.[10] Their capacity for wreaking such damage was increased by their superior intelligence which, according to Isidore, retained 'the keen perception of the angelic creation'.[11] Their capacity for foreknowledge and the length of their experience made the struggle against them a virtually hopeless one for mankind. They were tirelessly persistent: 'the devil never rests from his attack on the just man', who 'is sometimes reduced to the straits of despair'. So said Isidore.[12]

That was hardly surprising. The devil's aim was to make his victims feel that, as might happen in a war between two earthly lords, it might pay to buy off the attacker by going over to his side, or at least to try to get a foot in both camps. Not surprisingly, many came to feel that they had bought peace with the Devil at the price of damnation.

In such a situation the only recourse for those who took salvation seriously was constant vigilance. Life had to be an unremitting *agonia*, or struggle, against every attack, allurement and temptation, an *agonia* which would culminate only in the death agony, which was not just a fight against pain but the determined effort to remain faithful to God during the process of dying.[13] Psychologically, people were in a difficult position: the devil's forces seemed almost limitlessly powerful, and could make life almost impossibly painful. Yet the situation differed from that between two earthly lords because it was already certain that God would triumph eventually and that one's eternal destiny would depend on his judgment of one. Nevertheless, the nerve of some broke, and they gave way to what was later to be called 'wanhope' in England, that is, reconciling oneself to eternal damnation. Indeed that was one of the effects the devil was believed to produce in his victims.[14]

Clearly, the situation so perceived was bound to give rise to a great deal of strenuousness and heroic battling, not to say fear and anxiety, on the part of those who took it seriously, especially in view of the widespread expectation of the imminence of the final judgment, which will be discussed later (see pp. 129ff. below). Indeed preachers felt that fear was a necessary and salutary element in the Christian life. Gregory the Great, for example, taught that 'each man must live in fear, for he does not know what is to come, since we must never forget, but often repeat and ponder, the words, "many are called but few are chosen" '.[15] In his Life of Adalhard of Corbie, Paschasius Radbert approves of the fact that Adalhard 'walked anxiously with God',[16] and Agobard described fear as the nether millstone and hope as the upper; there is no flour without both, and God meant each to be used as the antidote to the other.[17]

(ii)

In this rather terrifying situation, however, resources were available which could enable believers to resist the evil powers and remain faithful to God, even if it was at great cost.

First, just as God's adversary the devil had his forces, so God, like any other lord, had his.[18] They were the angelic hosts, and they loomed particularly large in the Christianity of the ninth and tenth centuries. Angels were too prominent in the Bible for believers ever to have had any doubts about their existence,[19] and the Fathers regarded it as a truth of faith. Yet, being preoccupied with questions relating to the Trinity and the Incarnation, they did not devote much attention to the angels, until in about 500 CE some works appeared which, being attributed to one of Paul's original converts at Athens, Dionysius the Areopagite (Acts 17.34), enjoyed almost apostolic authority. One of these books, *Concerning the Celestial Hierarchy*, purported to give a detailed account of the angelic order, which it described as organized in three hierarchies, each consisting of three 'choirs', according to the following, strictly hierarchical scheme:

  (i) Seraphim, Cherubim and Thrones
  (ii) Dominations, Virtues and Powers
  (iii) Principalities, Archangels and Angels

(the titles are all derived from the New Testament). Gregory the Great reproduced this account in a slightly modified form, and so did Isidore, whose repeated discussions of the angels reflected the increased interest in them in this period.[20] This interest is also reflected in the art of the period.

For example, the archangels figure prominently on the altar frontal given by the Emperor Henry II to Basel Cathedral in 1019, and also in a sacramentary of about 870, probably from St Denis.[21] In the apses and domes of churches, St Michael the Archangel often ousted even the figure of Christ himself. The angels also came to occupy a larger part in religious observance at this time. In the canon of the mass, which long antedates this period, there is only a single reference to an angel, in contrast to the considerable number of saints who are named; but the offertory in the Mass for the Dead, produced around this time, includes the prayer '... that they fall not into darkness; but let the standard-bearer St Michael bring them to the holy light'. Perhaps more significantly, one of the first suffrages in the *commendatio animae*, which contains the prayers for the dying in use since the eighth century, asks all the angels and archangels to pray for the soul of the dying person. In the course of the haunting prayer which follows, the priest says: 'Go forth, O Christian soul ... in the name of the Angels and Archangels, in the name of the Thrones and Dominations, in the name of the Principalities and Powers, in the name of the Cherubim and Seraphim'; and later came the words, 'as thy soul departs from the body, may the glorious company of angels come to meet thee'. The angels are given a place of high precedence in these prayers, immediately after the persons of the Trinity and the Virgin Mary, and ahead of all the rest of the saints. The references to them, heard at a moment of heightened emotion, and combined with pictorial representations which often pictured Michael as receiver of the souls of the dead, and their champion, must have impressed on peoples' minds the vital role played by the angels in that most important of all matters, the issue of heaven or hell.[22]

Isidore describes the angels with some precision: 'Angels are of spiritual substance; they were created before all creatures and made subject to change by nature, but were rendered changeless by the contemplation of God. They are not subject to passion, they possess reason, are immortal, perpetual in blessedness, with no anxiety about their happiness, and with foreknowledge about the future. They govern the world according to command, taking bodies from the upper air; they dwell in the heavens.'[23]

How the angels were generally pictured it is extremely difficult to say. A learned and, for his day, sceptical man such as Agobard can say explicitly that the traditional representations were not to be taken as more than symbolic; and Isidore, as we have just seen, held that they were of spiritual substance. That did not prevent him, however, from believing that they 'veiled the face and feet of God'. Probably, as with the powers of evil, the traditional pictorial representations of them were taken more or less literally by the great mass of people. No doubt the details of the Dionysian account will have passed these latter by, but they will have been comforted by the faith that the evil forces arrayed against them were confronted by at least equally powerful forces on God's side. Isidore says that the Powers were so called 'because evil spirits are constrained by their power not to harm the world as much as they desire'.[24]

Daniel 7.10, which in the Latin version spoke of the angels as numbering millions, was frequently quoted, and these hordes were envisaged as being very much on a war footing. The Old Testament title 'Lord of Hosts' was interpreted as referring to the angels, and so was the word *mahanaim* (camps, or companies) in such texts as Gen. 32.1–2. When Fulk Nerra founded the monastery of Beaulieu-les-Loches in 1007, he dedicated it to 'the Holy Trinity and the celestial armies over which God reigns, namely the Cherubim and Seraphim'.[25]

The angelic host was thus pictured assembled at the Almighty's side, watchful and ready to descend on the enemy, just like the counts and generals who, with the bishops, flanked the person of the earthly sovereign. The comfort people derived from all this was all the greater in the light of current teaching about guardian angels, that is, angels specially detailed to look after particular nations and places (cf. Dan. 10.13, 21 and 12.1) and particular individuals (cf. Matt. 18.10 and Acts 12.15). Once again we see how much the doctrinal story was built on a scanty and obscure biblical basis. The doctrine of angels will no doubt have been more readily acceptable by the Franks, because of their immemorial belief in tutelary spirits and the like in their pre-Christian days, though interestingly, in this case it could also appeal to Greek thought (cf. Plato's *Phaedo* 108B and the frequent references to Socrates' *daimon*). Belief in guardian angels for individuals was a subject of some controversy among the Fathers and was first defined clearly by Honorius of Autun in the twelfth century; but it received liturgical expression much earlier (cf. the Collect for Michaelmas in the Leonine Sacramentary), and the eighth-century bishop Pirminius told a group of the newly baptized that 'a holy angel has been assigned to protect each of you'.[26]

Although the angels loomed so large in tenth-century Frankish religion, their help was not the only resource the church could offer in the struggle against the forces of evil. In addition to the sacraments, the Lord's Prayer and the sign of the cross were used, almost as charms, to ward off demonic attacks, and so were holy water and holy oil, and the repetition of certain prayer formulas. These were available from the clergy, whose custody of them added to the awe in which they were held.

The greatest resource of tenth-century Christians, the cult of the saints, has not yet been mentioned; but before we consider any other relationship with God, mediated through lesser supernatural beings, more must be said about the tenth-century understanding of direct relations with him.

8

Sin and Forgiveness:
The Work of Christ

(i)

How far was the the tenth-century picture of God which has so far emerged affected by beliefs about Christ's incarnation and what it achieved?

Paradoxically, the answer has to begin with some account of the contemporary penitential system. While, as we have seen, baptism cleansed candidates from the guilt of original sin and of their actual pre-baptismal sins, it was guilt for sins committed after baptism which would determine the issue of heaven or hell, and for these penalties had to be paid. By God's merciful dispensation, the necessary penalties *could* be paid, but in order to take advantage of this dispensation, the Holy Spirit's prompting was as necessary for penitence and penance as it was for coming forward to baptism. Such, at any rate, was the official teaching, though it probably had little impact in a situation where infant baptism was compulsory and universal, and penance an accepted and regular institution.

For by the tenth century regular confession to a priest, followed by the performance of the penance imposed, had become institutionalized, and was widely recommended for all.

In earlier days penance had been public, lifelong and unrepeatable, concerned only with major wrongdoing, and terminable only at the approach of death. Public penance was still advocated by some churchmen in our period; and as recently as the time of Charlemagne vigorous attempts had been made to promote it throughout the empire.[1] However, from the seventh century on-wards private confession, introduced into Francia by Celtic missionaries, had been increasingly recommended, until it eventually became compulsory, first for the clergy and then for all. It was one of the strongest forms of social control available to the authorities.

Just how widespread or frequent it was in the late tenth century is hard to tell, because the evidence is conflicting. There is a good deal to suggest that confession to a priest was something many people still postponed until the near approach of death, but Regino of Prüm (died 915) already envisages it as taking place at least once a year, on Ash Wednesday,[2] and Burchard's *Corrector* takes the same view.[3] In the eleventh century the pious emperor Henry III never put on his royal insignia without making a formal confession, and by the end of the century the Synod of Gran (Strigonia) demanded confession from all at least three times a year, at Easter, Whitsun and Christmas.[4] The precise date of the council is uncertain, and it must of course be remembered that it took place in Hungary.[5]

The process was held to involve four elements:

(i) Perception of sin and dread of God's judgment;
(ii) Regret (*contritio* or *compunctio*);
(iii) Satisfaction (*satisfactio*).[6]

The first two were known as *conversio mentis* (literally, a change of mind) and, as we have seen, were regarded as the work of the Holy Spirit,[7] though the Spirit worked through natural motivations, fear of merited punishment and longing for the heavenly fatherland.[8]

This *conversio* was supposed to involve continuing anguish (*dolor*) which, according to one tenth-century work, was expected to be lifelong.[9] For the forgiveness of some minor sins this *dolor* sufficed of itself, but for the great majority of offences confession to some other Christian was deemed necessary, and by our period this usually meant in practice one's parish priest, unless one belonged to some institution which maintained its own chaplain. As confession became regular and compulsory, the sense of the Holy Spirit's moving one to it must have become vestigial.

At first, when private confession was still a novelty and people were uncertain how to go about it, the clergy would ask questions to elicit what a penitent's sins had been. This practice is still presupposed in the early eleventh-century *Medicus* of Burchard of Worms, but it had tended to fall into abeyance because it sometimes suggested to penitents sinful practices of which they had previously been unaware.

When the sins had been confessed, the priest would lay down appropriate penances, and these had to be completed before absolution was granted and forgiveness obtained. Although for various practical reasons it had become common by the tenth century to give absolution at once, the making of satisfaction through penances was still seen as a condition of forgiveness; it was not until later that confession itself came to be regarded as the essence of the matter.[10] After the confession and imposition of penance, the penitent begged for the intercession of the confessor and of the saints. When absolution was given, it was deprecatory rather than declaratory in form – for example, 'mayest thou consent to be appeased (*placatus*), O Lord'. The priest then prayed alongside the penitent for forgiveness, and although Gregory, following Augustine, had taught that confession, penance and absolution really did 'strike off the bonds of sin',[11] the penitential practice of the tenth century cannot have dealt with a penitent's anxiety in the way a declaratory declaration of absolution is calculated to do; and it must have thrown great emphasis on the proper performance of the penances.[12]

The penances constituted what has been called 'an expiatory tariff',[13] so they are interesting to us as showing the general outlook of the period: in particular the sort of offences commonly committed, and the relative seriousness with which they were regarded.

We know about them as the result of the survival of a number of penitentials, handbooks for confessors containing exhaustive lists of sins, with the penalties appropriate to each. Of Celtic origin, these books spread over Europe with the Celtic and Anglo-Saxon missionaries, and were widely used in our period, despite reservations about them in some quarters. They varied widely in their provisions, and there could be a considerable disparity of practice between one confessor and another.

> It was partly on this ground that the authorities, some of whom still hankered after public penance, tended to oppose them. The synod of Chalons sur Saône of 813, for example, spoke of 'the *libelli* called penitentials of which the errors are certain, the authors uncertain', and the synod of Paris in 829 condemned them as uncanonical. However, Charlemagne ordered that every confessor should have a copy, and Regino of Prüm, writing in the tenth century, gave the same advice. The nineteenth book of the extremely influential *Decretum* of Burchard of Worms, produced in 1010, and known as the *Medicus*, was in effect a penitential. The title of Burchard's book is significant because confessors were encouraged to think of themselves as doctors of the soul, supplying the correct treatment for each condition.[14]

The penances prescribed in the penitentials consisted principally of fasting, though the saying of specified numbers of psalms, standing for long periods with arms outstretched, (self-) flagellation, giving alms and going on pilgrimage were also prescribed. In serious cases some combination of these might be ordered.

The penitentials are a subject in themselves, and without really extensive quotation it is difficult to make clear what they were like or what the impact of their prescriptions is likely to have been on penitents.

However, the following list may give some very rough idea of the sort of thing involved. The number in brackets after each offence indicates the amount of fasting prescribed; and the regimen to be observed during those periods was very precisely laid down. According to the so-called Penitential of Bede, for example, penitents were to go without wine, mead or flesh for three days each week, to fast completely until vespers (i.e. until after 4 p.m.), and then eat only dry food. During the penitential periods of the church's year (comprising some seventeen weeks) they were to eat only dry food, fast till nones (i.e. till about 3 p.m.) on three days in the week and till vespers on the other three. Sundays were exempt.[15]

> Extra-marital sex between a young man and a virgin (one year – or four, two of

them rigorous, if a baby had resulted); sexual relations between a monk and a nun (seven years), between a brother and sister (five years), between a mother and son (seven years and perpetual continence); sodomy (four years – or seven if monks or recidivists were involved); lesbianism (three years – or seven, if between nuns); bestiality (one year – or two if a monk was involved – and the slaughter of the animal); mutual onanism between children (forty days).

Killing through hatred or greed (seven years and retirement from the service of arms), in anger (four years), of a master or a wife (retirement to a monastery or a regimen involving the giving up of military service and participation in public affairs, lifelong abstention from meat or fat or alcohol, from all riding or bathing, from marriage or concubinage, from holy communion, except *in articulo mortis*, from contact with the other worshippers at church except to ask for their prayers); killing to avenge a brother (three years, one rigorous). Procuring an abortion (one year if less than forty days from conception; three years if later than that).

Drunkenness to the point of vomiting (twelve days for a lay person, more for clerics); fasting on a Sunday by inadvertence (one week); communicating after eating (one week).

Consulting a sorcerer (two years); worshipping the heavenly bodies according to pagan rites (two years).

Other miscellaneous offences provided for include violating a tomb to steal the clothes, having sexual relations in Lent or in the four or five days before a major feast, failing to communicate at such a feast, refusing the ministrations of a married priest, dropping a consecrated host, whether wilfully or by accident, having contact with excommunicate persons, failure to purify with holy water wine in which a dead mouse had been found, marrying within the degrees of consanguinity, swearing falsely and bearing false witness, lying or bursting out laughing.

This list, though only a minute sample, will make clear the wide range of sins covered and the way serious moral and criminal transgressions were included along with involuntary misdemeanours and what we should regard as contraventions of tabu. The predominance of gross and violent offences is what might be expected in a relatively primitive, rural society, and we may note the emphasis on outward and readily identifiable misconduct. The last point should not be exaggerated, however; the penitentials were concerned with inward evil desires as well as overt acts. For example the *Scarapsus* of Pirminius begins its discussion of sin with a list of eight principal vices, all, at least partly, dispositions of mind: greed, gluttony, fornication, anger, sadness, *accidie* (for which see pp. 191–2 below), vainglory and pride. In commentary on this list Pirminius warns against hatred, laziness and pride (which is defined as 'everything we do to promote ourselves or to win praise from others'), accepting favoured treatment, bias in judging, especially in return for money, running down one's neighbours and factious rivalries.[16]

It is difficult to tell how far the penitentials reflect the sort of penances that were in fact prescribed, let alone carried out. One wonders how far life would have been possible at all under the condition prescribed for someone who had killed a mother or wife; would anyone have been persuaded to accept such penance for long? Yet even if there is an element of the ideal about what they propose, the penitentials reveal what churchmen thought the situation should be, and no doubt reflect the reality to a considerable extent. When we remember what a large part confession played in the lives of many, it is clear that the penitential system must have moved forward the moral outlook and sensibility of early mediaeval men and women very considerably. At least it meant that they were encouraged to scrutinize their whole lives in search of sins and were induced to look for, and to recognize and mourn as sins, not only gross outward offences, but inner evil desires as well. As Harnack says of the change from public to private penance, 'there sprang from this a deepening of the notion of sin, since new sins, namely the "roots of sin" themselves, were put in place of the old mortal sins'.[17] By 'roots' he means, he says, 'intemperance, fornication, greed, anger, ill-temper, secret fear and dislike, presumption and pride'.

Still, by having attached to them the same sort of penances as those prescribed for more overt offences, these 'roots' were themselves to some extent externalized; and the prevailing impression made by the penitentials is of an emphasis primarily on the overt, outward act. As M.W. Baldwin says, 'there is as yet little evidence of any attempt to distinguish motives underlying acts, or the extent to which the will is involved'.[18] In that connection we may recall the wide variety of misdoing with which the penitentials dealt. It is revealing, for example, that the accidental dropping of a consecrated wafer should have been treated as a sin, or that the seriousness of extra-marital sexual relations should have been thought to depend on whether or not a baby resulted, something quite outside the couple's control. The idea seems to have been, at least in part, that certain species of behaviour were wrong *per se* and, as such, deserved punishment, even when they were involuntary or unavoidable. This must have deepened the sense of the supernatural as arbitrary; people could never know what might happen beyond their control that would land them in God's displeasure.[19]

Such a system was bound to suggest the idea that penances had objective value to God. In return for the undergoing of certain amounts of hardship, but not for less, he was able and prepared to remit the guilt of, and punishment for, such and such an offence. This impression could only be deepened by the very precise terms in which penance was defined – fasting until a certain time of day, and so on. The way was thus open for the belief that, provided the due amount of hardship was undergone in *some* form and by *some* person, the sin would be forgiven.

Right from the beginning, and largely for practical reasons – for example, because old and sick people or pregnant women could not undertake the necessary fasting – a twofold system of commutation was practised.

(i)(*a*) You could substitute some other form of penitential activity for that prescribed. For example, instead of fasting for so long, going barefoot, wearing a hairshirt or going on pilgrimage, you might give alms, say certain prayers (continuously and in large numbers), scourge yourself, strike your hands repeatedly on a stone floor, or stand for a long while with outstretched arms, repeating psalms. The principle was that you should undergo an equivalent amount of suffering, and the penitentials contain whole schedules of equivalents.[20]

(i)(*b*) You might pay money. A system of tariffs grew up: for example, three, ten or twenty denarii, according to means, would redeem seven weeks' fast. The money might be given to buy masses or for other charitable purposes.

It is disputed how far this development arose out of the old German system of *Wergild* described earlier (see p. 8). If it did, penances were seen as compensation or satisfaction for injuries done to God as the supreme Lord. However, Pelikan points out that theologians had spoken of penance as 'a way of making satisfaction to the Lord'[21] as early as the second century.[22] Whatever the truth of the matter, the way tariffs were employed in both cases will have led to the easy acceptance of the penitential system in Germanic societies, accustomed to the *Wergild* system.

(ii) You could actually get someone else to do the suffering for you. In support of this was quoted Gal. 6.2, 'Bear ye one anothers' burdens and so you shall fulfil the law of Christ', where many of the Fathers interpreted *onera* (burdens) as meaning 'failings'. An extreme example of this occurs in the canons published in England in about 967, according to which a (presumably rich) man due for seven years' penance could pay twelve men to fast for three days each, and then seven groups of one hundred and twenty men to do the same.

It must in fairness be repeated that one of the motives for allowing such commutations was to assist those too infirm to do penance themselves; and it must be added that those who employ others in this way are enjoined to be generous themselves, even to the point of giving away half their goods (Luke 19.8); and 'above all they are to cease to perpetrate injustice'. The rich man envisaged in the canons of King Edgar, for example, was expected to put aside arms, to go on a pilgrimage, to wear wool and a hairshirt, to give up sleeping on a bed and to forgive those who had sinned against him. It was recognized that many of the most effective penances would be beyond the reach of the poor, who would in any case have to discharge their penances in person; but that was justified on the basis of Gal. 6.5: 'everyone shall bear his own burden' (*onus*; see above on 6.2).

Another very important development, guided by the same principles, was that of *voluntary* vicarious suffering. Those who had not incurred any self-denial by way of penance could either forgo innocent pleasures and comforts or undertake penitential sufferings voluntarily, and thus put God in their debt to the tune of their 'innocent' penances.[23] Here we have the origin of the idea that the merits of good men and women could be available for others. The saints in particular, who had embraced self-denial and suffering beyond what their own shortcomings demanded, were said to have put God in their debt (*habent deum debitorem*), and their merits were thus available to provide satisfaction for the sins of others.

The upshot of all this was that there were a number of ways of dealing with post-baptismal sin. Sinners had their own contrition and *dolor*, the penances they undertook, the substitutes for these penances, particularly almsgiving, and the vicarious sufferings of others, particularly the merits won by the suffering of the saints. All these combined to provide the satisfaction necessary before God could forgive sins and remit the penalties for them.

It is easy to see how this led to a certain scrupulousness. Just as people who are ill take care to see that the treatment prescribed for their recovery is scrupulously carried out, so conscientious people of this period anxiously watched over the completion of the penitential regimen necessary for their forgiveness. Even so, there was little sense of assurance; and that was felt to be as it should be. There is a revealing letter from Pope Gregory to a lady of the court of the Empress Gregoria who had threatened to keep writing to him until he had been assured by a special revelation that her sins were forgiven. The pope replies that, quite apart from his unworthiness to be accorded a special revelation, it would not be good for her. She ought not to be certain of forgiveness until the last day of her life, when she would no longer be in a position to deplore her sins. Until then she must continue to fear, for certainty is the parent of indolence; she must not strive to attain it lest she go to sleep: 'Let your soul tremble for a while now, that it may afterwards enjoy unending bliss.'[24] There is considerable truth in Harnack's claim that this was a religion which 'set up fear and hope instead of faith and love, and for the grace of God in Christ substituted ... a complicated doctrine of merit ... God's sole concern was to be *satisfied*, since he was the requiter'.[25]

Faced with such a variety of mediators between their souls and God – Christ, the angels, the saints, substitutionary human agents – it is not surprising that people came to calculate what each could do for them and what each was good for;[26] and that fear of punishment tended to replace regret for sin. It is significant that Bede defined the confessor's task as being 'to absolve penitents from the *fear* of perpetual death'.[27]

A penitential system of this sort encouraged a contractual view of relations with God, all the more readily because of the way God was envisaged as a supreme overlord, and in a feudal, or semi-feudal society, relations with overlords were very much on a contractual basis. A good example of this attitude is the very frequent case where a rich man with a dubious past would decide, more or less on his death bed, to make generous provision for the clergy or the poor or some other deserving group. He would expect this to tell strongly in his favour after death and would make the provision quite explicitly with that expectation in mind.

The underlying emphasis on punishment, and the need to deal with it, could not help diverting attention from the heinousness of sin itself to the avoidance of penalties for it; the contractual view of divine-human relations was thus reinforced.

Still more revealing, if one stops to think about it, is the belief mentioned above that it was possible to live better than God demanded and so have merit over to pass on to others. Not only does such a notion imply a quantitative, and very external, view of human goodness; it presupposes that God is concerned, not with the moral health of the individual, but solely with the exaction of the amount of suffering necessary to enable him to pass over sin without any breach of justice. Suffering is here treated as a measurable commodity, and the transaction is so contractually conceived that it makes no difference by whom the suffering is undergone, provided it is sufficient in quantity.

On the other hand, it must be added that the official view presupposed a genuinely penitent spirit throughout the penitential process. We have already seen the emphasis placed on the anguish of contrition, and Jonas of Orléans, for example, wrote in the ninth century that 'penitence is assured, not by the length of time the expiation lasts, but by the degree of interior contrition'.[28] The sinner must go through the penitential procedure, but 'nevertheless it is from God alone that, in contrition of heart, with tears and groanings, he will ask pardon, in prayer to God whom alone he has offended by his sin';[29] and even when forgiven, he must not forget his offences. It is impossible to say how far teaching of this sort reached ordinary penitents and informed their attitude.

(ii)

Although this survey of penitential practice was undertaken with a view to understanding how the coming and work of Christ were understood in the tenth century, it has proved revealing about other aspects of religion at the time. The Christianity of the day, as it has emerged so far, was very much a do-it-yourself religion, according to which salvation largely depended on the conscientious discharge of certain clearly defined obligations. We have now to ask not only how the penitential system affected the understanding of Christ's work, but how far the understanding of Christ's work modified the situation produced by the system.

The Fathers never defined the doctrine of redemption in the way they defined the doctrines of the Trinity and the Incarnation. Various accounts of it were given, and most of these survived into our period. First there was the metaphysical account, which worked with the notion of substance current in Greek philosophy. According to this, every existent is constituted of some substance (*ousia*), and the substance of which it is constituted largely controls its characteristics and behaviour. To take an analogy from the natural world, a cube of a certain size made of the substance wood is lighter than one of the same size made of the substance iron, and will float in water, whereas the other will sink. According to this view, the substance of which human beings are constituted had become subject to corruption and death, and liable to be tempted to evil. The remedy was for this corrupt human substance to be united with divine substance in such a way that it took on the characteristics of that substance, rather as a cold, hard, grey piece of iron, if plunged into a hot fire, loses those characteristics and takes on the characteristics of fire instead, becoming hot, soft, red or white, and so on. (The analogy is one frequently used by the Fathers themselves.) What was needed, on such a view, was a close union between divine and human substance, and this was what was believed to have been brought about in Jesus, in whom both substances were united. In that sense the proponents of this view frequently used the language of deification. Following Athanasius and others, Augustine, for example, wrote that 'to make us, who are men, gods, he who was God was made man', or again, 'we are made gods'.[30] Similarly Pope Leo I claimed that 'unless the Word of God became flesh and dwelt in us, unless the creator descended to share the being of the creature (*in communionem creaturae*) and by his birth recalled the old humanity (*vetustas humana*, i.e. the corrupt human substance) to a new beginning (*principium*), death would reign from Adam right to the end'.[31] In emphasizing this primarily Eastern view of the matter, Leo was somewhat exceptional among Western Fathers, and he was careful to make clear that the Incarnation alone was not sufficient of itself to save us. 'Christ's passion contains the mystery of our salvation,' he wrote.[32]

> Although the metaphysical account of Christ's work was not explicitly canvassed nearly as much in the West as it was in the East, it lay behind a good deal of Western thinking, as we shall see. We have already seen how it resulted in a firmer grasp of Christ's divinity than of his humanity. In the analogy of the iron in the fire, the imagination naturally focuses primarily on the fire, the active element.

Leo shared this emphasis on the passion of Christ with other Western theologians. Some saw Christ's suffering as a price paid to the Devil (cf. Mark 10.45), but most taught rather that it was a deception practised on the Devil. Although God *could* simply have snatched mankind from the

Devil's control, he preferred that everything should be done in strict accordance with justice.[33] Assuming the characteristics of human substance, the Word of God deceived the Devil into taking him for an ordinary fallen man and bringing about his death, just as if he belonged to him and deserved such treatment. This was an abuse of power on Satan's part, and since he had struck one who was innocent, he deserved to lose his claims over those who were guilty; hence sinners could be freed without breach of justice. The formal and external notions of right and wrong in all this will be obvious enough. Such ideas were echoed by most Western theologians in the following centuries, and it is easy to see how they chimed in with the feudal concept of *diffidatio* referred to above.[34]

The idea of Christ as example was naturally stressed, and Gregory, who laid great weight on it, agreed with Leo that the death of Christ had not been strictly necessary; though he added that Christ willed to show us the greatness of his compassion 'by taking upon himself that from which he meant to deliver us'.[35]

Combined with these ideas, there was a fourth way of understanding the matter which, for reasons that will emerge later, was undoubtedly the dominant one. It received its classic formulation in Anselm's *Cur Deus-Homo?* (1097–8), and it rested on two convictions we have already met, namely that the sin of mankind had dishonoured God in a way that demanded *satisfactio*, and that God was not free simply to overlook sin; for had he done so, his mercy would have been in improper contradiction to his justice.

Yet if God thus had to have *satisfactio*, the situation of fallen angels and human beings was desperate. For since God is infinite, the satisfaction would also have to be infinite (according to principles such as those of *Wergild*). By definition, however, no finite creature could provide infinite satisfaction; and in this case there was the additional fact that the finite creatures involved were fallen. Even if, *per impossibile*, all human creatures after the Fall had completely avoided actual sin, that would have been no more than their duty, and would still have left the dishonour done to God by original sin untouched. So there could only be hope if an infinite being should live a perfect finite life and yet endure suffering. Since such an infinite being would be divine, and as such perfect, it would be free from original sin, and its suffering and death, which would be of infinite worth, would be enough to satisfy God and assuage his anger against his fallen creatures. As we have seen, God in himself was held to be impassible (incapable of suffering), so suffering would be possible for an infinite being only if it were so fully united to humanity that it could share in, or borrow, the human capacity for suffering. The resultant God-man would be representative of all human beings and contain them all, as it were, in himself. They would suffer in him.[36]

In arguing this, Anselm was in fact gathering together and setting out systematically and self-consciously ideas which had long been in the air.[37] In the pre-Anselmian formulations, however, the emphasis had tended to lie more on suffering-as-a-substitute than on suffering-as-a-representative.

It was not enough for the Word to become incarnate; the expiation of sin required that he should undergo the pain and punishment our sin deserved. In that way he took upon himself the responsibility for our sin and the punishment due for it. Writer after writer expressed what was in effect a doctrine of penal satisfaction. For example, 'he underwent the punishment for our sin so that, through his undeserved punishment he might do away our deserved fault'. 'His blood is the ransom and the price of our freedom.'[38]

The following account of the matter given by Gregory is revealing, both because of the unrelenting attitude it attributes to God the Father and for the relations it presupposes between Father and Son. Christ, he writes, 'because he appeared as the only righteous person among men and nevertheless, though without sin (*culpa*), faced (*pervenit ad*) the punishment of sin, both persuaded (*arguit*) man to sin no more and withstood (*obstitit*) God so that he should not smite ... By suffering he convinced both the one and the other, for he both rebuked (*corripuit*; or = took away?) the sin of man by inspiring righteousness and moderated (*temperavit*) the anger of the judge by undergoing death ... he exhibited to God deeds wrought upon himself by which he [sc. God] might be reconciled to men.'[39]

The death of Christ is thus a sacrifice, since our fault could not have been wiped out except by a sacrifice, of which the victim was not 'an irrational animal or a guilty man, but one spotless and holy'.[40] This was a sacrifice of which Christ was both priest and victim; and by it we have been liberated from our faults, freed from death and reconciled to God.[41]

Though Gregory does not speak explicitly of Christ's merits, that is in fact the concept with which he was working. For example, he writes: 'He shows himself the just man who merited indulgence (*indulgentiam mereretur*) for others.'[42]

What Gregory only adumbrated – a theory of Christ's merits, after the analogy of the merits which the saints and others can gain – was fully worked out and accepted in the subsequent period; and it will be obvious how well such an understanding of Christ's work fitted in with the ideas of *poena* and *satisfactio* as entertained in connection with the penitential system. For that reason alone it was bound to be popular at the time, and it obviously fitted in well with the conceptions of *Wergild* and compensation in Frankish legal practice. It exemplified the alternative: either punishment or satisfaction, especially as, according to Germanic law, vengeance did not have to be executed on the evildoer in person, but might be taken on a member of his or her clan. Indeed in some versions of Germanic law, according to Harnack, it was held a more severe form of vengeance to strike the best member of the clan instead of the miscreant.[43]

Christ thus in effect did penance for original sin on our behalf and so appeased the anger of God. The scope of his work extended beyond original sin, but if that is to be understood, other factors have to be taken into account. The Epistle to the Hebrews (7.24–25) pictures the ascended Christ as an eternal priest, continually making intercession for those he died to save. This picture was frequently elaborated in early mediaeval writing. The words of Gregory are typical: 'Our Redeemer offers a holocaust for us without ceasing, continually exhibiting (*demonstrat*) to the Father the flesh he has taken on our behalf. For his incarnation is the oblation which purifies us ... by the mystery of his humanity he offers a perpetual sacrifice.'[44]

The idea of purification, to judge by the surrounding passage, seems in practice to amount only to the mitigation of the *penalties* for sin, and the way such passages are formulated has led to the suggestion that what lies behind them is the transference to Christ of what was constantly done by the priest in the mass. Certainly the idea of Christ's intercession and the idea of the mass were closely associated.

There was an increasing demand at this time for frequent masses, and much emphasis on the church's continual offering of the mass. At the same time the belief that at the consecration the bread and wine actually became the body and blood of Christ was firmly established.

> There is sometimes a misconception about this, arising from the fact that, from the ninth to the eleventh centuries, scholars such as Paschasius Radbert, Ratramnus and Berengarius carried on a lively controversy about the *precise form the transformation took*. It is important to recognize that though Ratramnus argued against what seem to have been the virtually transubstantiationist views of Paschasius, neither he nor his ally Gottschalk had any doubt that a real change of the elements into the body and blood of Christ took place in the mass. Indeed such a conviction had existed long before this time.[45]

The way was thus open for the mass to be seen essentially as a sacrifice; not, despite the wording of the liturgy, just as a sacrifice of praise, but as a real sacrifice – in fact Christ's sacrifice on the cross. In the mass the passion of Christ was repeated for our atonement. Gregory wrote: 'The host offered ... on the sacred altar pleads in a unique way for our absolution, because he who, having risen from the dead by his own power, dies no more ... suffers again (*iterum patitur*) for us. For as often as we offer him the host of his passion, so often do we renew (*reparamus*) his passion to ourselves for our absolution.' Or: 'He is again immolated for us in the mystery of the holy sacrifice ... the sacrifice that is offered for us, ever reproducing in itself the passion of the only-begotten.'[46]

As a calling into action of Christ's sacrifice, the mass could, in the first place, wipe out the (post-baptismal) sins of the living. Bede, for example, wrote that, 'Christ daily washes us from our sins in his blood when the memorial (*memoria*) of his suffering is repeated (*replicatur*) at the altar.'[47] It is significant, however, that this is referred to as *laxatio* (mitigation); the emphasis seems, once more, to be on the remission of penalties.

Secondly, the mass could wash away the sins of the departed and free them from some or all of the punishments they would otherwise have had to undergo after death. The idea of purgatory, which was becoming more explicit during this period, led to a growing sense of the mass as an expiatory and propitiatory sacrifice.[48] Gregory writes that 'the holy sacrifice of Christ, our saving victim, brings great benefits to souls even after death ... for this reason the souls of the dead themselves often beg to have masses offered for them'.[49] He goes on to give vivid accounts of two cases where departed souls, known through appearances they made to the living to be in torment for their sins, were freed as a result of masses said on their behalf.

In addition to the remission of sins for the living and the dead, the eucharistic sacrifice could procure for those who needed them temporal as well as spiritual, blessings. For example, in Gregory's *Dialogues* we read of a man who was cured of serious illness, another who was released from imprisonment, and a third who was saved from drowning, when masses were said with their needs in mind.[50]

All this was bound to affect profoundly the perception of God and his way with the world. It meant that alongside his justice and wrath he had demonstrated his mercy. With the temptation he had also made a way of escape (*proventus* in the Latin, I Cor. 10.13). Whether the emphasis was placed on the Father's sending the Son and acquiescing in his suffering or on the Son's willingness to come and to suffer, the fact was that through his coming and passion, his perpetual intercession and the dispensation by which his sacrifice and its beneficent effects could be reproduced through the mass, mankind's desperate plight had been dealt with. The infinite satisfaction required had been provided, and together with it the means to wipe away post-baptismal sin and to deal with temporal needs and suffering.

Of all this there was grateful recognition. We have already referred to a number of hymns of thanks, and to them we may add one by Prudentius which was well known at the time, the *Corde natus*. It included the lines:

> He assumed this mortal body,
> Frail and feeble, doomed to die,
> That the race from dust created
> (*primoplasti ex germine*, i.e. from the seed of Adam)
> Might not perish utterly,

Which the dreadful Law had sentenced
In the depths of Hell to lie
Sing, ye heights of heaven, his praises;
Angels and Archangels sing!
Whereso'er ye be, ye faithful,
Let your joyous anthems ring,
Every tongue his name confessing,
Countless voices answering.[51]

Nevertheless, the situation just outlined conceals a good deal of confusion. Apart from the fact that 'forgiveness' and 'purification' seem in fact to have been limited to the remission of the *penalties* for sin, there is the question of how Christ's dealing with sin was to be reconciled with the need for penances and for reliance on the merits of other human beings. In practice, it would seem, Christ's redeeming work was only *one* of the means on which people needed to rely; and even Christ's work needed human efforts to make it effective. For example, it did not avail to bring relief to the people and souls described in Gregory's *Dialogues*, despite their prayers, until some human agent, moved by their need, caused masses to be said with their intention.

It was, as we have seen, through the mass that Christ's work was called into action; and even the mass was only believed effective, at any rate so far as those participating were concerned, if it was celebrated in the proper spirit. 'Whenever we offer mass,' said Gregory, 'we need to sacrifice ourselves to God in a sincere immolation of the heart; we who celebrate the mysteries of the Lord's passion ought to imitate what we enact. The sacrifice will truly be offered to God for us only when we present ourselves as the victim ... It was as the result of her steadfastness that Anna obtained her request (i.e for a baby. Note the appeal to her example, and see p. 38 above) ... it was because she kept the intention of her prayers always before her that she received the gift for which she prayed ... the offering will not be accepted unless discord is first removed from the heart.'[52] The reference to Anna's need for persistence is significant. Although admonitions such as this were salutary, as combatting an irresponsible *ex opere operato* attitude to the sacrament, in a situation in which the mass played so large a part in making Christ's saving work effective they must have increased the sense that 'it all depends on me'. The souls in Gregory's *Dialogues*, for example, would not have been profited by Christ's work unless they had taken the initiative and appeared to people able and willing to provide masses on their behalf.

Harnack may have exaggerated when he wrote that in this religious perspective, 'Christ as a person is forgotten. He is a great name in dogmatics ...; but the fundamental questions of salvation are not answered by reference to him, and in life the baptized has to depend on "means" which exist partly alongside, partly independently of him, or merely bear his badge.'[53] Nevertheless, it is easy to see what he means, and he is clearly pointing to an important aspect of the situation. When Gregory wrote that 'this sacrifice (sc. of the mass) alone has the power of saving the soul from eternal death because it presents to us the death of Christ',[54] he was thinking of the effect of the sacrifice in neutralizing the guilt of original sin. This only the sacrifice of Christ could do, and the fruit of it was appropriated through baptism. Where satisfaction for actual sins was concerned, although, as we have seen, the mass could be effective, other means also needed to be invoked, and in practice, we may suspect, it was on them that people largely relied.[55]

What is likely to strike a modern reader about the writers we have been expounding is their lack of reference to any close direct relationship with Christ or the Father. Even in their redemptive role, both these figures appear primarily as problem-solvers, concerned to find a way through a complicated calculus of sin, pain and punishment in order to achieve their own purpose by saving enough human beings to make up the number of fallen angels. It is true that the Incarnation involved Christ in the acceptance of suffering – and the appalling suffering involved in the crucifixion at that; but, as we have seen, his suffering was not much to the fore in tenth-century minds. That was partly because of the way in which the person of Christ was conceived. In him, as we have seen, human and divine were held to have been fully united; but the orthodox story made clear that there was only one self-conscious, personal agent present in him, and that was God the Son – God the Son existing under the conditions of human life. The Fathers insisted that his human experience had been real, and in no way illusory, and various verbal formulas were devised[56] which made it possible to say that God the Son suffered. Yet they *were* only verbal formulas. In himself the Son was, by the very nature of his substance, incapable of suffering, and we have seen how Cyril of Alexandria, one of the great pillars of orthodoxy, said of him that 'he suffered in a way that was not suffering' (*apathōs epathen*). Yet if *he* did not suffer the pangs of the crucifixion, who did? There was no other personal agent involved to whom such suffering could be attributed. Inevitably, therefore, Christ's suffering, and his closeness to us in his humanity, remained problematic. It is significant that in the nine long verses of the hymn quoted on pp. 72–3 above there is no reference whatever to Christ's suffering, and the only address to him is in the words:

Hail! Thou Judge of souls departed;
Hail! of all the living King.
On the Father's right hand throned,
Through his courts thy praises ring,
Till at last for all offences
Righteous judgment thou shalt bring.

Even in this context Christ had maintained his distance, and we are back with the *pantocrator*, the formidable judge, almost indistinguishable from the formidable lord, his Father.

The doctrinal intricacies retailed in this chapter will have been very largely a closed book to the great majority of believers; they will simply have gathered that they had God to thank for having removed the threat of original guilt and providing the means through which actual sins could be dealt with. It was for them, however, to make effective use of those means and to live blameless lives. For any sense of personal relationship or intimacy with the supernatural they will have turned to the saints; but before we discuss that we must briefly discuss the part played by the Holy Spirit in human relations with the Godhead.

(iii)

According to the official theology, there were further grounds for gratitude to God beyond those we have so far mentioned. God had not only provided the means of salvation, he had made possible the appropriation of them. According to the theologians, as we have already seen, the prompting of the Holy Spirit was necessary before anyone could seek baptism or make confession and seek forgiveness for actual sin.

The conviction was that in a fallen world human beings are too weakened and paralysed by sin to be able to seek or appropriate God's gifts by themselves; yet he has made it possible for them to do so by means quite independent of any initiative on their part. This action of God was attributed to the Holy Spirit and it was called *gratia*, the root idea of which was something totally free, unearned and unmerited – 'free *gratis* and for nothing', as we say (where *gratis* is a contracted form of the ablative plural of *gratia*). Without any approach from our side, God the Holy Spirit bestows what was called *gratia praeveniens* (*praevenire* = to precede), that is, grace which 'comes before' any movement towards God and salvation on our part. This prevenient grace was attributed to God's *superna pietas* (heavenly goodness, or piety), 'which effects something in us in advance of (*prius*) any approach on our part, in fact without any action on our part at all'.[57]

The effects of this grace will be described presently; meanwhile we note that it was a ground for gratitude to God and that it ran quite counter to any notion that salvation is something to be achieved by unaided human effort. No one could live and work in a manner that was truly the service of God (*in cultu piae actionis laborat*), wrote Othlo of St Emmeram, 'unless he was led by the grace of God alone'; and in the same vein Ratherius of Verona claimed that 'it is impossible for anyone to raise himself to the divine heights by his own powers, unless he is lifted up to them by the grace of him who for our sakes came down to the depths'.[58]

Nevertheless there were puzzles. The account of the matter current in the tenth century went back ultimately to Augustine, whose views were based on a very special experience. Having sown wild oats in abundance in his youth, he had been converted to Christianity while many of his boon companions had remained pagan, and yet he could not discover any way in which he had been a better man than they. He therefore saw himself vividly as 'a brand plucked from the burning', who had been singled out by the totally unmerited grace of God. Generalizing from this experience, he concluded that grace is bestowed *ante praevisa merita*, that is, completely without reference to any merits the recipients possess or are known by God to be going to possess, or to any special openness they may show towards it.

Though Augustine's views in this matter were by no means accepted *in toto*,[59] his general stance received a good deal of support in the subsequent period. In the ninth century a combative monk of Orbais called Gottschalk was notorious for holding Augustine's position in its most rigorous form; and though Gottschalk was eventually condemned, the controversy over his views revealed how much support there was for them from leading theologians of the day, even, apparently, from Pope St Nicholas I.[60] A respected figure such as Anselm could write that salvation comes 'by grace alone with no action of the free will', and Ratherius could go so far as to say that the forgiveness God has granted in his mercy is extended to me 'whether I like it or not'.[61] Support for this position was also drawn from the practice of infant baptism, now universal. Whether a baby was baptized or not was clearly something quite outside its control, and babies who received baptism, and with it the grace of God, obviously did so without any reference to their desires or disposition. The case of babies highlighted a problem which the doctrine of grace entailed. For it was agreed by all that babies who died unbaptized were 'subject to eternal torment' in hell, even if it was the mildest (*mitissima*) form of that torment.[62] From this one could extrapolate: if the bestowal of grace bears no relation to merit, the withholding of it cannot be attributed to any particular demerits on the part of those from whom it is withheld. Yet it is withheld from the great majority of the human race, who as a consequence are destined to suffer an eternity of torture in hell.

Cf. e.g Gregory, PL 76, 333: 'The number of the reprobate ... surpasses the limit of human calculation ... those who perish are innumerable, running beyond the number of the elect.' In the thirteenth century, the influential Berthold of Regensburg was to reckon the ratio of the damned to the saved at 100,000:1. The church was constantly likened to Noah's ark, and the fewness of those saved in it contrasted with the multitude of those who were lost. In thus regarding the elect as a small minority of mankind, writers could of course rely on the New Testament (e.g. Matt. 7.13–14 and 22.14, 'many are called but few are chosen', or Rom. 9.14ff.).

All human beings are guilty of original sin; why does God rescue some but not others? The question naturally occurred to the theologians, but they concluded that it was pointless to raise it. God's judgments in the matter are beyond our grasp; all we know is that he is just and merciful.[63] In a strict sense, no one can have him as a debtor. His justice is shown in that those who go to hell deserve it; his mercy in that he saves many from this fate. Isidore wrote: 'Grace is not conferred on the basis of any previously existing merits, but solely by the will of God. Nor is anyone saved or damned, chosen or rejected, save by the design of God who works by predestination (*predestinantis dei*) and who is just in regard to the reprobate and merciful to the elect.'[64] While theologians were content to trust that in some inscrutable way all this was just, those who were aware of such problems must have been left with a sense that there was no knowing the mind of the God with whom they had to do.

> The fact that those chosen must be equal in number to the fallen angels meant not only that the number of those to be saved was predetermined and strictly limited, but that it was determined by considerations not related to the well-being of the creatures.[65]

However, such passages as those I have quoted, if taken on their own, could easily give a false picture of the religious tone of the period. Augustine himself had warned that it could be discouraging to the hearers to preach openly on this matter,[66] and preachers of our period heeded his warning, so that the great majority of people will have been unaware of the details of grace and its predestinarian implications. Ideas such as Augustine's have been common among members of 'gathered' congregations, but in a situation where everyone was a practising Christian it must have been hard to have any vivid sense of the prevenient grace of God. For example, the first thing such grace was said to effect was faith, that is, acceptance of the doctrinal teaching of the church,[67] but in the circumstances of the tenth century, faith in that sense was universal, so awareness of its presence as being due to the special call of God must have been weak.

What is more, we have to distinguish prevenient grace from *gratia subsequens*, also attributable to the Holy Spirit. The effect of prevenient grace is to enable us to take advantage of the grace God subsequently offers us through prayer, sacraments and other means. Although this second sort of grace is often spoken of in language similar to that used about prevenient grace,[68] more characteristic statements attribute a vital place to human co-operation. (It is significant both that Anselm can report 'the contention of some that they can prove ... that man is not sustained by any free will at all' and that he should set out to modify such a view.)[69] For example, the passage quoted from Gregory on p. 75 runs in full: 'Heavenly goodness effects something in us in advance, without our agency, so that subsequently (*subsequente*) it may also affect with us by our own free will the good which we seek.'[70] Similarly Ratherius, also quoted above, could write elsewhere, 'heavenly gifts come only to those who, with the co-operation of the grace of God, have merited to obtain them by their industrious action'. Gregory says that if we co-operate in striving after the good, 'that which is a gift of the omnipotent God becomes our merit'.[71] (The passage quoted well exemplifies the notoriously difficult problem of identifying Gregory's precise view on this matter; but the above, taken in its context, is generally agreed to be the drift of his argument.) These, and innumerable other statements like them, make clear that a vital place was left for human effort and co-operation with divine grace, and for the merit they could earn. This comes out clearly, for example, in the voluminous controversy between Gottschalk and Hincmar of Reims, in which Hincmar was generally held to have won the argument. In fact, as we have seen, it was held possible actually to do more than is commanded and so earn a surplus of merit.[72]

The ambiguity revealed here is one which goes back to the New Testament[73] and has been present throughout Christian history, the emphasis varying at different times; but in view of the understanding of the mass we have described and of the large part played by the penitential system, there can be no doubt that in our period the merit gained by personal endeavour and co-operation with God, whether one's own or another's, was taken as a vital condition of salvation, understood as escape from God's wrath. Once again we have to recognize that the religion of the period was very largely one of personal achievement, with all the anxiety and strenuousness that entailed.

Here again it needs to be stressed that the great majority of people will have known nothing of the intricate doctrines we have been discussing. What they will have gathered from the sermons preached to them, as a number of these sermons bear witness, is that if they wanted to be saved, they must earn it by behaving in ways which conformed to God's will, as disclosed by the Bible and the church.[74] They were assured that they could rely on God's help in doing so,[75] and there was a lively sense of God's willingness to intervene in order to warn the pious of dangers and to strengthen their hand when they were tempted or attacked by the devil. The more instructed identified the Holy Spirit as the source of this help. In Dhuoda's *Manuel*, as we have seen, the Spirit plays a much larger part than Christ in helping those engaged in the battle against evil (see p. 48 and n. 17). Yet people thought in a very concrete way about religion, as about everything else, and the Holy Spirit was hard to envisage as a person, and could not easily be symbolized by any human figure from the contemporary world. It was difficult, therefore, to conceive intimacy or close personal relations with such a figure, and, as is clear from a number of the texts quoted earlier, the operation of the Spirit was envisaged less in terms of personal influence than in terms of an impersonal infusion of super-natural power, power available only to those who earned it by their co-operation. Once again, direct personal relations, or intimacy, with the Godhead were at a premium.

It must be added, however, that if the picture of tenth-century piety which has so far emerged were taken as complete, it would be very one-sided. For, as we shall see when we come to consider clerical, and especially monastic, spirituality, there were some who saw God primarily as goodness and love, and sought to enter into close personal communion with him. Before that is dealt with, however, we will round off this account of the religion of the generality by describing what was undoubtedly the most important part of it, and certainly the part to which they looked for any sense of intimacy and personal contact with the supernatural – the cult of the saints.

9

The Saints*

Given a Godhead so remote, unapproachable and threatening, there was bound to be a longing for more kindly intermediaries. The angels, as we have seen, fulfilled this role; but however benevolent, they were supernatural and faceless beings, and it is significant that the only one among them to achieve personal popularity was the archangel Michael, who gradually took on the status of a saint; for it was the saints who came to be the mediators *par excellence* between early mediaeval Christians and their God. They, after all, had known the same circumstances and hardships as their devotees and, in the case of local saints, the very same local conditions with which they were asked to deal. It is clear from the carving of the period, for example, that the saints took precedence over the angels, and the cult of the saints was at the very heart of popular religion. Luchaire did not exaggerate when he wrote that 'the true religion of the middle age, to be frank, is the worship of relics'.[1]

The word 'popular' needs defining in this context. It used to be thought that the cult of the saints arose spontaneously among the masses, who then compelled an unwilling hierarchy to accept it. However, the work of Peter Brown and others has shown that that is true, if at all, only to a very limited extent.

(i)

In the very early days, when the church was subject to persecution, it was accepted by all that martyrs, and others who had suffered for the faith, enjoyed specially close communion with God after death, and could be called on to use their influence with him in the interests of their fellow Christians. When persecution ceased, these expectations were transferred to another group who gave up all for God, those who poured into the Egyptian and Judaean deserts to practise asceticism there, often of a very rigorous kind. The Life of St Antony, one of the Egyptian hermits, written about 350, and traditionally ascribed to Athanasius, exercised very considerable influence on subsequent centuries, and so did the Life of St Martin of Tours by Sulpicius Severus (*c.* 400) and the second book of Gregory's *Dialogues*, which was in effect a Life of St Benedict. These three Lives all laid weight on the life, as well as the death, of the saint they described, and they established the pattern for the innumerable saints' Lives produced in the Middle Ages, especially in the two centuries or so after about 975. To influence the way saints' Lives were written was to influence the way saints were envisaged, and in this connexion the fact that all three were written by members of the ruling class is significant; the inclusion of numerous miracles in all of these three works was also important.[2]

The Lives of the saints were not biographies in the sense in which the word is now understood: Eddius's Life of St Wilfrid, which came nearer than most to meeting modern biographical requirements, got a very muted reception, to judge from the manuscript evidence.[3] For the most part these works deal with the subject only after he (women were rarely recognized as saints in this period, see p. 260 below) turned to serious Christian discipleship, almost always as a cleric and very often as a member of a religious order. Considerable emphasis was placed on the miracles performed during, and still more after, the saint's lifetime, and these miracles tended to be of certain well-defined types. In almost every case they bore a close resemblance to those performed by other saints and to those recorded in the Bible. Behind this lay an important concern of every hagiographer, namely to depict the holy man as a living example of an ancient pattern, fixed once and for all in the Bible, without regard for the kind of saint he was. His sanctity was determined by his conformity to the pattern. Sameness was proof of authenticity. The saint must perform acceptable miracles to enter into the glorious tradition.[4] Every reader of the saints' Lives quickly becomes aware of the extent to which the miracles ascribed to them have parallels in the Old and New Testaments;[5] being in the tradition helped to distinguish the miracles of the saints from pagan magic.

However, there was certainly variety. A saint might be a martyr, a confessor, an ascetic, a bishop, a monk, a member of the royal family or even a wild man of the woods, and he would display corresponding virtues. Over the course of time, the virtues ascribed to the saints changed, in accordance with what was admired in a particular period. Benedicta Ward writes, with reference to the capricious, and somewhat coquettish, behaviour ascribed to St Faith of Conques: 'It springs from the needs and imagination of the knights of the Rouergue.'[6] In our period, as we shall see, the Virgin Mary enjoyed nothing like the pre-eminence she was to enjoy later. The virtues she enshrined were not those characteristic of our period, which were rather such things as austerity, affability, patience and hard work. However, since it was the same God at work in every saint, the type of miracle performed was continuous from biblical times onwards. Gregory of Tours began his book on the *Glory of the Martyrs* with incidents from the life of Christ, and in answer to the question 'whether it is better to speak of the Life or the Lives of the saints', replied 'that it is better to say Life, because, though their merits and virtues differ, they are all sustained in this world by one bodily life'.[7]

If the primary concern of the hagiographer was not biographical, neither was it ethical, at any rate in the sense that he sought to provide an attractive model readily imitable, as it stood, by his readers. The holy was defined by what the holy man did, and loyalty to him, rather than how one behaved to others, was what won his patronage. Benedicta Ward again writes: 'St Faith was endowed by her devotees ... with a greater concern with devotion to herself than with the rules of society.'[8] As far as ordinary people were concerned, the saints put forward for their devotion were mainly male,[9] and even in the rare cases where they did not belong to the noble order, had practised sexual continence and an extreme asceticism such as were not within the compass of the great majority. The miracles which formed so large a feature of their Lives obviously could not be imitated by others; and in any case, although they earned their place by lives of superhuman effort, most of them were designated for holiness before birth, or at any rate before they had reached the age of discretion. For example, the Life of St Gerald of Aurillac reports that his father had a vision of his future glory before he was born, and there is something similar in the life of St Germanus of Auxerre, while the life of St Anskar describes how special revelations turned him to sanctity while still a child.[10] One cannot, therefore, claim that the saints of the Lives were object-lessons in living that the layman would do well to follow in detail.[11]

That is not to say, however, that these Lives made no moral impact. It is true, as Wallace-Hadrill says, that 'the common man listening to his own saint's life will learn the virtues proper to a saint, and some, but not all, of them may be meant to apply to him'.[12] Certainly, it will soon have become clear to such a man that 'the virtues proper to a saint' were very different from the qualities prized in a still brutal and rather barbaric society; and that the way the saints disregarded the world and sat loose to its success and enjoyments represented a way of life and scale of values the reverse of what had been generally accepted. The Lives of the saints were a powerful means of bringing such a message home.[13] Illiterate and uneducated people could appreciate and absorb the spirit of Christianity when it was exhibited concretely in the lives and acts of individuals, especially as these individuals were always portrayed as endowed with supernatural qualities and powers.

There was always the danger, never wholly obviated, that these supernatural powers would come to be the almost exclusive focus of interest in the saints, but the church tried to insist on the quality of moral sanctity and to keep it before the eyes of the faithful. This it did, not only through the saints' Lives discussed above and the accounts of their sufferings, known as *passiones*, but through the inclusion of matters relating to the saints in the liturgy – for example, in breviaries, sacramentaries, litanies, hymns, calendars and martyrologies. Appropriate pieces of this sort were frequently read aloud in the vernacular, with the intention, and often the result, of sustaining popular devotion; judicious selection ensured that those to whom this devotion was directed should be worthy of it, according to contemporary standards.

There was as yet no universally recognized procedure for determining which individuals could properly be made the objects of such devotion,[14] and popular acclaim, usually based on the alleged occurrence of spectacular miracles, played a large part in the development of local cults. The result was that on occasion the most unlikely, and in fact unseemly, characters came to be venerated.[15] However, the church authorities were well aware of the dangers, as witness the determined efforts of the French bishops to gain control of the matter throughout this period, and such directives as that of the Synod of Frankfurt in 794 to the effect that 'no new saints are to be the objects of devotion or invocations, nor are memorials of them to be erected in the streets; only those are to be venerated in the church who have been chosen on the basis of their sufferings and the merits of their life'.[16] The size of the problem is shown by the fact that, according to Cristiani, some 1300 saints were being honoured in France well before the Council.

In these ways the church sought to canalize popular devotion to the saints, maintaining it while at the same time keeping control of the forms it took and the choice of those to whom it should be directed; and incidentally, whether consciously or not, ensuring that those to whom it was directed all belonged to the upper orders of society, and mainly to the clerical order.[17] The saints were frequently represented as poor and labouring to get their own livelihood, but theirs was voluntary poverty, and the deliberate embracing of poverty was impressive to the peasants who knew what poverty was. They were also attracted by the way the saints had given to the poor and ministered to those in distress; but though the saints helped individual victims of need and injustice, there is no record of their having done anything to question or change the system from which the need and shortage resulted. Although asceticism is praised, wealth and authority are not attacked, and, so far from his status's being objectionable in itself, the powerful man, especially the powerful ecclesiastic, can be represented as a saint.

There was always a danger, as we have seen, that the supernatural powers of the saints would become virtually the exclusive focus of attention, and it cannot be claimed that the danger was very effectively met. Rosalind and Christopher Brooke have written that 'broadly speaking, the pious of the early Middle Ages expected their saints to be dead', meaning that the main interest was not in what the saints had done while alive, but in what they might be expected to do now that they enjoyed the immediate presence of God. As Christopher Dawson put it, 'in the ...

Dark Ages ... the Saint was not just a good man who was dead; he was a living power who took an active interest and share in human affairs'.[18]

In some cases, for example that of St Germanus of Paris or of St Anskar, Archbishop of Bremen, the blessings to be expected from saints were no more than a continuation of kindnesses and good works, often miraculous, they were said to have done in their lifetimes; but in many cases little or nothing was known of the earthly lives of the saints. Almost nothing was, or is, known, for example, about the history of either St Faith (or Foi or Foy) or St Benignus, yet both were the objects of extremely lively devotion during our period, in the one case centred on Conques and in the other on Dijon. It is now generally accepted that a number of those honoured as saints at this time had no historical existence at all.[19]

In view of the influence they now enjoyed with God as what Gregory of Tours called *amici dominici*, there was no limit to the blessings the saints might be expected to confer. Miraculous healing was the thing most sought after, but among other boons for which they were regularly entreated were military victory, the extinguishing of fires, improvements in the weather, increased fertility, the prevention of theft, the ending of pestilence or of cattle disease, foreknowledge of the future, the vindication of victims of injustice, and even the raising of the dead and the winning of pardon at God's judgment. In fact the saints were looked to to supply whatever human resources could not achieve. Many cases where these and similar blessings had been granted are recorded in the sources.[20] Without the conviction that such miracles had occurred in the past, people would not have gone on petitioning for them. In a situation in which so little was known about the workings of nature, it was easy for what happened to be *experienced* as a supernatural intervention. For example, Gregory of Tours says that he himself experienced cure from 'headaches, fevers, blocked ears, tiredness in the eyes and pains in my limbs', among other ailments. He also tells how he had been cured of toothache when he dowsed his head in the fountain of St Julian of Brioude, in which the saint's own head had been washed after decapitation.[21]

From this perspective the saints were seen as the courtiers of the heavenly court, vassals of the lord of heaven who stood in his presence and enjoyed his favour, and so were in a position to act as friends at court. This was an age of essentially personal government, in which a timely word to the authorities from a powerful patron could work wonders, and that was the model for people's approach to the saints; they saw themselves as *clientes* of a saintly *patronus*.[22] A saint could forward any case he or she took up, and prayers presented through a saint had a much greater chance of being effective.

In the Life of St Adelard we read that the saint 'has already come to Christ and is in paradise; there is no stain on him and so we can approach him as Jesus Christ'. In Helgaldus's Life of King Robert, St Benedict is described as 'a sure means of access to the common judge', and Queen Adelaide is said to have 'hoped to win for herself the favour of St [Denys] to whom God had promised by a faithful oath to grant him whatever he asked for anyone'. Ralph Glaber reports a vision in which the Virgin Mary told a devotee, 'It is I who take charge of your prayers and bring them to the notice of the merciful judge.' In a remark in one of his letters which is the more telling for being so casually included, Lupus of Ferrières speaks of a monk who had gone to Rome to obtain through the intercession of Saints Peter and Paul 'what he could not have obtained for himself'.[23]

The range of things the saints were believed willing and able to do was extremely wide, as we have seen, and many of them may sound surprising to modern ears. Gregory the Great, for example, wrote: 'If you had a case to be tried to-morrow before some great magistrate, you would surely spend the whole day planning for it; you would seek a patron and beg him earnestly to become your defender. Behold the severe judge Jesus is about to come; the terror of that mighty council of angels and archangels is at hand. In that assembly our case will be tried, and yet we are not seeking patrons who will then come to our defence. Our holy martyrs are ready to be your advocates; they desire to be asked, indeed, if I may say so, they entreat that they may be entreated. Seek them as helpers of your prayer; turn to them that they may protect you in your guilt; for the judge himself wishes to be importuned that he may not be obliged to punish sinners.'[24] This is an important theme. Not only could the saints assist a devotee to salvation by pleading their own merits on his or her behalf; it was believed that they would actually participate in the last judgment and influence its outcome. Thus, according to Frodoard, Charles Martel, condemned to the lowest hell, prayed to the saints 'who in the future judgment will hold the balance with the Saviour'.[25]

On the other hand, the favour of the saints was not to be too lightly taken for granted. 'Do not fail to keep the feast of All Saints,' writes Alcuin, '... for they have been entrusted with the keys of the kingdom, and can close heaven to unbelievers and open it to believers.'[26]

The patterns of ordinary clientage are clearly reflected in mediaeval people's relations with the saints. Many, for example, committed themselves to the care of one particular saint: the *Miracles of St Benedict* tell of a monk who 'appointed St Benedict the mediator of his prayers', while, according to Helgaldus, King Robert was specially devoted to St Anianus (Aignan), 'whom he desired to make, after God, his helper, protector and defender'.[27]

For those who adopted such a course, to change patrons at a later stage could be disastrous. A twelfth-century writer tells of a monk who preferred some other saint to the patron saint of his own monastery, only to find himself after death deprived of any saintly patronage, and therefore condemned to a very long period of torture in purgatory. The moral drawn was that 'it is no light thing to have no patron saint'.[28] Nevertheless, if one saint failed to answer prayer, people were not averse to going the rounds until they found one who would, as Bishop Withald is said to have done.[29]

Many saints were believed to specialize, often on the basis of their own earthly experience. St Roch, for example, who had died from plague, was specially helpful against it; St Eloi was particularly adept at healing horses, St Didier at destroying moles, and St Plouradon at stopping children from crying. St Faith at Conques, not so famous for healing as for rescuing soldiers and sailors, was constantly asked to bring about the release of captives, which she often did, interestingly enough, by encouraging their natural ingenuity through dreams. (A point I owe to Sister Benedicta Ward.)

Like earthly patrons, the saints had to be kept sweet. Einhardt refused an invitation which would have involved his being away from home and his large collection of martyrs' relics, because, he said, 'I have been warned by heaven not to be absent from them even for one week'; and in the hope of getting to heaven by their help, King Robert would 'betake himself to the presence of the saints, pray to them, honour them, and assail their ears with humble and saving (*salutaris*) prayers'.[30]

Where earthly patrons were concerned, the line between keeping them sweet and offering them sweeteners was a thin one, and this too is reflected in mediaeval converse with the saints. Queen Adelaide 'gave all sorts of presents to St Denys' in the attempt to win his favour and Ralph Glaber tells of a general who paid all he had taken in pillage to St Martin of Tours in a (successful) attempt to get him to paralyse opposing forces threatening the city.[31] Official theology, as reflected in the decisions of councils, was quite clear that the author of all these blessings was God, who should therefore receive the credit, the role of the saints being simply to pray for them on our behalf. Ermoldus Nigellus, for example, wrote that 'it is God we adore in his dear servants, whose prayers help us to reach heaven',[32] and Alcuin declared: 'It is God who is honoured through the relics of the saints ... it is better to imitate the examples of the saints in one's heart than to wear their bones hung round one's neck.'[33]

In practice, however, the saints were constantly regarded as independent wonder-workers. In the early eighth century the influential Greek theologian, John of Damascus, claimed that the saints were 'genuinely gods' (*alēthōs theoi*) and, as such, proper objects of worship (*proskynētoi*).[34] He explained and qualified his remarks in a way that brought them into line with orthodoxy, but it was dangerous talk nonetheless; and the saints were credited with such powers that they were in effect little deities, and their cult became almost a religion by itself. At the end of the Middle Ages the royal commissioners in France could write of the arm of St Antony that 'it is held more sacred than God Almighty'.[35] As Daniel-Rops says about our period, 'people admired the saints so much that in the end it made them forget the All-Highest'.[36]

In part, this may have been because of the way the cult originated. How far it was simply a superficially Christianized continuation of the hero-cults of late antiquity and the age-old worship of local pagan deities, associated with sacred sites and objects such as springs, rivers, trees and mountain-tops, it is impossible to say with any assurance. The matter is still the subject of much debate, but even so cautious a Roman Catholic scholar as Père Delehaye conceded in effect that, in part at least, this cult was something grafted on to the core of institutional Christianity, with some of its roots in the pagan cultural heritage.[37] It is hard to suppose that in the early days of Frankish Christianity the peasant who sought the help of the local saint was conscious of doing anything very different from what his forebears had done when they attempted to conciliate the *genius loci*.

(ii)

Right into the high Middle Ages the cult of the saints was predominantly a localized phenomenon. The saints were believed to be in heaven, but they were nevertheless present and active in and around their mortal bodies in a quite specific way. Their souls might be 'marching on', but their bodies were not simply 'a mould'ring in the grave'; in many cases, for example St Cuthbert, St Etheltrude, St Wynnibald or St Lull, they were believed to have remained free from corruption and to give off a pleasing scent from time to time. Whether or not that happened,[38] the saints' remains were believed to be a definite focus of their presence (*praesentia*) at which holy power (*potentia*) could be experienced. As Gregory the Great wrote, 'where the bodies of holy martyrs rest, it is certain that wonders occur'. That sort of belief is documented at least as early as 156 CE (*Martyrdom of Polycarp* xvii), and one of the key features of belief in the saints was the conviction that before and after their deaths they joined heaven and earth, straddled the division between the natural and the supernatural.[39]

Thus, the resting place of a saint was 'the place' (*ho topos* cf. *loca sanctorum*) where he or she was present, where earth joined heaven and the normal laws of the grave were held to be suspended. Accordingly, people earnestly desired to be buried – and indeed to live (cf. Einhardt at Mulinheim) in the vicinity of such tombs (*ad sanctos*) in order to benefit from the saint's *potentia*.[40]

The authorities were behind all this, and we hear of elaborate ceremonies at the tombs of saints during which, after the appropriate *passio* had been read out, the sense of the saint's *praesentia* was so vivid that the possessed cried out and the atmosphere was electric with expectation. There is still more than a hint of this in Ralph Glaber's account of concourses in 1000 CE and thereabouts when 'innumerable sick folk were healed ... and all were inflamed with such ardour that through the hands of their bishops they raised the pastoral staff to heaven while themselves with outspread palms, and with one voice, cried to God "peace, peace, peace!" '.[41]

(iii)

In the fifth and sixth centuries the church in the West refused to allow the bodies of the saints to be touched, and Gregory the Great declared it a sacrilege to move them from their tombs; but from the seventh to eighth centuries, when the tibia of St Genesius and the head of St Ferreol were subjects of dispute, it became increasingly common for the remains of saints to be transported. The process was normally a ceremonial and extremely elaborate one, known as *translatio*, in which the body, enclosed in a feretory of precious metal studded with jewels,[42] would be accompanied by eminent church dignitaries, monks, canons and other clergy, and large crowds, as well as musicians and choirs. It would be met and formally received at the boundaries of its new territory, and placed in a waiting shrine with great pomp.[43] In the course of the proceedings the crowds along the way did their best to touch the body, or at any rate the feretory or the clothes of the pall-bearers, in order to avail themselves of the holy power in a way they would be unable to do once it was enclosed in a shrine (see plate 10).[44] The shrine would also be an elaborate construction out of precious metal and precious stones, for this was an age which found difficulty in imagining spiritual grandeur unconjoined with material wealth. In the ninth century a woman went with rich offerings for some newly-installed relics at Prüm, 'but seeing that the saint's tomb did not glitter with gold and silver ... she rushed home and advised her friends to retrace their steps, saying "you will not find anything holy in that place" '.[45]

The recipients of a body translated in this way would expect to become the beneficiaries of the saint's presence and holy power; but there would be indirect advantages as well. Particularly if the body was that of some famous saint, or if it became known for the number and size of the miracles associated with it, it would attract pilgrims from far and wide. These would be expected to make offerings, and they would also need accommodation in the monastery or town holding the relics. Like modern tourists, they would be a source of commercial prosperity.[46]

One naturally asks what persuaded those living at the site of the original burial to part with their patron. In some cases they simply accepted money, often in order to be able to deal with some emergency, such as the burning down of a church or monastery; but in other cases what amounted to theft was involved. Perhaps the most famous theft of this kind occurred in 828 or 829 when the Venetians sent two merchants to bring back the (supposed) remains of St Mark from Alexandria, and a chapel, which subsequently evolved into the basilica, was built next to the Doges' Palace to house them. The Venetians, hitherto under the patronage of St Theodore, attributed their rapidly increasing prosperity to their new and more illustrious patron, of whom they have ever since been proud, adopting St Mark's symbol, the lion, as their own. Scarcely less celebrated is the incident which took place in the later seventh (or possibly the early eighth) century, when a party of monks from the newly-founded (651 CE) monastery at Fleury (St Benoit-sur-Loire), perhaps accompanied by representatives of the bishop of Le Mans, went down to Monte Cassino, then deserted and ruinous for many years, in order to dig up and take back what they believed to be the remains of St Benedict and his sister, St Scholastica. From that moment the monastery began to flourish, and the present Romanesque basilica was built in the eleventh century as a worthy shrine for the relics.[47]

Similar stories are told about the remains of other saints, for example those of St Foy at Conques and of St Hymerius at Amelia, which Liutprand demanded in 970 as the price for regaining the king's favour on behalf of the bishop. The writer who tells the story regarded it in an entirely favourable light: 'He found and graciously brought to Cremona the body of the great St Hymerius.'[48]

However strangely the morality involved may strike modern ears, it is important to set the matter in its contemporary context. There was, for example, a story known, and no doubt believed, by the Venetians that St Mark had anchored off their shores on a voyage from Aquileia to Rome and seen a vision in which an angel greeted him with the words 'Peace be with you, Mark my Evangelist; here your body shall rest.' The monks of Fleury will have heard in chapel the passage from Gregory's *Dialogues* (II, 34 and 37) which told how Benedict had been buried in an oratory he himself had built on the top of Monte Cassino in a tomb in which his sister had already been laid. It was, according to the later account, revealed to Abbot Mummolus in a dream that the site was now abandoned and desolate. Quite apart from the benefits they would bring to Fleury, could it be right that the remains of two such illustrious saints should lie unidentified and unhonoured?

The story of St Nicholas's 'translation' from Myra to Bari in 1087 tells us a lot about mediaeval attitudes. A highly coloured Life of the saint, produced by Methodius in the ninth century, gave him wide publicity, and will no doubt have had something to do with the matter. Although the theft was carried out with violence (crowbars were used), those responsible believed, or affected to believe, that their action was in obedience to a specific instruction given to the pope in a dream, and that the saint's failure to resist removal, and his performance of spectacular miracles on arrival at Bari, were evidence that he approved the translation. A new church was built at Bari to house him, and the pope himself (Urban III) was present at the inauguration.[49] The claim that a saint approved, or even demanded, the translation of his or her remains and specified the destination, and that he or she assisted the process with miraculous guidance and help, was a common one; the remains, for example, would refuse to settle until placed in the shrine of the saint's choice.[50]

The evidence suggests that justifications of this sort were often what we should call rationalizations. The absence of Mummolus's dream from the earliest account of the Fleury translation, for example, seems to show that it was an invention *post eventum*. Nevertheless, neither the credulity of the age nor its tendency to impute its own motives and preferences to the saints should be underestimated. The people of Bari, for instance, may well have been completely sincere in thinking that St Nicholas was dissatisfied with the inadequate veneration which was all depopulated Myra could offer him, and would perhaps welcome translation to a rich shrine in a prosperous city, where he would receive appropriate honours. Certainly, Nicephorus, the Italian Greek who narrates the story, believed in some such justification, arguing that the people of Myra had had the saint for over seven hundred years and that it was now Bari's turn. His comment is illuminating: the fraud (*fraus*), for such he admitted it to be, 'was a pious one, for, as Scripture says, "fraud is good if no one is injured" '.[51] Perhaps Nicephorus's account and comment give as fair a picture as any of the balance of feelings and motives involved in such transactions. One thing, however, is certain: they would never have occurred had it not been for a deep and almost universal belief in the very real spiritual and material blessings to be expected in the vicinity of a saint's remains. To attribute them entirely to commercial motives is completely to misunderstand the mentality of the age.

(iv)

The word 'relic' is used to describe the whole body of a saint, but it more commonly designates a part of such a body. When it became common to disturb and move the bodies of saints, it became customary to dismember them and distribute the parts, often tiny fragments, to different centres, the belief being that the presence and power of the saint were to be found as fully in any part, however small, as in the whole. The most valued relics were parts of the actual body, but in the case of Christ, and of the Virgin, after belief in her bodily assumption had developed, relics of this sort were obviously not available. However, in their case, as in others, things associated with them, such as clothes or possessions, served as relics. The Sainte Chapelle in Paris, for example, was built to house the crown of thorns which Louis IX bought from Baldwin II.

Our period saw the beginning of a quite concentrated interest in relics, translations and shrines, which lasted for some three centuries; and it is obvious that, once the minute dissection of saints' bodies came to be practised, the number of relics available will have been virtually limitless, especially in view of the belief that in some cases God miraculously allowed fragments to be detached without any diminution of the whole.[52]

It is significant that Guibert of Nogent, one of the very few men at the time to have reservations about the cult of relics, attributed the problems associated with it to the partition of bodies. 'All the evils of contention over relics,' he wrote, 'would be avoided if we permitted the saints to enjoy the repose of a proper and immutable burial place.'[53]

The demand for relics was insatiable. For one thing, they were guarantees of political prestige and spiritual authority, and kings, as well as leading churchmen, were more or less compelled to form large collections of them; for another, the Second Council of Nicaea in 787 decreed the use of relics in the consecration of new churches and altars, and laid down that any church which had been consecrated without them should acquire some as soon as possible. Also, relics were an essential element of social and political life, inasmuch as oaths, the chief guarantee of peace, and the principal way of settling disputes, were taken on them, in the assurance that perjury would then be avenged. The ordeal, another form of adjudication, also took place in their presence.

Rome was an almost inexhaustible source of relics, but collectors, such as Angilbert, abbot of St Riquier, got them from all parts of the Christian world. His collection, catalogued in 801, consisted of 138 items, including 23 associated with Christ (for example, a fragment of the cross, part of the sponge used at the crucifixion, and articles of clothing), 4 with the Virgin, 8 with apostles, and some hair of John the Baptist.[54] The abbey also possessed among its treasures the pillars of the flagellation, pieces of the Holy Sepulchre and some drops of the Virgin's milk. Very soon many churches had more than 500 relics, and in addition collections large and small were in the hands of leading laymen such as Einhardt, as well as of individual churchmen and rulers. Private relic collections were in some ways like the art collections of the modern world.

That may give some idea of the number of relics in circulation. The phrase is apt because relics served as assets which, as we have seen, were often realized when occasion demanded: for example, to pay for new or refurbished buildings. The variety among relics was almost equally great – from large items such as whole bodies, the Holy Lance used at the crucifixion, or Moses' rod, discovered at Sens just before 1000 CE, to minute quantities of filings from St Peter's chains, dust from saints' tombs or drops of oil from lamps that burned near them, and even particles of blood and spittle a saint had coughed up in his death throes, which were the only sort that poor pilgrims could afford.[55]

The official sale of relics at shrines was an important source of revenue. So strong was a saint's *potentia* believed to be that even a medallion bearing his or her image was valued as a vehicle of it; and there is a story of a man who got possession of a scrap of parchment on which St Germanus had written a couple of lines, and found that when it was boiled, the water proved a sovereign remedy.

Where the demand was so high, a regular trade in relics naturally developed, and professional relic-dealers, rather like modern art-dealers, went into business. Inevitably, some of them were dishonest, and it was recognized that relics were sometimes inauthentic.[56]

> However, this was a credulous and conformist age which did not readily accept doubts on such matters. Any educated churchman who raised them risked unpopularity or worse; when an abbot of Bonn expressed doubts about the authenticity of the remains of the patron saint of a nearby village he was cruelly punished by the saint until he offered his own body-weight in wax for candles at his shrine; even then he had to do annual penance for life.[57]

When doubts were raised, the only means of resolving them was by reference to the supernatural. Did a body remain incorrupt? Did it continue to work miracles? How did it fare when tested by fire or some other form of ordeal? In many cases the triumphant exhibition of a relic was enough to vindicate it in popular eyes, and even in the eyes of more sophisticated people, as in the mid-eleventh century when an imposing exhibition of the body of St Denys at his abbey, north of Paris, convinced a gathering of leading nobles and churchmen that it was genuine, despite the conflicting claim of the abbey of St Emmeram at Regensburg to have the true remains. At this period not even the educated were very adept at the critical sifting of evidence.[58]

It was, as Luchaire says, the *relics* of the saints which were the centrepiece of early mediaeval Christianity; and there can be no doubt not only that were the saints seen, in effect, as independent wonder-workers, and even minor deities or demi-gods, but that their relics were seen as independent vehicles of magic power, frequently being worn round the neck, for example, as *charms*.[59]

People slept in their presence, touched them, bound their heads with cloths in which they had been wrapped, swallowed dust or oil from the shrines in which they lay, washed in water which had been near them, in fact tried to avail themselves of their curative power by every conceivable means. Nor was healing the only thing sought through their aid. Theologians claimed that relics would neutralize poisons, control storms, rain, thunder and floods, and give victory when carried in battle. They were used to overcome robbers and stop fires and plagues, and carried through the fields to put an end to drought and ensure fertility. In fact there were a thousand uses through which they supplied the place of a virtually non-existent technology.

According to official theology, as we have seen, it was God who was responsible for all the changes wrought through relics, and the clergy claimed that his essential purpose was the strengthening of faith. Perhaps more widely accepted was the insistence that a worthy life was a condition of being helped through relics,[60] though, as we shall see, there were two sides even to that. It is worth reflecting on the fact that, even on the strictest orthodox view, God treated those who wore relics round their necks differently from those who did not. How will people have reacted, consciously and unconsciously, to such a fact and such a God?

(v)

Those familiar with the Catholicism of the twentieth century, or indeed that of the high Middle Ages, will perhaps be surprised that the Virgin Mary has not figured more prominently in the foregoing account.

Even before the fourth century, when her perpetual virginity was affirmed, Mary had been hailed as *theotokos* (literally 'mother of God', but more accurately 'she who gave birth to him who was God') and, as such, honoured above all other saints. Devotion to her developed more quickly in the East than in the West, but in the seventh century when there was a great influx of Easterners to the West and almost all the popes had an oriental background, the four feasts of the Virgin (Nativity, Annunciation, Purification and Assumption) replaced the single feast hitherto observed in the West, on 1 January. The Nativity, however, was not generally observed until the eleventh century, and only the Purification attained any real popularity in Francia in our period.[61]

The belief that Mary's conception had been miraculously exempt from original sin, although some adumbration of it has been claimed, somewhat implausibly, in the writing of Agobard in the ninth century,[62] did not become general till after our period, and was still denied by such leading theologians as Bonaventura and Aquinas in the thirteenth century.

From the seventh century onward the written sources show increased devotion to the Virgin. Alcuin, in the eighth century, was known for his attachment to her, and so were Hincmar, the influential archbishop of Reims in the ninth century, and Fulbert, the learned bishop of Chartres in the tenth. In the *Visio Wettini*, composed by Walahfrid Strabo about 826, Christ addresses his mother as 'most holy mother, you who have supreme command over earth and heaven', while at the end of the century she is addressed in positively fulsome terms in Abbo's poem on the siege of Paris: 'Illustrious mother of the redeemer and of the saviour of the world, brilliant star of the sea you whose glory surpasses that of all the stars.'[63] As to her status *vis-à-vis* her son, Peter Damian already called her *deificata* in the eleventh century, while by the early twelfth century Guibert of Nogent could write: 'The Virgin has with Jesus the power which a mother in this world has over her son. A mother does not pray; she orders. How then would Christ not listen to his mother?' Only a little later Bernard of

Clairvaux says in effect: If you fear the Father, there is Christ the mediator; if you fear him, who, though man, is also God, there is his mother, pure humanity. She will listen to you: the Son will listen to her, the Father to him.[64] The history of art mirrors the same development, the Virgin being more and more portrayed as the majestic *Theotokos*.

It will be noticed that all those quoted were monks, and it was in the monasteries that Marian devotion principally flourished at this time, the *Ave Maria* being added to the Lord's Prayer in the tenth century, though the usage did not spread throughout the church till rather later. Mary's close physical relationship to Jesus might be thought sufficient to explain her pre-eminence among the saints, but further explanations have been offered in modern times, for example, that it arose from popular hunger for an embodiment of female virtues in the supernatural realm. There is probably some truth in Mecklin's contention that when Jesus became a remote and, to the people, somewhat incomprehensible, figure as a member of the Trinity, the figure of Mary came in to fill the gap.[65] Such explanations must remain speculative, and so must the suggestion that the cult arose in part as an outgrowth of the need of monks for compensation for their unmarried state and lack of female companionship; though in favour of it is that a high view of Mary was always popular with members of religious communities.

In our period they were undoubtedly ahead of general church feeling in the matter, as was admitted at the time in the case of Fulbert of Chartres, for example. The Marian cult was only just beginning to penetrate the popular consciousness, and although seen as the head of the saintly company, the Virgin was not yet completely detached from the rest in the way she was later to be when she was pictured in a quite exceptional place alongside her son. She is not so much as mentioned in the comprehensive manual Dhuoda wrote for her son in 841-2, despite the fact that it was the work of a woman. The earliest collections of Miracles of the Virgin date from the twelfth century. There is no mention of pilgrimages to her shrines in the West until the tenth century. In 862 it took a miracle, according to the *Annals of St Bertin*, to persuade the inhabitants of Thérouanne to observe the feast of the Assumption.[66]

As Rosalind and Christopher Brooke suggest, this relative lack of enthusiasm was no doubt partly due to the fact that the virtues for which the Virgin stood, such as mercy, charity and chastity, were not as highly prized in the violent eighth, ninth and tenth centuries as they were to be later. It must also be remembered that, since her body was believed to have been assumed into heaven, there could be no central shrine which housed it and could form a base from which devotion to her might have spread. By the same token, few bodily relics of her were available, an important fact for people whose religion was highly concrete and specific. Later, this was to make her cult more generalized, but in our period her cult was just as localized as those of other saints, locks of her hair, drops of her milk or fragments of her clothing doing duty as relics.[67] An example of a typical miracle attributed to the Virgin is quoted by Benedicta Ward:[68] 'He washed the enclosed relics in water and wine and poured the liquid over the head and face of the aforesaid young girl and gave her some of the liquid to drink and ordered her to lie down under the feretory; then bending the knee he began to pray earnestly to Our Lady.' The result was a miraculous cure, which was, as Sister Benedicta says, 'typical ... and could have come from any shrine of the period'. Statues of Mary were also believed to work miracles, and churches dedicated to her ('Our Lady of such-and-such a place') served as centres of devotion to her. In that connexion it is worth noticing that she, like other saints, would often do at one shrine what she would not do at another. Of numerous examples we may quote two. In the *Miracles of Our Lady of Chartres* we hear of a woman who was cured of a skin disease through prayer to the Virgin. When she was about to set out for Our Lady of Soissons to return thanks, the Virgin appeared to tell her that it was by Our Lady of Chartres that she had been healed.[69] Again, a Norman called Vitalis arrived at the 'insipid conclusion that the Blessed Mary of Bayeux and the Blessed Mary of Coutances were one and the same person, that is, the mother of God, and that consequently the Virgin of Coutances could not possibly be more merciful or more powerful than the Virgin of Bayeux'. He therefore refused to join a pilgrimage to Coutances, only to be severely punished by the Virgin for his refusal.[70]

As a result, Our Lady of Bayeux, for instance, would be given a different profile from Our Lady of Coutances, say, or Our Lady of Rocamadour, and come to be seen, to all intents and purposes, as a separate saint. The same could be said of other saints, for example of St Faith at her different shrines. At this time devotion to the Virgin, as to other saints, was an essentially local phenomenon.

It is worth noting one feature of the Virgin's activities, and indeed those of other saints, even though it did not manifest itself to its fullest extent till later. It may be introduced by way of the legend of Theophilus, which originated in the East, but became widely known in the West from the ninth century onwards, until it became in fact the most popular legend of the Middle Ages, actually finding its way into the regular office of the Virgin by the eleventh century. Theophilus and the devil signed a contract by which Theophilus sold his soul in return for the succession to a bishopric he coveted. Repenting subsequently, he could find no way of setting aside the contract, but, in response to his assiduous prayer, the Virgin intervened, wrested the contract from Satan and returned it to Theophilus.[71] What is typical of the Virgin's intervention here is its amoral character. She saves Theophilus simply because he calls upon her. In a similar way she saved from drowning two boys on their way back from paying their devotions at Rocamadour who had fought their way on to a boat that was already full, and fallen overboard.[72]

Comparable examples are legion, and what characterizes them all is that, as Lord Melbourne would have said, 'there was no damned merit in them'. Benedicta Ward writes that the Virgin 'is portrayed as an arbitrary patron ... bringing mercy into a power-dominated society simply because she chose to do so. She intervenes to save those whom human and divine justice alike condemn ... stress is laid on how undeserving the suppliants were.'[73] No wonder she was hailed in the hymn at her office as *Mater misericordiae* (mother of mercy). Jonathan Sumption, making the same point, adds that 'she offered an escape from the rigorous teaching of the church on the subject of damnation and punishment'.[74] It is no doubt this which accounts for the proliferation of tales in the later Middle Ages recording the Virgin's intervention on behalf of thoroughly bad lots, whose only redeeming feature was that they prayed to her.[75] Nor was such behaviour exclusive to Mary; St Faith, for example, behaved in a similarly capricious way. 'She helped her people "juste et injuste" and gave assistance to the least deserving.'[76]

No doubt from one point of view, all this increased the sense of the capriciousness of the supernatural world; but in an age which put little emphasis on 'justification by faith, quite apart from works of the Law' (cf. Rom. 3.28), it must have come as a great relief to peasants and others who for various reasons could have little hope of meriting salvation, to feel that they, like those in the tales of the saints, might be helped and saved despite their lack of merits. It is perhaps significant that, according to the *Miracula* of Rocamadour, many of those who paid their devotions at this famous Marian shrine belonged to the *populus simplex et rusticanus* or were people of the flighty sort. No doubt all these found in the saint's acceptance of them, and her willingness to win them similar acceptance on the part of her Son, at least a chink in the dark contemporary doctrine of the strict justice, not to say wrath, of God.

(vi)

The vast majority of people had no opportunity of travelling any distance, and their devotion inevitably focussed on the local church or monastery. Here might lie the remains of some local worthy who had captured the popular imagination for some reason, and then confirmed his or her saintly status by continuing to be a source of healings and other miracles; or there might be remains or relics brought from elsewhere. In either case, the local saint was the centre and bonding-factor in local life. In that connexion it must be remembered that, according to the ideas of the time, the saints were in a very real sense the owners of any shrine, or indeed church or monastery, dedicated to them, and of all that pertained to it. Documents confirming gifts to shrines constantly speak of the gifts as made to the saint whose the shrine was; when Maieul of Cluny got near Rome, we are told that tears came into his eyes 'because he knew he would shortly behold the glorious apostles (i.e. Peter and Paul, whose shrines were in the city), as if he were standing face to face with them'.[77] People saw the local saint as their common *patronus/a* and, as we have seen, used the language of vassalage to describe their relationship to him or her.[78]

High and low alike, the inhabitants of a particular manor or village would see themselves as all under the patronage of Saint so-and-so. Free men would voluntarily give up their freedom to become *homines sanctorum*; the serfs of St Germain-des-Prés, for example, were described as *homines sancti Germani*. Patron saints thus personified the communal identities of towns and villages, and their continuing patronage linked the generations across time as well as individuals across the community. If the analogy does not sound too bizarre, the relation of a community to the local saint was rather like that of a modern English town to its football team. There was the same intense local feeling, local loyalty and local pride; and the same conviction that the local product was better than any of those of neighbouring places.[79] The community would accompany the saint's remains as they were carried through the village with an enthusiasm like that of modern fans who turn out to greet their team as it proceeds through the streets on an open-topped bus after some signal success (see plate 10). There are even accounts of *compotationes* (drinking bouts) 'for love of such-and-such a saint', and of physical violence.[80] On the other hand football supporters will not continue loyal indefinitely if their team consistently fails to win; and in the same sort of way mediaeval villagers expected results from their saint as the price of their devotion. There was a distinct air of bargaining and business transaction about the whole matter. We have many stories of devotees berating or deserting saints who failed to meet their needs, and even doing violence to their shrines. The monks of Fleury had occasion to note, in this connexion, that 'the vulgar mob is very fickle and bends like a reed in whatever direction the wind blows'.[81]

A few examples out of a large number must suffice. In about 977, when the members of a monastery founded by St Rudesind were oppressed by the king and got no redress from the saint, a lame old monk struck the shrine with his crutch and complained, 'Why have you brought us here, Rudesind? Why have you deceived us under a show of religion which we now see to have been false ...? Why have you torn us from our homes, where we led lawful lives, to serve, not God, as you promised, but tyrants?'[82] Ralph Glaber tells of a devastating fire in Rome in which St Peter's was endangered. Unable to put out the fire themselves, the crowd marched on the church 'crying with a terrible voice ... and crying ... with curses that if the chief of the apostles did not watch over his own, or emerge as a present defender of his church, many throughout the world would fall away from their profession of faith.'[83] The *Miracles de St Benoit* are full of such stories. For example, when burglars stole some of the church ornaments, a monk called out to the saint, 'Are you asleep, you layabout? ... since you cannot defend these ornaments, I don't care if the thieves take your breeches!' An old woman who got no satisfaction from the saint 'ran to the church, tucked up the altar cloths, and beat the altar with rods, crying ... You wretched old Benedict (*Benedicte vetustissime*). What are you up to? Why are you asleep?'[84] The villagers of Villeneuve-St-Georges used to take the saint down from the altar and plunge him in the Seine if he brought them too much, or too little, rain. Examples could be multiplied almost indefinitely,[85] and the tone of many of them is such as to justify Mecklin's comparison with the attitude of 'the savage who beats his fetish when it fails to work', and his reference to the 'essential crudity and semi-barbaric nature' of such a religious attitude.[86]

If the devotees thus expected the saints to keep to their bargain, the expectation was reciprocal. The saints expected to be duly honoured and to have their reliquaries and shrines not only maintained, but made increasingly magnificent; they expected offerings of wax so that they could be surrounded with lighted candles, and records of such offerings were kept.[87] They expected their remains to be treated with pomp and ceremony and to have continual attention paid to them. If all this was not forthcoming, they would retaliate by working no wonders, or even, in extreme cases, by leaving the shrine altogether. St Benedict, for example, was seen leaving Fleury because he was being dishonoured there.[88] If, however, they were properly treated, the saints would promote and defend the interests of the local community, both material and spiritual. In the eighth century an unknown poet wrote about the city of Milan, 'How fortunate and happy she is to have deserved as defenders saints like these, whose prayers make her unconquered and prosperous.'[89]

The relics of St Wigbert effectively protected Fritzlar against repeated assaults by the Saxons, who tried in vain to burn the monastery, while other saints secured good weather for their communities, or warded off human enemies and natural disasters. The Life of St Wigbert also tells of the saint's help in warding off attacks by the devil and his forces.[90] Help to individuals might include rescue from fire, flood, falls and the like. St Pirmin, for instance, saved a layman who fell into a well, and a nobleman who had been wounded by some Saxons,[91] but in a society devoid of means to combat disease, healing was what was valued above all. Healing stories are simply legion.[92] The (local) saint might also be concerned with social justice in the community, intervening, for example, in law suits or the liberation of captives.[93]

Punishment on God's behalf was also an important part of a saint's activity; it might be directed against a member of the community, for example, one who left mass early and mocked at those arriving, or one who joked during the saint's translation, or who failed to fulfil a vow.[94] More often, though, the saints directed their punitive measures against those who attacked or injured the community under their protection. In so doing, they showed a fierce and often, it must be admitted, rather chauvinistic loyalty to their protégés. For example, according to the Anglo-Saxon Chronicle, the Virgin Mary ridded London of invading enemies, but only at the expense of allowing them to 'do the greatest harm that ever an army could do' to the hapless people of Essex, Kent, Sussex and Hunts, who were not her particular concern.[95]

Since, as we have said, a client community and its property were seen as belonging to the saint, much of this punitive activity seemed in effect designed to protect the saint's own domains and interests. Thus, when St Remigius afflicted all the people of a village *and* their descendants with hernia (in the case of the men) and swelling of the throat (in the case of the women) it was because they had set fire to some corn he was storing against a famine. Or when a huge Norse warrior was shrunk to the size of a baby and dispatched to hell by St Germanus, it was for stealing a cloth from his altar to use as a bed sheet.[96] Sometimes the saints' concern for their honour and interests seems to us petty and predatory, as, for instance, when a child jumped over the grave of St Rigobert and was paralysed for life in one foot. In Dorset, people who mocked at St Augustine by fastening fishtails to his garments were given tails themselves, and so were their descendants after them. Frodoard tells of a marauder who chased a woman right to the parvis of a saint's church. Not only did the saint cause him to be horribly crippled for life, but refused to prevent his death until a present was made to him of the man's horse and absolutely everything else he possessed.[97]

Since those responsible for churches often had no physical means of preventing attacks and thefts, such stories as these were widely disseminated in order to frighten off marauding lords or other would-be robbers and desecrators.

In the official theology and the writings of scholars, the cult of the saints was formally integrated, as far as possible, into the Christian system. According to this, the saints are concrete individuals – as concrete and individual after death as before it[98] – who have achieved a place in God's immediate presence. They are the objects of his love and, as such, in a position to move him and to plead their merits before him on behalf of others. Officially, this was their only role in the matter, the miracles and other benefits associated with the cult of the saints being, as we have seen, wholly attributable to the working of God himself.

The means by which the saints had come to their present glorious position had been meritorious living. Since thinking on this subject derived largely from Augustine, that meant that they had led lives of heroic sanctity; they had been spiritual venturers, whose attitudes and behaviour mirrored the deepest aspirations of contemporary church leaders. Their attention had been entirely focused on the other world, and they had sat as loose to this world and its concerns as is compatible with bare survival.[99] In that sense they were ascetics, and it is noteworthy that there was virtually no saint who had not, at least after conversion, practised chastity and poverty, with all the lack of concern for the world that implies. Indeed sanctity, at any rate of the highest kind, was thought impossible without those virtues, and their companion virtue, obedience. They are ascribed, for example, even to such a military, lay saint as St Gerald of Aurillac.[100] The church authorities were anxious that the moral qualifications for sanctity should be stressed in connexion with the cult of the saints. For only so could the saints define the Christian manner of life and serve as examples in the way many leading churchmen wished them to do. Bishop Rimbert, for example, wrote of his predecessor, St Anskar, 'if anyone will follow the examples he left, he will lead, while on earth, the life of heaven (*coelestem conversationem*); if anyone will recall his teaching, he will be able to walk the way of God's commandments without failure'. Similarly, Bernard of Clairvaux told a congregation that St Martin was to be imitated in his demonstration of the Beatitudes rather than in his performance of miracles.[101]

It was all part of this piece of social control that the Synod of Frankfurt (794) attempted, as we have seen, to introduce a moratorium on the emergence of further saints[102] and that the French bishops worked so hard to reserve to themselves the right to decide who should be regarded as saints and have devotion paid to them. Ralph Glaber severely criticizes three bishops in southern France who had failed to exercise a sufficiently strict control in the matter, and his reason for doing so is revealing. Their carelessness had allowed a charlatan to pass off as a saint a man whose remains he had just dug up in a local paupers' cemetery.[103] Guibert of Nogent, no great champion of the cult of the saints, makes the situation very clear. Left to themselves, he says, the ordinary people would venerate as saints men and women about whose lives nothing was known, not even whether they were now in heaven or hell. Whereas the hierarchy would not even declare formally that the Virgin Mary had been assumed into heaven 'for the reason that it cannot be proved by the necessary arguments', the populace, if it were left to them, would willingly pay honours not only to people about whose lives nothing at all was known, but to completely unworthy characters such as the so-called 'St Pyro, who in fact met his end through falling into a well while in a drunken stupor.[104] The greatest care should therefore be taken to see that honours were paid only to those whose lives were known to have deserved for them a place in heaven; and by the same token, the authenticity of relics should be a matter for careful scrutiny. Guibert has no difficulty in showing that the need for such scrutiny was often ignored, with the result that there were, for example, two alleged heads of St John the Baptist and two bodies of St Firmin in currency.[105]

Guibert was by no means the only one to be critical in this way. In 794 the French bishops opposed what they believed (wrongly) to have been an imprudent recommendation of the worship of images by the Second Council of Nicaea in 787; and, as we have seen, the *Admonitio Generalis* forbade the cult of false martyrs and doubtful saints. The process of holding an enquiry before the proclamation of a saint goes back to the ninth century at least; in 864 the bishop of Constance permitted payment of honours to Othmar, former abbot of St Gall, and the translation of his relics, only after an examination by his diocesan synod and three days of prayer and fasting.[106] The scepticism of Adhémar of le Puy about the Holy Lance, allegedly discovered during the first crusade, is well known; and his namesake of Chabannes offers a critique of the head of St John the Baptist claimed by the church at Angély which has a very critical modern ring about it.[107] Many other examples could be quoted, and Sumption goes so far as to say that such an attitude 'was probably fairly typical of educated churchmen of the day'.[108]

There were not lacking church leaders who were doubtful about the role assigned to relics in general and saw dangers in the cult of the saints as a whole, if not carefully controlled. Among these was the scholarly Agobard, Archbishop of Lyon, who, in his treatise *On Images* distinguished sharply between the shrines of the saints (*memoriae*) and the real houses of God (*templa*). He also distinguished between the forms of devotion known as *pietas* and *servitus*, and argued that there is no other mediator between God and man than the God-man Jesus Christ, who alone is worthy of religious honours.[109] The defence of the cult of the saints by Ermoldus Nigellus makes quite clear that there were those who opposed it,[110] while Einhardt, though an avid collector of relics, confessed to certain doubts, on theological grounds, about addressing prayers to the saints. 'Is it right to direct our ... prayers ... to the apostles and martyrs? May we invoke those whose souls, we know well, are ever in the presence of God? If the problem were not one which touches God, I should call it one proper for Hercules; and with that I must leave it.'[111]

Even Augustine, apt to be credulous about such things, advised caution, and, as we have seen, his attitude of reserve was fully shared in the eleventh century by the learned and attractive scholar, Guibert of Nogent. However, as Guibert himself makes clear, it was a position difficult to sustain in the face of popular hostility and the vested interests of possessors of relics. When the representatives of a famous church were engaged in a money-raising campaign and were exhibiting what they claimed was some of the bread used at the Last Supper, he confesses to having been browbeaten into supporting their claim against his better judgment. He also bears out what we know from other sources, that the populace would resort to physical violence in defence of the authenticity of treasured relics.[112] The original discovery of relics was often attributed to revelations made in dreams, and similar revelations were quoted as guaranteeing claims to authenticity. To doubt such revelations could easily be represented as sheer faithlessness and, apart from the stigma attached to such an attitude, there was a widespread belief, as we have seen, that it might well bring horrible retribution from the saint in question. Giraldus Cambrensis claimed that 'those who despise the relics of (Welsh) saints are usually punished', and of the one hundred and thirty-nine miracles recorded in the *Miracles of St Benedict* a considerable proportion is directed against those who showed lack of faith toward him.[113] Guibert and Adhémar of Chabannes were quite exceptional in their ability to handle evidence critically, and the weight of opinion was pretty solidly against them and their like. For the populace, and indeed many of their leaders as well, miracle was evidence which admitted of no argument (Gregory the Great had been influential here), and in a society which had no difficulties about the occurrence of miracles, this meant that innumerable men and women were authenticated as saints in the absence, or even in the face, of historical evidence about their lives.

Miracle settled everything; and it was in the miracles wrought by the saints, and in their other acts of succour, that the great majority were predominantly interested. 'The refinements of saintly piety, as outlined in the great Augustinian tradition, never touched the life of the masses for whom the church ordinances were merely magical contrivances for manipulating the forces of evil that threatened them at every turn.'[114] Far more than the mass, or any other institution connected directly with God, it was the activity of the saints which represented salvation for the overwhelming majority in all walks of life. The saints were the real saviour-gods to whom you brought your needs and troubles. Whether you got any relief depended on their decision, and in practice they were regarded as the sources of it, however much the official teaching might attribute everything to God. Most people, if asked how they linked such ideas to the rest of the Christian faith, would have had no very coherent answer.[115]

The contents of this chapter may help to explain both the quotation from Luchaire with which we began and his comment on it: '... how could men of that time raise themselves to the metaphysical and moral conceptions of Christian doctrine? To the masses religion was the veneration of the remains of saints or of objects which had been used by Jesus or the Virgin. It was believed that divine intervention in human affairs manifested itself especially through the power of relics. Therefore, hardly anything was done, whether in public or private life, without having recourse to the protection or the guarantee of these sacred objects ... Relics were brought to councils and assemblies; on them the most solemn oaths were taken, treaties between entire peoples and conventions between individuals were sworn. They were the shield and buckler of cities. Was there need of asking God to end a long-enduring rain? A procession was held and the relics were shown. Whoever undertook a distant pilgrimage, a dangerous voyage, or a campaign of war, first went to pray to a saint, to see and touch a relic. The chevalier put some relics in the hilt of his sword; the tradesman, in a little sack suspended from his neck.'[116]

As that makes clear, it would be almost impossible to exaggerate the centrality of the saints and their cult in tenth-century religion. Not only were the saints constantly kept before people's minds through the liturgy and paraliturgical devotions of the church, through the names they bore and gave their children, as well as their visits to shrines, but the days dedicated to various saints were important time-markers. One celebrated the feast of the saint after whom one was named, and in addition many legal obligations and customary practices were tied to feasts of the Virgin and of other saints, such as Peter (Lammastide), Hilary, Andrew, Laurence or Denys. The saint was deeply embedded in everyday life but also in folklore, and if we wanted a parallel to help us understand some of the attitudes involved, we might perhaps say that mediaeval Catholics felt the same pride and enthusiastic loyalty in relation to their chosen saints as some modern people feel in relation to a favourite actor or pop-star. At the same time, they had the sort of feelings of admiration and respect that modern non-scientists tend to have for an eminent scientist. Like the mediaeval saint, the modern scientist, as popularly conceived, is something of a stereotype. People are very much aware how far their life and well-being depend on the activities of such white-coated men and women, yet they do not understand the method by which they achieve their results or how their work fits into the total cultural scene. Without understanding any of these things, they are content to accept an image of scientists which approximates to folklore, and then get on with using the electricity supply they make possible and the antibiotics they supply. The attitude is essentially pragmatic, and so was the predominant mediaeval attitude to the saints. What people were interested in was the results the saints and their relics produced; and if those results were forthcoming, it made very little difference whether the saint who produced them was one of the great spiritual heroes of the past or an obscure local saint with little or nothing to commend him or her except his or her miracles.[117] Who shall blame them in an age when they had virtually no other resource to help them deal with an unpredictable but always threatening and dangerous environment?

Sir Richard Southern writes: 'The deficiencies in human resources were supplied by the power of the saints ...'. As human beings, men were powerless. They could only survive through their dependence on the supernatural ... relics were the main channel through which supernatural power was available for the needs of ordinary life.' Consequently, 'it is scarcely too much to say that the popular religion of these centuries was centred not on the sacraments, not on God or the life of Christ, but on the saints and their relics'.[118]

All that needs to be added to the quotations from Luchaire and Southern is a warning that the word 'popular' should not be too narrowly construed. Root-and-branch opposition to the cult of the saints was quite lacking. Even Guibert, for all his criticisms, was not fundamentally opposed to it. On the contrary, he was clear that the veneration of genuine relics was entirely proper. He also believed that a genuine prayer to a false saint could be of avail, if the petitioner honestly believed in his or her sanctity.[119] What he, and such other critics as there were, opposed was an over-easy acceptance of spurious saints or relics, or any approach to their cult which exaggerated its place in the Christian life or treated it as a magical way of getting what one wanted out of all relation to inwardness and a spiritual relationship with God. Guibert laid great stress on this last,[120] but, like other similar critics, had no doubt that the saints had God's ear and were the proper channel through which to approach him. Ermoldus Nigellus spoke for them all when he wrote (in the passage following the one quoted on p. 86): 'of course Peter is not God, but I firmly believe Peter's prayers can obtain for me the remission of the guilt of my sin'.[121]

So, however variously interpreted, the cult of the saints formed a vital, and indeed quite central, constituent in the religious faith and practice of everyone in tenth-century Francia.

10

The Past

In the early Middle Ages religion permeated all departments and aspects of life and thought. Every age is deeply influenced by its conception of the past, and this was particularly true of the tenth century, as we shall try to show. The point must first be made, however, that the conception of the past which so influenced the period was itself very largely the product of both the religious faith and the material conditions of the time.

Tenth-century people knew comparatively little about the past. Apart from what they could discover from the Bible, the Fathers and certain classical historians, history was for the most part a closed book to them.

The influence of the ancient Latin historians was mainly on the style and form of historical writing; for example, it gave currency to the biography of the individual. Some ancient historians, Sallust and Suetonius, for instance, were quite well known, though classical writings were seldom read *in toto*. History was regarded as a branch of grammar,[1] and grammar was taught by taking students through literary texts from Latin antiquity and explaining the allusions to history, myth, cosmology and the like *en passant*. It was in this way that a budding scholar picked up his bits and pieces of historical knowledge. He would thus be familiar with historical examples rather than complete historical texts.

Such knowledge as people had was confined to the biblical and Graeco-Roman worlds and, so far as the more recent past was concerned, to Christendom. Scholars did not know or understand the classical world well enough to comprehend it as a cultural whole, alternative to their own, and they knew nothing of any other foreign cultures beyond what could be gleaned from the odd traveller's tale. There was therefore no question of their having the sort of insight into a fundamentally different culture or religious system which might have raised questions about their own, or set it in a new perspective.

If the Bible was one of their chief historical sources, it also controlled the way they understood the historical process. No one can read the biblical account without receiving the strong impression that God is in continual and more or less direct control of events. This impression was, if anything, heightened by what the Fathers wrote; and the pagan authors, with their accounts of omens, sacrifices and interventions by the gods, did nothing to diminish it. It was also strongly reinforced by the Lives of the saints, works well known to almost everyone because they were often read aloud in the vernacular. These Lives not only represented God as constantly intervening through the miracles performed by the saints; they portrayed the lives of the saints themselves as controlled by God from start to finish. Many a saint, for example, was reported to have behaved, even as a baby, in ways which showed him or her to be already predestined by God for sanctity.[2]

For tenth-century people, supernatural agents and their activities were, as we have seen, an accepted part of the cultural scene, and the past was interpreted in corresponding terms. Disasters, public and private, were seen as God's punishment for sin, and periods of prosperity as signs of his favour.

Such a view of history informs all writing on the subject. Mediaeval accounts of the past were expressly designed to trace God's hand in events, to praise him for what he had done and to stimulate others to do the same.

> Ordericus Vitalis (1075–?1142) says more than once that history should be 'sung' like a hymn in honour of God who created the world and governs it with justice. He also says that it should provide examples of the kinds of behaviour God rewards and punishes.[3]

As this suggests, there was no place for the modern assumption that all historical events can in principle be accounted for on the basis of some combination of previous historical events and circumstances. The principle of historical causality as we understand it went largely unrecognized. Historical events, like natural events, were understood, not as so many links in a chain of inner-historical cause and effect, but as independent and discrete. The mediaeval chronicler did not see the materials he recorded as constituting a continuum of action. Every page of the clerical chronicle was, potentially at least, a new beginning. Of one such chronicler W.J. Brandt writes: 'He did not see in human experience the causal processes fundamental to modern experience. He saw human action, as he saw natural action, as an endless series of events, frequently related but at the same time possessing a unique structure that kept them discrete. His experience of the human world was consequently, not comparable to ours.'[4] Brandt adds: 'Of course reality did not ... present itself ... as an endless succession of events existing in splendid isolation from each other; events were frequently interrelated. But they did not, for that reason, lose their event-character.'[5] Peter Burke points out that this way of viewing the past was linked with the origins of mediaeval historiography, which seems to have begun with the writing of brief notes on events which had happened in a particular year, in the margins of Easter Tables. When independent histories began to be written, they kept the chronicle framework and tended to organize the facts in a one-after-another, rather than an explanatory, way. As Burke says, the favourite connective was not 'because', or 'as a result', but 'meanwhile'.⁶ Gurevich makes the same point: 'Mediaeval historians had neither the words nor the concepts to express the continuity of the historical process.'⁷

Such a discrete view of what had happened in the past made it easier to believe in the occurrence of frequent supernatural interventions; there was no sense that a miracle would involve a whole chain of natural and historical consequences in addition to the one it directly transformed. By the same token, however, such a view made it impossible to see the present situation as the product of (identifiable) historical forces and to cope with it accordingly. If the situation was thought to need changing, the only intelligent way of dealing with the matter was by appeasing God and thus changing the way he was directing events.

Brandt stresses another important fact. He points out that according to tenth-century ideas, actions did not originate in the precedent situation. They acted as a disturbance of that situation, originating in some peculiar way outside it. Ordinarily, in the view of the chroniclers, the cause of an action could be identified with a quite specific human character or human ambition or, at least, human action. Where it could not, fortune might be invoked as the agent, though a pious writer could of course substitute God himself for this causal agent. 'But ... the hand of God or the inscrutable, personified, working of fortune, was inherent in the clerical view of action.' In the same vein, Burke writes that 'mediaeval histories lacked a middle ground between the ascription of motives to individuals ... and extremely general interpretations of history in a theological manner'.⁸

It may seem strange that in a society so strongly orientated on God, *fortuna* should have played the large part it did in historical explanation, even in clerical writings.⁹ An important influence here was the sixth-century writer Boethius, who saw himself as a victim of fortune. Although a Catholic, he served faithfully for many years in the civil service of Theodoric, the Arian king of Italy, but was then thrown into prison, and eventually executed, on suspicion of involvement in an anti-Arian plot. During his imprisonment he mused on his fate and wrote a book in which he attributed it to *fortuna*, whom he personified as a woman. The book, known as *The Consolation of Philosophy*, was extremely influential throughout the Middle Ages, and with it the idea of fortune and her wheel.

On the mediaeval view, action and change were not implicit in, and natural to, human existence and institutions. Just as in pre-Newtonian science a state of rest was taken to be the natural condition in physics, so in human affairs the natural state was, for the tenth century, the pre-existent ground; action and change were disturbances of the norm, and thus unnatural states of affairs. What God was believed to want was peace and stability – that is, in effect, absence of change in which the church could carry on its mission with the minimum of disturbance. In a period of warfare and turmoil such as the tenth century, this meant that most of the events the clerical chroniclers had to record seemed to them regrettable. Hence the pessimism characteristic of their works. As Brandt puts it, 'the chroniclers were engaged in reporting events which should not have happened'.[10]

(ii)

If the tenth-century historians knew nothing of alien cultures, they knew very little about the history of their own. This was basically due to lack of evidence. Apart from what could be known from the Bible and the Fathers, the past was largely unknown and unknowable. Records existed for some limited areas of it,[11] but even where they could be trusted as free from forgery, bad communication made them difficult to consult, especially for monastic writers – the great majority of those who wrote about the past – most of whom seldom stirred from their monasteries.

> Ordericus Vitalis, a conscientious, early twelfth-century historian, who exerted himself to discover original documents, confessed that 'though they contain great wisdom, they are hard to find'.[12]

What is more, such sources as were available were full of mythical elements.[13] These were often of a very bizarre kind and strained even contemporary belief; yet the age found it difficult to reject them. This response has often been described as credulity, but with only partial justice. A critical spirit was by no means lacking. Agobard of Lyon, for example, was well known for his scepticism with regard to unlikely tales; and so, at a later date, was Guibert of Nogent, while Flodoard knew how to mount a well-argued critique of his sources.[14] Isidore correctly derived *historia* from the Greek word *historein*, which he took to mean 'seeing', and argued that the only satisfactory accounts were those based on eye-witness.[15] Other accounts could be no more than compilations from sources, and what he thought of such compilations is clear from another passage, where he wrote (in John Treviso's charming translation): 'We shall not blame makers and writers of stories that diversely speak and write; for long passages of time and elde (antiquity) of deeds maketh them unknown and writers to err.'[16]

A good scholar such as Lupus of Ferrières took the point, more than once apologizing for his temerity in attempting to write about events which had occurred further back than living eye-witnesses could reach.[17] This critical spirit was stultified, however, by the lack of tenable criteria. The Bible was held to be beyond criticism, and it contained accounts of prodigious interventions by God; for example, his having kept the sun and moon stationary in the sky for twenty-four hours in order to help Joshua and his army (Josh. 10.12–13). If this was the God who was still in control of events, who was in a position to deny confidently even the most extraordinary stories in more recent sources? Would not such a denial constitute a faithless refusal to credit God's, or the saints', ability to work such wonders? Historians were bound to ask themselves the question, and it was pressed home by those who had an interest in the continued acceptance of the stories at issue – for example, the custodians of relics by which remarkable miracles were reported to have been effected. We have seen the social pressures that were brought to bear, for example, on the abbot of Bonn and on Guibert of Nogent, when they ventured to express doubts in such matters.[18]

The only alternative to reliance on the sources was to admit complete ignorance of the past, and few were willing to do that. So there seemed nothing for it but to accept Jerome's advice; 'The best course is to believe what they [sc. historical sources] say unless it is to the prejudice of sound faith and morals, or contradicts known truth.'[19] Tenth-century people were the more ready to do that because in an age when books were still extremely few, and writing still a rare accomplishment, there was a strong tendency to suppose that if a thing was written, it must be true. Every 'author' was an 'authority', and what he said 'authentic'. Eye-witness testimony was taken to be in a class by itself – it was in fact seriously overrated – but, that apart, there was little attempt to distinguish the relative trustworthiness of sources.[20]

One factor which contributed to distortion in the accepted picture of the past may perhaps be described as the canon of appropriateness. It was felt that if God was in control of history, he could be trusted to have seen that things fell out 'fittingly'. For example, the monastic life was taken to be so important an institution, and so obviously in accordance with the will of God, that it 'must' go back not just to Benedict or Antony of the Desert, but to the apostles themselves.[21] Similarly, the shorter of the two creeds in common use was so fundamental that it must have gone back to the original apostles, each of whom had contributed one of its twelve clauses.

Examples abound: for instance the tradition that the great abbey of St Denis (Greek: Dionysius) outside Paris had been founded by Dionysius the Areopagite, or that the city of Paris itself had been founded by a large contingent of Trojans in the ninth century BCE and named after the son of Priam. Especially where the glorification of rulers through their genealogies is concerned,[22] it is difficult to be sure how far we are dealing with conscious propaganda; but the very fact that it was plausible to advance such claims shows the substructure of attitudes which underlay them. A Parisian monk felt that to question the authenticity of the relics of the city's patron saint was a crime so heinous that God must have dealt with it in condign fashion. He therefore represents the guilty party, Manasses of Orléans, as having been deprived of his diocese and struck dead soon after, whereas in fact he lived for another twenty-five years and died at an advanced age in full possession of his see.[23]

This tendency to put forward as factual what 'must have been' the case helps to explain an otherwise puzzling feature in so deeply religious a culture, namely its frequent resort to what by modern standards can only be regarded as forgery. We may take as our one example the best known forgery of the early Middle Ages, the so-called Donation of Constantine.

> Though it is the best known, it is only one out of very many. The whole document in which it is included, known as the False, or Isidorean, Decretals, claims to be the work of Isidore, but was in fact compiled in the ninth century, and contains a lot of spurious material alongside genuine elements. Hardly a monastic chronicle was free from forged documents and falsifications of history.[24]

From the later eighth century it came to be believed in some monastic circles that the pope was not only the religious ruler of the world but also the temporal ruler, even if he normally elected to delegate the exercise of his temporal authority to the emperor and other secular rulers. That being so, it would have been passing strange, it was felt, if God had not revealed as much to the fourth-century emperor Constantine, his chosen agent for bringing the world to Christianity. It was therefore believed that Constantine had indeed recognized God's purpose and acted upon it, formally declaring the pope's worldwide religious supremacy and his temporal sovereignty over the West. Since that was what he 'must have' done, there seemed no harm in stating definitely that it was what he *had* done, and indeed producing a document which recorded his action. 'Such documents,' says Sir Richard Southern, 'did not have the vulgar associations of modern forgeries ... [they] provided documentary proofs for claims which, in the minds of those who made them, scarcely needed to be justified.'[25]

It is difficult for us to enter into the precise mentality that produced such documents, a mentality described by Carolly Erickson as 'inhabiting a middle ground between fantasy and self-delusion'.[26] In claiming that forgery of this sort belonged 'in the ranks of the virtues'[27] Beryl Smalley perhaps went too far; Burke seems nearer the mark in writing that 'we simply lack the evidence to decide exactly how much innocence and how much unscrupulousness went into the making of a document like the Donation of Constantine'.[28] We may suspect that in that particular case the canon of appropriateness played a larger part than it did in the case of innumerable forgeries produced to establish the claim to some property made by a lord or a monastery, or the authenticity of suspect relics.

A further factor which underlies a lot of what has been said above is the failure of the early Middle Ages to appreciate the *differentness* of the past. Obviously it was recognized that in some ways the past had been unlike the present – the ancient Greeks and Romans had not been Christians, for example – but the differences were not taken very seriously and there was a tendency to dismiss them, where possible, as due to individual faults and eccentricities; Virgil, for example, was explained as a necromancer.

> Lack of a historical sense of this kind is characteristic of primitive societies, and no doubt in this case it was partly due to the fact that the slowness of social change made such change as did occur difficult to notice; and also to the fact that the differences between the age and many of its predecessors were small as compared with the great differences which make us so aware of our remoteness from almost the whole of the past. Furthermore, accounts of the past had in many cases been orally transmitted, and oral tradition is always vulnerable to revisionary handling in the light of contemporary conditions.[29]

There was little sense of any radical discontinuity; the past was seen in terms of the present, and people projected themselves back on the men and women of earlier times. In the art of the period figures from antiquity were pictured as dressed and accoutred in mediaeval clothes and armour, and as surrounded by mediaeval buildings.[30] However exactly that is to be understood, it is symptomatic of the sense that the historical figures depicted and those who depicted them inhabited essentially the same milieu. Commenting on the lack of recognition of the major changes that had occurred in the course of history, Beryl Smalley wrote that this was an age when it was possible to 'converse with Adam and Eve or Julius Caesar or Charlemagne as though they were neighbours'.[31] Mediaeval people could feel at home in even the distant past in a way quite impossible for us to-day.

(iii)

This had a considerable effect on the outlook both religious and secular. Human life, it seemed, would remain basically the same from Creation to Doomsday – a period, it must be remembered, calculated at only some seven thousand years – and that meant that what had been valid in the past was valid for all other ages, exactly as it stood. Particularly as the age was so conscious of its cultural inferiority to previous ages, the institutions and authoritative pronouncements of the past were taken as binding precedents for the present. In practice the form in which such precedents were applied often involved considerable modifications of the original; but there was no theoretical justification for such modifications, or, usually, awareness of them.

The age was one in deep thrall to the past, an age largely controlled by custom and precedent. Religious writers were careful to forestall any accusation of originality and to insist that they were advocating only traditional beliefs and established Catholic practices.

Such an understanding of the past naturally tended to make people suspicious of change, and their suspicion was deepened by another aspect of their thought. The mediaeval understanding of God's participation in history went far beyond belief in his individual interventions. He was thought to have an overall plan for his creation; and the idea was taken over from Augustine and other patristic writers that history had been preordained by him to consist of a certain number of distinct periods, in each of which he would accomplish one part of his plan. The details varied (see p. 133), but according to the commonest form of the idea, which carried the authority of Augustine (and of a work by Bede entitled *On the Six Ages of this World*), there were six such periods, corresponding to the six days of creation and the six stages of which an individual human life was believed to be made up, if it reached full term.

> The first five world-periods were generally thought to have been Creation-Flood, Flood-Abraham, Abraham-David, David-Babylonian Exile, Babylonian Exile-Christ. They were commonly estimated to have lasted in all some five thousand years, partly on the basis of II Peter 3.8, 'with the Lord one day represents a thousand years'; investigation of the detailed chronological notices in the Bible appeared to suggest roughly the same figure. The six ages of the individual were childhood, youth, adolescence, maturity, old age and decrepitude.

The coming of Christ had ushered in the last period of history, and that was the period in which mediaeval Christians believed themselves to be living. On the analogy of individual ageing, it was thought to be a period of irreversible deterioration and decline. It had already run a considerable part of its course, and was not expected to last much longer, especially in circles where Augustine's interpretation of Rev. 20.6, as limiting the duration of the earth to a thousand years was taken literally. Meanwhile, as in the later stages of old age, any change could only be in the direction of greater decline.

> So strong was this feeling in the earlier Middle Ages that when in the twelfth century change became too pronounced to be ignored, and some of it had to be admitted as good, scholars were surprised and exhilarated, but also deeply puzzled.[32]

The fact that the entire course of history was not expected to last for more than some seven thousand years at most made it all the easier to see history as a divinely planned and supervised drama in six acts. The beginning had been revealed in the Bible, as currently interpreted, and so had the gist of the plot, even if many of the details remained unknown. Nor was there any doubt how it would end, namely with the complete victory of God over all forces opposed to him.

We have already explained in general terms how this drama was believed to have unfolded. The most influential account of it was that contained in Augustine's *City of God*. He pictured two rival cities, the city of God and the earthly city, existing side by side throughout time and space. The drama of world history had begun with God's decision to create a set of independent spirits, the angels, with whom to share the blessings of existence. Thus began the city of God; but when a number of the angels defected and fell, they constituted the earthly city, whose origin and principle were thus essentially sinful. Humankind was created, as we have seen, to make up the heavenly choir, depleted by the fall of the renegade angels; but when the first two humans defected as well, they and their posterity also joined the earthly city, with its institutions, customs and tabus designed to control the lust of sex, the greed of barter and exchange, the distinctions of class and divisions of labour, none of which existed in Paradise. Although such institutions were ordained by God to cope with the human condition, they had been necessitated by the Fall and were marks of the fallen condition.

The cosmic blunder of sin called out the resources of God's infinite love, and we have described earlier the measures he took to make it possible for some of Adam's guilty posterity to return to the primal condition and become members of the city of God. Meanwhile the two cities remained hopelessly intermingled, and would continue to do so until the Last Day, when the sheep and the goats would finally be separated, and the unreality and specious attractiveness of the earthly city unmistakably unmasked for what they were.

> Although almost every detail in Augustine's long and rather rambling book could appeal to some biblical text in its support, the thesis as a whole goes far beyond the teaching of the Bible, for example in its account of the fall of the angels. and is a good example of the way the doctrinal tradition arose from the embroidering, filling out and synthesizing of biblical material (see p. 381).

This tale of two cities was the background to all thinking and living in the Middle Ages. The understanding of the past in the tenth century was thus an understanding derived from theology, not from empirical historical study. Even if the evidence necessary for such study had been available, poor communications would have prevented the examination of most of it, and the scientific procedures necessary for the fruitful evaluation of it were entirely lacking. Diplomatic, for example, was a thing entirely unknown.

(iii)

Since, as a result, ideas of history, though clear, were largely erroneous, there was little awareness of the broad forces and influences which in fact shape the course of history, and little appreciation that the current situation was the result of a particular combination and interplay of such forces. The ordinary causalities of history gave no guidance as to the origins of the situation in which people found themselves, or about the best way of dealing with it. That is not to say that people of the period lacked common sense and could not draw lessons from their past experience. It was, for example, a recognition of the importance of strong central government that led churchmen and others in 833 to oppose Louis the Pious when his plans to bequeath his kingdom to his sons seemed likely to weaken it. Nevertheless, ignorance of historical – and natural – causality made the course of history seem very arbitrary. Where everything seemed to depend on the unpredictable interventions of supernatural forces, good or bad, or of *fortuna*, and on the equally unpredictable whims of individuals, it is small wonder if the course of things seemed incomprehensible and unpredictable in comparison with what were taken to be the ordered certainties of the world above. The vagaries of history seemed likely to remain for ever beyond the capacity of the human mind to fathom.[33] The essential truth about history was already known, and the only legitimate reason for writing about it was to bring that truth out.

There was little concern with the past for its own sake. No doubt there were scholars who got interested in the past as such, but any purely archaeological or antiquarian interest was liable to be frowned on in the same sort of way as curiosity about the facts of nature. As Lupus of Ferrières makes clear, it fell under the category of love of letters, which, he says, was regarded by most people as 'a horrible waste of time'[34].

The Middle Ages had inherited from the classical world a view of history as a branch of rhetoric, and it was a rhetoric of edification. The aim of most writing about the past was to stimulate readers – or hearers – to virtue and sanctity and to exhibit God's saving and punishing hand everywhere at work. Robert of Torigny, for instance, justifies his continuation of Sigbert's chronicle as being 'recorded for the benefit of those who follow after'. The aim, he says, 'is to record divine punishments for sin in the past so that those in a like situation in the future may know that they must make their peace with God through penitence and confession'. He makes clear that what historical writers and moralists are doing is 'to praise virtue, censure vice and admonish us to love and fear God'.[35] Ordericus Vitalis was to write in the same vein, explicitly using the language of edification.[36] Inevitably such motivation led to the exercise of a certain amount of poetic licence with regard to the facts, and it certainly led to a high degree of selectivity. Lupus of Ferrières, for example, writes that he will 'omit those matters which may tend to discredit the rest ... and merely attempt to narrate what is worth recording'. What such words could mean is revealed in Helgaldus's Life of Robert the Pious, a masterpiece of selectivity, which, in its concern to present the king as a saintly figure completely leaves out, for example, the matrimonial troubles which led to his excommunication.[37] The point must not be exaggerated: Lupus recognizes that a 'history does not allow itself to be obscured by colourful deviations from the truth', and Laetaldus of Micy explains how he sought to verify the facts, 'leaving out things which seemed to me less probable'[38].

Such an understanding of history was bound to produce conflicting feelings. So far as the future of this world was concerned, the effects must have been depressing and discouraging. Those who took the matter seriously must have felt rather like people living at the beginning of an ice-age. God's periodization of history meant that the world had only a short future and that it was bound to deteriorate, whatever human beings might try to do to improve it. The metrical Life of St Alexis, for example, written in the eleventh century, opens with the lines:

The age was good in the time of the ancients.
Then one found faith, justice and love.
Belief too, of which very little remains;
Everything is changed, has lost its colour
Will never again be such as it was for our forebears
At the time of Noah and the time of Abraham
And of David whom God loved so dearly
The age was good; it will never have such worth again:
It is old and frail; everything is in decline,
Has grown worse, no one does good any more ...[39]

Such language was common at the time, and it was not just an expression of romantic nostalgia; nor was it simply based on empirical recognition of the cultural superiority of classical antiquity, although that was something of which those who knew about the past could not be unaware. It sprang primarily from theological conviction. As we have seen, an analogy was drawn between the six ages of the world and the six ages of an individual life. The sixth and last period of human life is one of degeneration, weakness and declining powers, and people of the tenth century believed the same about the historical period in which they lived. *Mundus senescit*, it was repeatedly said, 'the world is getting old'; and the word *senescit* carried all the overtones it carries in relation to an individual life. The state of the world was far worse than it had been in its prime, and it could only be expected to deteriorate further, because, as in the case of the individual life, the periodization of history and the characteristics of the successive periods were not a matter of accident; they were rooted in the will of God, who must intend the final period of history to be one of decline and degeneration, just as he willed 'declining years' for ageing individuals.

Apart from its human occupants, the future of this world was somewhat obscure. Certain passages in the New Testament might suggest that it would be gloriously transformed in the end, yet it was clear that even animals had no souls, and there was a sense in which the world seemed ultimately expendable, with no prospect of continuance after the – relatively imminent – Last Judgment. If so, any attempts to improve it, as distinct from exploiting it more fully for spiritual ends, would be so much waste of time. If there was to be any fundamental change in its condition, it would be brought about by God, not by men. Not surprisingly, therefore, concern for the future concentrated on the supernatural world. E.K. Rand wrote of Gregory the Great that for him 'our existence has just two stages, the immediate human present and eternity. Inattentive to the past, he builds not for human progress, but for life everlasting,'[40] and according to Robert Meagher, what was arbitrary and perverse, in Augustine's eyes, was 'not the desire for blessedness ... but rather the denial of the desire for [true] blessedness and the calculated reduction of one's expectations to what "reasonable" mortals may devise and accomplish', that is, by natural means in this world.[41]

On the other hand, as these quotations make clear, at the supernatural level, the situation was full of hope. Daniel-Rops is right to claim it as a 'profound service of Christianity that it gave a sense of direction to the drama of people's lives instead of leaving them alone and distraught before an abyss at the bottom of which they could see nothing'.[42] Unlike the ancients, most of whom viewed history with deep pessimism, the mediaeval Christian was able to believe that the time-process as a whole had a meaning and that within that meaning the individual life could have real and lasting significance. The dénouement of the whole process was known in advance through revelation, and it was a supremely happy ending which would include an eternity of bliss in the celestial city for those who availed themselves of the means to it.

However, availing oneself of those means depended critically on lifelong self-denial and vigilance, and even then could be frustrated by falling into sin *in articulo mortis*; and since Augustine's two cities were so inextricably intermingled in this world, no one could be absolutely sure to which he or she belonged. It would be a great mistake to suppose that the outlook was one of unclouded hope.

> For those like Gottschalk who took seriously the strict Augustinian doctrine of predestination, there was also the realization that they might not be among the elect, and that, if so, there was nothing they could ever do to alter the fact. As we have seen, however, such strict predestinarianism was not common, and for most people the hope of salvation seemed to be there if they chose to avail themselves of it. About 850, Amolo, the archbishop of Lyon, described Gottschalk's view as 'having a pagan hardness, with nothing of the Christian about it'.[43] Many would have agreed with him.

The general failure to appreciate the extent of discontinuity with the past also had important consequences. As we have seen, human life seemed likely to remain basically the same for all time: unlooked-for divine interventions were to be expected in the future as in the past; human sin would continue to be rewarded with famine and other natural disasters.[44] People's attitude to the story of the past could be summed up in

Horace's epigram *de te fabula* (*Satires* 1.1.70: 'Change but the name, of *you* the tale is told'). What had been valid in the past was valid for all other ages, more or less exactly as it stood. Particularly as the age was so conscious of its cultural inferiority to previous ages, the institutions and precepts of the past were taken as determinative for the present. Instead of casting round independently for the most suitable way of responding to their circumstances, people simply assumed that the appropriate response was to be found somewhere in the past, and that their task was to look for it there. As we have seen, writers were careful to forestall any accusation of originality; leaders both secular and ecclesiastical had to represent any new measures they proposed as either a return to past precedents or a more correct interpretation of them. That is why the temptation to invent such precedents was so strong.

If the age was thus in deep thrall to the past, and largely controlled by custom and precedent, not least in the religious sphere, the past by which it was controlled was to a considerable extent a past of its own devising. It was a past unhesitatingly interpreted in the categories of the Bible and the orthodox tradition; and since the means were lacking to recover it accurately, it was a past consisting for the most part of what 'must have been' the case, given contemporary presuppositions. Having little or no sense of cultural development, people supposed both that ancient institutions and ways of doing things could and should be reproduced in the present, and that they were in fact reproducing them faithfully. To some extent the similarity of tenth-century culture to cultures of earlier days enabled them to do this; but often they were forced by what were in fact the changed circumstances of their day to deviate significantly, if unconsciously, from their models. Knowledge of the past was for them a vehicle of edification, and they took little interest in history for its own sake. Apart from the great events of 'salvation history', their sights tended to be on the future rather than the past.

11

The Influence of the Non-Christian, Germanic Past

One aspect of the past affected Frankish religion in the tenth century very considerably. The writings of the time contain abundant evidence of rites and practices which they describe as 'pagan' and 'superstitious', and which clearly derived from pre-Christian religion and practices.

The evidence comes mainly from the records of councils, synods and secular assemblies which sought to suppress these practices, and from the penitentials, which direct confessors to interrogate penitents about their participation in them, giving lists of the items about which they should ask. The fullest evidence comes from two documents of this sort, the *Ecclesiastical Discipline* of Regino of Prüm (*c.* 906) and the *Decretum* of Burchard of Worms (*c.* 1008).[1] Both these works originated in Germany, where such practices were no doubt especially prevalent, in view of the people's relatively recent conversion to Christianity. There is plenty of evidence, however, to show that they were also widespread in northern Francia into – and indeed well beyond – our period. Evidence is also found in sermons which attack these practices, and in lives of laymen or clerics who either indulged in them or criticized them.[2]

The beliefs and practices in question were far too numerous and various to be discussed at all fully here. Some of them amounted to no more than commonplace superstitions such as the belief that seeing a monk or a cripple or a blind person early in the morning meant bad luck, or that it boded ill if someone sneezed nearby or if a bird flew past on the left-hand side or a mouse or a hare ran across one's path.[3] There was also a belief that certain days were bad for beginning to plough or to plant or to travel; and many couples were careful to get married on Friday, formerly the day sacred to Venus. Of the same sort were the customs of keeping iron in the house to ward off demons, of wearing amulets and phylacteries for the same purpose, or of reciting hallowed formulas over snake-bites, cramps, abscesses and the like.[4]

Most significant areas of life attracted such practices. The weather, for example, was important in an agricultural society, and there were various practices designed to modify it, some of them under the control of *tempestarii* or *immisores tempestatum*, individuals who were believed able to conjure up weather that might ruin the crops or make their fruit available to mysterious supernatural beings.[5] Human destiny was believed to be deeply influenced by the heavenly bodies, and attempts were constantly made to predict the future on the basis of their relative positions. Any apparent interference with their normal working inspired terror, and we have vivid descriptions of how the peasants reacted to eclipses of the sun or moon, beating metal vessels and shouting to encourage the heavenly body in its fight against what seemed to be an attempt by some monstrous beast to devour it.[6] The prosperity of the forthcoming year was thought to depend on the performance of certain rites at the beginning of it, many of them involving dressing up in the skins of calves, stags and other animals.[7]

Love was the focus of many of these practices, which were designed to arouse it, to stifle it (for example on the part of an unwilling bride who wanted to prevent the consummation necessary to the validity of her marriage), to get rid of its fruits, and so on. Potions were produced, often according to complicated recipes including human semen, urine and menstrual fluid, designed to increase potency or to destroy it; and there were recipes and incantations for bringing about abortions.[8] Health likewise looms large; for example, Agobard gives a vivid account of the propitiatory offerings people made during an epidemic.[9] Sick children were placed in ovens or on roof-tops and treated with herbs cooked to the accompaniment of traditional incantations. Models of limbs were hung from trees or placed at crossroads to procure the healing of an arm or a leg. As all this implies, certain sites were regarded as sacred, and prayers were said at them, particularly at crossroads and over certain stones and fountains. Among such places were burial sites, and there were many rites aimed at appeasing the dead so that they would not trouble the living. Funerary watches were held, culminating in dancing, singing and eating.[10] Wax dishes of food and wine were buried with baptized children, while unbaptized infants and women who had died in childbirth were often buried in a secret place, transfixed with a stake.[11]

Ways of foretelling the future are looked for in every culture, and in addition to reading the stars, tenth-century people – often including those at court – practised various forms of augury and had recourse to individuals believed to have the power of divination.[12] Attempts to ensure a prosperous future included fertility rites, sometimes involving the use of chrism and holy water, or even a consecrated host.[13]

On a personal level sorcery (*maleficium*) of various kinds was widely practised, and spells were cast by people believed to have special skill with them.

In a society such as that of the early Franks which had no police force or rapid means of communication, and in any case lacked the ability to weigh evidence objectively, it was often felt necessary to seek supernatural guidance over disputed matters which could not be decided in other ways. A common method for dealing with such matters was the ordeal, which took a number of forms. One of these was the ordeal by fire: the parties to the dispute were required to walk through fire, and the one who appeared to suffer less serious and permanent injury was adjudged to be in the right. Variant forms required the parties to walk on, or hold, hot iron, or to plunge their bare arms in boiling water and lift out a stone which had been thrown into it. Alternatively, the parties might be thrown into cold water, the one who was rejected by the water, and floated, being assumed guilty. In cases involving freemen judicial combat was sometimes the method chosen, the assumption behind all these procedures being that the heavenly powers would not allow the guilty to prevail.[14]

The list could be extended almost indefinitely, to include, for example, a vivid belief in witchcraft. What are we to make of such beliefs and practices? There is no doubt what contemporary writers and ecclesiastics made of them. They saw them as so many instances of failure to trust in the power of God and the saints, and in the efficacy of the sacraments, and did everything in their power to suppress them.[15] By and large this attitude has' prevailed, and modern scholars often speak of pagan superstitions and survivals, which they distinguish sharply from the Christian religion.

> There were differences of opinion among contemporary writers about the extent to which these rites and practices had any real efficacy. Among the sceptics were Agobard and, on the whole, Burchard, who took most of them to be delusions, the mere belief in which merited penance. Hincmar, on the other hand, betrays a clear belief in the power of magic,[16] and so, apparently, does Liutprand.[17] The same is true of many of the penitentials; indeed the constant repetition of the questions they contain ('Have you *done* this or that?') must surely have confirmed the conviction of penitents that something effective was involved. The standard view of those who accepted the efficacy of magical practices was that they were the work of the devil; and where non-Christian deities or spirits were involved, they were identified by the church with demons.[18] Coulton may have been exaggerating somewhat when he wrote that 'nobody whatever doubted the actual existence of these old pagan gods',[19] but in general the point is well taken. Alcuin went so far as to suggest that God allows auguries to be fulfilled as a way of testing the faithful.[20] This was surely a dangerous suggestion; even so limited a positive assessment of magic could easily have misled the simple.

This contemporary way of regarding the matter could well be misleading, however. What we are dealing with is people surrounded by extremely harsh circumstances and an environment which they found terrifying,[21] without any technological resources on which they could rely. The only available ways of dealing with the situation were symbolic ways, which meant in fact resort to the supernatural.

To many aspects of this situation traditional responses had been handed down by fathers to sons from time immemorial.[22] These responses, which were taken to enshrine the wisdom of the ages, were simply part of the culture, things one did – in many cases quite unselfconsciously – as part of the routine of agriculture or health care or whatever it might be. Those who adopted them will often have been as little conscious of any incompatibility with the rest of their beliefs as are people today who touch wood to ward off ill-luck, avoid walking under ladders, or throw a pinch of salt over their left shoulders when salt has been spilt. No doubt mediaeval people took their practices more seriously than those trivial modern examples might suggest, but the motive will have been the same, a compulsive fear of what might happen if they were omitted; they would not have persisted so long, people will have felt, unless there were something in them.

Can people really have been so unaware that what they were doing ran counter to the church's teaching? In many cases we must certainly allow for a certain perverse pleasure in disobeying the commands of the church, and the spice of danger it brought; but in general we may suspect that people will not have been aware of any sharp division in their religious behaviour such as many modern writers presuppose.

As we have seen, church leaders made a sharp distinction, but there is ample evidence that 'for the most part the parish clergy must be regarded as splinters from the same wood as their parishioners, sharing their misconceptions and their simplified view of life'.[23] In fact we know that the clergy commonly took part in magic practices themselves.[24] The truth is that the tenth-century church lacked the educational resources to control or direct popular religion, and most people will have received few hints that elements in the religious practice they inherited were inconsistent with their baptismal faith.

They can be forgiven for being largely unaware of it themselves, because the differences between Christian and non-Christian rites must often have been hard for uneducated people to detect, especially as the church had deliberately taken over many pagan rites, with only a thin Christianizing veneer. If, for example, at Rogationtide – itself a Christianized version of the old Roman Robigalia – unintelligible Latin prayers could help to improve the harvest, why should not other traditional incantations do the same?[25] If swallowing dust from the tomb of a saint could cure illness, why should not the eating of other things prepared with appropriate rites? If herbs collected to the accompaniment of the Pater Noster and the Credo were health-giving, why not herbs collected in accordance with other hallowed rites? If there were such beings as angels and demons, why not kobolds and brownies?[26] To people with little instruction and less Latin, the words and manual acts of the Catholic rites can have been little more than mumbo-jumbo; and one sort of mumbo-jumbo is hard to distinguish from another.

We have seen how far the practice of Christianity in the tenth century was orientated towards the production of concrete results, but there were many areas of life in this world to which official Christianity provided no specific responses. Partly for that reason the religion of the great majority was an amalgam of practically-orientated rites and practices, some of which would be described today as Christian, others as pagan.

We might indeed want to say something of the same sort about much of the religion that was officially sanctioned. The church set itself to Christianize the general sense of a supernatural environment which underlay a lot of popular religion, and in the process introduced a variety of paraliturgical rites, especially blessings and exorcisms, which are almost as difficult for us to distinguish from pagan practices as they were for contemporaries. There were blessings for bread, water, oil, fruit, boats and fish nets, for example; others provided protection against natural disasters, wild beasts or the hazards of travel. Candles blessed at the shrine of St Blasius protected from thunder and hail, while a swarm of bees could be called in the Lord's name and secured by the repetition of three Paternosters. We have already noticed the invocations over the crops in early summer; stones and springs hitherto sacred to pagan spirits were transferred to the patronage of saints, with only superficial changes to the rites practised at them.

Eclipses and other unusual phenomena were still regarded as portents of what was to come, though this was now attributed to the will of God; and astrology, with its postulate of the power of the stars, was recognized and practised by church leaders. Both Charlemagne and Louis the Pious got leading ecclesiastics such as Alcuin and Dungal to interpret the position of the stars for them,[27] while Nithard, for example, attributed significance to a number of meteorological phenomena, including the path taken by a comet, and so did that pillar of orthodoxy, Florus the Deacon.[28] A cultivated man like Lupus of Ferrières was puzzled that the scriptures had nothing to say about the significance of comets, but was convinced nevertheless that the Gentiles had been right in seeing their appearance as foretelling disaster.[29] Year after year chroniclers noted the meteorological events which they took to be prodigia.

Divination by the casting of lots was frowned upon, and so, for a time, were the sortes biblicae or sortes sanctorum. These were variants on an ancient custom whereby a book by some poet, usually Virgil, was opened at random and the first words on which the eye alighted were taken as a prophecy of the future and a guide to action. In the sortes biblicae a (part of a) Bible was substituted for Virgil, while the sortes sanctorum utilized a collection of scriptural passages specially selected for purposes of divination. The so-called Penitential of Egbert, the Burgundian Penitential and the Penitential of Silos[30] follow Augustine[31] in condemning the practice, but the church found increasing difficulty in objecting to the consultation of lots which made use of holy books, and by the twelfth century we find the Pope himself (Innocent III) employing the practice.[32]

Rather similarly, there was a certain amount of objection to the ordeal as a pagan practice, but Christians could accept the principle that God would not allow the wrong to prevail, and even in the early sixth century the so-called Synod of North Britain recommends ordeal by fire as a means of deciding between two parties who persistently accuse each other; from the early ninth century (or even a little earlier) when Charlemagne legally recognized it, this method of settling questions of guilt was not only generally accepted, but surrounded with liturgical rites.[33] Specifically Christian forms of the ordeal were introduced, for example, the ordeal of the cross: both parties stood with arms outstretched to see which collapsed first. There was also the ordeal by which both parties partook of the sacrament, the idea being that divine vengeance would fall on the guilty one. Hincmar approved the use of the ordeal by hot water to test orthodoxy of belief[34] and the ordeal came to be preceded by a mass, after which the objects to be used were solemnly blessed. Though the ordeal was not favoured in Rome itself, hagiographical literature in Francia frequently refers approvingly to the ordeal by fire; for example, it enabled St Ricardis to establish her virginity. We even hear of priests giving the chrism to people about to undergo the ordeal so that they could drink it, or anoint themselves with it, and so achieve a favourable result. Such a practice was condemned by synods, as was the use of chrism for magical and medical purposes.[35]

So far as it can be reconstructed, the religion of the Franks before their conversion was not a coherent, theologically worked out system, but a matter of courting a variety of deities and spirits in ways dictated by custom.[36] The rites were expected to produce specific results and to contribute to the well-being of the individual and the community by promoting military success and worldly prosperity.[37] They had become so interwoven in the fabric of everyday living, so much part and parcel of the accepted methods of fighting, farming, housekeeping, child-rearing and so on, that life would have seemed virtually inconceivable without them. To have omitted the rites connected with agriculture, for example, would have seemed as fatal to success as failure to sow the seed. Customs so entrenched could have been eradicated only by an intensive programme of religious education and an exceedingly effective system of social control. Recognizing this, the church attempted both, but the educational process was largely frustrated by the incomprehension of the recipients and by the lack of priests adequate to the task. The system of social control, exercised through preaching and catechizing, and the imposition of laws, backed by the secular power, and above all through the penitential system, was rather more effective. The effect was cumulative, and the situation in the tenth century was significantly different from that in the seventh. Such a system could never be completely successful, however, and at least from the time of Gregory the Great the church adopted a complementary strategy. In a famous letter addressed to Augustine of Canterbury, through Mellitus, in 601 CE the Pope observes that 'it is impossible to eradicate all errors from obstinate (*duris*) minds at one stroke, for anyone climbing to the top of a mountain climbs gradually step by step, not by leaps and bounds', and goes on to recommend the gradual substitution of Christian for pagan rites, suggesting that, as far as possible, they should be assimilated to the rites they replace.[38] This policy likewise was quite effective over the course of centuries, but it met with two difficulties. The first was stubborn opposition to change. As late as the seventh century, a group of northern Franks, who included several notables, roundly declared to Bishop Eligius: 'Although you are always bothering us, you will never uproot our customs, but we will go on with our rites as we have done before, and we will go on doing so always and for ever. There will never exist a man who will be able to stop us holding our time-honoured games to which we are deeply attached (*gratissimos*).'[39] By the tenth century the mood had softened, but by no means changed completely. Michelet may be right in suggesting that the women especially treasured the old gods and religious ways. 'Good Christian women though they may have been, they had a corner in their hearts for them.'[40]

Despite its practical concerns, traditional Christianity was predominantly interested in the supernatural realm; but in a period of great hardship and very poor technology, religion was bound to be looked to for prosperity in this world as well. It was precisely with results of that sort that traditional Germanic religion had been concerned, so it is easy to see why, especially in areas for which the new religion made no specific provision, people felt it best to hedge their bets, to keep a foot in both camps, obeying the church but at the same time paying tribute to the powers of grove and stream.[41] In fact they will not usually have seen it quite in those terms. Since the traditional Germanic religion did not form an overall system, there will have been no sense of confronting the Christian system with a rival;[42] there will have seemed little harm in supplementing the Christian rites with some practices which were 'known' to work, and which, for the reasons given above, will not necessarily have been perceived as anti- or even non-Christian. What James wrote of a rather earlier period will still have been applicable: 'They thought that their [pagan] festivities were justified because of the ancientness of the custom; there is no indication that they worshipped pagan gods ... they were Christians who still continued rituals closely bound up with the rural processes of sowing, harvesting and so on.'[43]

The second difficulty the church encountered arose because even so far as, in the course of time, the Franks took wholeheartedly to the new rites, they almost inevitably transferred to them some of the magical, or quasi-magical, attitudes associated with the old practices. For them the church ordinances were, in the words of J.M. Mecklin, 'merely magical contrivances for manipulating the forces of evil that threatened them at every turn'.[44] We have already seen, for example, how the chrism was used, with the connivance of the local priests; holy water was also taken for 'magical' purposes – for example, to be sprinkled over the crops – until the fonts had to be locked; and, as Mecklin again says, 'even the mass itself ... became a mechanical contrivance for tapping the magical saving energy stored up in the church'.[45] Thus the host was used to rid cabbages of caterpillars, to restore health to a hive of bees or to act as a love philtre. The Creed and the Lord's Prayer were employed, in the unintelligible Latin version, as magic formulas.[46]

While these were practices of which the church leaders disapproved, Frankish custom also brought about officially sanctioned changes in traditional Catholic faith and practice. The hierarchy's policy of substituting Christian for pagan rites led to the introduction of many new forms of devotion. For instance, it was largely in response to the currency of pagan rites for the dead that the observance of All Saints' Day was introduced, or at any rate popularized, in the West in the ninth century, and the commemoration of All Souls promoted by Odilo of Cluny in 998, pagan customs in honour of the departed being transferred to it, many of them with very little change.[47] The *Memento* of the dead was introduced into the canon of the mass at about the same time.

In the same sort of way there can be little doubt that the Franks' familiarity with, and demand for, lesser divine beings contributed significantly to the intense preoccupation in this period with both angels and saints. 'The real saviours and intercessors of the lower classes,' writes Mecklin, 'were the ubiquitous demigods, the saints. They peopled the world of the medieval man much as did the lower deities of paganism.'[48]

The ordeal became so firmly established that by 1076 the Synod of Worms actually decreed its use in monasteries, in certain circumstances and it thus found its way into canon law.[49] The *sortes biblicae* likewise gradually gained official recognition until they could be used by cathedral chapters in instituting a bishop or a canon, and even, as we have seen, be employed by the pope himself. As for portents, a work by a deeply orthodox writer such as Paul the Deacon's *History of the Lombards* contains numerous accounts of meteorological and other phenomena taken as forecasts of the future, and Liutprand makes clear that the 'skill of drawing auspices' had come to be regarded as a gift from God, not from the devil.[50]

However, the influence of primitive Frankish religion in making tenth-century Christianity what it was must not be exaggerated. Anyone familiar with the writings of Gregory the Great, for example, will recognize that in the very early Middle Ages the official Catholic faith, the faith into which the Frankish nation was baptized, already contained considerable elements of what to-day can only be regarded as superstition. Confining ourselves to examples from Gregory's *Dialogues*, we may note how the celebration of masses was believed capable of effecting a man's release from chains at a very great distance, how a gesture of Benedict could shatter a glass jug (of poison) without his knowing it was poison or intending to produce the effect, how the sign of the cross was effective against demons even when made by a non-Christian, or how the cloak of Eutychius, when held aloft in the fields, would produce rain in time of drought.[51]

Consequently the religion of the period, even the religion of the learned, was, though to varying degrees, what appears to us as a mixture of the genuinely Christian and the magical or superstitious. Père Vauchez may perhaps oversharpen the distinction a little, but his comment is illuminating: 'In fact – and it is an element of the greatest importance for the later evolution of Christianity – the spirituality of the clergy and that of the rest of the faithful do not at this period constitute two worlds without contact. Apart from a very small élite of bishops and abbots who do their best to remain faithful to the patristic tradition and make the vain attempt to oppose the evolution taking place, the clergy share in the same culture – or lack of culture (*"inculture"*) – as the laity and are subject to the same mental climate. Thus in the Carolingian period we see the church, for long very cautious with regard to various aspects of popular piety, welcoming such of them as seemed compatible with Christian doctrine.'[52]

This religion should be looked at as the integrated totality it must have appeared from within; there is important truth in the comment of J. C. Schmitt: 'The theory of the survival of paganism is invalid (*caduque*): nothing "survives" in a culture; everything is either experienced or does not enter the picture. A belief or a rite are not the combination of a jumble of left-overs and innovations, but an experience which makes sense only in its present cohesiveness.'[53] From this perspective it may be argued that among the influences on the accepted theological and liturgical tradition considered in this section of the book, the pagan religious heritage deserves to be taken very seriously. It was largely with this in mind that Père Vauchez wrote: 'Between the eighth and the tenth centuries a certain conception of the Christian faith finally disappears. It gives way to a combination of representations and practices of clearly different inspiration.'[54]

12

The Future

As we have seen, apart from certain crucial events in the history of salvation, such as the Exodus, the Crucifixion and the Resurrection, early mediaeval people were more interested in the future than in the past, more interested in the end of the world than the beginning. They had ideas about how the future would unroll which, without being fully specific, were definite, and held with absolute conviction, because for the most part they were rooted in the accepted theology.

(i)

The entire life-course of the universe was believed to be under the direct providential control of God, who had distributed it in a number of discrete periods. As we have just seen, by the tenth century it seemed reasonable to suppose that the sixth and final period had not long to run, so at various plausible dates around this time, especially just before 1000 CE or 1033 CE (a thousand years from the death of Christ) or in 1009 CE (when the Holy Sepulchre in Jerusalem was totally destroyed by the Caliph Hakim), a vivid belief arose in some quarters to the effect that the end was imminent. While specific expectations such as these were never anything like universal, and never achieved the status of official belief, it was universally agreed that the end could not be far off. People's attitude was rather like that of a very old person who knows that he or she cannot have very long to live, but has no means of knowing precisely how much time is left.[1]

Already when the western Roman empire fell, many writers saw in what was happening the fulfilment of St Paul's announcement of the end of the world (cf. e.g. I Cor. 10.11), and such expectations persisted. For example, in the seventh century, chancellery acts contained the formula: 'as disasters multiply, clear signs show that the end of the world is getting near'.[2] In the eighth century the Life of St Pardulfus (787), for example, betrays the same conviction; and though it is slightly less well attested for the tenth century, evidence for it is by no means lacking. For instance, charters founding or endowing monasteries use almost exactly the language just quoted;[3] and if that were thought to be simply traditional, Abbo of Fleury, who was born in 940, says that, when young, he heard a preacher announce the coming of Antichrist and the end of the world for 1000 CE.[4] He had also heard it said that the end of the world would come when the Annunciation and Good Friday occurred on the same day, which happened in 970, to the accompaniment of considerable excitement in Lorraine, and in 992.[5] Misled by one exaggerated sentence in Ralph Glaber, the nineteenth-century historian Jules Michelet popularized the idea that almost everyone had expected the end of the world to arrive precisely in 1000 CE; but in the light of much evidence to the contrary, that view has now been abandoned.

In his *Apology* of 998,[6] Abbo argued against the view he had heard in his youth, and in an influential book of 954, Adso of Montier-en-Der had done the same. On the basis of the Book of Daniel, he argued that world history would contain four empires, of which the Roman empire would be the last. However, like his contemporaries, he regarded the Christian empire of his own day as a prolongation of the Roman empire, from which it followed that the history of the world would not end before the death of the last Christian emperor, who, Adso thought, would be the greatest of all the Roman emperors and, after a triumphant reign, would go to Jerusalem to lay down his sceptre and crown on the Mount of Olives.[7] Neither papal nor royal documents of the period just before 1000 CE show any sign that the end of the world was expected in that year; indeed in 998 the Council of Rome imposed a seven-year penance on king Robert, and the following year Pope Sylvester II recognized the right of the archbishops of Reims to crown all future Frankish kings; and it was precisely in 1000 CE that the emperor Otto III established himself in Rome with the intention of governing the empire from there in the future. Numerous wills and documents founding or endowing institutions, which were drawn up in the late tenth century plainly envisage a continuous future, and it seems clear that that was the general expectation. In fact the approach of 1033 CE seems to have caused considerably more stir than that of 1000; but even so, the tendency to associate the coming of the end with a particular date should not be overestimated. Thietmar of Mersebourg actually wrote, *à propos* 1000 CE: 'When the best year since the Immaculate Virgin gave saving birth arrived, a brilliant dawn was seen to shine upon the world.'[8]

Relying on such sayings as those in Mark 13.32 and Luke 17.20, many writers resisted all attempts to predict the precise date of the end, but that does not mean that they, or anyone else, expected an extended future for the world. In the ninth century an angelic message to a monk called Wetti contained the warning that 'the destined day is approaching for the world when the order of history will finally be ended',[9] and a tenth-century hymn stated baldly,

Veniet, prope est, dies irae supremae
(The day of the final wrath is coming very soon).

At the Council of Trosley in 909 the bishops were urged to hold themselves ready to answer for their acts, 'since the day of judgment is just about to come'.[10] That fairly represented the general belief right down into the later Middle Ages, as witness, for example, Bernard of Cluny's mid twelfth-century rhythm *de contemptu mundi*, with its well-known lines:

> The world is very evil; the times are waxing late;
> Be sober and keep vigil; the Judge is at the gate.
> (*Hora novissima, tempora pessima sunt, vigilemus,*
> *ecce minaciter imminet arbiter ille supremus.*)[11]

(ii)

These passages make clear that the end of the world was expected to coincide with the Last Judgment. This would be an unspeakably awesome event when Christ would appear in majesty with his angels and saints.[12] Whatever clemency he might have shown in the past, on this occasion he would function as a completely objective judge, whose verdict would be based solely on the merits of those who appeared before him.[13] These would comprise all members of the human race; and whatever possibilities of amelioration and purgation might have been available hitherto, even for the dead, would now come to an end. Every individual would be irrevocably consigned to an eternity of unspeakable bliss or unspeakable torture. There was no middle way: the starkness of the contrast is brought out in the art, as well as the writing, of the time – for example, in the sculpture on the tympanum of St Foy's church at Conques.[14] The apprehension aroused by such a prospect would have been acute enough, even had it not been that, as we have seen, the great majority were expected to be condemned, particularly if they belonged to such an evil and degenerate age as the tenth century was thought to be. Hence the reference above to 'the day of the final *wrath*', and Bernard's *minaciter imminet* ('the *threat* of his presence draws near').

Inevitably, the circumstances likely to surround such an awe-inspiring event became a focus of intense interest, and on the basis of various enigmatic and highly symbolic passages in the New Testament, speculation tended to run riot.[15] The End, it was said, would be preceded by famine, earthquakes and other natural disasters; in particular, it was widely believed that before his final triumph, Christ would be confronted by an evil power, generally known as Antichrist, who would be born in Babylon, and who, although he would not ultimately prevail, would rule the world until the descent of Christ and his saints, causing utter havoc and the most terrible suffering for a period of years. Attempts were sometimes made to identify the Antichrist with historical or contemporary persons or groups, for example with Muhammad, whose name was quoted as

Maometis to make it conform to the number of the Beast (666) in Rev. 13.18. It is noteworthy that a writer such as Odo of Cluny (879–942) expected the arrival of Antichrist in his own lifetime.

The matter was further complicated by the mysterious reference to a period of 1,000 years in Rev. 20.6, which, as we have seen, preoccupied Augustine.[16] Following one of his interpretations, some writers suggested that before the coming of Antichrist there would be a sort of golden age on earth, a reign of peace in which the last emperor would govern the world. Details varied widely, but in contrast to some of its later manifestations, the expectation as put forward in the tenth century did not envisage a transformation of the existing order so much as its extension. Indeed, in the form put forward by Adso of Montier (p. 128 above) it had a strong political colouring, the thesis being that there was no call to expect the appearance of Antichrist so long as the kingdoms remained attached to the Frankish emperors, the last of whom, as we have seen, would govern with supreme wisdom and eventually lay down his crown in Jerusalem. Not surprisingly, the Frankish authorities were inclined to foster that sort of expectation.

(iii)

What will it have been like to live with such a picture of the future? First, it must be recognized that little or nothing of the detailed speculation just described found its way into established teaching.[17] As we have seen, many interpreted Mark 13 (esp. vv. 32 and 21) and parallel texts as putting a question-mark against all such enquiries, and warnings were given against prophecies which might unnecessarily alarm the masses. What most of these last, and indeed many of the uneducated clergy who taught them, will have imbibed was the certainty of the final judgment, and perhaps the sense that it would come sooner rather than later. There is evidence that, especially on the part of preachers who expected it imminently, it was put forward as a motive for repentance and amendment of life, and its terrors exploited; and those exposed to visual representations of it, whether in painting or sculpture, will have been left in no doubt of the terrible finality of it and the appalling consequences for those who received the thumbs-down. All this will particularly have struck terror into the hearts of peasants and others whose circumstances and way of life gave them little chance of acquiring the merits required for a positive verdict.

However, most people did not apparently connect the judgment with any particular date or event, and there was not the sense of immediacy there was in the New Testament church. We may suspect that for most people, desperately preoccupied with the struggle for sheer survival, the whole matter was no more than a background to more immediate fears and concerns. Certainly there are no signs, such as appear in some cultures with a vivid expectation of the end of history, of people's downing tools and abandoning the ordinary business of living.[18] To say that, however, is not to deny that these eschatological expectations did a great deal to mould the character and outlook of the age. Ralph Glaber associates the millennium of Christ's death in 1033 CE with outbreaks of heresy, the holding of peace assemblies and movements for monastic reform.[19] The need for repentance in such a situation was vigorously preached, and monks especially, with their constant exposure to the scriptures and writings of the Fathers, were bound to be alive to eschatological expectations and speculations. The belief that the End would come in 1000 CE was particularly strong, for example, at the newly-founded abbey of Cluny, whose abbot, Odo (927–942), was one of those who spread the expectation by his writings. Not only did the monks feel the need for personal purification before the end; many of them were determined to make their common life so perfect as to be a veritable anticipation of the life of heaven, and this was undoubtedly an important factor in the movement for monastic reform which gathered strength at this time.[20] In such circles at least, the feeling was strong that the carnal world had to be rejected, and that it was impossible to belong simultaneously to the imperfect earth and to 'the land without evil'. A story about Odo of Cluny shows how far this attitude could be taken. When a baby nephew of his who had been rescued from the hands of Viking raiders was brought to him, he had it baptized, and then prayed that it might die, which it did three days later.[21] In a degenerate world, Odo felt, with the final judgment so near, the greatest blessedness was to die very young, before the sinless state produced by baptism could be lost.

However, as we have seen, such an extreme view was by no means typical, and Delisle Burns perhaps exaggerated somewhat when he wrote that 'the very fact that the Last Judgment was believed to be at hand led men and women to care little for a world which was soon to perish'.[22] There is certainly truth in that, but the full reality was more complex. Alcuin, for instance, was quite clear that he was living in the last dangerous period of history,[23] and his terror in the face of the Last Judgment[24] aroused in him a deep sense of sin and turned him to inwardness in his last years. Yet he still counselled concern for the nation's future (*Epistle* 123), and his poetry, derivative though it may be, certainly betrays observation of, and love for, the natural world.[25]

Nevertheless, the expectations we have described were bound to produce what Le Goff calls 'the fundamental pessimism which impregnated all mediaeval thinking and feeling'.[26] Since the declining state of the world was part of God's providence, there could be no question of any new flowering of culture after the disappearance of classical civilization: the authority of the Fathers had already settled that. Nor was any fundamental change to be expected from the military or political doings of the nations; and there could be no question of utopian visions for this world or action to give them effect. Any attempt to reverse the world's decline would be contrary to the intended nature of things, rather like attempting to arrest the ageing process in the individual by the administration of drugs. Consequently, comprehensive and co-ordinated attempts at eliminating injustices and sufferings in the present life were not so much as contemplated.[27]

By the same token, originality was at a discount. 'We are *homunculi* (dwarfs) at the end of all time,' wrote Alcuin; 'there is nothing better for us than to follow the teaching of the Apostles and the Gospels. We must follow these precepts instead of inventing new ones or propounding new doctrine or vainly seeking to increase our own fame by the discovery of new-fangled ideas.'[28] The function of a writer was to hand on the tradition of the past uncontaminated with foreign matter. A physician, it was pointed out, does not produce the ingredients of his medicines himself; he makes them from God-given herbs and other materials already to hand. The theologian should follow suit.[29] So far did this go that theologians such as Bede, Alcuin or Hincmar were content to stitch together quotations from the Bible and the Fathers without even attempting to reconcile inconsistencies. Hrabanus Maurus explicitly defended the lack of originality in his writings,[30] while Amalarius of Metz, who expressed his own ideas in what he wrote – *scripsi quod sensi*, he said – was condemned at the Synod of Quierzy in 838 because some of his teaching could not be substantiated directly from the Bible or the Fathers.[31]

Perhaps the best word to describe the mood is 'resignation'. People must obey the will of God by combatting evil and relieving suffering wherever it was in their power to do so; for the rest they must endure the progressive decline of the world until God in his mysterious providence saw fit to bring it to an end. That day was not likely to be so very far off, and the important thing was to be prepared for it when it arrived.

Where the rulers, lay and ecclesiastical, were concerned, the duty laid on them by God was not only to be prepared themselves, but to ensure the preparedness of their people, the one group through their legislation and example, the other through ecclesiastical enactments, preaching, writing and pastoral oversight, as well as by personal example. For the rest of the people, their duty was to make and keep themselves ready for the judgment, and to do anything they could, by prayer, personal example and persuasion, to help those close to them to do the same.

(iv)

As we have seen, no one would be allowed to cease to exist at death. The body would remain in the grave, awaiting resurrection and reunion with the soul, at the Last Judgment; but meanwhile the soul – the essential person – would continue in a fully conscious condition.[32] In the case of all human beings who died unbaptized, their share in original sin condemned them irrevocably to eternal damnation; and nothing they or anyone else could possibly do could alter that. So far as the baptized were concerned, if they were to obtain a favourable verdict, they must be worthy, and that, as we have seen, was a matter of personal or vicarious merit. In a world where life was short, and sudden death frequent, the matter was one of constant concern, because those who died in a state of grievous sin would be condemned to eternal damnation immediately on their death, whether or not they were actually despatched to hell before the final judgment. Similarly, those who died in a state of sanctity or perfect righteousness would immediately be adjudged worthy of heaven, and either admitted to it at once or kept in some agreeable ante-room of it until the Last Day.[33] Since no one could know for certain who belonged to these two groups respectively, the church prayed for all the departed, but in the case of the groups just mentioned without effect: prayer for the damned was of no avail; for the saints it was unnecessary.[34]

What of those whose lives had been neither entirely good nor out-rageously evil? During our period beliefs about their condition were crystallizing, though no fully-fledged or formally defined doctrine seems to have emerged until later.[35]

If it seems strange that no agreed doctrine should have emerged on so important a topic, the main reason no doubt is that the Bible had no clear or unequivocal teaching on the subject, as Tertullian conceded in the third century.[36] Broadly speaking, the Jews of the Old Testament period did not believe in life after death at all,[37] while the writers of the New Testament addressed a situation very different from that of early mediaeval Christianity.

Paul certainly expected the End to come in his own lifetime, and even later New Testament writers expected it to come very soon. Mark 9.1, for example, shows that even around 70 CE it was still believed that some of those who who had heard Jesus speak in the days of his flesh would survive on earth until he came in his glory. In such a context, the question of what was happening to the relatively few who had died before the End could be represented as a foolish one which scarcely needed raising (cf. I Cor. 15.36). As Paul saw it, the real problem was how the majority of Christians, who would be alive on earth at the last trumpet, would be changed into a heavenly form (I Cor. 15.51ff.). Those who died were simply asleep (I Cor. 15.51 and I Thess. 4.13), and at Christ's coming would be awakened to join their brothers and sisters. Consistently interpreted, Paul's doctrine of justification by faith apart from works of the Law meant that saving faith, not works, would be the decisive thing at the judgment; and even where a doctrine of judgment by works prevailed, as, for example, in Matthew, Hebrews and indeed parts of Paul's own epistles as we now have them, the vivid sense of the Holy Spirit's guidance and assistance made it possible to hope that all believers would achieve salvation. So long as the Christians were a small, self-selected and devoted minority, often suffering for their faith, such a hope made sense, and the prayer was that the faithful departed would await Christ's coming in a place of refreshment (*refrigerium*), often thought of, with reference to Luke 16.22ff., as Abraham's bosom. It was only when Christianity expanded and then became the majority religion of the Roman empire, and the church had come to include numbers of *hommes moyen sensuels*, that the question of their destiny after death seriously arose. By then theologians no longer understood the eschatological orientation of New Testament Christianity and, lacking all sense of the historically relative, found difficulty in arriving at a synthesis on the basis of what were in any case enigmatic, and sometimes incompatible texts.[38]

However, from an early date, the church, with its strong belief in the efficacy of prayer, had found it natural to pray for its departed members and to celebrate the eucharist and perform works of mercy on their behalf, though for some time this practice was not linked with any very clear picture of the situation of those it was designed to help.

By the fourth century the different degrees of faith and discipleship among Christians were clearly apparent, and, on the basis of various New Testament texts, especially I Cor. 3.11ff., Augustine argued that there were some whose lives, though not perfect, had been good enough to deserve that they should be purified by fire (*per ignem quemdam purgatorium*) before the Last Judgment. It was these souls whom the prayers of the church could help. He also distinguished *homines scelerati*, people guilty of very serious sins such as inescapably bring damnation, from those guilty of 'light' (*levis*), minor (*minor*), or moderate (*modicus*) sins, who might be thought worthy of purging by fire. Augustine does not state all this dogmatically, but puts it hypothetically and concludes, 'I will not deny it; it may be true' (*non redarguo, quia forsitan verum est*),[39] and it is clear that such ideas were by no means central to his own thinking.

In the following period, however, they were discussed and to some extent clarified. Gregory the Great cleared up certain difficulties he found in Job 14 by postulating different regions in hell, the upper regions in which the righteous rest in peace, and the lower in which the wicked are tormented;[40] and in his *Dialogues* he answered the question 'whether we must believe that there is a purgatorial fire after death',[41] first by argument and then by relating a number of stories, or *exempla*, which impressed on the memories and imaginations of subsequent generations the idea of purgatorial sufferings which would render departed souls acceptable to God, and which could be mitigated and shortened by the action of the living in praying for the sufferers, and holding masses and doing good works on their behalf. In some cases this purgatorial suffering took place in this world, at the site of the crimes it was intended to purge.[42] Gregory's views were echoed and in some respects developed by writers such as Isidore, Julian of Toledo, the (Irish) author of the seventh-century *Liber de ordine creaturarum*, Bede, Alcuin, Hrabanus Maurus and Haimo of Halberstadt.

However, it is clear that even by the tenth century there was no formally defined teaching on the subject, and the emerging consensus was often expressed in very tentative terms, for example, 'it is not incredible that ...',[43] 'it may be, as some suggest ...', 'this has led some to the opinion that ...'.[44] The allocation of each soul to heaven or hell, which would be announced at the Last Judgment, was made at the moment of the individual's death, and no one was to suppose that the departed could do anything further to alter that. If, however, they had lived good enough lives to deserve it, a period of purgatorial punishment might atone for certain sorts of sins they had committed while alive. It was made quite clear, however, that the sins in question could only be *leviora* and *minima* – such things as the 'idle use of legitimate marriage, excessive pleasure in useless things, anger leading to abusive language, exaggerated interest in personal affairs, inattentiveness during prayer, oversleeping, bursts of laughter, gossiping and the like'. Serious sin could not be dealt with in this way. It was also emphasized that the purgatorial suffering involved, which might include subjection to extremes of heat and cold alternately, would be of the severest sort – far worse than anything that could be experienced in this world. It would last as long as the amount and gravity of the sin required, unless it was shortened through the intervention of the living with prayers and masses. Although, as we have seen, their bodies remained in the grave until the Last Judgment, the souls deemed worthy of purgatorial punishment were believed to be endowed with a special materiality – *similitudo corporis*, Julian of Toledo calls it – such as would enable punishment to be inflicted on them.

(v)

What impact all this made on ordinary Christians of the tenth century it is difficult to say. As yet few, if any, efforts had been made to locate purgatorial suffering on any map of this world or the other, and the noun *purgatorium* was not apparently used before the twelfth century; what has no name is not easily popularized.[45] The ideas we have been discussing found little or no place in the liturgy in the tenth century, and the canon of the mass made no mention of expiatory punishment beyond the grave. Although the phrase 'the first resurrection' (cf. Rev. 20.6) occurs frequently in liturgical texts, the reference appears to be to an intermediate place of repose, a gentle paradise in which redeemed souls wait for the day of resurrection, and nothing in this conception suggests the idea of Purgatory. Warnings were continually given against relying on purgatorial cleansing hereafter as a means of getting to heaven, instead of striving to deserve it now; for example, Ratherius of Verona makes the point strongly, reminding his readers that such cleansing is effective only for lesser sins; criminal sins cannot be purged after death.[46]

On the other hand, accounts of a number of visions were in circulation in which the purgatorial process was vividly recounted, and well-known figures were pictured undergoing it. Such visions were regarded as genuine revelations of truth and must have done much to spread the idea of purgatorial punishment, though the emphasis in them on the terrible tortures involved will hardly have encouraged readers to rely too heavily on the purgatorial process as a way of dealing with their sins. One other thing will certainly have spread such ideas: prayers and masses for the dead were constantly said, and there was continual encouragement for everyone to take part in them and make them available for deceased friends and relatives. As the idea of purgatorial cleansing after death spread and clarified, it was progressively linked with the practice of prayer for the dead, which was now understood as shortening, mitigating or even obviating purgatorial suffering. The latter was thus kept regularly before the minds of a great many people. However, there is little to suggest that purgatorial punishment was much in evidence in teaching and sermons in our period. It was not yet part of official doctrine, and it may have been handled cautiously as liable to weaken the feeling of moral responsibility. Even if they felt that purgatorial suffering after death and the prayers of the survivors might be of some assistance to them, most people in the tenth century are likely to have been struck mainly by the accounts and portrayals of the Last Judgment and its irrevocable consequences. Since few, and those mainly monks and nuns, were expected to receive a favourable verdict, Rosalind and Christopher Brooke seem justified in talking of 'the dark hopelessness of tenth and eleventh century ... eschatology'.[47]

(vi)

The portrayals of the afterlife which moulded the mediaeval imagination were in writing as well as in painting and sculpture. In the nature of the case, total bliss is harder to portray visually than extreme suffering. That comes out, for instance, in the portal of Bourges cathedral. The quiet and satisfied smiles on the faces of the righteous, as they are led away to bliss by Peter, hardly convey total blessedness, nor do the tiny human figures representing departed souls wrapped in a cloth on Abraham's bosom; by contrast, the devils torturing the damned clearly mean business. It is safe to generalize: there is no doubt that such representations had more impact in inculcating a fear of hell than in conveying the brighter hopes. Caesarius of Heisterbach explicitly noted the significance of the fact that 'in almost all visions that have been vouchsafed of the pains of the wicked and glories of the elect, the vision of the torment has almost always come first'.[48] Since heaven is so difficult to picture, visual representations tend to concentrate on the Last Judgment and its immediate aftermath, showing the blessed being led off to heaven by Peter or some angelic guide, while the damned are corralled into a monstrous hell by hideous demons armed with all manner of instruments of torture.

Written accounts could range more widely, and from the third century onwards a long line of documents described visions of the whole world beyond. If some of these are more or less faithful reports of genuine dreams, the dreams themselves must have been influenced by a literary tradition to which all the accounts seem to belong, and which appears to go back to origins in Jewish and oriental sources as well as, to some extent, in classical and Celtic mythology.[49] Certain motifs are to be found in most of these accounts. The person having the vision is frequently represented as ascending in the company of a guide to a point from which he can survey the world beyond, a constant feature of which is a stinking fiery stretch of river over which a bridge leads from this world. Sunk screaming in the river up to their chests or chins, or even their hairline, are men and women being tortured, while the bridge is a means of judgment; the righteous find it easy to cross, whereas sinners find it slippery and narrow in proportion to the gravity of their sin, and many fall from it into the river. In many of the reports the pains suffered in the river seem to be purgatorial. Hell itself is usually pictured as a deep valley, or as darkened by threatening-looking woods; and the tortures endured in it are extreme forms, or extensions, of the treatment then customarily inflicted on the defeated in battle, or those being persecuted or severely punished in this world, in addition to such things as attacks by dragons with mouths full of burning sulphur and pitch.

Among those suffering, either purgatorially or eternally, were many eminent rulers and churchmen: for example, Theodoric, Charlemagne, Louis the German and his brother Lothar.[50] Church leaders naturally publicized, even if they did not encourage, such visions, which provided a means of exerting pressure on secular authorities and on ecclesiastical subordinates who showed signs of getting out of line.

The descriptions of hell leave little to the imagination, but where the *refrigerium* of the saints, or heaven itself, are concerned, the descriptions tend to be conventional and rather flat. For example: '... the bridge led to pleasant meadows beyond, covered by green grass and dotted with richly scented flowers, in which were various groups of people dressed in white robes. The fragrant odours pervading the region were a delight for all who lived there. Everyone had his own dwelling, which gleamed with brilliant light ... and the bricks were made of gold.'[51] Those who had enjoyed these visions are often reported as saying that they must not, or cannot, describe the glories they have seen;[52] the fact is that it is not possible to convey a quite novel condition of perfect blessedness simply by eliminating what we do not like in this world and piling on what we do, particularly when the new situation is supposed to be one of complete changelessness.[53]

The heaven and hell of the mediaeval imagination are really extrapolations of this world; heaven, as we shall see, is envisaged as a hierarchically ordered community comparable to the Frankish kingdom; the saints gathered before God are like the members of an earthly court surrounding their king, and the heavenly choir is modelled on a monastic choir singing the office before the high altar. It must be remembered that for the people of this period, the realm of God and the departed was really 'another world', with the emphasis as much on 'world' as on 'another'; its reality-status was as high as – or rather, higher than – that of this world, and it was as firmly anchored in space; heaven above and hell below.

(vii)

That brings us to the much-discussed question how far mediaeval people interpreted the accounts and portrayals of the other world literally. There is no simple answer. Peter Comestor (or Manducator) makes clear that by the middle of the twelfth century, at any rate, mediaeval thinkers themselves held differing views,[54] and some years before that, Honorius of Autun argued against the view that the spiritual world existed materially. He declared that heaven is not a corporeal place, but the spiritual abode of the blessed situated in the intellectual heaven, where they may contemplate God face to face[55]. There can be no doubt that this was a minority view, at any rate in our period. Even in the thirteenth century, Aquinas insisted on the physical reality of hell-fire, and as we have seen, Gregory the Great thought of it as located beneath a volcano in or near Sicily.[56] He had met the view that the bodies of the departed are impalpable in Eutychius, patriarch of Constantinople, but had won him round to the belief that, though subtle, they will in fact be palpable. Eriugena, much the most sophisticated thinker in the ninth-century West, believed hell-fire to be corporeal, though of a subtle nature,[57] and at the end of the tenth century, Gerbert, the leading scholar of the age, formally declared his belief 'that the resurrection comes with this flesh which we wear'.[58] According to Bede, Cuthbert actually saw Aidan (of Lindisfarne) going to heaven,[59] and Aidan himself was fed by angels with 'loaves of the sort eaten in heaven' during his lifetime.[60] Already in the third century, Tertullian had argued that if the departed soul can taste punishment or refreshment, it gives proof of its corporeality;[61] and even those who denied corporeality of a literal kind, agreed that the departed must exist in some form which allowed them to feel pain or refreshment. On any showing, the beings and proceedings of the other world, including the rewards and punishments, were completely *real*; that was the vital point. No doubt the great majority envisaged the joys and sufferings of the other world as being, except in intensity, very much the same as those experienced here; and even the most sophisticated were fully convinced of their actuality.

Expectations were not only realistic, but in some cases quite detailed. Not only would individuals be recognizable in the hereafter; they would appear as they were, or would have been in their prime, at the age of thirty, Christ's age at the resurrection.[62] On the basis of John 14.2 it was believed that the blessed would enjoy different positions and degrees of blessedness in heaven in proportion to the degree of their sanctity while on earth. Augustine, who took this view, argued that everyone in heaven would be satisfied with such an arrangement because all would then want total justice to prevail.[63] According to some – for example, the author of the Penitential of Firmian – the departed from among the laity would occupy lower positions than those allotted to the clergy.[64] The appeal to absolute justice was also used to answer the question why the blessed did not pray for the damned, and were unmoved, or even pleased, at the thought and sight of their sufferings. The matter had been raised at least as early as the third century in Tertullian's *de spectaculis* and was discussed by Augustine, among others. Appeal was made to such texts as Ps. 57(58).11, but the main thrust of the argument was that the eternal damnation of the wicked was what God's justice demanded and that the blessed could therefore only acquiesce, and indeed rejoice at it.[65] In Mark 12.25 (and parallels) Jesus is represented as teaching that there is no marriage in heaven, and on the basis of that, and of such passages as Rev. 14.4, the joys of the Christian heaven, in sharp contrast to those of the Muslim paradise, were portrayed as entirely sexless. It must be remembered that those responsible for the mediaeval picture of the other world were all celibates, who found difficulty with a positive view of sex, even in this world.

(viii)

What sort of impact are the expectations described in this chapter likely to have had on the mass of ordinary people? We meet a serious obstacle in attempting to answer that question.

In the early days it was natural for the members of a persecuted minority such as the church to think that the mass of mankind would be damned, and the belief persisted. It was strengthened in as much as those who believed God's purpose in creating the human race had been to produce substitutes for the fallen angels naturally assumed that the number of the elect would be limited. Even those who did not subscribe to that view were clear, on the basis of such texts as Matt. 7.13–14; Luke 13.24; Matt. 20.16b (Vulg) and 22.14, that the elect would comprise not only a minority of the human race, but a minority of the Christians. Augustine had taught that very emphatically, and argued moreover that it was in accordance with the providential will of God. With very little modification, this became the general mediaeval view, later mediaeval thinkers saying that the proportion of those saved would be as low as one in a thousand or more.[66] Among monks and nuns the conviction was strong that the monastic way of life was the only one really acceptable to God,[67] and they did not burke the corollary that few but Religious would be saved. That was certainly the view of Gregory the Great, and it was the opinion at Cluny, for example, in our period: Abbot Odo felt justified in 'rescuing' a young woman from the married state to which she was pledged in order that she might become a nun and so stand a chance of salvation.[68] In the light of such beliefs, many lay people who could afford it gave large sums to Religious houses and took the cowl in them in their later years, so as to die members of the Religious order. This was known as joining a monastery or nunnery *ad succurrendum*, and no-one had any doubt that it would confer monastic status at the Judgment. Odo of Canterbury, for example, who died in 959, wrote: 'All peoples and nations, tribes and tongues, run to St Benedict in order to receive his benediction; so that even the mockers who in their lifetime vilify this Order, when they come to death, then feel themselves not secure without the Religious habit of the cowl, if only *ad succurrendum*.'[69] As in the cases of Lothaire and Odo, for example, it was often done only just before death was expected.

To the extent that ordinary people were aware of such ideas, they will have found them extremely depressing, for their chances of being included in the saved minority would have seemed minimal. They had no way of approximating to the monastic way of life, and many of what were regarded as the more effective lay methods of achieving merit, lavish almsgiving, founding or endowing churches, monasteries and shrines, dying *sub cucullo*, benefitting from numerous votive masses (which had to be paid for), were beyond their reach. It was very well for an aristocrat such as Dhuoda to reflect that departed relatives of hers, who had cut a powerful figure in the world, 'might well be in God's presence *pro meritis dignis*';[70] the general sense of inferiority which, as we shall see, the culture inculcated in the peasants must have made them seem, even to themselves, unlikely candidates for inclusion in a very small élite.

It is, however, uncertain whether they were aware of the ideas in question. Later in the Middle Ages the fewness of the elect was certainly used by preachers as a means of 'shaking their congregations over the pit', but the evidence is less clear for our period. Augustine, although he held passionately that the elect would be a small predestined minority, had urged caution in disseminating such views, for fear of their possible discouraging effect,[71] and it may be that there was hesitation about disturbing the masses in this matter, comparable to the doubt mentioned above in connection with the end of the world (see p. 136).

Uncertainty on this point affects a further question. G.G. Coulton once wrote that, in contrast to the mystery religions, 'Christianity ... succeeded ... in bringing home to the multitudes of average men and women the eternal importance of truth and right conduct', fixing, as it did, 'a literally immeasurable gulf between religious success and religious failure'.[72] There is certainly truth in that, but no one familiar with the appalling atrocities and lawlessness recorded by Gregory of Tours and later chroniclers will gainsay the blunt comment of another modern scholar that, 'in fact fear of hell did not make them good'. Coulton himself wrote elsewhere of 'the gulf that separated the ordinary peasant, in his inmost nature, from the established religion of the day'.[73] If it is true that 'you cannot make people good by act of Parliament', it must also be true that you cannot alter their inner characters and motives by the use of supernatural sticks and carrots. Even when people kept the prospect of heaven and hell before their minds (which cannot have been all the time), it cannot have changed their fundamental mind-set; and we have to allow for the possibility that lay people will have despaired of salvation and felt 'in for a penny, in for a pound' where wrongdoing was concerned. We have also to remember the availability of subsequent penitence and satisfaction as a way of dealing with contemplated breaches of morality. A good example here is Fulk Nerra, in whom, according to Sir Richard Southern, 'the alternation of headlong violence with abrupt acts of remorse and atonement, which characterize the early feudal age, has its full play'.[74] Even when allowance is made for the amount of legend that gathered round his name, it is clear that his tumultous life was a constant alternation between appalling brutality and atrocities, and attempts to expiate them by public penance, pilgrimages and lavish gifts to religious institutions.[75] Again and again it was the fear of God's terrible vengeance that led him to make reparation, and at the end of his life, when nearly seventy, he embraced the rigours of a third pilgrimage to Palestine (in the course of which he died) in the hope of winning forgiveness and salvation.[76]

It will greatly have affected the mood of the age to know that death-bed repentance was always available, at any rate for those who had the opportunity (hence the great fear of sudden death), and in fact the Middle Ages were a time deeply preoccupied with death. After all, it was for each individual the moment when the irreversible decision between an eternity of hell or heaven (whether or not preceded by purgatorial suffering) would be declared.[77] That being so, the process of dying was naturally taken with full seriousness. People on their death-beds would be surrounded by relatives and friends, there to help them through their agony without loss of faith or virtue,[78] and the priest would also be present to administer rites of various sorts. As we have seen, the intervention of saints and angels on behalf of the dying person was sought in prayers and litanies, and other rites were designed to ensure that he or she passed through death in a state of grace. The narrative sources for this period do not suggest the existence of a fixed liturgy of the sick; but anointing, which, from the early ninth century was normally reserved for the mortally ill, was prescribed in a number of ecclesiastical and secular decrees.[79] In practice, ordinary lay people at this period seem mostly to have been content with confession, absolution and the *viaticum*, that is, Holy Communion given as a way of strengthening the soul on its journey (*via*) to the other side. So vital was this last taken to be that in some cases the host was put into the mouths of those already dead: whether as a substitute for the Holy Communion they had not had time to receive, or as a sort of magic talisman, comparable to the coin put in the mouth of the dead to pay for the ferry over the river Styx, it is not possible to say.

Especially in view of the universal absence of privacy, all this must have meant that everyone had plenty of opportunity to observe the efforts which were necessary, but also forthcoming, to secure the salvation of the dying. How far this offset the feelings of pessimism and discouragement other factors may have induced, it is now hard to know, though there were some occasions when hopes of avoiding damnation seem to have been abandoned, for example in the case of the former papal legate Arsenius who, as we are told, 'left for the place that was appropriate for him still conversing with the demons, and without the *viaticum*'.[80]

However much or little people knew about the details of eschatological doctrine and speculation, preachers, confessors, sculptors and painters ensured that everyone was made vividly aware of the fact of the Last Judgment and the momentous and stark alternatives to which it led.

Accepted as unquestioned fact, all this cannot have failed to have a deep influence on the decisions people made and the way they behaved; but since the great majority had no prospect of adopting the means most highly recommended for ensuring a favourable verdict, a great deal of fear and anxiety were engendered, and it must have been difficult indeed to think of God as a loving father to whose merciful care one could confidently commit oneself and one's future.

13

The Church and the Divisions of Society[1]

(i) Male society

Our question is what it was like to be a Christian in northern Francia in the tenth century. In order to get nearer to an answer we must now look at the social groups into which Francia at that time was divided. The matter is of direct interest for our study for two reasons. First, the divisions were regarded at the time as being religious in origin and character; also, they were so deep and far-reaching that the members of the different groups must have had very different attitudes to their religion, as well as to practically everything else.

We have already seen that whereas the Frankish tribes were originally divided into three classes, developments in methods of warfare from the eighth century onwards had the effect of blurring the distinction between the second and third classes, until secular society came to consist in effect of two groups: those who could afford arms and horses, and those who could not and were therefore dependent on the first group for their defence and security.

When the Franks became Christians, the clergy formed a third group, and for centuries after that, male society in France was taken to consist of three groups, though the lines between them were somewhat differently drawn at different times. Until about the tenth century, the lines were drawn between the Religious, the rest of the clerics and the lay aristocracy, the mass of the people being regarded as too amorphous and insignificant to figure in any formal classification.

Just about the time with which we are concerned, however, a new classification was coming into currency, which divided society into:

(a) *Oratores* (Those who pray)
(b) *Bellatores* (Those who wage war)
(c) *Laboratores* (Those who toil)

That particular formulation has not been traced back beyond Aelfric, abbot of Eynsham from 1005 to about 1020, but the idea was already current in our period, though the third group were usually referred to not as *laboratores* but by some less specific term such as *servi* or *agricolae*, tillers of the soil.

How were these groups made up?

The *oratores* comprised the whole clerical order, including the Religious. Nearly all the learned, and a large proportion of the literate, belonged to this group, membership of which depended not on birth but on ordination or on 'conversion', as it was called, to the monastic state. It therefore included people of very different social backgrounds, from the great prelate to the humblest parish priest, who might well have come from the class of *laboratores*, and be indistinguishable, socially, from other members of it. We must beware of preconceptions based on the social standing of clergy in the modern West.

The *bellatores* were also known as *pugnatores* or *agonistae*, and it is significant that they should have been thought of primarily in their warlike role. However, that was by no means their only role. They were also *rectores* or *potentes* ('rulers' or 'powerful ones'); they were the secular section of the ruling class, and as such, known as *praelati* (the foremost ones) or *praedicatores* (those with a right to speak). As with the *oratores*, there was wide diversity and gradation in their ranks, from the magnates who formed the king's entourage[2] down to the impoverished sons of the lesser nobility who by this period were often landless and without prospects, banding together to rob and pillage – little better than brigands.

The word *laboratores* does not mean simply 'workers', but rather 'toilers': *laborare* is sometimes replaced by the word *insudare* (to sweat, cf. Gen. 3.19) and it signifies those whose activity is hard and painful (cf. the idea of a woman 'in labour'). *Labor* was often juxtaposed with the word *dolor* (pain or grief). Once again, these terms covered a wide spectrum so far as property and prosperity were concerned, but they nevertheless designated a clearly differentiated group. They were sometimes referred to as the *pauperi* (poor), and poor most of them were; they were also defenceless, as we have seen. Their time was entirely taken up with boring, backbreaking labour such as no member of the superior classes would ever undertake.[3]

By the time they are classified as *laboratores*, at the end of our period, the idea is beginning to emerge that they, like the other two groups, have a vital function to perform in keeping society going. As we have seen, they were allowed to keep only a proportion of what they produced for themselves and their families, and to expend only part of their labour for their own benefit, the surplus being used to feed, house and heat the other two groups. That was their contribution to society.

Earlier, however, they had tended to be regarded just as a rabble; no specific function in the scheme of things was attributed to them; they were simply *servi*, serfs or slaves, whose only duty was to keep silent and to obey, passive and abject. Duby describes the attitude to them thus: they were limited to a passive role, bleating lambs in need of protection from predators. They did not constitute an order – because they were not actors ... they had no specific duties ... they fulfilled no function. They sweated and stank and coupled like animals.'⁴ In his *Libri Sententiarum* Isidore regarded the poor neither as active participants nor as having any particular obligations, but rather as passive – potential victims, to be protected.⁵ At any rate among the more old-fashioned, such views were still current in our period.

These three groupings cannot quite be described as castes because *some* movement from one to another occurred, though it was limited. The degree of social mobility in this period is a subject of some disagreement, Duby arguing that it was greater than many have supposed. One source of it was the action of kings in raising able men from humble backgrounds to high office in the church. A notable example of this was Ebbo, a royal serf, freed and educated by Charlemagne and raised to be Archbishop of Reims through the influence of Louis the Pious, in about 816. It is significant that throughout his tenure of the archbishopric, which ended in disaster, he had to contend with indignant opposition from many of the aristocracy. His enemies told him, according to the aristocratic Thegan, 'the Emperor gave you liberty, not nobility ... for that would not be possible'.⁶ Waldo, the abbot of Reichenau and a relation of the Carolingians, once swore that he would never acknowledge a superior of lower birth than himself so long as he had three fingers on his right hand;⁷ however, Walahfrid Strabo, who began his studies at Reichenau and eventually became abbot there, not long after Waldo, was an Aleman of very poor parentage.

Yet, if not to be described as castes, these groupings were not simply classes in the modern Western sense. In the first place, the threefold division of society was regarded as rooted in the will of God and the basic framework of creation 'from the beginning'. It was a primordial structure belonging to the time of myth rather than to the time of history, and simply taken for granted as part of the way things are.⁸

As the Bible showed,⁹ three was a special, even a sacred, number. God himself was threefold, and the heavenly hosts were believed to be organized in orders of three, a view reinforced after the work of Dionysius the Areopagite became available in the West in the middle of the ninth century.¹⁰ Thus any attempt to alter the threefold division of society was thought to involve opposing the will of God and attempting to overthrow the essential nature of things by putting this world out of its proper correspondence with the world above.

Not only was all reality meant to exhibit a threefold structure; the structure was meant to be hierarchical. It must be remembered that earth and heaven were seen as one vast, inter-related reality, and that the church was perceived as a single whole, including the dead as well as the living. Throughout this whole a system of hierarchy prevailed and was *meant* to prevail. Archangels, for example, were above angels, and Dionysius exhibited the whole celestial world as a hierarchical system which he believed himself able to plot in some detail. Revelation 5.8–10 suggested *ordines* in heaven, and Bernard of Clairvaux interpreted 1 Cor. 15.23 (*unusquisque in ordine suo*) in the same sense.

Thus *inaequalitas* was an essential principle of reality, and there were strong reactions against even the slightest suggestion for mitigating it. Gerard of Cambrai, for example, in the early eleventh century, argued that to abolish it would threaten the equilibrium of the universe, and Wallace-Hadrill writes of Hincmar of Reims (*c.* 806–882) that 'he felt the work of the devil was disruption ... social classes seemed to him to have divine approbation. Freedom lay in fulfilling God's purposes by assuming the responsibilities proper to one's own class.'[11] According to Gregory the Great, basing himself on John 14.2, it was God's will that a certain *inaequalitas* should prevail even in paradise, though he hedged the idea round with a number of qualifications.[12] Bernard of Clairvaux in the early twelfth century regarded the orders as absolutely immutable, and at about the same time Hildegard of Bingen stoutly defended the exclusion of all but the daughters of the nobility from her nunnery. It was, she said, 'the will of God that the inferior estate should not rise above the superior, as Satan and the first man had done, seeking to fly higher than their place ... God orders persons on earth just as in heaven, where he distinguishes angels, archangels ...' 'What man,' she asked, 'would gather all his herds in one stable, cattle, asses and sheep together?'[13]

Not only was the threefold hierarchical structure of society directly attributable to the will of God, so was the place of each individual within the hierarchy. We must now examine the three sections more closely, noting a certain asymmetry between them.

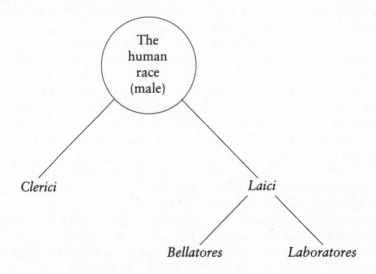

You became a clerk through ordination, and all clerks were members of a quite distinct *ordo* (*the ordo*, according to one important use of a word with many uses), though, as we have seen, this did not at all mean that all clerks belonged to the same social grouping (see p. 144 above). Membership of this group was, at any rate in theory, brought about through a call to the clerical or monastic state, and the distinctiveness of it from the rest of society thus had clear religious backing.

Other members of the church (which, as we have seen, was virtually co-terminous with society) were all alike *laici* (lay people), and what divided them into two groups was *natura*, rather than *ordo*. The terminology here is somewhat confusing. The church did not lose sight of such texts as I Cor. 12.13 or Gal. 3.28, or deny that all the baptized were capable of salvation; in that sense Jonas of Orléans in the mid-ninth century could warn the 'leaders' against believing that their subordinates were inferior to them by the nature of their being; they were inferior 'by virtue of *ordo*'. Since in this sense all men are equal, the leaders have a duty to provide for the religious well-being of the whole people; all the various manuals written at the time for the guidance of rulers are clear about that.

Nevertheless the distinction between the *bellatores* and the *laboratores* was real, clear and supposedly God-given. As Augustine put it: 'In the church this *ordo* is established: some precede, others follow ... and those who follow imitate the leaders.'[14] When it came to the question of the basis on which individuals had come to be members of the group to which they belonged, there was uncertainty and a feeling that the problem was beyond human solution. It was agreed, however, that at the heart of the matter lay an order of merits. Some people were less tainted by sin than others, and by nature less inclined to it. Good and evil, the heavenly and the earthly, were unevenly distributed among human beings. There was a natural inequality residing in impurity. Thus Gregory the Great taught that evil made different inroads on different people, and claimed that the reason was a *dispensatio occulta*, a mysterious distribution, on the part of God.[15] Isidore went further. 'Although,' he wrote, 'remission of original sin is granted to all the faithful by the grace of baptism, the just (*aequus*) God has introduced discrimination in human life (*discrevit hominibus vitam*), constituting some slaves, others lords, so that the freedom (*licentia*) of slaves to do wrong may be checked by the power of those who bear rule.'[16]

This was the basis on which control of the third group by the first two was understood to rest. Since by God's will human beings differed in their sinfulness and tendency to sin, it was only right that the less culpable should assume the responsibility for leadership. They were meant to exercise it with care and affection (charity, which involved an essential element of condescension) as well as firmness; but such was the wickedness, ignorance and stubbornness, verging on bestiality, of the third group, that repression and the sternest measures might often be necessary in order to restrain them and make them work. Fear, according to Isidore, was salutary for the rustics, because it kept them from sinning.[17]

So far as the two lay groups were concerned, membership of one or the other was thus by birth, and was dependent on a divine choice which, so far as human understanding went, seemed arbitrary.

The point was put rather differently by saying that the *virtus* or charism, and consequent illumination, necessary to exercise control was carried by noble blood. The nobles were warriors in virtue of their genetic qualities, the blood in their veins being responsible for their beauty (important for a successful noble), their impetuosity and martial qualities. These things could only be inherited; and consequently, even if a member of the nobility fell on hard times, he was still, according to Gregory the Great, distinguished by his inherited capacity to rule. Conversely, the eleventh-century chronicle, the *Miracles de St Benôit*, expresses horror over an occasion when men of the people mounted horses and sought to usurp the place of knights at a battle by the river Cher.[18] Their blood was unsuited to such a mission, lacking, as it did, the genetic qualities that gave a knight his valour; and the result was a disaster. Likewise, to have allowed rustics to take part in deliberative assemblies would have been to flout the essential constitution of things.[19]

It is now possible to understand Charlemagne's directive: 'every man shall keep his own life's purpose, and his own profession, *unanimiter*'.[20] The last word (which presumably keeps some of its root meaning, 'of one mind') is important, and a good deal lies behind it. The lot of the poor was so grim that even the dominant classes could make sense of it only by positing a doctrine of *concordia*. It was assumed that, as in a family, a village community or a monastery, all hearts were bound together by ties of affection, the community being a single body, the various parts of which had different functions but worked together in co-operation.[21] Walahfrid Strabo wrote: 'The house of God is built in unity by the love and charity of each order: in this way the unity of Christ's body is constituted; each member has a function, the fruit of which is shared by all in common.'[22] The image of society as a harmonious household was thus common, and its unity was held to derive, like a family's, from reciprocal giving. What the rulers had to give was the ordered society which it was their vocation to provide (though they must do it with condescension and without undue strictness), and also alms.[23] The contribution of the labourers was to be willing to respect and serve their masters.

The theory is set out concisely by Gerald of Cambrai. The *oratores* are able to enjoy the 'holy leisure' they need through the efforts of the *pugnatores*, who guarantee their security, and of the *agricultores* whose *labor* provides for their bodily needs. The *agricultores* are defended by the *pugnatores*, and owe forgiveness of their sins to the prayers of the *oratores*. The *bellatores* live on the rents of the *laboratores* and the taxes paid by merchants; and the work of the *oratores* cleanses them from the sins they may have committed in the course of their armed struggles.[24] Such was the theory; a later formulation of it added a further point. 'Servitude is ordained by God,' it said, 'either because of the sins of those who become serfs, or as a trial, in order that those who are thus humbled may become better. For servitude is of great help to religion in protecting humility, the guardian of all virtues.'[25] There was a widespread view which put a redemptive interpretation on the peasant's *labor*. Just as the redeeming work of Christ could sometimes be described as *labor*, so the physical pain and misery of the peasant's *labor* might be an instrument of redemption, in the same sort of way that a warrior, by giving his life for a good cause, might redeem the less grievous sins by which he was tainted. Only let the peasant submit abjectly to his lord, who thus, mysteriously, became God's minister to him. The poor were thus supposed to venerate the ways of life from which they were excluded.

How far all this was, consciously or unconsciously, rationalization designed to promote and protect the interests of the ruling classes is a question which will be discussed later. At the time the situation was seen as the result of the Fall. Servitude was not part of the way things were meant to be, and manumission of serfs was preached as a good work, pleasing to God. We may refer, for example, to the eleventh-century act of manumission cited by Southern: 'Whoever, in the name of the holy and undivided Trinity, moved by charity, permits any one of his servile dependents to rise from the yoke of servitude to the honour of liberty, may surely trust that in the last day he himself will be endued with everlasting and celestial liberty.'[26] Liberty was prized in practice, and rather more than a century later, Gerald of Wales stated bluntly: 'There is nothing which so stirs the hearts of men and incites them to honourable action as the joy of liberty (*hilaritas libertatis*), and nothing which so deters and depresses them as the oppression of servitude.'[27]

Certainly the unfree had a lot to depress them. Serfdom was universally admitted to involve degradation and indignity. We have already seen how the Middle Ages inherited from the classical world a contempt for the *banausoi*, those occupied in manual work; and for the Bible one may cite Ecclus. 38.25 [Vulg. 26ff.]. Such an attitude continued current. In innumerable passages the peasants are represented as little more than animals. Even a liberal cleric could write of *rustici qui pecudes possunt appellari* (the rustics who may be described as cattle), and their families were regularly referred to in legal documents as *sequela*, a word designating an animal's brood. The peasant was constantly described in literature in a positively Hogarthian way as stupid, dark-skinned, deformed and hideous: in Coulton's words, 'a mediaeval Caliban'. According to one description, 'he was large and marvellously ugly and hideous. He had a great mop of a head, blacker than coal, the space of a palm between his eyes, broad cheeks, a great flat nose with cavernous nostrils, large lips redder than underdone meat, and long hideous, yellow teeth.'[28] The many similar descriptions quoted by Luchaire and others fully justify his conclusion that 'it was the tradition that the villein could not, even in physique, be anything else than disagreeable to the eyes, and different from others'.[29] In the *Miracles de Notre Dame* the peasants are said to have 'such hard heads and stupid brains that nothing can penetrate them'.

What is more, the lords constantly breached the peasants' rights and broke the agreements relating to them; free families could easily find themselves illegally reduced to serfdom without redress, as happened, for example, to the sister of one of Anselm's correspondents.[30] In practice peasants were almost entirely at the mercy of their lords' will and whims, and had little defence against extra demands and exactions laid upon them; there is no reason to think that ecclesiastical landlords were any less demanding than others. In fact the good organization of their estates, and the continuity of administration of which they were capable, tended to make it particularly difficult for peasants to escape the demands of monastic landlords.[31] All this explains Luchaire's comment that to the peasants' physical hardships 'there must be added the shame of servitude which is an hereditary blemish; the odious and humiliating exactions, the legal disability of marrying, of moving about and of making wills'. He adds: 'even then we have an inadequate idea of the complexity of the misfortunes and the miseries in which the peasants struggled.'[32] Their sense of isolation was all the more marked, and constantly reinforced, because this was a society much attached to outward ceremony and symbolism, so that people's social category was indicated by their clothes, the shape of their footwear, the cut of their hair, and so on, and also by their appointed place in the numerous parades and processions which accompanied all sorts of occasions. The poor people's feeling of inferiority extended to the religious sphere, and indeed feelings of religious inferiority may well have been experienced by all lay people, except the very highest, in a world dominated by the clergy, in which it was often said that the full Christian life could be lived only in the monasteries.

So far as the church was concerned, the peasants had to pay tithes to their parish church, in addition to their other payments, and they were forbidden to work on a number of feast and fast days in the year, something which was much resented, to judge from the constant complaints by bishops and councils that it was being ignored;[33] the church also did its best to restrain a good deal of the peasants' rustic merry-making.

There was a good deal of rustic merriment, including singing, dancing, wrestling, cockfighting and bull-baiting, and there were games of primitive football and hockey. The locally-brewed ale was cheap and there was a great deal of drunkenness and loose talk. Being traditional, the peasants' games kept many traces of paganism and for that reason, among others, the church was suspicious of them, especially as they often took place on Sundays and feast-days.[34]

We must remember, too, the profound ignorance of the *laboratores*. They were completely illiterate, and in any case church services were all in Latin. They rarely received instruction in the vernacular, and then it was of the sketchiest kind; and they had little leisure or privacy for private devotion. So far as they learned their religion from painting and sculpture, these commonly depicted Christ as a stern judge separating the sheep from the goats. While in theory a peasant could be among the sheep,[35] it emerges from the writings of influential authors, such as Peter Damian (*c.*1040) and, later, Anselm that the chances of salvation were thought to be slight for any but Religious. God's real good pleasure, and the highest places in heaven, were reserved for ascetics, and certainly for those who avoided all sex. This had already been argued by Augustine,[36] and in our period Abbo of Fleury, among others, was quite clear that indulgence in sex (which was more or less *required* of the laity) impeded progress towards perfection. The question could be raised in all seriousness whether there would be the same reward for all. In the mid-tenth century Duke William of Normandy asked: 'the church is organized in *tripertito ordine*; men are distinguished by different functions (*dispares ... officiis*). Is it possible that there is the same reward for all?' He was told by Abbot Martin of Jumièges that 'each will be rewarded according to his *labor*',[37] but this meant that even in the hereafter the expectations of the laity, and especially of the peasants, who lacked access to the most effective means of satisfaction, were distinctly limited.[38] Fichtenau writes that in 'God's fortress' – which is how heaven was conceived by the Franks – 'there were to be found separate apartments for important people such as the saints and the magnates of the empire', while Ntedka points out that 'the society of the beyond is conceived as a continuation (*prolongement*) of the community here below'.[39] If that was how the heavenly society was to be, the prospects for the peasant were poor indeed, and it is no surprise to find a Goliardic poet writing that 'the peasants are always in a state of anger and their heart is never content'.[40] They are bound to have felt confused and depressed about their lot, both in this world and the next. They will not have known or understood the theological niceties of the matter, but actions speak louder than words; and, given the way they were treated, they can hardly have avoided a profound lack of self-respect, even of religious self-respect. It would have been difficult to have a lively sense of the love of God, or of your worth in his eyes, if he had placed you in such a position, and loaded you with such numerous handicaps. Although, as Southern says, 'hard words break no bones', he rightly adds that the effect of the low view of them, and the contempt in which they were held, must have helped to make the peasants assimilate to the stereotype of them. Being a Christian was obviously a very different thing for them from what it was for an archbishop, let us say, or a monk at Cluny. As Christianity was understood at the time, 'the full Christian life could be lived only in the monasteries'[41] and it would be surprising if lay people, and particularly those at the lower end of the scale, had not felt a sense of discouragement and near despair. Riché points out that a need was felt at Cluny to try 'to reassure the laity, who, in a world run by the clergy, suffered from a sort of "inferiority complex", and to convince them that they had an important role to play in the Christian community'.[42] He cites a passage from Paulinus of Aquileia which speaks volumes: 'there is a great confusion in the minds of the laity, who say: "What business is it of mine to listen to the reading of the Scriptures or to learn from them, or even to keep going to the priests and the churches of the saints? When I become a clergyman I will do what the clergy are supposed to do." '[43]

In the nature of the case, we have no direct evidence of the feelings of the peasants, but we know of their support for a number of heretical, or semi-heretical, movements which began to emerge at this time, and which tended to preach equality in sin and in the need for penitence, and also advocated abolition of social differences, even the one between the sexes. Women took a full part in what were to become egalitarian fraternities which minimized the need for clergy and for the sacraments of which they were the indispensable celebrants. We know, for example, of an (abortive) rising of Norman peasants in 977, which was inspired by hostility to all lords, both spiritual and secular.[44]

Where direct evidence in writing is lacking, the evidence of archaeology is the more valuable, and the words of Wallace-Hadrill, based on the remains of the Merovingian village of Brebières, near Douai, are worth quoting. After describing the finds, he writes: 'Privation, disease and misery explain the tenacious hold of the villagers everywhere on the only comforts that were left to them: the soothsayer, the wise woman, the medicine man, the gods of the countryside and the saint in his shrine. Men reduced to nothing will tend to draw together to make themselves something as a unit bent on propitiating the seen and unseen sources of their wretchedness. In the enslaved *rustici*, therefore, I detect what is entirely characteristic of the time: the capacity of the group to identify itself in a common purpose and to maintain its private privilege against the world of outsiders – in this case, the privilege of suffering. His kin, his neighbours and his gods lift my *rusticus* to membership of a little community which is itself and not any other community. How it lives is conditioned not only by hunger and exhaustion but also by its common view of good and evil, gods and demons ... Everything else, and everyone else, was hostile until proved otherwise.'[45] Although the period referred to is somewhat earlier than the one we are considering, the situation will not have changed greatly, as Wallace-Hadrill himself points out.

(ii) Women and Slaves

We may begin our discussion, as Suzanne Wemple does, with a quotation from a ninth-century writer, Haimo of Auxerre. He writes: ' "I do not permit a woman to teach" (I Tim. 2.12). In her own home, a woman is allowed to teach members of her own sex, and boys as well, but in church she is forbidden. Why this prohibition? Because she must be subject to the man, for she is made of his body. Moreover, she is forbidden to teach because her sex is weaker than that of the man; hence it must be feared that, as Eve, seduced by the snake, brought death into this world, she too, lapsing so easily into sin, should lead others into the same sin.'[46]

The Middle Ages inherited a low view of women both from classical antiquity and from early Frankish times. The degree of women's emancipation varied from time to time in the ancient world, but, broadly, the ancients were convinced of the weakness and light-mindedness of the female sex; even physicians felt that male dominance was nature's intention. In the second century CE the anatomist Galen, one of the greatest medical figures of classical times, whose work was extremely influential in the Middle Ages, traced woman's inferiority to physiological causes, arguing that, from a sexual standpoint, a woman was a man turned inside out. The birth of a female child was attributed to some defect in her parents or to some external influence such as a humid wind blowing from the south at the time of her conception.[47] The woman's place among the pre-Christian Franks was definitely subordinate; and though women, at any rate of higher social rank, had considerable rights – for example, to hold and administer land, defend themselves in the courts, make donations and the like – women in Frankish society were strongly associated with magic. Tacitus already says that the Germanic peoples attributed to their womenfolk magic powers denied to the men;[48] though this might enable them to prophesy and divine, the reputation was obviously a dangerous one to have, once the Franks had been converted to Christianity.

The Jews also had a low opinion of women. If Socrates was reputed to have said that the three blessings for which he was grateful to fortune were not having been born an animal, a woman or a barbarian, orthodox Jews have to this day a prayer to be said by men in the official daily service which runs, 'Blessed art Thou, O Lord our God, King of the Universe, who hast not made me a woman.'[49] This low view was stated bluntly by Philo,[50] and it found expression in a number of Old Testament texts;[51] and on the basis of the Old Testament more than one Christian teacher gave a list of holy men who had been led astray by women, for example, Samson, David and Solomon. Jezebel's name usually featured prominently in such lists.

Although from some points of view, the New Testament stressed the equality of women,[52] it gave rather an uncertain sound on the subject, and many New Testament texts were quoted which seemed to emphasize the inferiority of women and the need for them to be subject to men.[53]

Much the most influential text in this connexion, however, was the story of the Fall in Genesis, on which, after Augustine, the Western church laid extremely heavy emphasis. On the basis of Gen. 3.1ff. or I Tim. 2.14, for example, Eve was regarded as responsible for sin and the Fall; and since all were believed to be involved in the guilt of it, she was seen as the source of all human guilt and misery. Already in the third century the influential Western theologian, Tertullian, had written of Eve as 'the gateway through whom the devil gained entrance, the *resignatrix* (meaning uncertain: "unsealer" or "traitor"?) of that forbidden tree, and the first rebel against God's law'.[54] What is more, he identifies all women with Eve and her transgression. 'Do you not know,' he asks them, 'that you are (each) an Eve? The sentence of God on this sex of yours lives on in this age; the guilt must of necessity live too.' Subsequent Fathers fully endorsed what he said, particularly the even more influential Jerome in his *adversus Jovinianum*. Not only was woman virtually identified with temptation and sin, in innumerable decrees, sermons and treatises, but since sexuality in its present unbridled form was held to derive from the Fall (e.g. Gen. 3.16), woman was held responsible for that.

We shall not understand the outlook of the Middle Ages unless we recognize that the church, or at any rate its clerical spokesmen, really hated – the word is not too strong – sex and sexual intercourse. Odo of Cluny, for example, regarded sexuality as the principal means by which the devil secured his hold on creation; sex was unworthy of the Christian. According to Augustine, the essence of shame lay in the inability of the mind to master the body, and for him and those who followed him, this was precisely what characterized the sexual act.[55] Sexual intercourse was bad, whether in or out of marriage, and as late as 1022 there were men of high culture who doubted whether the church should get involved in the profane rites of marriage; to them marriage was a carnal, and hence contemptible, matter.[56] Marriage was at best a solution of the last resort, a remedy against lust for the lowest moral category in society, the *conjugati*. Both the continent, or virgins, and widows rated above them in the moral scale, Matt.19.10–12 being taken to mean that the best course was to avoid marriage.

At least it could be said for marriage that it prevented promiscuity, but sexual intercourse was not only degrading; whatever the context, it was the means by which the entail of original guilt was passed on. It was clearly necessary for the continuance of the race, which was God's will, but no pleasure, or at any rate no excessive pleasure, was to be taken in it. Gregory of Tours, for example, praises Gregory of Langres because 'he had known his wife solely for the sake of propagating children',[57] and in the same vein Augustine had argued that since the experience of sex is now inseparable from the sense of shame, the wise man wishes he could have children without it, and uses it solely for the purpose of procreation, being as moderate as possible.[58]

Lupus of Ferrières felt called upon to explain how Christ could seem to have approved of marriage through his attendance at a wedding at Cana (John. 2.1–11). He insists that Christ clearly put virginity above it, being himself a virgin and a virgin's son.[59] According to Eriugena, if Adam and Eve were united in paradise, it may not have been *sine coitu*, but it was *sine ardore*, without the heat of pleasure; and that is how it should be now. Husbands should recognise that intercourse is a sort of sin, to be indulged in with disgust.[60] We have already quoted the example of the elephant who was believed to turn his head away while having sex, from disgust at what he was doing, and Peter Damian insists that God intends him for our guide.[61] Accordingly, to be passionately in love was literally a work of the devil, and frequent sex was condemned, wives who indulged in it being dubbed *meretrices* (harlots).[62] The whole endeavour of the church was to limit sex in whatever way possible; Jerome, for example, was clear that any man who loved his wife too much was an adulterer. The trouble seemed to be that men were no longer able to propagate simply as an act of rational will, 'in tranquility of body and soul', as Adam did if he had intercourse with Eve in paradise.[63]

Concupiscence had reduced human beings to the level of the animals, and, being the result of the Fall, it was the responsibility of Eve. For Augustine and his followers, concupiscence was by no means limited to sexual desire; as we have seen, it originated in the mastery of reason by passion, and was the conglomeration of all the bent tendencies awakened in human beings by the Fall, in which the revolt of the flesh against the spirit vents itself. The attitude of the age to sex was all part of its sharp dichotomy between spirit and flesh, and its distrust of the latter.

Women, it was believed, were more lustful and sexually aggressive than men, and aroused them to intercourse, and to concupiscence within it, both by their natural charms[64] and also by various wiles which they practised, including use of spells and other kinds of magic.

Women were thus deeply suspect by church leaders; Augustine wrote that in a woman the good Christian 'likes what is human, and loathes what is feminine'.[65] The question could seriously be raised whether in the original state of innocence any female children were meant to be born.[66] The answer, according to Aquinas, was in the affirmative, and he rejected Aristotle's view that a woman was simply a man gone wrong; but he followed Augustine (and many others) in holding woman to be less intelligent than man.

The male was the norm. Everyone knew that God was male, and not female, and Augustine drew the conclusion that physically man is more like God than woman, whose body 'cannot have imaged God even in paradise', and who 'was nearer Satan than Adam could be'.[67] One of his followers denied flatly that women could be said to be in the image of God.[68] It was also held that woman is less rational than man. As we shall see, she was below reason and above it, but she was not rational.[69] Womankind was regarded as weak. The collect for the office of Virgins called them *sexus fragilis*, and a sermon of pseudo-Bede clearly betrays surprise that women could achieve martyrdom, 'rising superior both to the world and to their sex ... thus doubling the glory of their warfare' (as compared with male martyrs).[70] Frodoard, when describing a woman of great character in charge of a nunnery, calls her 'a woman with the heart of a man'. In many Lives of female saints it is regarded as a signal act of God's goodness to have produced virtues in the women in question despite the weakness of their sex.[71]

Alongside this theological depreciation of women, and no doubt partly dependent on it, went a general picture which is less easy to document. It may be, as Samuel Laeuchli, for example, has suggested, that the repressed sexuality of Western clerics gave rise to 'a constant desire to punish women with whom they came into contact';[72] certainly the documents produced by the clerics suggest a very dark view of womankind. In general accounts of the universe women are put in the same category as night, water, the moon – all that is cold and blue – and yet they were seen as so ardent that men could not cope with their sexual demands. Women did not play fair; they pretended and dodged, they were frivolity personified, fickle and chattering, even in church when they should have been attending to the service. The clerical writers are aware of being cut off from the women's world, which was out of bounds to them, 'confined to the household where men and women coupled and had children, where children were raised, food prepared, and the dead prepared for burial'.[73] It was a world foreign, but fascinating, to men, who imagined the strange and perverse practices which they supposed went on there. If children died in that world, infanticide was readily suspected, and so were abortion and prostitution.[74]

Both Bible and tradition suggested that women should be kept in subordination and, given the view of them just outlined, it was felt that this subordination should be strictly enforced. As with the *laboratores*, women's inherent sinfulness demanded as much, and meant that they had no right to a voice in any decisions of government. Any suggestion to the contrary met firm opposition, as at the Synod of Nantes in 895, which stated: 'it is astonishing that some wretched women, acting with impudent effrontery, against both divine and human law, attend general assemblies and public gatherings (*conventus*), thus disrupting, rather than settling, the business of the kingdom and the good of the state (*respublica*). It is improper and reprehensible, even among barbarians, for women to deal with the cases of men. Those who should be discussing their spinning and weaving with the residents of the women's quarters ought not to usurp the authority of senators in public meetings, just as if they were palace officials.'[75]

A woman's husband was her lord, *dominus*, and it must surely have been significant that this was the word also used for God; the overtones it could carry are shown by the Latin version of Psalm 45 (44.12), where the king is described to the queen as 'the Lord thy God to whom worship belongs'. All this was taken to be the result of the Fall, after which the more or less equal union of love which had existed in Eden was no longer possible. In the Christian era the woman was not exactly a slave, according to Augustine, but she must never give orders to a man, for men carry the power, and 'unless the due order is followed, nature will be more completely distorted and sin will increase'.[76] It is significant that Augustine went much further than the Roman law texts of his day, which no longer mention any subordination in their references to marriage contracts. In fact he reacted against the progressive emancipation of women in the society of his time.

No doubt husbands varied very widely in their exercise of their lordship, but we have plenty of evidence that wives were sometimes badly maltreated and subjected to savage brutality.[77] Our detailed evidence relates mainly to royal and noble families, but there is no reason to suppose that peasant husbands behaved better. It is only fair to add that a good deal of our information comes from churchmen such as Hincmar, relatively speaking a champion of women, who strongly criticized such cruelty, and sought ways to mitigate its effects, for example by making churches available as sanctuaries.

Only just before our period, married women had considerable control over property which belonged to them personally, most notably their husbands' betrothal gifts to them (*sponsalia*); but by the end of our period the husband's power over the whole of the couple's property was becoming so great as to make the wife's prerogatives largely fictitious.

The formal position at the end of the eighth century is succinctly stated in the Caroline Books, sent by Charlemagne to the pope in about 792, probably on the advice of Theodulph of Orléans. 'The frailty of the woman's sex and the mutability of her mind do not permit woman to place herself in supreme authority in matters of faith and rank. She is compelled ... to submit to the authority of the male.'[78] However, the breakdown of central authority in the subsequent period meant that by the time we are considering the position of women, at any rate of the upper class, had changed a good deal, and in practice they sometimes exercised considerable power, especially in local affairs. For example, during the absence of her husband on military campaigns, a woman might find herself responsible for the management of his domains.

The change was limited, however, and there were many positions and opportunities absolutely barred to women. Pseudo-Augustine wrote that a woman 'is not allowed to have any authority. She cannot teach, testify, act as a surety or serve as a judge; hence she certainly cannot rule.'[79]

So far as religion was concerned, the question of priesthood for women was not so much as raised by the Fathers or early mediaeval writers. In addition to the reasons already mentioned, there was the matter of ritual impurity. A synod at Auxerre in about 585 claimed that women are impure by nature, and so must be veiled in the presence of the sacraments. When they receive communion they must have a cloth over their heads, and also over their hands, whereas the men may have the host placed in their bare palms.[80] In fact women must not touch anything that is consecrated or sacred. The West, even more than the East, separated women from active participation in liturgical worship; already in the fifth century Pope Gelasius I directed that women must be kept away from the altar area.[81] A lot of this centred on menstruation, with its sexual connexions and Old Testament connotations of impurity. The penitentials make clear that menstruating women were not supposed to enter a church, nor might a woman enter church for forty days after childbirth. Gregory I discounted much of this, and took the various Old Testament provisions (eg Lev. 12.4–5; 20.18, etc.) as a *mysterium*, arguing that the sin lay in the pleasure of intercourse, not in the delivery, which was pain and punishment enough.[82] The other attitude continued to prevail, however, and was an effective bar to any active participation by women in church services or the church hierarchy. In the ninth century we find Theodulph of Orléans writing. 'Let women never approach the altar when the priest is celebrating mass, but let them stand in their own place, and there let the priest receive their offerings ... for women ought to be mindful of their weakness and of the infirmity of their sex, and therefore fear to touch anything holy in the ministry of the church.'[83] The *tabu* element in all this hardly needs stressing.

Woman's equality in pursuing the ascetic ideal was recognized, and many women found release and fulfilment in the Religious life, where they could wield considerable authority in the nunneries and could gain a thorough education and give expression to their own ideals, emotions and spiritual aspirations. We may think, for example, of Hroswitha, or of Hildegard of Bingen a century later. In this, as in other respects, woman's lot was rather better than it was to become in subsequent centuries, though even at this time the Benedictine Rule had been imposed on Religious houses in such a way as to isolate women Religious from the mainstream of religious and intellectual life; and they were able to play little part in the revival of learning in these centuries.[84]

All this might seem to add up to a fairly clear picture. 'Men and women are equivalent in the Gospel, yet woman is subordinate to man in history.'[85] In fact, however, this topic is a good instance of the limits of historical knowledge. It is impossible to know how things worked out in practice, how people responded to the models offered to them, and to what extent the prescribed rules were obeyed. How far did women interiorize the ecclesiastical account of them, and what was married life actually like?

In general it is difficult to think that women did not yield to the intense pressure to which they were subjected, and interiorize the accepted picture to a considerable extent, simply on the principle that if a thing is said often and emphatically enough, some of it is bound to stick. There were so many contexts, ecclesiastical and secular, in which women's (alleged) status was brought home to them. Being expected to practise charms and wiles would naturally lead many women to do so, especially as they had no overt and recognized way of influencing the course of events. The penitentials suggest that they did resort to spells and incantations, often enough at any rate for specific penalties to be prescribed. For example, they would anoint themselves with honey, and then roll in flour, using the mixture to make cakes for their husbands; or they would concoct potions containing their menstrual discharge or their husbands' sperm, the aim being to change the man's attitude (*mens*) from hate to love or vice versa.[86]

On the other hand women did sometimes wield very high authority, as we have seen – often with conspicuous success. For example, during the minority of the emperor Otto III his mother Theophano and, after her death, his grandmother Adelaide ruled the empire effectively and wisely. In a humbler sphere, free women who married serfs could continue to own and manage their property on behalf of their children. Still, woman's place was firmly regarded as being in the home, and if a woman exercised public power, it was only as an extension of her role as mother and property-owner.

If women were below reason, they were also to be seen, at any rate somewhat later, in the literature of courtly love, as above reason, standing for a higher principle than reason, love. Many married couples enjoyed a relationship of mutual affection satisfying to both. Wills often speak with great affection and respect of the testator's spouse, and women's signatures frequently appear alongside their husbands' on documents making joint charitable gifts. Yet we must beware of importing anachronistic ideas of romantic love into the picture. John Boswell was surely exaggerating somewhat when he claimed that 'apart from the monastic clergy, love does not appear to have been a concern of tenth-century Europeans in any context, theological, moral, sexual or emotional'.[87] Yet it is true that the church teaching of our period treated sexual relationships as simply a matter of physical pleasure – to be avoided – or simply as a technique of reproduction on a biological level. Even the layman's intuition that there was more to it than that was apt to be rejected by the authorities. Some time later, Robert de Courson could write that if you asked married people why they had sexual relations, they would reply: 'because I love him or her, and I am married'. 'What are you to do?', he asks, 'they know no better.'[88]

With this went the patristic commonplace, based on classical teaching, that, as Aquinas put it, 'the purpose of woman as helpmeet is just to assist man in the work of generation, not to help him in everything; for in all other fields he is more effectively assisted by another man than by a woman'.[89] This may well have been a case where the laypeople felt that they knew better in practice than the clerics, and simply went on their way unperturbed.

The idea of a woman standing for love was no doubt incubating in our period, and the whole subject must have been considerably affected by the growing veneration for the Virgin Mary. Although this veneration had not yet by any means reached its apogee (see above pp. 93f.), it had gained strength in the ninth century, as the artistic evidence shows.[90] As by one virgin, Eve, sin had come into the world, so it was through another virgin, Mary, that the Saviour and salvation had come, a fact emphasized by the frequency with which the Eve/Mary typology was reproduced in art and liturgy. This must have helped to mitigate the image of woman simply as Eve; but even so, the Virgin Mary was pictured, as we have seen, in an essentially maternal and domestic role; and even devotees of the Virgin, and comparative champions of women, such as Jonas of Orléans and Hincmar, still insisted on the weakness of women and the need for their subjection to men.[91]

As in the case of the peasants, it must largely be left to readers to envisage for themselves what it would have been like to be a female Christian in such a context. Admittedly, few of the women would have known any of the texts quoted above, but we can perhaps imagine something of the feeling of a young girl growing up in this culture. She would, for example, be bound to notice that she was always expected to wear long clothes, in contrast to her brothers. If she asked why, the answer was that her clothes were meant to hide her flesh. Eve the temptress was seen in every woman – still deluded, she approached Adam with an illegal fruit to be shared, the fruit now being her own body. Adam still needed protection against her advances. A girl would notice how her mother was expected to bow to her father in all things, and how carefully she and all other women and girls were kept at bay in church. She would see the terrifying doom pictures, and could not help knowing that, according to church teaching, she and all her sex were responsible for the damnation threatening so many, and for all the other ills of a fallen world. She could hardly fail to become aware, at least implicitly, that at heart the feeling of church leaders was: 'What a wonderful world it would be if there were no women!' How could women fail to distrust their own femininity in such a situation? Anselm could envisage the possibility that 'women might despair of having a lot in the share of the blessed, since from a woman so great evil proceeded', and felt the need to encourage them.[92]

Against this background, reinforced in sermons and church art, as well as in constant custom and prohibition, it must have been difficult for a woman to take to heart Paul's teaching that 'in Christ there is neither male nor female' (Gal.3.28), and to feel anything more than a second- (or even third-) class citizen, with second-class status and prospects, even in the eyes of God. Small wonder that women played such a large part in developing the cult of the Virgin Mary. Here was a member of their sex who really counted in the scheme of things, before whom even the highest Christians – popes, bishops and emperors – bent the knee, and who was presumably on the side of the other members of her sex. Small wonder either that heretical, or semi-heretical, groups which played down or denied the significance of the distinction between the sexes found so much of their support among women. However, we must not oversimplify. There was a strand in church teaching which did keep the equality of all Christian souls before people's eyes; and though the egalitarian sects did not emerge on any scale till later, they must have had their origins in the ideas of some earlier thinkers who diverged, to a greater or less extent, from the majority view.

If, in the light of all this, it should seem that women will have had an even lower estimate of themselves than male peasants, the importance of social distinctions must be borne in mind. Women of the noble class will have seen themselves as members of an order altogether superior to the peasants; and, whether separately or with their husbands, they will have had the means to give alms, endow churches, monasteries or votive masses, and perform all the other good works which were held to avail for the salvation of souls. Rather similar considerations will have applied to women members of the Religious order. Almost all of them came from the noble class; and since women were held to be more highly- sexed, the sacrifice they made in accepting virginity was thought to be the more pleasing to God. As *continentes*, they belonged to the highest moral stratum in society and the one whose way of life was thought most likely to lead to salvation.

This seems the most appropriate place to say something briefly about slaves. So far as it can be discovered, their position was dire indeed. There is very little evidence about the view of them as a separate group, and none at all about their view of themselves. Texts such as Gal.3.28 and I Cor.12.13 implied that slaves, if baptized, shared an equality with all other Christians, but the limitations on that insight we have observed in the case of peasants applied, if anything, more strongly to slaves. If to be born a peasant was a sign of inferior moral character, to be born a slave was even more so. As we have seen, the distinction between slave and free was nothing like as strong and definite as we might be inclined to expect; but so far as it existed, slaves would have had even less opportunity than other peasants to behave in the ways that were thought effective in making satisfaction and winning a place in heaven.

Even to try to envisage the religious self-understanding and prospects of, let us say, a Hincmar on the one side and a hereditary slave in a poorly-served rural parish on the other, is to realize how wide a gap separated being a Christian in the one case from being a Christian in the other. The difference was not simply a subjective matter of different apprehensions of the faith; it involved quite objectively different statuses and prospects in the eyes of God. So too, in practice, did the other distinctions which have formed the subject of this chapter.

14

The People of God

In its capacity as the church, the population of West Francia was as sharply divided as it was in its secular capacity, but the divisions were along somewhat different lines. The main division was that between clergy and Religious on the one side, and the laity on the other. This division was so deep and sharp that we could speak of a quite separate clerical caste, except for its not being hereditary.[1] According to the official view – and we must remember that this was largely the product of clerics and is known to us almost exclusively from their pens – the clergy, although only a small proportion of the population,[2] were superior to everyone else, rulers included. In fact the laity are constantly said to be subject to the clergy (*subiecti*). This was because the difference between clergy and laity was thought to have deeper roots than any worldly distinctions. It was often said to be a difference analogous to that between body and soul.

At their ordination God took the clergy to be his own servants, and that set them apart from the feudal hierarchy and exempted them from the jurisdiction of secular judges; their affairs were regulated in accordance with their own canon law. Ordination – or in the case of the Religious, their *conversio* – also gave them a special charism, in virtue of which they alone could know and teach what is, and is not, Christian. As repositories of what 'the divine authority teaches',[3] the priests had the prerogative to declare where equity and justice lay, and then it was for rulers to give effect to it.[4] It must be remembered that relatively few lay people were literate, so there was little chance of any theoretical challenge to clerical opinion.

Ordination also conferred what, for want of a better word, may be called a tabu character. An ordained man was 'pure', and his purity had to be preserved. This set him apart as a sacred person and meant that his calling was incompatible, for example, with serfdom, marriage or sexual relations, or with certain types of work.[5] It also meant that he could count on obtaining a superior place in the hereafter, supposing that he got to heaven.[6]

Parish priests by no means made up the whole clerical body, and we have already seen some of the reasons why the tenth century was prepared to maintain so many economically unproductive members.[7] The clergy were the intelligentsia of the age, the only people who could explain the nature of reality and the way it worked. They were also the technologists, the only people believed capable of understanding what was going on and of producing – by their prayers and sacramental activities – the results which the age desperately needed but had not the knowledge to produce by secular means.

The clergy also fulfilled another role. The way in which mediaeval people sought to bring their ideals into relation with the actual world was by fashioning an institution in which these ideals might become concrete. They sought to establish a visible church, a great society embracing all the various activities of the human spirit and claiming to be the highest expression of its purpose.[8] Indeed it seemed at the time that ideals could not be realized, nor salvation achieved, outside this body; the church was what German scholars call a *Heilsanstalt*, an, or rather the, institution and vehicle of salvation; and, as such, it was of direct divine foundation. Christ, it was believed, had not only founded it; he had laid down the way in which it should be organized to the end of time. The apostles whom he had appointed were intrinsic to its existence, and unless it was governed by them, or by successors in direct line of descent from them, it would cease to be what Christ had intended, and no longer function as the vehicle of salvation.

(i)   The bishops

We shall begin this account of the clerical order with the bishops, because they were taken to be the successors of the apostles, the priests being the successors of the other disciples. It was believed that an unbroken line of succession could be traced back from them to their original predecessors. Although the order of clergy embraced men of different statuses and 'orders' – deacons, sub-deacons and others in so-called minor orders –[9] bishops and priests were in a class apart, for they alone disposed of sacramental powers.

As the successors of the apostles, the bishops were constitutive of the church,[10] and they alone could guarantee its continuance by consecrating other bishops to carry on the all-important succession. Bishops administered the sacraments of baptism and eucharist, essential to salvation, and they alone had the power to ordain priests by whom these sacraments could be made available throughout Christendom. Other essential functions peculiar to them were the blessing of the holy oils – necessary for baptism, confirmation, extreme unction and other purposes – and the administration of the second part of the initiation rite, which had by the early Middle Ages become quite separate from baptism, and was known as confirmation.[11]

Bishops were thus of the essence of the church and were frequently described as *vicarii Christ et clavigeri regni caelorum* (proxies for Christ, who carry the keys of the kingdom of heaven).[12]

Important non-sacramental roles were also traditionally assigned to them. As guardians of the faith, they had a theological role, being responsible for declaring what the faith was and settling disputed questions in the areas of doctrine, discipline and liturgy. To discharge these responsibilities, they met together for deliberation, in provincial and national conferences, known as councils or synods.[13] Secondly, they had an educational role: not only were they expected to provide such schooling as there was for children, but they had to maintain a supply of sufficiently educated men to serve as priests and local teachers, and to instruct their clergy and people themselves through a preaching ministry. Thirdly, they were assigned a pastoral role, being responsible for the charitable work of the church, ensuring that the poor, the sick, fugitives and others in special need were catered for.

In the early centuries of Christianity, when society was still essentially city-centred, many bishops were able to fulfil these roles personally for the relatively limited urban populations for which they were responsible; but as city life gave way to rural conditions, in which the population was widely scattered, they were compelled to work more and more through intermediaries of various kinds.

What impact is a tenth-century bishop likely to have had on the people in his diocese? In order to answer that question, we need to take account of an important historical development. As imperial power declined in the West, the bishops had, from the fourth century onwards, taken over many responsibilities of a social, administrative, and even military sort previously undertaken by the secular authorities. Consequently, when the Germanic invaders settled in Western Europe, their rulers naturally turned to the bishops for help in governing their realms. The bishops were the only people with the education, experience and administrative organization necessary for many of the things that had to be done. Thus, from Merovingian times onwards, the bishops in Francia occupied a position very similar to that of the counts: they were expected to attend the king's court and to act as his advisers, to take an active part in legislation, both ecclesiastical and temporal, to act as the king's emissaries and to exercise what was called *iudiciaria potestas*, which included the right to command obedience and to raise various taxes. They were also expected, as major landholders, to raise troops for the king and, on occasion, lead them personally in battle.

All this not only limited the amount of time and energy the bishops had for their strictly ecclesiastical work; it largely determined what sort of men would be chosen for the office. If the bishops were to have an important political role, they needed to be the sort of men who understood the workings of the political world and the minds of the other *optimates* with whom they would be working. Accordingly, the bishops of this period were almost uniformly drawn from the landed families.

These families were prepared to go to almost any lengths to keep control of the bishoprics. In 928 the Count of Vermandois persuaded king Raoul to appoint his son to the archbishopric of Reims at the age of twelve; and according to Frodoard, a child of under five years of age was made archbishop there in 925, 'for fear that the bishopric should fall into the hands of those outside the family'.[14] In the tenth century the bishopric of Poitiers had virtually become hereditary in one family.

Men from the lower orders were occasionally made bishops, for example Ebbo, who became Archbishop of Reims in 816 (see p. 145 above), and Gerbert of Aurillac, who, after being Archbishop of Reims and then Ravenna, became Pope Sylvester II in 999. In both cases, however, there were exceptional circumstances, and, even so, their humble origins were held against them both, and caused them grave difficulties at important moments in their careers.

It also followed that if the bishops were to be important officers of state, the king would want to choose them. Although vestiges were allowed to survive of the way bishops had been chosen in earlier times – by a combination of popular acclamation, the votes of the cathedral clergy and the advice of neighbouring bishops – the kings had gained effective control of all episcopal appointments long before our period;[15] and not only did the king choose the bishops: as in the case of the counts, he provided them with the resources needed for their task. In one of its meanings the word *episcopatus* came to stand for the *res ecclesiae*, the property a bishop held in order to be able to perform his duties. When bishops were appointed, the king handed this over to them, under appropriate symbols, and it had become customary for him to invest them with the symbols of *episcopatus* in its religious aspect, the ring and the pastoral staff, at the same time. This was the origin of the investiture controversy which loomed so large in the following centuries.

Although in substance this arrangement continued, it should be added that, as the royal power weakened in Francia in the ninth and tenth centuries, the bishops, with their education, their considerable resources and their effective organization and well-defined aims, gained a growing sense of their corporate power. By about 840 it was becoming customary to anoint a bishop's head at his consecration, and at the same time the bishops were insisting that the gift of the Holy Spirit at consecration gave them superior charismatic qualifications and an unchallengeable right to determine the divine will for the community. It was for the bishops to tell both rulers and people what should and should not be done. Even a morally bad bishop was to be revered and obeyed.[16] Already in 833 the bishops had sought to make clear to all 'how great the strength and power and the office of the bishop is, and what sort of damning punishments await him who is unwilling to obey sacerdotal admonitions';[17] and their part in the deposition of Louis the Pious had implied some sort of claim to make and unmake kings (though see further pp. 220 below). When Charles the Bald became king of Aquitaine in 848, he was the first Frankish ruler to be anointed – and also crowned and handed a sceptre – by the body of bishops, which clearly pointed forward to Hincmar's claim that 'the episcopal dignity is greater than the royal, for bishops consecrate kings, but kings do not consecrate bishops'.[18]

Indeed in Hincmar's time the Frankish bishops under their metropolitans made great claims for themselves, and for independence from royal and also, as we shall see, from papal control.[19] However, this was something of a rearguard action, for in the absence of a strong king, the bishops found that, however great their spiritual powers might be, they did not avail to stop the control of the church from passing to the secular nobility. It was now often dukes and counts, rather than the king, who appointed bishops. The only alternative source of power to which bishops could turn was the papacy, to which, as we shall see, many suffragans had already begun to look for defence against what they regarded as the oppressive behaviour of such overwhelming metropolitans as Hincmar.

The end of the tenth century was thus a period of transition and difference of opinion in regard to episcopacy. There were forces at work that would produce support for an extreme assertion of papal sovereignty such as was to be put forward in the following century. On the other hand, conservative elements which looked back to the traditional law, and viewed with dismay the erosion of episcopal power involved in greater papal sovereignty, still continued to exalt the office of a bishop.

Bishops constantly complained about the weight of extra-ecclesiastical activity laid upon them, but they submitted to it. In practice they had no alternative, yet they could hardly help being aware of all that was expected of them on the pastoral side. In his widely known and immensely influential *Pastoral Rule*, Gregory the Great not only described in uncompromising terms a bishop's pastoral obligations, but insisted on the amount of prayer, self-denial, self-discipline and withdrawal from the world which they demanded. In the eighth century his views were reinforced by Alcuin, for example, who recommended the constant reading of Gregory's work;[20] and in the ninth century Hincmar elaborated the same themes in his *de officiis episcoporum*.[21] Meanwhile royal capitularies insisted that bishops should stay in, and perambulate, their dioceses, ensure that the people knew the Lord's Prayer and the Creed, and that the clergy were equipped to minister to them, and be active in promoting education, building churches and ensuring the payment of tithe.[22]

Little time was available for the personal discharge of these duties, and when bishops did travel round their dioceses, they were bound to be seen as the grandees they were. They were frequently faced with huge numbers of candidates for confirmation, whom they often confirmed without dismounting from their horses, while their officers controlled the crowds.[23] This may seem to us impossibly *de haut en bas*, but we must remember that this was a very hierarchical age which associated lordship with God, and outward show and display with lordship. Those who saw the lord bishop pontificating with splendid vestments and accoutrements will have been put in mind of the grandeur and glory of the Lord God and of the grace he made available through the bishop's sacramental activities.

Yet if the bishop could be a symbol of God's glory and generosity, people must also have seen him as a symbol of God's stern and demanding character. As we have seen, the bishop was responsible for ensuring that tithes and all other church taxes were paid in full, and his visits often had an inquisitorial side. By what Chélini goes so far as to call a 'totalitarian and coercive arrangement',[24] villagers were constrained to reveal the ill-doing of their fellows, and this could be visited with excommunication. Although such matters were usually dealt with in a pastoral spirit, and the aim was to prevent the spread of such contagions as incest, adultery, parricide or fratricide, excommunication was deeply feared. For the parish priest and others involved, visits by the bishop must have meant great expense and great strain; and those who were tenants of a bishop, or directly under his control, will often have found him an extremely exacting master. Of one eleventh-century bishop, for example, we hear that he was 'very exacting about the payment of rents, to such an extent that he often forced his peasantry to pay by violence'. While the bishop's biographer is slightly uneasy about this, he apportions at least part of the blame to the tenants for being 'untrustworthy and cunning'.[25]

The bishops were certainly quite as willing as anyone else to press their legal claims, but this was not always due to greed or self-aggrandisement. A bishop was sometimes known as the 'husband' of his see,[26] and his identification with it will have made him feel an obligation to uphold its interests. In particular he will have felt an obligation to the patron saint(s) of the diocese to preserve, and if possible augment, their patrimony, even by means which might have been held unworthy in another cause.[27]

So far as concerns the parish clergy, their relations with their bishop were largely conducted through archdeacons, rural deans and other diocesan officers. However, all parish priests were required to wait on the bishop at least once each each year, shortly before Easter, to collect the holy oils which he had just blessed. In the case of a pastorally-hearted bishop this will have provided an occasion for advice and encouragement; but the numbers present were large, each priest had to pay the fee required at such visits, and the occasion was sometimes used as an opportunity for enquiring into the educational level of the priests and their general fitness for office. All this must have detracted from the personal character of the occasion, and one suspects that the social gulf between the bishops and most of the parochial clergy was too deep to allow of any very helpful contact. All in all, though a bishop was known as a father in God, he is likely to have appeared to the priests, as he did to other people, as *dominus episcopus*, the lord bishop.

Mediaeval churchmen often showed a remarkable ability to find time for prayer and reflexion in the midst of constant practical activity, as the example of Bernard of Clairvaux makes very clear. This was exemplified by many bishops; thus Bruno, the young archbishop of Cologne, was the brother of the emperor and deeply involved in political affairs, yet he made it a regular practice to reserve the early morning and the period after supper for meditation and study. Not all bishops were of that stamp; some were scoundrels, even by the rough and ready standards of the age. The military man Archambaud, who became Archbishop of Sens in 958 through the machinations of his relative, Count Renaud, made his home in a monastery which he mulcted of its property and turned into a centre of orgies and debauchery; he trafficked in churches and church property, and on the profits kept falcons, dogs and courtesans.[28] On the other hand, his successor, Anastasius, was 'a father to his clerics, the friend of the monks, the consoler of the afflicted and the defender of the poor, the orphans and the widows'.[29] He was succeeded in turn by Saguinus, a conscientious, reforming archbishop, who did a lot to restore the Religious life, and also the discipline of the clergy, in the diocese.[30]

In fact each bishop had his own style, emphasis and way of interpreting his office. Yet the life-style of most tenth-century bishops differed little from that of lay lords; they had their dogs and falcons, they entertained lavishly, they raised troops for the king and sometimes led them in person. Some of them had little Latin and officiated only on the major feasts – and then for congregations made up entirely of members of the ruling class. By no means all of them were models of celibacy.

Ordinary people, so far as they were aware of the bishop's life-style, will not have found it any great incitement to devotion and self-abnegation. Even those who received the bishop's charity will have found it institutional, conveyed through the hands of subordinates. Of direct instruction from the bishop most people will have received little or none. The bishops regarded the instruction of the people as the duty of local priests, and in any case felt it should be of the most elementary kind. Their main influence on the content of it came through the homiliaries which some of them wrote, and which will be discussed later.

There can be no doubt about the great importance of bishops in early mediaeval Francia, or of their considerable, and often decisive, influence on the general course of events. So far as the religious sphere is concerned, their sacramental activities were believed essential to the very existence of the church, as we have seen. On the non-sacramental side, the decisions they arrived at in common made a good deal of practical difference. In Carolingian times they presided, for example, over a major change in the forms of service, condemned various heresies, admitted the *filioque* clause to the Creed, pronounced on the use of images in worship, sanctioned a major tightening of monastic discipline, and in the long controversy over Gottschalk sought to work out the church's position on predestination and free will. If the chaotic situation after the middle of the ninth century made it difficult to discuss major dogmatic issues, local synods still pronounced on matters of discipline, resisting the marriage of the clergy, for example, adjudicating on the degrees of impediment to marriage, and attempting to establish the Peace of God. This, and a lot of similar episcopal activity, served to determine the way the faith was understood and practised, even if the ordinary people were scarcely aware of it as doing so.

What the bishops did individually was also significant. It could make a great deal of difference, for example, how well a bishop chose and trained his clergy and supervised their work, or how vigorous he was in building new churches, or in acting as a peacemaker between the magnates in his diocese.

So the bishops wielded great influence in the church, even if their direct impact on individuals was not very great, and their personal example not a major factor in deepening devotion and self-discipline. It was unfortunate that the purposes for which, and the way in which, they were chosen tended to put holiness of life at something of a discount. Even such vigorous and conscientious bishops as Hincmar seem seldom to have been very kindly or sensitive men; and in general, as Southern says, 'the great weakness of the Carolingian episcopate lay in its alienation from the people'.[31] Many tenth-century bishops are likely to have purveyed an image of the God they represented as a powerful autocrat rather than a father.

(ii) The Papacy

The status of the episcopate in the tenth century was in fact a matter of some confusion and dispute, especially in Francia. This was because it was tied up with the question of the bishops' relation to the pope, and that also was a matter of uncertainty.

The rise of the papacy is too complex a subject to be discussed here. Suffice it to say that it is not really till the seventh century that the history of the papacy, in any full sense of the word, can be said to have begun; and that by then a primacy universally accorded to the Roman church almost from the beginning, had been extended to the Roman bishop as well.

According to the popes, this primacy was based on the words of Jesus in Matt. 16.17–19, interpreted as meaning that Peter was appointed by Christ, and that the powers and authority of the other apostles were conveyed to them through him. Since the popes identified with Peter – to a degree and with a realism difficult for us to comprehend – this meant that the pope alone was God's vicar (*vicarius dei*), from whom all other bishops derived their power and authority. In fact the papacy claimed to be the fountain-head, the *exordium*, from which the whole life and activity of the church flowed out. By the will of Christ, Peter and his successors, or proxies (*vicarii*), were constitutive of the church: no pope, no church, no vehicle of salvation. Pope Hadrian I (772–795), for example, claimed that Rome was the source of all episcopal power; and in the tenth century Abbo of Fleury based the primacy of the popes on the fact that they 'occupy the position (*vices gerere*) of blessed Peter who is the head (*princeps*) of the whole church'.[32]

Such claims were broadly accepted in the West, and it was into the Western church that the Franks were converted. The early Christian Frankish rulers accepted that no people could regard themselves as orthodox Christians unless they were in communion with the pope, in the sense of holding to the beliefs, traditions and discipline current in the church at Rome. With that in mind, Charlemagne asked Pope Hadrian I for a detailed account of what those beliefs, discipline and liturgical practice were, receiving in response a collection of canon law which the Frankish church accepted in 802 and a contemporary Roman mass-book (now known as the *Hadrianum*) which Frankish theologians took over and elaborated.

This acceptance of the Roman primacy was maintained in Francia, even by churchmen such as Hincmar of Reims, who were often critical of the papacy; but the question remained what prerogatives such a primacy conferred. It was generally agreed that councils should not be held, nor their findings taken as binding, without papal approval, and that the pope was to be consulted on disputed questions of faith and morals; and many held that he possessed appellate jurisdiction over religious disputes in all dioceses. By the tenth century, however, papal claims had gone beyond that. It was now claimed that the canons of councils actually owed their force to the papal approval and that the formal decisions of popes had exactly the same validity as the decisions of councils. The popes in fact claimed to hold legislative power in their own right, to have a *principatus*, or monarchic power, in the religious sphere parallel to that of emperors in the secular sphere.[33] From the fifth century the office of pope was increasingly distinguished from the office-holder, and this was soon taken to mean that decisions and actions of popes in their formal capacity were beyond criticism.

In fact what the popes claimed was a universal supremacy, a Petrine monarchy, directly willed by God. In the words of Gregory the Great, the apostolic see was 'the chief of all the churches, whose bishop is responsible for the government of the whole church and has the duty to correct any bishop or patriarch guilty of heresy or any offence against the canons, whether or not the matter has been referred to him by others'. In part this was propaganda against the claims of a possible rival, the Patriarch of

Constantinople, or 'new Rome'.[34] As that suggests, papal claims were by no means universally admitted, and they were not without critics in Francia. Before that is considered, however, we must discuss papal claims in the secular sphere.

Although the decline of imperial power in the West had meant that popes had often had to undertake secular responsibilities of various sorts, they remained for many centuries loyal subjects of the emperor at Constantinople, accepting that he played a part in their appointment, and dating their letters, for example, by the years of his reign. However, Constantinople proved increasingly incapable of providing Rome with effective protection against barbarian invaders, as well as showing signs of what Rome regarded as theological deviation; and eventually the popes decided to break the connexion. They were still in desperate need of protection, however, and as we have seen, in the middle of the eighth century Pope Stephen III[35] journeyed to Francia to throw himself on the mercy of the increasingly powerful Franks. He received a positive response from Pepin III, and from then on, popes could generally reckon on continuing, if unevenly effective and enthusiastic, protection from the Carolingian rulers and later the early Ottonian emperors. They were also guaranteed lands in central and northern Italy to compensate for lands they had lost in the south, and to provide them with a patrimony.

Meaning as it did that as holders of lands within the Frankish domains the popes were vassals of the Frankish rulers, this created a paradoxical, and potentially controversial, situation. For, as we have seen, the spurious document known as the Donation of Constantine made bold secular claims on behalf of the pope. According to it, in addition to his religious primacy, the pope had received secular lordship over the Western world from Constantine I. Though the popes chose not to exercise this secular lordship directly, the fact remained that secular rulers derived their authority from the pope, and that he had a right to a say in their appointment. Such was the claim. It was a new claim which would not have been possible had not circumstances led the popes to withdraw from their long-established relationship with the Eastern emperors in favour of a relationship yet to be defined, with a Frankish régime which itself had not yet established any clearly defined relationship with the political world into which it had broken.

On Christmas Day 800 Pope Leo III crowned Charlemagne as emperor of the Romans in St Peter's. Whatever else may have lain behind this still very variously interpreted event, there must have been a conviction on the pope's part that the making of emperors was his prerogative. If so, it was not a view Charlemagne accepted with much enthusiasm. It suited him to seek, and eventually gain, recognition of the imperial title from Constantinople, but he himself continued for the most part to rely on his position as king of the Franks. While his domains were by this time large enough for them to be plausibly represented as a successor to the old Roman empire in the West, Charlemagne felt that he ruled them by right of inheritance and conquest, and not by papal appointment. In fact, after the Frankish manner, he regarded them as his personal family possession, over which he held spiritual as well as secular authority, like his Germanic forebears, and also like the Old Testament kings whose successor and antitype his religious advisers proclaimed him to be. According to such a typology, the pope would have corresponded to Zadok or one of the other court priests of the Old Testament; and while it is going too far to say, as one scholar has done, that Charlemagne treated the pope as a sort of superior court chaplain, he certainly regarded papal prerogatives as circumscribed. As we have seen, he fully recognized the importance of being in communion with the pope, but he believed his position as spiritual leader entitled him to appoint his own bishops and theological advisers; and he frequently presided over their synods and councils, even when doctrinal matters were under discussion. On occasion these synods declared the pope to be in error and called on him to change his position.[36]

Charlemagne had no hesitation in telling the pope what his duties were and admonishing him to carry them out properly. In a famous letter of 796 he defined his, and the pope's, respective responsibilities thus: 'it is our task ... to defend the holy church of Christ everywhere from the attacks of pagans without, and to strengthen it within through the knowledge of the Catholic faith [note the claim that the promotion of the true faith is the *king's* duty]. It is your duty, O holy Father, with your hands raised high to God, after the manner of Moses [see Exodus 17.11] to aid our armies, so that by your intercession ... the Christian people may always and everywhere be victorious over the enemies of his holy name ...' He goes on to urge the pope 'to adhere everywhere to the canonical laws, and to follow always the statutes of the holy Fathers', advice not calculated to encourage independent papal legislation.[37]

In view of all this it is not surprising to find Charlemagne claiming to be 'lord and father', 'king and priest', 'the governor of the Christians', or to find his counsellors calling him vicar of Christ and ruler (*rector*) of the people of Christ.[38] Alcuin was representative of the Frankish view when he wrote to the king: 'there are three persons most high in this world. There is the apostolic sublimity which customarily governs in the capacity of vicar the see of the Blessed Peter the Apostle ... another is the imperial dignity, the secular power of the second Rome [that is, the Eastern emperor]. The third is the royal dignity in which the ordering of Our Lord Jesus Christ has placed you, the ruler of the Christian people, in power more excellent than the other dignitaries mentioned, more clear in wisdom, more sublime in the dignity of your government. For lo, in you rests the entire safety of the churches of Christ.'[39] Even when we allow for the element of court flattery here, it is noteworthy how Alcuin exalts the royal dignity over the papal and the imperial, and emphasizes its religious character. He adds: 'May the ruler of the church be rightly ruled by you, O king, and may you be ruled by the right hand of the Almighty.'

Charlemagne's pious successor, Louis, seems to have been equally unhappy with the pope's secular pretensions. Although he allowed Stephen IV to officiate at his coronation at Reims, he regarded the papal intervention simply as a religious consecration of rights acquired from other sources, and in 817 he pointedly crowned his son Lothar as co-emperor with his own hands, although he agreed to Lothar's coronation by the pope five years later. However, by the later tenth century, coronation by the popes had come to be accepted as the means by which an emperor entered on his office, though it is not at all clear how far it was taken to be constitutive of the office. It is also true that tenth-century emperors no longer laid emphasis on the spiritual aspect of their function in the way that Charlemagne had done. None the less, in Germany and West Francia rulers and their nobles continued to appoint their own candidates to bishoprics and other ecclesiastical offices, without reference to the pope. The popes were in no position to resist; indeed some of them seem to have approved of the arrangement. John X (914–928), for example, rebuked the Archbishop of Cologne for appointing a bishop of Tongres: 'According to an ancient usage,' he wrote, 'no one but the king can confer a bishopric on a clerk.'[40]

By this time appointment by rulers had extended to the papacy itself. Charlemagne had made no attempt to appoint popes, but emperors had increasingly insisted on at least a veto over papal elections and on the pope's taking an oath of loyalty to them when he took office; and the early Ottonians, as Focillon says, actually 'disposed of the tiara', making and unmaking popes in what they believed to be in the best interests of the church, even though they often had to enter into rather dubious negotiations with the Roman aristocracy in order to do so.

Popes could be forgiven if they preferred this situation to what had preceded it in the previous sixty or seventy years, when the papal elections had been entirely controlled by aristocratic factions at Rome, in particular by the family of the corrupt Theophylact and his scandalous daughter Marozia. They had made popes of corrupt relatives and other immoral characters, entirely from considerations of personal advantage and dynastic connexion. Pope succeeded pope with bewildering rapidity, only to be deposed or murdered in what has been called *the* dark age (*saeculum obscurum*) of the papacy.

Roman Catholic historians in particular have warned against giving too much credence to scandalous stories told at the time, especially by Liutprand,[41] and have pointed out that on the whole the business of the papacy went forward smoothly. A conscientious tenth-century abbot such as Abbo of Fleury could speak of the papacy, if not the pope, as 'shining brightly throughout the entire church'.[42] However, as we shall see, the heads of large monasteries like Abbo had an interest in promoting the papacy, and the undoubted facts are scandalous enough. Popes blinded and mutilated their dignitaries and ran what amounted to a house of ill-fame in the Lateran. Even the pro-papal *Liber Pontificalis* records that simony reached a point where bishoprics were sold to the highest bidder on the open market – on one occasion, apparently, to a child of ten.[43]

The sexual conduct of many of the popes was scandalous, on any showing. John XI, for example, was the illegitimate son of his predecessor and Marozia, while according to the *Liber Pontificalis*, John XII 'spent his whole life in adultery and frivolity' – to which Benedict of Mount Soracte adds that 'women swarmed round him' and that 'his whole body burned with a passion of which the results are impossible to enumerate'.[44] Even if we do not accept the report that he was stricken with a fatal illness while in the arms of his mistress, and refused the last sacrament,[45] the record is dark enough. The situation remained much the same in the early eleventh century. Although it may not be strictly true that Benedict IX (1032–1044) was appointed as a child of ten or twelve,[46] the very fact that such stories were given credence in Francia at the time shows the light in which the papacy was regarded there. Benedict's personal life was certainly scandalously violent and dissolute.[47]

Between 882 and 996 there were no less than thirty-two popes and anti-popes, a number of whom were murdered by their rivals or successors in peculiarly brutal ways. The relevance of all this to our subject will become apparent presently.

The picture which emerges is of a situation in which there was no generally accepted understanding of the secular rights and prerogatives of the pope. The successors of Leo III (795–816) in no way abated the claims he had made, and strong popes such as Nicholas I (858–867) greatly augmented them, holding that while the spheres of church and state were distinct, and princes had no right to interfere in the former, the church did have a right to oversee and influence the state. They protested against what has come to be known as 'the lay domination of the church', that is, the making of ecclesiastical appointments and the holding of ecclesiastical offices and church property by lay people. When circumstances were favourable, they could sometimes give effect to their claims, but for every strong pope there were several others who were either weak by temperament or prevented by circumstances from pressing papal claims.

From the middle of the ninth century both popes and secular rulers were preoccupied for nearly a hundred years with other matters – the rulers with the new wave of barbarian invasions, the popes with the problem of the withdrawal of imperial protection which this entailed. The general situation was altogether too chaotic for serious discussion of papal claims to be carried on, or for the claims adumbrated by Nicholas I to be followed up.

It would be a mistake to think of tenth-century rulers as deliberately infringing what they knew to be the pope's rights, from motives of personal and political aggrandisement. No doubt there was an element of that, and no doubt the popes disliked a lot of what they saw happening; but the emperors had their own views about the pope's status – Otto III, for example, was aware that the Donation of Constantine was a forgery – and for the most part they will have been doing no more than dealing with a difficult problem as best they could, conscious that they were following centuries of custom in acting as they did. On the whole they had the support of their theological advisers.

All this will be the more intelligible if it is recognized that even the popes' claims in the religious sphere had by no means been universally accepted. Many of them were never accepted in the East, where the deliberations of councils were regarded as the proper means for deciding theological questions; at the most, the Eastern patriarchs regarded the pope as some sort of *primus inter pares*.[48] A not dissimilar view had been common in Francia. Matthew 16.17–19 could be interpreted in other ways than that adopted by the popes. Apart from the suggestion – almost universally accepted, according to Jonas of Orléans[49] – that the word 'rock' in v. 18 refers to Peter's faith rather than his person, the passage was often interpreted in the light of Matt. 18.18 and John 20.22–23 as implying that although, as a matter of historical fact, the divine commission was given first to Peter, the commission received by the other apostles was identical with his; and that it was on the whole body of bishops, as the successors of the apostles, that the church rested.

On this view, issues of faith and morals were to be settled by the bishops meeting in general or provincial councils, and the primacy of the pope, so far as it went beyond ceremonial precedence, consisted in the fact that Rome was the depository of conciliar decisions and the pope the authoritative interpreter of them. Any decisions he issued must be in conformity with such conciliar pronouncements, and normally no more than extrapolations from them, or applications of them to particular situations. He certainly had no right to sit in judgment on them. He had only the most limited right to legislate independently and no authority to intervene in the diocesan affairs of his fellow bishops. Bishops were answerable to their metropolitans, and according to some the pope had not even the right to receive appeals from the judgments of provincial synods. What was involved here was a clash between the old canon law, traditionally followed in Francia, and the new canonical position put forward in such documents as the Donation of Constantine and the rest of the False Decretals, which gave the pope far wider powers than he had traditionally enjoyed.

Right from the beginning, the Frankish bishops had shown a certain independence of the pope. As we have seen, they openly declared the pope to be in error at the Synod of Frankfurt in 794; and at an assembly in Paris in 825 they expressed themselves even more strongly, accusing the pope of 'opposing the truth' and of having come within an ace of 'toppling over into superstition'.[50] In 833 they threatened to depose Gregory IV, writing to him simply as a brother bishop, and urging him to subject himself to the emperor, 'to whom the whole *sacerdotium* is subject'.[51] At about the same time Jonas of Orléans and others were writing that popes could be excommunicated if they went beyond the ancient customs; and later in the ninth century Charles the Bald addressed a severely critical letter to Pope Hadrian II in which he reminded him of the fate of Pope Vigilius who had been condemned for heresy in the sixth century.[52] A similar line was taken by leading Frankish churchmen such as Hincmar of Reims, the undoubted leader of the Frankish church in the second half of the century, who consistently opposed what he saw as the new papal pretensions, resisting any claim to infallibility, and standing for the rights of metropolitans against attempts by the popes to usurp their authority. On the other hand, some bishops and lower clergy who felt that their privileges were being infringed by metropolitans such as Hincmar saw a possible source of redress in papal power, and initially welcomed the extension of it. So did the larger monasteries, which received *privilegia* from Rome exempting them from their traditional subjection to the jurisdiction of the local bishop, and from all lay domination. However, as it was borne in on the bishops that any major extension of papal power could only be at the expense of their independence, many of them became alarmed; and when in 1007 a papal legate consecrated the new abbey at Loches, contrary to the wishes of the local bishop, they cried sacrilege, accusing the pope of transgressing the ancient canons, which made clear that no bishop could exercise power in the diocese of another without his permission. They called the pope's action 'insolent', and insisted that 'all orthodox bishops are in some sense the spouses of their sees and represent Christ equally'. Lemarignier comments: 'To the thesis of effective papal primacy, they opposed, without qualification, a thesis of episcopal equality, granting the Pope only a precedence of honour. The quarrel over the structure of monasticism was calling into question the entire organization of the church.'[53] The Councils of Anse (1025) and Seligenstadt (1023)[54] took much the same line, and in 1008 the Bishop of Orléans and the Archbishop of Sens claimed the right to make the powerful Abbot of Fleury burn papal bulls which claimed to exempt the abbey from their jurisdiction. The learned and moderate Fulbert of Chartres confessed that he could find 'no shadow of reason' for the papal claim to exempt the monastery.[55]

Such doubts about papal claims were bound to be fuelled by the scandalous character and behaviour of most contemporary popes, and a series of events just before the end of our period shows that they were. When the condemnation of Arnulf, the Archbishop of Reims, for treason against his sovereign, Hugh Capet, was referred to the pope for confirmation, no reply was received, possibly as a result of bribery. A council was therefore held in the monastery of St Basle at Quierzy in 991 to depose Arnulf and appoint Gerbert of Aurillac in his place. When Abbo of Fleury and other abbots refused to agree, because of lack of papal approval, another Arnulf, this one the bishop of Orléans, made a long speech, probably composed by Gerbert, of which a full and apparently accurate version has been preserved.[56] It is a remarkable utterance. Not content just to deal with the immediate crisis, Arnulf raised the question of the pope's right to judge. He argued that where the facts were undisputed and the issues clearly covered by law, a synod could judge a bishop without recourse to Rome. Since the pope was bound by the law, he could not but uphold the council's action; otherwise no one need obey him, for judgment is not just a matter of power: it presupposes the appropriate moral and intellectual qualities. These, he said, were just what was lacking in contemporary Rome ('it is notorious that there is no one at Rome with enough knowledge of letters to qualify as a doorkeeper'), and he went on to describe the gross venality of the papacy and to chronicle a number of scandals and crimes of the kind described above. 'It cannot be to monsters like these, utterly dishonourable, devoid of any knowledge either of things divine or things human, that countless priests of God throughout the world, conspicuous for their knowledge and virtuous life, should be legally subjected ... Let us therefore be as patient as we can with the sovereign pontiffs, and meanwhile seek the nourishment of the divine word wherever it can be found, for example in Belgium and Germany. If anyone claims, with Gelasius [pope from 492 to 496], that the Roman church is judge of every church and that it is not itself subject to anyone's judgment, let him establish in Rome a man whose judgments need no correction.' Arnulf does not hesitate to use such expressions as 'Antichrist', 'man of sin' and 'the mystery of iniquity'; and, after referring to the African church, which, he claims, had never known Roman jurisdiction over its bishops, he adds: 'She [Rome] has already lost the allegiance of the East; Alexandria, Antioch, Africa and Asia are separate from her; Constantinople has broken loose from her; the interior of Spain knows nothing of the pope's judgments.'[57]

These may seem surprising sentiments, but Gerbert said very much the same in some of his letters[58] and in his speech at the Council of Chelles in 993.[59] At this council, held in response to the pope's protest, the bishops stuck to their line, declaring that papal decrees which contradicted the decrees of the Fathers were null and void, and that any pope who issued them would run the risk of being treated in accordance with Titus 3.10, *haereticum hominem et ab ecclesia dissentientem penitus evita.*[60]

We must allow for an element of rhetoric in all this, and remember that the abbots present at St Basle, and the president of the council, the Archbishop of Sens, disapproved of the line taken; also that at the German Synod of Moozon in 995 the pope succeeded in having the decision overturned: for various reasons Hugh Capet now found it politic to fall into line, and Arnulf was reinstated at Reims. By a strange twist of fortune, Gerbert found himself pope (Sylvester II) four years later!

Nevertheless, taken with the other evidence we have quoted, the proceedings at these two councils show that, in Francia at any rate, there was at this time no agreed understanding of the papacy and its relation to the rest of the episcopate. Most of the Frankish bishops, while unhesitatingly conceding primacy, and a measure of judicial sovereignty, to the pope, took a minimalist view of that primacy. For them it was the college of bishops as a whole on whom the church rested, and the pope, for all his pre-eminence, was one among them.

The niceties of the pope's status, important though the matter was, must have been a subject in which only a very small minority of tenth-century Christians – emperors, bishops and theologians – were concerned or interested. To the great majority of lay people and, one imagines, most priests as well the pope was simply, as Rosalind and Christopher Brooke put it, 'a remote, prestigious, charismatic figure presiding over the immense treasury of Roman relics, Peter's successor sitting on Peter's tomb'.[61] Poor communications meant that it was often possible for reformers to appeal to the standards of Christian conduct advocated in collections of canons and the letters of popes without any very accurate knowledge of the real situation in the Roman church of their day.

For us it is important not to be misled by hindsight. Relatively speaking, the question of the papacy was still a new one in the tenth century. Those who opposed the new papal claims had no sense of fighting a rearguard action or swimming against the tide of history. For them the verdict of history on the matter was still an open one.

(iii) Priests

The great majority of priests in West Francia in the tenth century were parish priests serving some four thousand parishes, of which the boundaries had been drawn in such a way that everyone in the kingdom belonged to some parish and was reasonably close to a church.[62] Those in a parish had to attend their parish church and no other. Priests were forbidden to minister to those from other parishes, apart from *bona fide* travellers and pilgrims.

In the light of what was said above about the clerical caste, we should expect the clergy, or at least the priests and deacons, to have been set apart from the rest of the community, and many official enactments of the period presuppose that it was so. The clergy were to be revered for their learning, chastity and general holiness of life; in addition to their sacramental functions, they were to spend their time instructing, visiting and encouraging their parishioners, hearing their confessions and ensuring the presence in every parish of at least one life which instantiated contemporary Christian ideals. They were to devote themselves to reading, prayer and spiritual concerns, to expounding the biblical readings for the season and inculcating the Christian way of life, ensuring that their people knew by heart the Creed and the Lord's Prayer, caring for the poor and sick and providing schooling for the children of the parish. They were to live chastely, with no women, or none but very close relatives, living in their houses.[63]

In particular, great emphasis was laid on preaching. As we have seen, the Carolingian rulers made a determined bid to turn their people's nominal Christianity into a fully absorbed and living faith. To this end they relied heavily on regular preaching, and scholars such as Walter Ullmann and Rosamond McKitterick have argued that it proved a quite effective instrument for the purpose.[64]

Enough sermon material from the period has been preserved to give us some idea what contemporary preaching was like.

Only *some* idea, because the evidence is difficult to assess. Many of the sermons we possess are in Latin, the work of learned men and intended for those with some pretensions to learning. Important in this connexion are works called *homiliaries*, collections of sermons and addresses by learned bishops and others.[65] Some of these consist of discourses meant for individual reading and reflexion by monks and other educated readers; they are full of patristic quotations and complicated allegorizations such as no peasant audience could have understood. Others appear to contain sermons preached to popular audiences, or intended for translation into the vernacular and adaptation to popular needs. In the nature of the case, it is impossible to know exactly what a sermon as actually delivered to a rustic congregation will have been like. A large number of homilies by Aelfric of Eynsham (*c*.955–*c*.1020) have been preserved in the Anglo-Saxon vernacular; they expressly say that they were intended for lay, and comparatively uneducated, people; but most of them at any rate seem too long and complicated to have been preached to simple congregations, especially as we have evidence that short sermons were all that people would tolerate.[66]

By the late tenth century a preacher could presuppose in most of his hearers familiarity with the basic items of the Christian faith, such as those included in the Creed. It was the duty of parents and godparents to pass these on to the children;[67] and most people seem to have known about the trinitarian nature of the Godhead (at any rate in very general terms), about the Fall and its results, and about the incarnation of God the Son in the person of Jesus, his death as a sacrifice for sin, his resurrection and ascension. They were also aware of the end of the world and the Last Judgment as a not too distant prospect, and of the eternity of either heaven or hell which awaited them thereafter.[68] What the preacher tried to do was to fill out this faith and give it greater existential relevance. Sermons usually started from some biblical passage, often one of the readings for the day, or from the Life of some saint whose feast was being celebrated. Preachers sometimes repeated the stories in simple and vivid language, and then allegorized them, most often along tropological lines (see p. 36 above).

If, for example, the text reported the Jews' attempt to stone Jesus,[69] the application might be that Christians must at all costs avoid 'stoning' him by their evil thoughts and deeds.[70] Or if the reading was about the coming of the Magi with their gifts, the preacher might emphasize the long and dangerous journey they willingly endured in order to visit and adore Christ, and suggest that his hearers should show a like enthusiasm and urgency about coming to worship Christ in church, and should offer as their equivalent to the Magi's gold, frankincense and myrrh, 'hope, charity, patience, humility and chastity', gifts equally acceptable to him.[71]

Such applications were seldom original; they were drawn from a common homiletic stock which went back eventually to the Fathers. Something was usually said, *en passant*, about the theological significance of the events narrated; and since all the key events were treated in the course of the liturgical year, the hope was that the whole Christian story would be expounded, at least summarily.[72]

Whatever the subject, the content of sermons always remained strictly within the bounds not only of traditional orthodoxy but of current assumptions and social practice.[73] When, for example, the preacher was speaking of Simeon bearing the infant Jesus in his arms (Luke 2.28), he was at pains to make clear that this Jesus was at the same time impassible Godhead. 'Simeon bore in his arms him who preserves and rules over all things. Little he there appeared, yet was he, nevertheless, very great and infinite.'[74] As for current assumptions, the preacher always presupposed, for example, the accepted divisions of society, assuming that Christianity would mean one thing for rulers, another for the rich – who were comforted by the Vulgate version of Luke 11.41: it was only their 'overplus' (*quod superest*) they had to give in alms[75] – another for the 'middling sort', and yet another for the poor, who were to 'be patient in their indigence and ever to rejoice'. There is scarcely ever a hint of Christianity as providing any serious critique of existing structures, even in the case of serfs, who are to 'serve with all their heart', and expect no easing of their condition, except for the fact that 'every servitude will be ended with this life'.[76]

By way of a sanction, there was an undercurrent of reference to the hearers' latter end, and they were reminded of the appalling consequences of condemnation thereafter.[77] While there was not infrequently reference to the power of Christ and the Holy Spirit as 'casting down vices in us and rearing up virtues', in general the tone was decidedly Pelagian. For example, in closing words which carried all the force of a peroration, Aelfric urged: 'Men most beloved, consider this discourse and with great care eschew unrighteousness; merit with good works the eternal life with God' (I, 28). Love of God and friendship with him were defined in terms of 'fulfilling his behest', and the impression generally given was of Christianity as hard, lifelong struggle to win a favourable verdict from God by good works and strict conformity with all the rules of the church – for example, paying one's tithes promptly, and abstaining from work and from sexual contact at the times prescribed.

Sermons were supposed to be preached once a fortnight, or even once a week, but this was a rule honoured more in the breach than in the observance, even in cathedrals, and it would probably be a mistake to exaggerate the influence of sermons where the mass of people were concerned. Even official pronouncements were compelled to recognize that many priests were in no position to preach at all; and even those who could, had little theological grasp and must have been 'only one step ahead of the class'. Their sermons can have consisted of little more than elementary moral teaching. Their ability even to translate the liturgical readings will often have been very limited.[78]

To enable parish priests to carry out their duties, every parish had to be provided at its foundation with a *sponsalitium*, or *dotalitium*, consisting of a house, at least a specified minimum of land, and the servants necessary to manage and work them, as well in many cases as a deacon and/or parish clerk. In addition, priests were entitled to one tenth of the gross income of every parishioner (*tithe*), and to other dues and offerings. With this provision went certain secular responsibilities: for example, that of disciplining murderers, thieves, highwaymen and those who committed adultery, if necessary by means of excommunication.

The majority of parishes were small and isolated,[79] and to prevent complete isolation of priests from their colleagues and the church authorities, rural deans regularly gathered the members of their deaneries for what were called 'calendar chapters', to discuss matters of common concern. At these gatherings, each priest would report on the condition of his church and its appurtenance, on the moral condition of his parishioners and on any gross or incorrigible sinners there might be among them. Also, as we have seen, all priests had to wait on the bishop for a more prolonged gathering at least once a year.[80] and a parish could expect an episcopal visitation from time to time.

The canons prescribed outward signs of respect to be shown to the clergy, and a writer such as Dhuoda evinces the sort of reverence for them that accords with that.[81] She advises her son: 'With your whole soul fear God and honour his priests; love them, revere them; they are indispensable to our well-being in countless ways.' However, Dhuoda, as a member of the ruling class, might be expected to reflect the official view of the matter, and the priests she met were no doubt of a higher quality than most. The reality was in most cases somewhat different. There were certainly many educated and highly competent clergy in monasteries, at court and in the cathedrals and bishops' entourages; but most parish churches had been built by local lords in the vicinity of their halls to serve their families and the people working on their estates.[82] Parishes were usually very small, and, despite the opposition of the bishops, the founder tended to regard the church on his land as his property, to be served by one of his servants for whom he demanded ordination; by this time bishops found such demands difficult to reject.[83] Claiming the right to appoint (*commendare*), and not wanting rivalry or insubordination from the priest, the lord normally chose one of his own workers (often a serf) to be trained, and then ordained, to serve in his church; once appointed, a priest was required to stay permanently in the same parish.

What is more, by the tenth century the lords had appropriated to their own use a great deal of the *dotalitium* and other resources in many parishes, including the tithes; and the amount the priests were allowed to retain was so small that they were obliged to undertake secular work of various kinds in order to get a living, the more so because the bishops were allowed to make some claims on parish resources, and often claimed more than their due. Some of the work priests were reduced to doing was very demeaning,[84] and the lord, to whom they had to do homage on appointment, expected them to provide him food and other services just like the rest of his dependants.[85] For example, they might be expected to wait at table or to lead the dogs for the hunt, and, if disobedient, they risked corporal punishment, if not dismissal.[86]

This meant that it was in effect impossible for anyone of noble birth or real education to serve as a parish priest, and the parishes were therefore served quite largely by serfs, or ex-serfs, with an absolute minimum of education, and none of the qualifications which would have enabled them to give a real lead.

Lords often press-ganged serfs into ordination, whether they wished for it or not; and even a man who willingly accepted ordination was more likely to be motivated by a desire of bettering himself than by anything that would be recognized to-day as a 'vocation'. Whatever their attitude, the education these ordinands received was of the meagrest, and even so, few of them had the background to absorb it. The majority of priests were quite woefully ignorant, unable, in some cases, to understand even the Latin they repeated in the mass. There is ample evidence that some of them could not even construe the canon, the central prayer of the service, which is barely long enough to take up more than a page and a half of the present book.[87]

Those of them who were serfs, or ex-serfs, naturally shared the culture, or lack of culture, of the circles from which they came,[88] being as credulous as their fellow peasants and as susceptible to the religious eclecticism described above.[89]

Strong efforts had been made to differentiate the clergy and to raise their status in the eyes of the people, and in the ninth century an attempt was made to apply something approaching a monastic type of discipline to them,[90] an attempt supported by the powerful authorities at Cluny in the tenth century. They were supposed, for example, to wear distinctive clothing, but this, like much else in the reforms, was ignored by many,[91] and some neglected even the tonsure. The evidence is clear that many priests frequented taverns[92] and indulged in hunting, falconry and similar lay pursuits. It must be borne in mind that parishioners would have known their priest as one of themselves since his childhood, and that his relatives would still be working alongside them. Familiarity tended to breed contempt, and many parishioners were certainly resentful at having to give tithes and other offerings to one who was essentially one of their number, despite the fact that officially they were 'subject' (*subiecti*) to him as their superior. The tithe may have been less unpopular at this time than it became later, but there is little doubt that it was unpopular; things would no doubt have been different if a larger proportion had been known to go to the poor, who were registered in each parish and whose relief was ultimately the responsibility of the priest. However, people seem to have been very attached to their church, which was in fact *the* public building of the village, in and around which all sorts of activities, sacred and profane, took place.

It did not help that many priests, in their poverty, broke the rules and charged for their services,[93] or that they exercised some judicial and disciplinary functions, and were known to report to their ecclesiastical superiors on their people's conduct. They seem to have done little or no pastoral visiting.[94] Socially, parish priests were, as David Knowles said, 'absolute nobodies', and this cannot have assisted their work in such a highly hierarchical society, where people were judged according to their property and independence.[95]

Such feelings on the part of the laity were reinforced by the fact that the great majority of priests had wives or, more commonly, concubines. Having no special vocation to the priesthood, or particular aptitude for celibacy, most priests felt quite unable to embrace continence, despite the fact that centuries of church pronouncements had enjoined it upon them, and that the demand for it was constantly repeated by synods, councils and theological writers. The arguments for and against clerical celibacy were often brought out into the open, and I Cor. 7.9 was quoted in favour of clerical marriage, until Gregory VII (*c.*1021–1085) finally forbade any further study of the matter. Whatever the clergy might feel, lay people seem increasingly to have disapproved of clergy who were not celibate, though in all probability this sprang not so much from moral disapproval of their failure to live up to the standards expected of them as from fear that the holy power conveyed through the sacraments might be impaired by the impurity of the officiating priest. There was a tabu element here. Congregations frequently refused to attend the masses or accept the sacramental ministrations of non-celibate priests, an attitude frowned on by the authorities, who insisted that the unworthiness of the minister did not hinder the effect of the sacrament.[96] Burchard's *Corrector* prescribes penalties for such refusal to accept the ministrations of non-celibate priests, and certainly it was an attitude which would effectively have deprived most parishes of the sacraments; for the proportion of celibate priests was comparatively small and would have been nowhere near sufficient. For most of the Middle Ages clerical celibacy remained an aspiration rather than a reality.

In many cases it will have been through the confessional, rather than through teaching or example, that parish priests exercised their main influence on the moral character of their parishioners; and although many of them no doubt followed the penitentials fairly slavishly, their influence as confessors was, as we have seen, a considerable force for good, unconsciously inculcating, as it did, the duty of self-examination and of avoiding the aggressive and self-assertive habits which had hitherto come naturally to a still half-barbarous population.

The religious consequences of such a situation were considerable. Members of the ruling class would not have been prepared to accept any radical criticism of their code of behaviour or ways of life from priests such as these, even had the priests dared, or been competent, to offer it. Any of a nobleman's family who wanted deeper religious insight will have had to look elsewhere. As for the ordinary people, it was undoubtedly as a provider of sacraments, what Vauchez calls 'un spécialiste du sacré', that the priest made his chief impact on them. Vauchez describes the priest as 'a man of prayer and sacrifice rather than of preaching or witness' (*'homme de la prière et du sacrifice, plus que de la prédication ou du témoignage'*) and makes the interesting suggestion that this was connected with the assimilation of the Franks to the 'people of God' of the Old Testament.[97] The idea of priesthood, he suggests, was strongly influenced by the Mosaic model of cultic service. The sacramental side of the priest's activity will have been given added prominence by the increasing emphasis being placed on the 'miracle' of the mass, and the spread of vicarious penance with its corollary, a greatly increased demand for masses. So far as teaching went, the most that people will have got from it will have been the bare bones, at best, of the central theological tradition, and a sense that the Lord of lords was just and righteous, but an exacting taskmaster, as might be expected of one so powerful, whose will had to be faithfully carried out as the essential prerequisite for enjoying his favour, in the next life, if not in this. The priests, for the most part, will have had neither the training nor the imaginative creativity to present the faith in any novel or exciting perspective.[98]

Few priests provided a shining personal example to their people, and yet, as Fichtenau says, 'men of that age were dependent upon personal example, the place of which could not be taken by books'.[99] He goes on to suggest that 'perhaps the enormous appeal which the worship of relics made to the people in this time of crisis was due, in part, to the fact that in an age devoid of saints, people desired the bodily presence of the saints of earlier ages'. If so, it is a rather sad comment, especially in view of the fact that, as we have seen, many of the saints of earlier ages failed to provide either an imitable or an altogether edifying model for ordinary people.

(iv)   The Religious [100]

The Religious need to be considered quite separately from the clergy, because, as was clearly recognized in the tenth century, their aims and way of life were very different. Originally, only a small minority of Benedictine monks were in orders, and even in the tenth century quite a number were not. Women Religious shared the aims and way of life of their male counterparts, but were never in even minor orders.

Christian asceticism has taken many forms and been inspired by many motives in the course of the church's history. It may perhaps be said to have emerged first in the third and fourth centuries, when a large number of believers retired into desert areas round the Mediterranean basin, because they felt they could attend fully to the things of God, and achieve salvation, only if they cut all ties with civilization, resisted the demands of the sexual impulse and subsisted on the minimum amount of food and drink compatible with survival.

Such a denial of all worldly contact seemed to them to be the only way of concentrating the mind on God and showing him the devotion he deserved. Only those who shut themselves off from all other enjoyments could give themselves wholly to the enjoyment of communion with God. As far as possible, everything that could give occasion to sin or interrupt contemplation was to be avoided.

Astonishing feats of self-abnegation were achieved, and reported to an admiring Christian public by Athanasius and others; yet experience fairly soon showed that such heroic forms of self-denial were only for the few (who even so, sometimes exhibited alarming signs both of pride and of fantasy and hallucination), and that most aspiring ascetics would be well advised to live a communal life, in which the support and example of companions would help them to avoid sinning, and a superior would do the same by counsel, discipline and enforcing a rule.

Ascetic communities of many sorts grew up in both East and West, guided by different leaders on different principles; but experience was husbanded and, on the basis of it, Benedict of Nursia in the sixth century drew up what he called 'a little rule for beginners' (seventy large pages in modern print), which has formed the basis of monastic life in the West ever since.[101]

Benedict was, for his time, a kindly man, a man of moderation and common sense, and in his Rule he made reasonable provision for the needs of the natural man. Nevertheless he demanded of a monk complete abstinence from sex, total renunciation of property (even the clothes a monk wore and the books he read belonged to the monastery) and, in particular, obedience. It was to be obedience to the spiritual guidance of the Bible, obedience to the Rule and above all implicit, immediate and ungrudging obedience to the abbot 'who is believed to hold the place of Christ in the monastery'.[102] Benedict also insisted on stability (*stabilitas loci*); once a monk had been accepted into a monastic community, he was to stay in it for the rest of his life, fighting the forces of evil from inside the enclosure, as if he were under siege.[103] Benedict was not concerned to develop the individualities of his monks; his aim was rather to habituate all alike to a particular pattern of existence and conduct taken to be pleasing to God, through an unceasing round of recurrent duties, ceremonies and prayers. The overall aim was, quite unashamedly, to enable them to save their souls in a violent and vicious world, where it seemed almost impossible to save one's soul outside the cloister.

The author of the Rule seems to have been a layman and to have envisaged monks who would be laymen for the most part – and not necessarily scholarly or sophisticated laymen at that. He had no intention of founding an order. Each community, as he conceived things, would be a small independent unit (of say, fifteen members) under its own elected abbot, living under such a version of the Rule as suited its particular location and circumstances.

By the eighth century, cenobitic (from the Greek *koinos* and *bios*, life together) groups, living under various rules, were scattered all over Francia; and in this matter, as in so many others, Charlemagne decisively influenced the course of events. He himself founded a number of important communities and he took steps to ensure that all the communities in his realm, both for men and women, conformed to the Rule of Benedict, of which he sent to Monte Cassino for what he believed to be the original text. In the ninth century Louis the Pious, in conjunction with the monastic reformer Benedict of Aniane, tightened the policy further, at the same time elaborating the Rule, so that it controlled the common life in much greater detail. (He also took steps in the direction of imposing it on cathedral clergy and other semi-monastic groups of clergy, known as canons. In certain respects he sought to impose it on the secular clergy as well, see p. 279 n. 90.)

This reform proved less effective than its author hoped because of the chaos and the breakdown of central authority in the ensuing period (see pp. 10ff.). As we have seen, the Vikings often pillaged and burned monasteries, destroying their books and treasures and forcing the monks to flee. In the confusion many monks left their communities to wander off in search of food and livelihood. Some monasteries erected fortifications and gave refuge to the local people, while a greater number threw themselves on the protection of some powerful local lord. In return for such protection a lord often sought some control, and even ownership, of the monastery; and this accelerated a process of secular control of monasteries which had already begun. Just as a rich man who built a parish church tended to regard it as his own (*Eigenkirche*) and expected to exercise control of it, so one who founded a monastery often regarded it as his own (*Eigenkloster*), and either put in abbots of his choice or acted as abbot himself. Many abbeys came under the control of lay abbots[104] (sometimes having a religious abbot as well); and although some lay abbots managed an abbey's affairs conscientiously, in the interests of the inmates, many applied monastic property to their own uses, as even Charlemagne and his predecessors had sometimes done. The founding and funding of monasteries became increasingly common, so that a great deal of property came to rest in their hands and in many cases they became very large landowners. In a period when resources were stretched to the limit, and the supply of booty had largely dried up, it was inevitable that monastic property should often be used for secular purposes. So much capital could not be allowed to remain in what was, from a military and political perspective, idleness. As a consequence, the century or so after about 850 CE was one of grievous loss and degradation for many religious houses, and for almost all, one of secular control of their personnel and resources.[105] Nevertheless reform was in the air, but before that is discussed, we must notice a vital shift which had taken place in monasticism during the Carolingian period.

As we have seen, Benedictine monasticism had originally been designed for individuals who sought their own salvation through total renunciation of the world; and *ex hypothesi* monasteries had wherever possible avoided, and indeed spurned, contact with things secular. Charlemagne, with his vision of a reformed society, saw things differently, envisaging the Religious as having a part to play in his reforming plans. He looked to abbots to assist in the work of government, in the same sort of way as bishops; he looked to monks to take part in his programme for education, and to produce the books his educational and liturgical programmes required. He expected monasteries to play a part in the care of the poor and sick, and to provide quotas of troops for his armies in proportion to the size of their properties. Above all, he saw the Religious as a spiritual *militia*, who would fight the spiritual enemies of society as the secular nobles fought the earthly enemies, and who would win God's favour and support for the kingdom by their merits and prayers. It was in line with this that the reform of Benedict of Aniane greatly increased the amount of prayer, both corporate and individual, the Religious were expected to undertake.

The tenth century saw a number of initiatives in the direction of monastic reform, apparently undertaken independently, along these lines. The most important of these arose from the founding, in 909, of a new monastery at Cluny in Burgundy – a district, it will be noted, relatively untouched by the incursions of Vikings or Hungarians.[106] Significantly, although Cluny was founded by a single nobleman, Duke William the Pious of Aquitaine, who might have been expected to see it as an *Eigenkloster*, he in fact vested the proprietorship of it in the apostles Peter and Paul, and placed the monastery under the immediate protection of the apostolic see, thus freeing it from intrusion by any secular power.[107] As a result, the monks were guaranteed the right to elect their own abbot without outside interference. Under a succession of outstanding abbots, Cluny became large and exceedingly influential, shaping the character of monastic observance even in monasteries such as Fleury, which did not join the Cluniac family.[108]

The upshot was an increasing number of monasteries, in Francia and elsewhere, dedicated to a return to the strict Benedictine observance, but it was now Benedictine observance as understood in the light of the Carolingian reforms. Detachment from the world was still a central concern, but now the monks also saw themselves as having duties to the society around them – especially, at Cluny, the duty to glorify God on their own behalf and that of their fellow countrymen, through elaborate buildings, church decoration and ritual observance. They also saw themselves as obliged to promote the well-being of the Frankish realm, and of certain individuals within it, by frequent masses and unceasing prayer.[109]

Other differences from the original Benedictine programme were that the tenth-century monks and nuns came exclusively from the upper classes, and that the majority of them, in fact the very great majority, had entered the cloister very young as child-oblates.

Serfs were not free to leave the land. In theory the Religious were drawn from all the free classes, but in our period there was a very strong aristocratic element. The resources of even the highest families were limited, and the cloister provided for sons, and especially daughters, for whom no adequate endowment could be found, a home where they could expect aristocratic companionship and a reasonably aristocratic way of life. Such offerings of children also earned merit with God. Religious houses made no excuse for such limited membership; indeed they gloried in it. For example, the monks of Reichenau wrote to the pope in 1029: 'In the monastery there always have been, and are now, only monks of illustrious and noble birth ... from its foundation there have been none but the sons of counts and barons.'[110] The grounds advanced for such discrimination are clear from a chronicler's report that a queen who founded a nunnery justified the exclusion of all low-born women on the grounds that 'those who are well-born are highly unlikely to become degenerate'.[111]

As for child-oblates, they were envisaged in the original Rule (§59), though Benedict did not envisage communities very largely made up of members who had joined in this way. The tenth century was not sentimental about children, and it saw no more difficulty in undertaking lifelong monastic vows on behalf of a child than it did in confessing the Christian faith on its behalf at baptism; in fact entering the monastic life was seen as a new baptism.[112] As children entered early upon training for the military life, no difficulty was felt about their joining the monastic *militia* in the same way, especially as the *opus dei* was seen as work of a very practical kind, and 'a personal vocation was no more necessary for this work than for any other'.[113]

Inevitably, all this meant that many Religious had no particular *attrait* to the monastic life, which had thus become, as David Knowles put it, a profession rather than a vocation.[114] In the case of most Religious it therefore makes no sense to ask what had attracted them to the cloister; where the relatively small number of late vocations[115] were concerned, motives varied. Some, no doubt, were moved by the traditional Benedictine concern for the salvation of their own souls, or by fear of hell;[116] others were accused of hiding away in fear; while yet others saw in the cloister the only chance for study, reflection and deep communion with God.[117] For those who could accept the basic renunciation required, conditions in the cloister were not altogether unattractive. In accordance with Benedict's directions, the food, though normally including no meat, was reasonably plentiful, and wine was supplied; certainly these aristocratic Religious were far better fed than serfs. The surroundings were often beautiful, and as comfortable as those outside, and there was freedom from hard manual work and from the anxieties involved in making one's way in a violent and insecure world.[118] A noble 'convert' could rely on having the company of his or her own sort, and Religious who worked their way to the top of the hierarchy could expect interesting responsibilities and spheres of activity.

In order to get the feel of monastic life it is necessary to know something of the *horarium*, the timetable by which the life of the cloister was closely controlled. The original Rule had divided the monk's day, in roughly equal proportions, between corporate prayer, manual work and reading or private prayer. By the tenth century, as we have seen, manual work had been reduced to little more than some household chores. According to the Cluniac *horarium* at least half a monk's waking hours, and sometimes a good deal more, were devoted to services of worship.[119] The original Rule prescribed the liturgical obligations of the monks in great detail. It imposed what it called the *opus dei* (work of God), a daily round of seven services ('offices' or 'hours'), based on certain biblical texts,[120] beginning an hour or two after midnight and occupying in all some three and a half or four hours. In the course of time this 'office' (duty), as it was called, was greatly expanded. The services were sung to increasingly elaborate chants, which involved a great deal of repetition; and the heightened concern for the dead[121] meant that masses and prayers with their intention took up a great deal of time. At Cluny there were two elaborate and lengthy communal masses each day, in addition to the one or more which each priest would say for specific people and causes;[122] and on some days the entire psalter (150 Psalms) was chanted in the course of the offices. In addition, the monks met daily in chapter, for business and disciplinary purposes. It is not clear whether all the monks were involved in all these activities, but if we take account of the time that must have been spent in preparing for services,[123] it will be clear that corporate worship was by far the largest charge on a monk's time and energy.

By the tenth century monastic properties had become so extensive (though they were less scattered than they later became) that in large monasteries, at any rate, the administrative work connected with them and the activities undertaken for the king and others are calculated to have occupied a great deal of the time of some half of the monks. Of the others, some will have had to take part in teaching the novices, others will have been involved in the arrangement of the services or in the care of the poor and sick, while others had to copy and illuminate service books and other texts. These and similar activities will have taken up so much time that relatively little will have been left for study and private prayer or reflection. It is difficult to estimate how much those with a will to it would have been able to achieve in that direction, but Cluny never had any great reputation for scholarship. A scholarly monk like Anselm, for example, believed the Cluniac life would have left him insufficient time for his studies, though, as that implies, some monasteries, such as his, gave more opportunity for scholarly work.[124]

By the tenth century Frankish monasteries, many of which had grown large by Benedict's standard,[125] had come to be seen as great power-houses promoting the general welfare through ceaseless sacramental and intercessory as well as practical activity.

It is difficult to judge what it must have been like to be a member of such a community. What would have been the effect of such ceaseless immersion in corporate and private prayer, and such exclusive concern with the religious side of life?[126] How far will participation in worship have become simply mechanical? It is perhaps significant that later monastic reformers drastically reduced the amount of liturgical activity required. We hear a good deal about a peculiarly monastic temptation known as *accidie*, a kind of boredom resulting in sluggishness and loss of will-power. Given that many Religious had no special vocation for the sort of life entailed, some found the required continence and self-discipline beyond their powers. There was a good deal of homosexuality, either open or manifesting itself in monastic friendship (*amicitia*),[127] and in some cases monasteries sheltered concubines and courtesans; in others abbots and monks alike gave themselves to secular pastimes such as hunting or falconry.[128]

The relative isolation of the Religious from ordinary life had undesirable consequences in some cases, leading to distortions of normal human instincts; it also led to a certain lack of realism in some of their writings, which was a matter of importance at a time when most theology was produced in monasteries.[129]

There was thus a deep ambiguity about tenth-century monasticism. The Religious were taught to regard the Rule as the very charter of their way of life, and it was constantly read aloud to them, for example during their otherwise silent meals. It clearly presupposed that avoidance of all contact with the world in the interests of saving their souls was the essential basis of monasticism. Yet in practice a very great deal of what tenth-century Religious did related to the world, whether they were in church, praying and saying masses for it, or mixing with it as dispensers of charity and hospitality, as statesmen or as landowners, with all the entanglement in the feudal system landowning involved.[130] Hauck put the point succinctly: 'The more the monasteries became nurseries of civilization, the less did the monks represent the ascetic ideal. The latter denies the lawfulness of the former; the former hinders the realization of the latter. It is impossible to reconcile the two. In the great royal abbeys St Benedict's Rule was current; but the life in these houses was in open contradiction with the decrees of the Rule. Men knew this but they looked upon the written law as limited by a customary law which had gradually grown up in deviation from the Rule.'[131] Despite the texts Hauck cites in support of his last statement, the ambiguity was keenly felt by conscientious men such as the great abbots of Cluny or, later, Bernard of Clairvaux, who saw their vocation as obliging them to be freely available to give guidance to popes and secular rulers. Obviously, such advice could only be effective if it was based on a thorough knowledge of what was going on in the world.

Whatever the devotion (and it was often great), or the feelings and temptations of the Religious, how did their presence affect their contemporaries? They undoubtedly exercised a great influence, greater in some ways than that of the secular priests, if only because of their virtual monopoly of learning and spiritual doctrine. It was in fact from monastic usage that the obligation of reciting the seven hours each day was extended to the secular clergy in the ninth century. Degenerate though many of them became in the ninth and early tenth centuries, the monasteries did preserve the traditions of both secular learning and Christian devotion amid the darkness of the invasions; and it was largely due to them that civilization at this time 'got through by the skin of its teeth', as Kenneth Clark put it.[132] Their very existence was a sign to a still violent and only half-civilized people that order and stability, based on regard for others, and harmonious co-operation, were possible, and that the most imperious passions and aggressive instincts will yield to discipline and self-denial. Significantly, it was largely from monasteries that the attempts to limit and civilize warfare in the late tenth and early eleventh centuries developed.

> The so-called Peace of God and Truce of God were attempts to limit or suppress the evils of private war and feudal lawlessness. Although the movement seems to have originated with the bishops of central and southern France (Synod of Charroux 987), Cluny was associated with it from the beginning, and Abbot Odilo, with another monastic reformer, Richard of St Vannes, helped to extend it north and east.

As Colin Morris puts it, 'It is not too much to say that in the tenth century the monastic reformers offered to the aristocracy the one alternative way of life and system of values.'[133] People needed a public manifestation of a higher way of life in order to be reminded what can be done in the moral realm. That the aristocracy sometimes got the message is suggested by the confession of Ranier, the Marquis of Tuscany, who is reported by Peter Damian as saying that no emperor could put such fear into him as a mere glance from the monastic reformer Romuald, founder of the Camaldolese Order.[134]

No doubt the influence of the Religious was imbibed unconsciously for the most part, and the age was probably quite unconscious of a further element in the situation. If, to be sure of salvation, one had to embrace the ascetic way, then there could be no assurance of salvation outside the cloister. From the fourth century onwards the claim was often implied, and indeed made explicit, that there was no sure way to salvation, or indeed any way at all, without at least the renunciation of sex. Chastity was regarded as the quintessence of the monastic life.[135] Higher places in heaven were thought to be reserved for virgins of both sexes, and only slightly lower places for those who, having known sex, had then permanently forsworn it.

Since lay people were expected to get married, this view, so far as it percolated to the laity, inevitably made them feel that they had little hope of heaven on the basis of anything they themselves could do, and no hope at all of the highest heavenly rewards. They were at best irretrievably second- or even third-class citizens of the kingdom of God. Their only hope lay in hitching themselves to the monastic star or climbing on to the monastic bandwagon. This they could do in various ways. One was by imitating the monastic life as far as possible under secular conditions. As we shall see, monastic thinkers had no ideal for lay Christians except as pale reflections of themselves. Odo of Cluny, for example, wrote a completely unrealistic, indeed faintly ludicrous, Life of Gerald of Aurillac, in which the knight is portrayed as maintaining lifelong virginity and behaving in other quasi-monastic ways which would have been totally incompatible with the real situation of a military man.[136] In reality it was only to a very limited extent that a lay person in a world such as that of the tenth century could copy the life of the cloister. A more practical way of identifying with the Religious was to support them by gifts of treasures and land, to undertake the protection of their lives and interests, to offer one's children as oblates and to promote their practical interests by any available means; and, as we have seen, one could throw in one's lot with them just before death by taking the cowl and reckoning thereby to merit a monk's or nun's reward.[137] Above all, one could seek to share in their merits by procuring their intervention with God on one's behalf. Their total renunciation meant that they had merit to spare and that their prayers were especially efficacious; people constantly sought to take advantage of these facts. In return for gifts, or promises of legacies, they got their names and those of their relatives inscribed in the lists of those for whom a religious house prayed regularly, or joined societies and confraternities of prayer which were beginning to be associated with monasteries. A number of comparable arrangements were available, but all involved gifts to the monasteries concerned, and that gave a clear religious edge to the rich over the poor.

So far as this situation prevailed, it meant that the overwhelming majority of people in Francia were forced to see themselves as second-rate Christians whose hope of salvation lay not through a direct relationship with God, or even a direct pleading of the work of Christ, but through their ability to persuade more meritorious Christians to offer their merits and plead on their behalf.[138]

Once again the impersonal and contractual nature of most people's relation to God is well to the fore. As for the Religious themselves, more will be said later about their private devotional life, but this may be the place to explain their corporate view of their condition. From early days the word *isangeloi* (cf. Luke 20.36, 'like the angels') had been applied to them; but such language needs to be properly understood. If Bernard of Clairvaux could write of the monastic state that 'it makes those who live it and love it stand out from other men as rivals of the angels and as hardly men at all',[139] he was not so much claiming moral perfection for individual Religious as suggesting that the condition into which their *conversio* brought them was one entirely pleasing to God. As communities organized on what were taken to be purely Christian principles, monasteries were thought of as so many colonies of heaven on earth.[140] They were spoken of as paradises[141] and as anticipations of the heavenly condition here on earth. The reference of the word *isangeloi* in Luke was to the non-sexual character of life in the hereafter. Only in the heavenly Jerusalem would even the Religious be fully perfect, but the monastery was, in its measure, the heavenly Jerusalem brought forward into time.[142] The Religious were like the angels in offering continual praise and worship, and it was thought only fitting that the context of their offering should be as like that of the angels as possible. Nothing was too beautiful or too sumptuous for their churches, where the glitter of gold, the brilliant twinkling of lights and the scent of incense combined to give a foretaste of the heavenly splendour.

According to theorists of the monastic life, not only did the Religious renounce the world in order to build up the new man called to stand in the presence of God; at the same time they returned, at their 'conversion', to the original state of perfection, and they anticipated the life of the world to come. Inevitably a certain triumphalism, with more emphasis on the Transfiguration than the Incarnation, tended to creep in,[143] and there was a temptation, at least, to look down on those outside the cloister; yet, as we shall see, there was a noble vision here, calculated to arouse and maintain a high level of devotion.

15

The Higher Spirituality

Even the most practically-orientated Religious had more opportunity for private prayer and contemplation than most other members of society, and their spirituality tended to be of a different sort. Whereas for most people God was a stern lord, and religion consisted of the attempt to fulfil the conditions on which he granted well-being, the Religious were more likely to start from an idea of God as the *summum bonum*, who embodied all possible perfections and was thus supremely lovable. Human beings were made in his image, and union with, and enjoyment of, him were the only things that could ultimately satisfy them. 'Thou hast made us for thyself and our heart is restless till it finds its rest in thee.'[1]

It was recognized, however, that although this might be the truth of the matter, it was not how ordinary men and women in a fallen world saw it. The Fall meant that instead of seeking their satisfaction in God, human beings could and did find it in a whole range of this-worldly objects and states, sexual relations, possessions, reputation, the exercise of power, food and drink, hunting, falconry and so on.

The Religious felt that so far as they had been rescued from this condition, it was through compunction, a word of great importance in their vocabulary. In its original profane use, *compunctio* seems to have been a medical term designating an attack of acute pain or physical illness,[2] but in Christian usage it came to mean pain of the spirit, an act of God in us by which he awakens us to the truth, by means of what was variously described as a shock, a blow, a sting or a sort of burn.[3]

This pain was believed to take two forms. The first arose from a terrifying recognition of the true state of affairs: fallen attitudes amounted to a denial of God, and could only lead to disastrous consequences at the Last Judgment. This recognition was known as 'the compunction of fear' (*timoris, formidinis, paenitentiae*), and closely associated with it was humility, 'the virtue which renders a man vile in his own eyes by a true understanding of his present condition'.[4]

Those to whom compunction was granted in its second form were deeply affected (and often reduced to tears) by the recognition of a possibility they were in danger of denying themselves, namely the fulfilment of a longing too deep for satisfaction by any objects in this world. This was 'compunction of desire' (*amoris, dilectionis, cordis*), though when it first arose, those who experienced it were often only vaguely aware of its true nature or proper object.

Once aroused, how was this longing, which was in fact a longing for God, to be brought into clearer focus, deepened and maintained as the mainspring of a whole life? The devil was ever present, ready to reactivate the attractiveness of earthly delights and use them as a means of temptation. His advances could be fended off with the appropriate rites and formulas, but to those who took the Religious life seriously it seemed that the safest course – perhaps indeed the only safe course – was to put oneself in a position where yielding to temptation was impossible. Those who did this by entering the cloister were denied all contact with the other sex and required to renounce private possessions of every kind. They were allowed only modest amounts of simple food and drink such as were not likely to lead to gluttony or inebriety; and they were required to wear a plain habit which fully covered the whole body and gave no opportunity for bodily vanity or sartorial display.[5]

> Measures like these were believed to have far-reaching effects because according to the moral psychology of the day evil impulses were linked in a causal chain, so that frustration of one impulse also dealt with others which derived from it. Thus, for example, if you avoided gluttony by eating less, you also went a long way towards conquering lust.[6]

To make assurance doubly sure, Religious were required to give up all control over their own lives and futures. All decisions about the way they lived and occupied their time, and even about what they believed, were taken out of their hands and vested in an abbot or abbess, who was charged with seeing that their way of life was such as to keep God always before their eyes.

Interpreted in this way, the commitment to obedience was perhaps the most radical requirement of the monastic life. That is suggested, for example, by the repeated emphasis on it in Benedict's Rule; and Gregory the Great said with reference to it: 'It is a lesser thing to renounce what one has; it is an exceedingly great thing to renounce what one is.'[7] Obedience was to be immediate and given with complete willingness, the commands of a superior being carried out as promptly as if they came from God himself (c.5). A monk was to obey commands for which he could not understand the reason, and even those which to his eyes looked wrong. Although the Rule does not refer specifically to vows of poverty, chastity and obedience, the requirement is there in the most stringent form. Such renunciation involved negating not only personal inclinations, but the social institutions which were held to presuppose the reign of sin, the family, the state and private property. This was acknowledged, but occasioned no surprise: had not Jesus taught that no one could be his disciple unless he hated all the members of his family;[8] and had not the earliest Christians had all things in common, 'none of them claiming that anything he possessed was his own'?[9]

Indeed, interpreted in this way, the monastic requirement of renunciation could claim a good deal of support from the New Testament.[10] More extreme attitudes were also believed by many to be demanded by the New Testament. Texts such as I John.5.19, 'the whole world lieth in the evil one'; James 4.4, 'friendship towards the world is enmity with God'; Gal.5.17, 'the flesh lusteth against the spirit and the spirit against the flesh',[11] could suggest an attitude of contempt and active hatred towards the natural world, and in particular towards the body, as the seat of evil impulses. In the attempt to frustrate these impulses, enthusiastic Religious often positively maltreated their bodies, hoping thereby to imitate Paul, who had said, 'I torment and subdue my body' (I Cor.9.27).

In the eyes of Jerome and other founders of monasticism, renunciation of the monastic type was essential for those who sought to be true Christians; for according to the apostle Paul, 'those who are Christ's have crucified the flesh with the affections and lusts thereof' (Gal.5.24). If the world was indeed in opposition to God, then to fight it was meritorious, and the more savage the attack on it, the greater the merit. In the early days of Christian asceticism many of the hermits in the desert had vied with one another to see which of them could inflict the greatest amount of suffering on his body; and though the *Rule* did little to encourage such an attitude, many of the more ardent Religious went beyond the Rule in their efforts to crucify their bodies, especially the sex-urge. At the best of times the lack of cleanliness in the monasteries was proverbial; the monks were allowed few baths and they rarely shaved or used a comb. Many went far further. In the middle of the ninth century, for example, Ardo writes of Benedict of Aniane that: 'When he became a monk he proceeded to damage his body with incredible fasting ... endangering his own flesh, as if it were a bloodthirsty beast. He took scanty food ... bread and water enough to avert death but not hunger. Sometimes, when excessively exhausted, he rested prostrate on the bare earth, but only in order to weary himself further with such "rest". Often spending the whole night in prayer, he kept himself awake by standing with bare feet on the pavement in the icy cold ... a colony of lice grew on his filthy skin, feeding on his limbs emaciated by fasts.'[12] Benedict of Aniane may have been unusual in taking things quite so far, but his biographer clearly counted it to him for righteousness, and very similar things are told of Bernard of Clairvaux some three hundred years later.[13] Even Gregory the Great taught that in order to reach God one must love, desire and wish for death (though never induce it); and from the time of Chrysostom there was a tradition that Religious ought never to laugh. Despite the moderating influence of the Rule, the attitude of many Religious towards a great deal in the world, especially sex, can only be described as one of abhorrence, and there was sometimes a danger of a slide into a more or less Manichaean dualism, though the church set its face steadfastly against any such thing: the world might be a source of temptation, and present itself as an alternative object of desire to God, but the very fact that it could do so showed that it was not intrinsically evil; rather, it was a corruption of what had once been very good.[14]

All this could be no more than preparatory. Their withdrawal from the world was intended to leave the Religious free for God (*vacare deo*) and to give them the time and elbow-room (*otium*) to cultivate relations with him. How was this done?

According to the Rule, monks were to spend three or four hours a day on reading (48), which was said to be 'the right path by which we may reach our Creator'.[15] The translation 'reading' gives an inadequate idea of what the Rule meant by *lectio* or *lectio divina*. It must be borne in mind that books were rare, awkward to handle and often difficult to decipher. They were so expensive that even the richest monastery could afford only a limited number, and there could be no question of providing each monk even with a Bible. At the beginning of Lent each year, every Religious was issued with one book from the library, which he or she was expected to read right through in the ensuing twelve months.

It must also be remembered that, even when reading in private, tenth-century readers, like those in antiquity, read the text aloud, or at any rate enunciated the words sub-vocally. Such reading was inevitably slow – especially if the text was hard to decipher – and approximated to learning by heart. At intervals the reader paused in order to master what had been read so far. This was known as rumination (*ruminatio*): just as animals which chew the cud, regurgitate what they have eaten for further chewing, readers recalled to mind what they had read, for further mastication (a metaphor used at the time) by which the full meaning and flavour would be released.

Religious read comparatively few books, but read them very thorough-ly; the result was that everything that was read became deeply impressed on the mind – so deeply that when similar topics or sentiments were encountered in subsequent reading, texts already read would recur to the mind and play their part in interpreting the new text. Readers became, as it were, walking concordances, in whom any passage could trigger off memories of other relevant texts which they had read and could usually quote with reasonable accuracy. (The habit of quoting from memory explains the frequent inaccurate quotations and false attributions to be found in the books of the time.)

The aim of such *lectio* was not the discovery of new truth: novelty was deeply suspect in a society which believed God had already revealed everything that it was needful or salutary to know; nor was it critical or analytical: the day of scholasticism was not yet, and few readers had access to the books requisite for the necessary comparing and contrasting. The aim was said to be *sapientia* (wisdom) rather than *scientia* (knowledge).[16] Wisdom came by making one's own the picture of God provided by the Bible and authoritative later commentary on it. Clearly such an uncritical approach to reading was only possible where the amount of reading matter was relatively small, confined to the same small group of topics, and believed to be completely true and completely consentient. The Bible and subsequent Christian literature – virtually the only texts the monks read – were assumed to speak with a single voice, if appropriately interpreted; and the object was to interiorize the single, coherent message they presented in their different ways, and allow oneself to be permeated by it through and through. This seemed relatively straightforward because, as we have seen, no serious cultural gap was perceived between past and present.

The amount of time spent on *lectio* was calculated to keep the attention of the Religious constantly preoccupied with the supernatural; they were to 'contemplate' the picture presented to them, to see it steadily and see it whole. The clearer and more adequate your picture of God, the more lovable he would appear and the keener would be the desire for him. The purpose of this type of reading was thus the arousal and deepening of love rather than the extension of knowledge.

Sometimes, it was believed, the longing for God aroused by this meditation might be partially satisfied here in this world. A long tradition which reached back both to the Bible and to Plato and subsequent Greek philosophy described the enjoyment of God in terms of sight (*visio dei*) or contemplation (*theōria*).[17] Just as a great picture or a sublime landscape can bring peace, joy and self-forgetfulness to the observer, so the vision of God would bring total and lasting blessedness to those to whom it was granted, though in this case something much more than an external relationship was involved. The New Testament spoke of Christians 'becoming partakers of the divine nature' (II Peter 1.4), and the goal was believed to be nothing less than that, provided the phrase was not interpreted in pantheistic terms as implying the absorption or transformation of human individuality into the Godhead.[18]

In heaven the angels and the saints beheld God face to face, and it was believed that in response to righteous living and faithful contemplation some share in this vision of God was sometimes granted here below.

Whether the full heavenly form of *visio dei* had ever been experienced by anyone while still in the flesh was disputed. Even if it had, it was only by a handful of quite exceptional people such as Abraham and Moses; others could at most expect to experience it only in a partial form – *in aenigmate* (I Cor.13.12, perhaps = 'indistinctly').

One analogy used for such partial vision of God was the light coming into a dark building through the splay of a narrow window, in contrast to the full light of day outside. Partial though it was, such a vision of God was beyond description, and those who believed they had experienced it felt quite unable to give an account of their experience, though they were clear about the rapture and unspeakable joy it had brought. Those still on earth could not sustain even such partial vision for more than a very short time; and when they returned to the level of ordinary existence it seemed flat and empty by contrast, though that served only to set this world in its true perspective: earthly delights were as nothing in comparison with the joy of the vision of God, and to prefer them to it was revealed as the madness it truly was. By the same token sin appeared in its true colours and its full heinousness.

Though some such experience was to be the objective of all *lectio* and contemplation, it was granted only to some; but even the majority to whom it was never granted in this world had no doubt that their contemplative study was abundantly worthwhile. Not only did it keep their minds on things above and deepen their desire for God; the witness of those they read convinced them of the possibility and transcendent worth of the vision of God and gave some inkling of what it would be like; and they were kept in mind of the godly life required as a condition of it, and so made ready for it if it were granted them hereafter. Their appetite was whetted, although in their measure they already partook here below of the contemplation which was the occupation of all who achieved heaven hereafter. In this sense, too, the life of the Religious was *isangelos*, like that of the angels.

The texts a monk read might be a rather random selection, dictated by what was available in the library of his particular monastery; but that caused little concern. Most of the literature in question was endlessly repetitive, little more than centos of biblical texts, and of interpretations of them by previous writers; so it mattered little whether a reader got the ideas at first, second or third hand. Most of the books had been designed for monastic *lectio*, or something very like it, and, whatever the aspect dealt with, they all reflected the one Catholic faith. So the feeling was that one text would lead towards God as well as another.

Particularly for unscholarly monks, four hours reading a day was a considerable amount, even if it often passed over into private prayer and meditation, which were generally regarded as legitimate ways of spending part of the period allotted for *lectio*. It also seems that certain other activities, for example the copying of manuscripts or the education of young monks, were sometimes allowed to take place in this time. Nevertheless, in view of its importance, it continued to have a significant, if somewhat reduced, place in the monastic timetable.

However, the overwhelming emphasis placed on liturgical activity in the reforms of Benedict of Aniane in the ninth century, and the practice of Cluny in the tenth, undoubtedly gave a very different balance to the monk's day. Whereas in the Rule *lectio* was allotted as much time as liturgy, and in fact slightly more,[19] at Cluny and associated houses the time taken up by liturgy increased dramatically, while that formally allotted to *lectio* decreased; and even then, paraliturgical and other activities were allowed to encroach on it.

By way of compensation, however, the Religious were encouraged to make the words of the liturgy, and of the texts read to them in the refectory, the basis for rumination and meditation. Benedict had written 'let us so take part in the psalmody that our mind is in accord with our voice' (§19), meaning apparently that the monks were to pay close attention to the meaning of what they chanted, and make the sentiments of the psalms and lessons their own. The liturgy thus became a means through which they interiorized the faith of the church – and a very effective means it was. The constant daily repetition of the words made them part and parcel of the monk's personality, and the impressive architectural and musical settings of many of the services must have increased their impact.[20] The psalms, chants and biblical readings of which the Office consisted were intercalated with short antiphons and anthems, and with collects and readings from the Fathers, which contextualized them in such a way that, whatever their original meaning, they came to express the faith of the church. For example, it was made clear that Christ was the subject of all the Psalms, and they were interpreted christologically in a way that served to reinforce the church's teaching about his life, death, resurrection and second coming. The language of the liturgy thus came to form a large part of the monk's mental furniture; and his private prayers consisted to a considerable extent of the vocal, or sub-vocal, repetition of verses from the psalms, and other texts, in their liturgically contextualized, ecclesiastical sense. In this period the Office was thus a staple, or perhaps the staple, of monastic spirituality.[21]

How is this monastic spirituality to be assessed, and fitted into a general picture of tenth-century religion? So far as the monks' own study of the Bible was concerned, the omnipresent use of allegory will have made it possible to come to terms with many biblical texts which, if unallegorized, might have seemed inconsistent with the picture of God as supremely lovable. On the other hand, monastic beliefs had to conform with the orthodox tradition as totally as anyone else's, so that Religious had to find ways of reconciling the idea of God as *summum bonum* with his willingness to damn the great majority of his human creatures, and other apparently contradictory traits. This was done by balancing the various qualities which went to make up the divine perfection. God's love must not contradict or nullify his justice, and so on. In this way love came to have a very special meaning in God's case.

Anyone who has read sermons preached at this time by Religious to other Religious will have noticed that, despite a certain difference in tone, they differ little in practice from the instruction given to those outside the cloister. God may be the sum of all perfections, but he is still an exigent Lord, whose favour has to be won, and his wrath appeased, by meritorious living, by penance, by the intercession of the saints, by the saying of masses and other sacramental means.

Most people will in any case have been unaware of this type of spirituality. To people outside them, monasteries appeared principally as owners of land and employers of labour, as dispensers of charity and guardians of powerful relics, and as power-houses of prayer which was peculiarly efficacious on account of the great sacrifices the inmates had made for God. Many Religious themselves justified their existence in similar terms. They felt they were doing their duty by honouring their patron saints, and maintaining and extending the estates needed to support devotion to them, by helping the poor and the sick, by pleading for the souls of the departed, and by maintaining on behalf of the whole people the continual round of praise the church owed to God as supremely worshipful. For many of them who had no special vocation or attrait to the monastic life, anything beyond duties such as these would have been hard to undertake with enthusiasm. The programme of spirituality described above was the preserve of an élite.

However, the attempt to justify the monastic life in terms of what it did for others was a far cry from the motivation that brought it into existence (and was presupposed in the Rule), which was, quite simply and unashamedly, to save one's soul. A modern Religious would want to add at once that this way of saving one's soul is only for a few; others, with different vocations, are called to save their souls in other ways. To some extent, this was accepted in the early Middle Ages as well. Cassian, for example, whose writings were very frequently read to the Religious, taught that 'men advance toward God in many ways, and so each man should complete that one which he has fixed upon'.[22] Nevertheless, it was universally accepted that the monastic life was superior to the secular. Mary and Martha in Luke 10. 38–42 were regularly allegorized as standing for the contemplative and the active lives respectively, and in their case Jesus had made clear that 'Mary hath chosen the better part' (v.42). Jacob's wives, Rachel and Leah, were similarly allegorized; it was admitted that there was an obligation on the church to win souls for the kingdom, just as Leah had borne children; yet it was the beautiful Rachel whom Jacob had preferred and loved, even though, like a Religious wholly given up to contemplation, she had produced no children (converts).

The superiority of the monastic life was clearly stated by Abbo of Fleury, for example, who towards the end of our period worked out a complete doctrine of the three estates: the state of the laity is good, that of the clergy better, that of the monks best.[23] A century or so later Hugh of Flavigny claimed to know what the order of precedence would be at the Last

Judgment: the Religious would come just after the apostles, and ahead of bishops, priests, laymen, and lastly, lay women.[24]

However, that was not the only, or even perhaps the majority, view. There were many who felt that practising contemplation simply with a view to saving one's own soul smacked of egoism, and that God might call those who had had some glimpse of his perfection to share what they had seen with others, and to express it in concern for the sick and the poor and for the good government of society. From Augustine and Gregory onwards, there was a good deal of support for what was called the *vita mixta*, that is to say, a life in which contemplation was combined with practical activity in preaching and good works. Like Plato's philosopher-kings, contemplatives were to put their experience at the service of their fellows. Some of the most influential figures of the early Middle Ages, such as Gregory the Great, or Bernard of Clairvaux, just after our period, were men who, with whatever (professed) reluctance, added deep involvement in practical affairs to the contemplation which they regarded as the real business of their lives.[25]

No one claimed that contemplation was the exclusive preserve of the Religious. The secular clergy could practise it, and were expected to do so, and it was also held up as the highest aim for the laity, appropriate forms of prayer and reading being produced for their use. In fact lay practitioners were few, and almost entirely confined to the upper class; contemplation was virtually impossible for the great majority who were illiterate and lacked the requisite leisure and the resources to buy books. Their way of life, even at its best, was taken to be inferior to the mixed and contemplative lives, and to lead to lower heavenly rewards; the most they could do to improve their religious prospects was to throw themselves on the mercy of the Religious in the hope of profiting from their prayers, and sharing the merits their renunciation had won. Even here, as we have seen, the rich, who could win the gratitude of the Religious by gifts or endowments, were at an advantage. In general, lay people accepted the view that the Religious life was the highest, indeed the only fully satisfactory, form of Christianity (see p. 150–2). Since it demanded the renunciation of precisely the things with which they were constantly engaged, the effect this must have had on their spirits and outlook will be obvious.

As for those who followed the contemplative life, it will be clear that, given the assumptions lying behind their *lectio*, their outlook was bound to be deeply conservative, a fact of great importance when it is borne in mind how overwhelming was their influence on the culture as a whole. Monks, and former monks who had become church leaders, were the opinion-formers of the age *par excellence*.

Their spirituality clearly embraced contradictory elements. If, for example, total world-renunciation of the monastic type was a necessity for union with God, then the conversion of all believers to a serious attempt to attain such union would have meant the end of the human race, a point once taken up with Augustine, who could only say: 'That would be a blessing; for it would mean that the number of the elect would be filled up and the Kingdom of God accomplished.'

In practice, neither he nor anyone else really accepted such a radical doctrine, but the result was a somewhat confused situation. The outlook of the time was largely formed by men who had forsworn some of the basic human drives, often at the cost of considerable suffering and of a measure of impoverishment and dislocation of their personalities. Such men found it difficult to give any positive account of the part God intended these drives to play in the lives of those outside the cloister. These latter *enjoyed* sexual relations, family affections, the pleasures of the table and the chase, and so on, but within the framework set by the Religious could only do so with a bad conscience. In the circumstances, there could scarcely be a positive theology of this-worldly relationships, activities or institutions.

In the early Christian centuries, when enthusiasm for asceticism ran high, the hermits had often felt that moral perfection and the capacity for mystical union with God made the sacraments superfluous, and this idea lingered on in some circles in the East. There was perhaps a certain logic in it, and even in the Benedictine Rule there is no daily mass; it may well be that the eucharist was celebrated at Monte Cassino only at infrequent and irregular intervals; very few of the monks were in holy orders.[26] As the emphasis on liturgy increased, the monks not only came to see the offering of votive masses as a large part of their *raison d'être*, but came to believe that the virtues were impossible of achievement without the sacraments, and that progress in contemplation depended on them. Monastic spirituality was thus a combination, perhaps not fully thought through, of the mystical and the sacramental.

We saw at the beginning of the chapter that the idea of God from which ascetic piety started was different from that which lay behind the reward-seeking religion of the people. Yet the question can be raised whether in the last resort ascetic piety, being concerned with the salvation of the individual soul, was not itself reward-seeking. Certainly the Religious asked less from God by way of reward in this world; indeed, as we have seen, many of them welcomed hardship and suffering as a means of union with Christ in his suffering, and sometimes induced it voluntarily. Yet it must be recognized that theirs was an eschatological piety in the sense that for it the true hierarchy and true rewards would be manifested only in the hereafter.

How far, though, was the desire for those rewards the motivation for their lives of self-denial? That is always a difficult question in relation to religious faith and practice of any sort, and no doubt in this case the answer will have varied from person to person. Some – and perhaps in certain moods, all – will have seen their self-denial as highly meritorious and been inclined to ask, with Peter in the Gospel, 'We have left all and followed thee; what therefore shall we have?' (Matt.19.27). The chief consideration for others – and perhaps in some moods for most – will have been that God is good and that all creatures ought to seek the good. Man, they will have felt, is so made that he can find no full or lasting satisfaction except in the good, but if united with the good, he will be totally and lastingly satisfied. That duty and satisfaction coincide in this way will have been seen simply as a result of the way God has made the world and thus as a cause for deep gratitude on the part of his creatures.

16

The Secular World and Lay Life

Various aspects of tenth-century attitudes to the secular world have already been discussed, and in the light of what has been said, we should hardly expect the church to have had any very positive attitude towards it.

The world was believed to have been created initially simply as a setting for human beings, in which a specific, but unknown, number of them were intended to find their way to heaven as substitutes for the fallen angels. According to the general belief, it had only a relatively short time still to run, and all the non-human creatures it contained would prove to have been expendable in God's eyes. Meanwhile the world shared in the disastrous results of the Fall, and the human society which grew up in it was simply the 'earthly city' of Augustine's *De Civitate Dei*: being the product of Adam's sin-stained descendants, it was shot through and through with injustice, violence and oppression. God's only concern for it was that such peace and order should be imposed upon it as would enable the church to do its work, and its members to practise their religion and save their souls. As Augustine had made clear, such order could be imposed only by the exercise of force, and the church accepted the use of armed force provided it was with this end in view. According to many, though not all,[1] force was also justified if used in God's cause, that is, in order to force unbelieving peoples into the Christian fold. This was one of the justifications put forward for Charlemagne's wars of Saxon conquest, for example. The content of the Old Testament, interpreted as direct divine revelation, made outright disapproval of war unthinkable. The use of force in self-defence was also accepted, but fighting for personal gain or aggrandisement was frowned upon, and the church at this time increasingly sought to limit the scope of warfare, the times at which it was legitimate and the kinds of suffering inflicted.

We have already seen how the church discouraged study of the world for its own sake; and in general it had no positive doctrine of the secular world or of secular life within it, either individual or corporate. The best attitude was that advocated by St James, 'to keep oneself unspotted from the world' (James 1.27). So the ideal stance was that adopted by the Religious, who had the minimum possible contact with the world, and particularly with the body and its lusts, which were the vehicle by which original sin was passed on.

Yet, if the human race was to continue, only a minority could be Religious, or celibate clerics. The rest, known indiscriminately as *laici*, were expected to marry and have children,[2] and, whatever their work or status, this necessitated their involvement in the world and its activities. Inevitably, the *laici* were the overwhelming majority, yet the church had no positive evaluation of their life and activity, and no lay spirituality to propound. The best it could suggest was that they should abstain from the world and live like Religious as far as they could. To the extent that that was impossible, they were generally regarded as second-class Christians who could scarcely expect to please God fully or attain eventually to the highest places in heaven. All this has been denied or at least played down in modern times, but it is hard to see on what grounds (see below, n. 4). There is no evidence for any pattern of specifically lay spirituality or sanctity, and that is no accident. If full Christian discipleship involved the renunciation of the world and the flesh, then the lay way of life, the only function of which was to provide economic support for society, and to engender for the church, could only be a *pis aller* at best. The only models put before lay people were ascetic models they could copy only to a very limited extent. As we have seen (p. 193–4 and n. 136), the monks' model layman was one who *avoided* typical lay activities rather than one who undertook them in a Christian spirit. There was no positive doctrine of what it should mean to be a lay person, and no suggestion that there might be a positive vocation to being a farmer, a knight, a yeoman, a serf, or even a married person. Odo of Cluny could present Gerald of Aurillac as a saint only by making him a celibate. The Religious, who largely constructed the thought-world of the time, did not really believe in social values at all.

There was not even any attempt at a positive Christian understanding of sexual relations. They were regarded by many simply as a consequence of the Fall, and marriage was treated as a second-best, a concession to the weakness of the flesh,[3] and the sexual act, even within it, as stained by sin. It was to be studiously avoided at the many proscribed times, and no pleasure, or at any rate no undue pleasure, was to be taken in it. There was little sense of its being an expression of the mutual love of husband and wife, and there was little appreciation of the joys of home life. Many of the men, especially, were coarse and brutal to their wives, and found difficulty in distinguishing between love and lust; the church had a scant basis of understanding for dissuading them.[4]

Early in the eleventh century several members of the entourage of Constance, the consort of Robert the Pious – responsible and highly spiritual men – actually expressed disapproval of any church involvement with marriage, which they took to be a carnal and contemptible matter, unsuitable for association with the sacred.[5] They were highly suspect in some quarters, but they represented a Manichaean, or quasi-Manichaean, attitude to sexual union which had a long history in the Christian tradition. In the fourth century Jerome, who in this matter was followed by Gregory the Great in the sixth, held that to marry was a sin, and he fought frenziedly against women and marriage;[6] although Augustine saw virtue and positive value in the marriage tie and family relations, he too took the sexual act to be a sin, albeit in the case of married couples a venial one which could be redeemed.

In the ninth and tenth centuries, however, as Père Toubert points out,[7] this sort of anti-matrimonial rhetoric was comparatively little heard.[8] Many writers took the view that marriage was a God-given institution within which grace was available to help a couple overcome lust and provide support and legitimate love for each other and their children.

The early Christians had been content to follow the normal Roman procedures for contracting marriages, though the church insisted strongly on monogamy and exogamy. The German tribes, when they appeared on the scene, had marriage arrangements in many ways similar to those of the Romans. Like them, they distinguished clearly between betrothal (*desponsatio*) and marriage proper, but they also made a distinction between *Muntehe*, which was marriage in the full sense, and *Friedelehe*, which was a sort of cross between marriage and concubinage, and was normally contracted in private. A *Friedel-frau* was definitely a wife, but she received no dowry, her offspring had only.a weak claim to inheritance, and she could be repudiated if her husband or his family so desired. Such an arrangement was popular with the Germanic aristocracy: their chief concern was with passing on family wealth and also *valor* of body and soul, believed to be transmitted through the blood, and it was convenient to be able to replace a wife who proved infertile or otherwise unsatisfactory with one more fertile, wealthy or nobly-born. Accordingly, many noble families clung to such arrangements right down into our period, though it was against the increasingly successful opposition of the church, which had quite quickly won over the lower-order Franks to its point of view.[9]

According to this, marriage was indissoluble, must be contracted publicly, and depended on the free consent of both parties, whereas Frankish custom had allowed a bride to be bestowed without her consent, where an alliance seemed advantageous to her family or her guardian. The church was almost obsessively concerned with the danger of incest and forbade marriages within four degrees, and later seven degrees, of kinship, that is, between couples who had a common great-great-great-great-great-grandfather. In relatively isolated communities, at a time when godparents counted as relatives, such prohibitions were impossible to observe and were in fact constantly broken, with or without official dispensation.[10]

Perhaps as a relic of early Christian practice, and partly no doubt because of the church's ambivalence with regard to marriage, the role of the clergy in the contracting of marriages was relatively limited. From the ninth century onwards the church more and more took over what pertained to marriage,[11] and official teaching increasingly required that first marriages should take place at the entrance to the church (*in facie ecclesiae*) and be followed by a nuptial mass inside which, according to the Roman rite increasingly used in Francia, included a specific nuptial blessing.[12]

However, it was universally agreed that *consensus facit nuptias* (it is the consent [of the pair] which makes a marriage),[13] and no one claimed that a nuptial blessing was a *sine qua non* of a legitimate marriage.[14] In fact second marriages, and certain others which the church allowed as legitimate, were excluded from the possibility of a nuptial blessing, and we have no means of knowing how many first weddings enjoyed the benefit of clergy, though undoubtedly a large number did not. When they did, the couple were expected to abstain from sexual intercourse for one night (or three) 'out of reverence for the blessing', and not to attend church for thirty days. Notions of ritual impurity were still influential.

Although the word *sacramentum* was used in this connexion,[15] there was no question at this period of marriage's being regarded as a sacrament in the full sense of the word. The first time a specific marriage *ordo* was composed seems to have been in 856, when Hincmar produced a form of service for the wedding of Aethelwulf, king of the West Saxons, and Judith the daughter of Charles the Bald;[16] but this service combined wedding and coronation, and there is no indication that such services were used for ordinary weddings in our period.

Opinions varied about whether consummation was essential to a valid marriage; even Hincmar was not consistent on the point. Theologians felt hesitation with regard to the matter because consummation had never taken place between Mary and Joseph.

At least from the time of Charlemagne, divorce was forbidden, but the evidence of the penitentials shows that divorces continued to be common, and indeed were allowed in certain circumstances. Apart from the penitential disciplining of individuals, the church had no mechanism for dealing with the problem.[17] The evidence also shows that contraception, although forbidden, was widely practised, particularly in the form of *coitus interruptus*.

It is unusually difficult to generalize here, but there can be no doubt about the fact that the married state was regarded by theologians as second-best, or about the inferior status of the wife. Once her consent had been given, marriage involved her being handed over from the control of one male to the control of another, who had the right to discipline and punish her. It would be wrong, as Toubert insists, to ignore the positive value placed on marriage and on the relationships within it, but it is also true that it was regarded as a dangerous state needing to be hedged round with safeguards against the ever-present threat of lustful excess; and *moderatio* and *discretio* were the virtues associated with it. Augustine had more than once defined the ends of marriage as *fides* (fidelity), *proles* (offspring) and *sacramentum* (solemn obligation), and it was in the second of these, the procreation of children to be additional members of the church, that married couples, and particularly the women, were expected to find their principal satisfaction. The absence of love from Augustine's list is noteworthy, and although it was among the blessings prayed for in the nuptial mass, mediaeval attitudes to it should not be interpreted in the categories of the romantic movement. Whatever exactly it meant, Jerome's statement that 'any man who loves his wife too much is an adulterer' should not be forgotten.

One of the few preachers to show some awareness of the lack of a lay spirituality was a monk who had himself had a previous career in the secular world, Ambrosius Autpert. In a sermon to lay people he envisages the objection that the kind of discipleship he had been advocating could only realistically be undertaken by Religious. He agrees, but says that for his lay audience too there is a strait gate and a narrow path 'according to the restricted measure (*modulum*) of your order and the scope of your powers'.[18] His account of this path is worth transcribing in brief. 'You are to avoid coveting or taking other people's property,' he says, 'and to avoid falsehood of all kinds; you must practise moderation and avoid luxury. You must avoid sex outside marriage, and even within it abstain in the proscribed periods. You must fast in Lent, go regularly to church, and above all give alms generously as a way of redeeming small daily delinquencies.' The advice given in innumerable other sermons was similarly limited; and when in the twelfth century Gratian summed up centuries of Christian law and tradition in his *Decretum*, he wrote: 'Lay men are alowed to have a wife, to cultivate the earth, to judge and promote lawsuits, to lay their offerings on the altars, to pay tithes. If they do this they will be able to be saved, on condition that they avoid evil by well-doing.'[19] None of this can really be called a spirituality for the laity, and the same is true of the more detailed advice as to what should be taught to the laity given by Theodulph, bishop of Orléans:[20]

> What this amounts to is that in addition to the Creed and the Lord's Prayer, lay people should learn certain one-line prayers, e.g. 'Thanks be to God' (for making them in his own image and distinguishing them from the beasts, §32); on Sundays they should attend mass and the morning office, and refrain from work; they should give alms, practise hospitality to strangers, avoid lying, perjury, and other gross sins, and regularly confess such sins as they might have committed. It is true that in his *De institutione Laicali* (*c.*830), Jonas of Orléans sought to provide the basis for an *ordo laicorum*, and that Dhuoda's *Manual* presupposes a pattern of lay religion as an unremitting struggle against vice, in which the soul climbs the fifteen degrees of perfection and triumphs over evil by penitence, prayer and almsgiving. Such a pattern of piety, however, was designed for the upper class, and in any case was largely negative and external; it provided little advice on direct personal relations with God.

In part this minimalist, and rather grudging, attitude to the lay state was an outcome of the general attitude to the world described above. Those whose work involved their continual immersion in such a world were inevitably besmirched by it. On the other hand, it may be questioned whether any more refined or sophisticated spirituality would have been intelligible, let alone acceptable, to the great majority of the laity.

A group as large and heterogeneous as the *laici* defies easy generalization. At the one end we have someone like Dhuoda, a woman whose culture and learning equalled that of many Religious, not to say parish priests, and who was in a position to practise a world-renouncing spirituality more or less as she chose; at the other end were the totally uncultured, uneducated, illiterate peasants, whose long hours of backbreaking labour can have left them little time or energy for anything but eating, sexual intercourse and sleep. However, the likes of Dhuoda were quite exceptional, even among aristocratic lay people; apart from Nithard, she is one of the few lay writers who can be cited for the period after the time of Louis the Pious.[21] The deacon Amalarius went so far as to say that only those who kept themselves from marriage and possessed no lands or beasts had time or wit for study; and certainly the laity have left us without much direct indication of their feelings about religion or anything else. We can only piece together their religious situation from indirect evidence of various sorts.

It is important to realize how little impact five centuries of Christianity had had on the Frankish mind, and how uncivilized most Franks still were. Even in the eleventh century, Robert Guiscard, a Norman baron of insensate cruelty, consuming greed and a total contempt for morality, was not untypical. Such men despised study.[22] As for the peasants, many of them were still in the barbaric stage, little more than undisciplined children,[23] who gave free rein to their instincts and appetites; they were often coarse, brutal and totally uncultured, though, as we have seen, the self-examination associated with confession had begun to introduce a degree of moral consciousness into some minds.

It is small wonder (even if inexcusable) that the more refined among the clerics dismissed them as *contemptibiles personae*, as an errant mob,[24] and even as human cattle (see p. 149). Not that religious equality was denied in theory. We have already heard Jonas of Orléans on the matter, and Alcuin, writing to a layman, is even more explicit. 'Do not be worried about being a layman living in the world,' he writes, '... the kingdom of heaven is open to every sex, age and person equally, according to his or her deserts. There is no distinction there as to who has been lay or clerical, rich or poor, young or old, slave or master in the world, but each will be crowned with eternal glory according to his or her good works.'[25] Practice did not always match theory, however, and it is in any case significant that the letter is addressed to a count. The sting is in the tail: given the current belief that salvation was a matter of merit, and that the most efficacious good works involved complete renunciation of the world and of sex, lay people were obviously at a great disadvantage, especially if, unlike the count, they were in no position to engage to any extent in the other leading good work, charitable giving.

In addition to the advantage this gave them, the clergy regarded themselves as inherently superior in virtue of their holy status (see p. 163). They had the knowledge to direct the others whom they described as their 'subjects', and from their point of view, lay people were seen simply as the beneficiaries of their pastoral care, who received and did not give, who were defined religiously not by any active role, but as sheep needing shepherds.

9. Resurrection of the dead

10. Translation of the relics of St Alban

11. St Martin du Canigou

12. Frescoes, Müstair, Switzerland

Mappa mundi

14. The devil devouring a man

15. Tenth-century reliquary

It was in fact difficult for the majority of lay people to rise above this level and get beyond the bare and rather external minimum laid down for them. The deep things (*profunda*) of the faith, which might have made it a coherent and attractive whole, were not thought suitable to be entrusted to them; for them only the *aperta* and the religious stories were proper. Some of these they knew, but mainly as separate incidents, not as interrelated episodes which combined to constitute a coherent *Heilsgeschichte* (story of salvation). We must remember that they normally had no access to the Bible, even through their parish priest; and the various incidents of which they heard in the lections at mass, or saw depicted in wall-paintings, were not theologically contextualized. It is true that the mass was understood by theologians as reproducing the life of Christ and the episodes of his passion, and as embodying a philosophy of history in which all past times were contained; but the evidence suggests that expositions of all this to the laity, so far as they were provided, were usually muddled and unsatisfactory in the extreme; and although the sacrifice of Christ was said to be 'reiterated' at the consecration, it was in practice the reading of the Gospel on which stress was laid, while the consecration attracted little attention.[26] The communion might represent the common meal of Jesus and his disciples, but congregations were not encouraged to communicate at all frequently, for fear of their being impure. In any case the service was in Latin, which lay people could no longer understand, and it was at about this time that the priests began to celebrate from the westward position, with their backs turned to the people, thereby widening the gap between what they were doing and an almost non-participating congregation. The laity no longer brought their gifts to the altar at the offertory, and the mass could scarcely be seen as a corporate activity; the priest prayed for the people in both senses of the word.[27] Though compelled to attend mass regularly, people seem generally to have been bored by it, and there is plenty of evidence that they gossiped and jostled in the course of it, not surprisingly since it was all unintelligible, except sometimes for a vernacular translation of the Gospel for the day. If there was a sermon, it was virtually certain to be some variation of one of the standard themes: paying tithes, restricting sex, avoiding perjury and the like. The other services were equally incomprehensible to most, though members of the upper class sometimes followed them, and in some cases recited offices themselves. One of the features of the period was the comparatively small emphasis placed on the mass. Thus, although baptism, charity, love of God, recitation of Psalms, almsgiving and other good works were frequently referred to in the Penitential of Egbert, for example, as means of redeeming sins, there is no reference to the mass in this connection. As Chélini says, 'it played only a secondary role in the positive religious observances of the day'.[28]

As for prayer, it was conceived as essentially a corporate activity, where the laity were concerned. They were taught to take over and repeat such parts of the liturgy as they could, rather than to engage in personal and individual devotion. That would have involved exploring and making their own an understanding of the revelation they did not possess, and would in any case have required a privacy few of them could command.[29] The budding vernacular contained no terms in which to express any but the simplest religious sentiments.[30]

This rather negative account seems broadly justified, though shortage of space has made it difficult to do justice to some nuances. For example, as we saw in Chapter 13, there was an awakening realization in the late tenth century that the *laboratores* had a positive and indispensable role in society; and where powerful laymen were concerned, they were held to have the positive function of protecting and supporting the church, backing its canons with secular sanctions, putting down magic and superstition and providing for the poor, the sick and the Religious. Some of them shouldered these burdens faithfully, and it would be cynical to suppose that they were motivated solely by the thought of the merits they might earn in the process.

It must also be pointed out that from the second century an allegorical interpretation of the figures of Noah, Daniel and Job in Ezek.14.14 (taken together with Luke 17.34–36 and Matt.24.40–41) had led to the belief that God intended there to be three orders of believers, each with a distinctive and praiseworthy (*laudabilis*) role. These orders were often identified as *prelati, continentes* (celibates) and *boni conjuges* (good married people).[31] However, although some argued that there were no intrinsic moral distinctions between the orders (Daniel was not to be thought better than Noah, for example!), they came to be linked with the different yields referred to in Matt.13.8, etc. (hundredfold, sixtyfold, thirtyfold), with the corollary that the laity could expect at best to be the lowest, even in the hereafter.[32]

Lastly, it should be mentioned that, according to Rosamond McKitterick and others, there was more literacy among lay people than had until recently been supposed.[33]

In sum, we may say that from a religious point of view, the lay people were entirely dependent on the clergy. The great majority had no access to devotional books or any other independent source of enlightenment, so they lived, willy-nilly, in a thought- and belief-world entirely constructed by clerics. The more independent-minded of them no doubt indulged in a certain amount of scepticism, but they could have no alternative to put in place of the clerical system; and unless they were prepared to risk an eternity of damnation, they had no alternative but to follow the precepts of the church. Implicit obedience to these was constantly inculcated; indeed it has been said that obedience was more emphasized than faith, which in such a society could be more or less taken for granted.

In the case of the great majority, however, it was largely an implicit faith. Since the priesthood on which lay people so depended was mostly represented in practice by parish priests who were ex-serfs, themselves uneducated and often unable to preach, many of the laity can have had only a very confused and incoherent picture of the faith. Perhaps the best way of describing their state of mind would be to say that they found the world a mysterious and rather awful place, in both senses of the word. There was no way of predicting how things would turn out, or of understanding why they turned out as they did. The explanation was generally held to lie with the activity of supernatural beings of various kinds, whose ubiquitous presence gave an awesome quality to existence; and much lay religion was a matter of traditional gestures and periodic rites designed to fight or placate these powers. (The mass had its place in popular piety in this context.) Many of these rites were so shrouded in mystery, and their *rationale* so little understood, that it was not always easy, with the best will in the world, to distinguish which of them were specifically Christian. It sufficed if they seemed to work. In such circumstances, people must often have felt, as they wrestled with the unseen powers, like soldiers fighting in a thick fog.

Churches themselves were described as *terribiles loci*, and if the Lord was above it all, missing nothing, and ever ready to intervene, he was a terrible and hidden God, whose ways were past finding out. It was vital to catch his eye, if one hoped for a place in heaven, but that was best done through his special friends and intimates, the angels or the saints.

In practice the confessional was probably the point where church influence was primarily brought to bear, and it would be a mistake to underestimate the extent to which it promoted inwardness and moral consciousness in a still semi-barbaric people; at the same time, as we have seen, it was largely responsible for promoting a contractual and external view of relations with God, and practice of it was far from universal.

Sumption's description of a rather later period hits off the tenth century as well. 'Christianity,' he says, 'remained in their eyes a vital framework of life, rather than a body of coherent beliefs or commanding ideals ... they recited prayers at fixed hours, uttered pious formulae when they were appropriate, gave alms when it was expected of them, and marked the passing stages of their lives by receiving the sacraments of the Church.'[34]

One further point, emphasized by Riché, is worth making. Being told that precisely the activities and contacts which distinguished them were second-best, if not indeed positively suspect, must have produced a real malaise and an inferiority complex, so far as church teaching was taken seriously, particularly on the part of the peasants who had no resources out of which to supplement their own endeavours by the merits of others.

17

Kingship, Government and Religion

If there was thus little positive evaluation of the religious status of lay people, exception must be made for one layman, if layman he can be called,[1] namely the king. To the question of his status, both in relation to God and to the church hierarchy, a great deal of thought was given; and it is in the context of kingship that tenth-century ideas about government and politics are best understood. The age was not one which devoted much time to general questions of political theory, but for purely practical purposes certain questions had to be addressed.

When the Eastern emperors could no longer guarantee peace and order in the West, and their writ effectively ceased to run there, the resulting power vacuum was an urgent practical problem. As a leading power, which had often acted in place of the Byzantine emperors, and was now itself badly in need of protection, the papacy naturally gave a great deal of thought to the matter. The obvious people to turn to were the Franks, by the eighth century a formidable power, who controlled almost all of what we call France and a large part of modern western Germany. An opportunity offered in the middle of the century, when the family which had long exercised the real power as mayors of the palace wished to take over the crown itself from the ineffective Merovingian king Childeric III.[2] The evidence does not reveal exactly how Frankish rulers were appointed before that time, but heredity and election by the nobles seem to have played a considerable part. Although the current mayor of the palace, Pepin, could claim election, in the sense that most of the nobles seem to have supported his move, he had no strong hereditary claim, and he was in any case taking the unusual step of usurping the throne of a living predecessor; he therefore sought wider support for his move. He wrote to the pope asking for his support, and Zacharias replied accepting the principle that 'it was better, in the interests of order, that the one who possessed the actual power should be recognized as king'. Papal support was signalized when Boniface anointed Pepin king on the pope's behalf, and then, two years later, when his successor Stephen personally anointed Pepin, and also his wife and sons, thus conferring legitimacy on his line as well as himself.

In return, as we have seen, the pope asked the Franks for military protection; he may also have hoped that papal anointing would become an integral part of Frankish king-making, so that the papacy would have an established role in the appointment of all future rulers in the West. Some such thought was probably in the mind of Leo III when he crowned Charlemagne emperor in St Peter's in 800. We should not lay too much stress on this, however. Charlemagne crowned his imperial successor, Louis, with his own hand, and Louis did the same to his successor, Lothar;[3] and the Carolingian crown several times changed hands without the accompaniment of unction.[4]

What clearly needed thought was the way in which the rulership of the West was to be envisaged and conducted. That it should be on monarchical lines was not questioned; neither the Franks nor the church had known any other system and, as we have seen, biblical precedent was decisive. When it came to more specific questions, the situation of the Carolingians was too different from that of the old Roman empire for much useful precedent to be found in that quarter; and for the same sort of reasons the Eastern emperors hardly provided a model. The papacy would certainly not have welcomed the caesaropapist ideology of the Byzantine court.

What was needed was a new pattern of government, suited to a novel situation; and throughout the centuries after Pepin we can observe rulers and church leaders working, on the whole amicably, towards such a pattern. In the nature of the case, those involved were feeling their way, and there were the variations, inconsistencies and loose ends that such an experimental situation would lead us to expect.

In a church-dominated culture which always sought to base its behaviour on precedents, the natural place in which to look for guidance was the Bible, and the anointing of Pepin as the successor to Childeric was based on the model of Samuel's anointing of David to succeed the unsatisfactory king Saul, even if the details of the precedent were not pressed as fully as some modern writers have suggested.[5] As we have seen, the Franks regarded themselves as a chosen people, strictly comparable to the Israel of the Old Testament; and again and again in the following years we find church leaders appealing to the Old Testament, often in considerable detail, as they seek for the appropriate pattern of kingship.[6]

Both Carolingian Francia and ancient Israel were communities of faith, in the sense that all the members of each community shared the common religious outlook of the group. Membership of the society and adherence to its religious faith were coterminous;[7] and in both it was accepted that the ultimate ruler was God, and that the earthly ruler was his deputy,[8] whose function was to ensure that the divine will for the community was carried out. In societies for which the supernatural was so intensely actual, the relationship between divine and human rulership was bound to be a matter of great concern. The matter was nothing less than 'God's rule over God's people'.[9]

The most prominent of the Old Testament kings was David, and it was recognized that his kingship had been an office or ministry. He had ruled, it was said, *propter ordinem*, and his remit had been to ensure, under God, the religious as well as the secular welfare of his people. The Carolingians drew the moral: if the whole purpose of the state was the salvation of its members' souls, the ruler's responsibility could not be confined to their material well-being, any more than David's had been. In fact Charlemagne, who was hailed as *novus David*, was content to see himself as a Davidic ruler, concerned to secure the religious and secular welfare of his people and to see that God's will for them was carried out.

To discover what that will was, he turned to his bishops and other religious advisers. He worked out policy in formal and informal consultation with them, and he was also the apparently willing recipient of unsolicited advice from such of them as Alcuin and Cathwulf about his royal duties.[10] We have already seen how much of his legislation was designed to maintain the order and stability God required (p. 107); to ensure, so far as legislation and reforming activity could, that all his subjects were faithful, practising Christians, and that life was lived in his realm according to Christian principles; and to effect the forcible Christianization of the new territories he subjugated, in particular Saxony.

If some of the methods employed seem to us strange, we must bear in mind the contemporary way of picturing the divine king whom Charlemagne sought to represent, and also that the warlike exploits of the Old Testament kings were taken as divinely guaranteed precedents. War, said Augustine, was inevitable in the earthly city, if God's cause was to be upheld; so wars on behalf of good causes, especially Christianity, were just wars, and those who died in them could look forward to a heavenly reward. God was seen, it will be remembered, as a triumphant, all-powerful, warrior lord who dwelt in a fortress, realistically conceived as the prototype of Charlemagne's palace at Aachen, and did battle for the souls of men and women. The *laudes* (praises) with which the kings were hailed at their inauguration, and on certain other solemn occasions, began with the repeated cry 'Christ is conqueror, Christ is ruler, Christ is in command' (*vincit, regnat, imperat*), and went on to address the heavenly king by such titles as 'our victory', 'our impregnable wall', 'our totally unconquerable defence'[11] It was this king and his hierarchy that the earthly king and his hierarchy were supposed to mirror (see pp. 44–5). Small wonder, then, that when Alcuin advised Charlemagne about his duties, he told him he must be a conqueror and subjugator of peoples, after the Old Testament pattern, and must not hesitate to reign through terror when necessary, because that would save bloodshed by leading to the surrender of the pagans over the frontiers, and would produce the *stabilitas* God desired (see p. 107). Admittedly, that was not the whole of what Alcuin said: the king must also convert the heathen, keep the kingdom free from heresy, correct wrong-doers and defend the victims of oppression.[12] Cathwulf added to the list: the king must be truthful, show patience, generosity and openness to persuasion; he must punish the wicked and exalt the good, be just in his judgments and moderate in his demands for taxes.[13] As morality was understood at the time, the moral content of all this was high, and it was expected that the king would display a high level of personal virtue and be a moral example to his subjects. He could expect God's help in his endeavours after good rulership, and if he succeeded, prosperity and fertility would attend the realm. It was recognized that no ruler was likely to be perfect, but on the whole Charlemagne's bishops were satisfied with their ruler; the success of his arms and the prosperity of his realm suggested that he had the requisite qualities, even if his private life sometimes gave cause for concern.[14]

Still, the matter could not rest there. For one thing, many of Charlemagne's successors seemed less satisfactory as rulers than he had done. At the death of Louis in 840, the Carolingian territory was divided among several rulers, and they and their successors waged wars on one another which seemed to have more to do with self-aggrandisement than with the maintenance of God's peace and order, and which, in combination with the inroads of the Vikings, meant a steady loss of power from the centre to the local magnates. In such circumstances the rulership of the West needed to be rethought.

At the same time the religious perspective was also changing. Charlemagne, as we have seen, regarded himself, and was regarded by his countrymen, including the clerics, as unquestionably the supreme authority in the empire. For all the ecclesiastical pre-eminence he accorded to the pope, and for all the importance he attached to conformity with Roman standards of faith and practice, the bishops, including the bishop of Rome, were seen as below him.[15] Since the eighth century, however, increased claims had been made for the papacy. Popes had claimed not only to possess supreme religious authority throughout Christendom, but also to have been invested with supreme secular authority in the West, even though in practice they exercised it through secular rulers. With the disappearance of the overarching authority of a Charlemagne, such papal claims became more plausible. From now on it was increasingly accepted that the pope was the embodiment of Christ and the head of the Christian society, and that all accounts of government had to be compatible with that.

Meanwhile the Frankish bishops had been gaining in self-confidence and the sense of their corporate authority. As they met together in councils and synods over the years, they developed a common mind – almost a corporate personality.[16] We have seen how the churchmen of Charlemagne's time had expected to be consulted, and had felt free to offer the king advice and directives about his duties. The Frankish bishops now felt confident in laying down the law to rulers about how they should behave. This was because they claimed to be repositories of knowledge about the way of life God expected of the people (they were *divinae voluntatis indices*), and so about the objectives at which rulers should aim. In 833 they had not claimed the right to depose the king (Louis the Pious), but they had judged him to be failing in his duties, and imposed on him a penitential status which was incompatible with his continued exercise of power, at any rate for a time. However exactly this action should be interpreted, it clearly implied some claim to pronounce on who was, and was not, fit to reign. From that it was a short step to a claim to have some significant say in the choice of rulers.

This was a point at which secular and religious considerations had to be reconciled. When a throne fell vacant, particularly in the turbulent and violent conditions of the later ninth and the tenth centuries, it was vital that the man chosen to succeed should be up to the task. If someone with a hereditary claim was available, so much the better, but he had to have qualities of leadership, administrative ability and a good measure of military prowess. Of all this the lay magnates were likely to be the best judges, and there is evidence that when a king was to be made, their approval of a candidate was sought, and shown by their hailing and acclaiming him, sometimes holding him up on a shield and even raising him to a throne, in the open space in front of the cathedral.

> There is a difficulty here, because the coronation *ordines* do not record the total process by which a king was inaugurated. For the secular proceedings we have to rely on such evidence as Widukind's account of Otto I's inauguration, when the *duces* and *milites* made him king *more suo* (after their own fashion), that is, in the sort of way just described.[17] Some Anglo-Saxon *ordines* refer to pre-coronation *conventus seniorum*, and there is some reason to think that the whole ceremony often concluded with a big feast. The available evidence is enough to convince most scholars that some form of lay 'election' was usually part of the total process, though it did not always take extended ceremonial form. It was probably regarded as a means by which God's will was expressed. For example, Louis the Stammerer described himself in 877 as *misericordia dei nostri et electione populi rex constitutus*.[18] The church certainly maintained that it was God who chose the kings.[19]

However, if a ruler was to measure up to the bishops' standards, it was felt that he would need special divine assistance, and so from the middle of the ninth century it became the universal custom for the secular 'election' to be supplemented by a religious service of which the essential element was a solemn ninefold anointing, regarded at that time as a sacrament which conferred on the king the grace of God that the due performance of his duties would require.[20] In addition to the anointing, the king was crowned by the bishops with a crown which was placed on the altar, and also invested with a dalmatic (the vestment of a deacon), the sceptre and the orb. He was expected to make a formal *professio* before he was anointed, and then to give certain detailed promises during the service. What these amounted to was a solemn statement of his intention to champion the Christian faith and uphold the *honores* of the institutional church and the interests of the people, as enshrined in the laws. In return, he received a promise of due obedience from all. These royal undertakings put a curb on any arbitrary exercise of power, and the analogy of the *professiones* demanded from bishops before their consecration (from which the royal *professiones* were probably derived) suggests that, as in their case, the penalty for failure to comply with them would be *privatio honoris* (deprivation of office). Hincmar certainly argued that case, but, as we shall see, failed to follow through the logic of his argument. Nevertheless, a record of the king's words was kept in the archiepiscopal archives and provided a firm criterion by which to judge his conduct of government. The kings in effect accepted the bishops' understanding of the royal role and were, in theory at least, content to be judged in accordance with it. Charles the Bald, for example, accepted that the judgments of God were given through the bishops ('who are called the thrones of God') 'to whose censures and reproving judgments I was prepared to subject myself and am at the present time subject'.[21] The evidence concerning these royal undertakings is difficult to interpret and still the subject of some controversy.[22]

The orders of service (*ordines*) for many of these ceremonies have been preserved, and they contain what might fairly be described as a job specification,[23] yet it is not easy to be sure what interpretation was placed on the ceremony. In fact it was probably understood rather differently by different participants.

Despite the investment with the dalmatic, and the fact that unction was a central element in royal inaugurations, as it was in the ordination of priests and the consecration of bishops, it is a mistake to see the royal ceremony as conferring any sacerdotal character. The anointing was probably seen, on the analogy of anointing at baptism, as marking the recipient's transition to a new status and membership of a new order, and as conveying the supernatural help the new position would require.[24]

There has been some confusion on this matter both in mediaeval and modern times, partly as a result of a misunderstanding of certain contemporary texts. The *Libri Carolini*, for example, describe Charlemagne as 'lord and father, king and priest', while in the tenth century the entourage of the emperor Berengar claimed it as 'beyond doubt that the head of the empire is called a priest'; and there was the repeated insistence that *rex non omnino laicus*.[25] It has also been noticed that the head-anointing of bishops at their consecration was coming in at just about the same time in the ninth century that the anointing of kings was becoming the regular practice. This was in fact no coincidence: in both cases the idea was to signalize that the one anointed was being consecrated to God in a special way and receiving certain spiritual powers; and also to emphasize the gap between the man and the office and thus the responsibilities involved. The religious status of rulers received special emphasis in Eastern Francia. A miniature in a Gospel Book from Aachen, for example (just before 1000 CE), shows the emperor enthroned above the earth, his head being blessed, or crowned, by the hand of God, which is reaching down from above to touch it. The emperor is shown enclosed in a mandorla ( ), a figure usually reserved for representations of Christ. The veil across the middle of the picture appears to symbolize that the king's head is in heaven, and the intention was clearly to present him as the vicar of Christ who, in a later phrase, had his feet on earth but his head in heaven (*pedes in terra, caput in caelo*). There appears to be nothing quite parallel to this in the West, though there are numerous representations which emphasize the semi-sacerdotal character of the emperor's dress and of the objects by which he is surrounded, and make clear that he is directly dependent on God, with ecclesiastical persons subordinate to him.[26] While all this makes clear the profound religious connotations attaching to kingship at the time, and serves to differentiate the king from all others, it does nothing to suggest any strictly sacerdotal role for him. Even Berengar was said to be a priest only in the sense that 'priests and kings are sanctified from the same horn of oil'. Certainly the anointing, at any rate in the context of the inauguration as a whole, came to be seen as constitutive of kingship.[27] One who had been through these ceremonies achieved a special status, set apart from all his fellows, a different person,[28] with the endowments necessary for the fulfilment of the royal role. A good king would ensure the peace and order God willed for his people. Paschasius Radbert, for example, quoted the Wisdom of Solomon 6.24 (26), 'a wise king is the upholding (*stabilamentum*) of his people',[29] and in 877 Pope John VIII is said to have described the emperor Charles the Bald as 'the saviour of the world, constituted by God, whom he established as the prince of his people in imitation of the true king Christ his son ... so that what Christ owned by nature the king might attain to by grace'.[30]

If these were the theological terms in which the bishops viewed a royal inauguration, others, perhaps including the kings themselves, probably saw it in less exalted terms – as what Wallace-Hadrill calls 'a piece of church magic'.[31] Everyone agreed that the king emerged from the ceremony as 'the Lord's anointed' (*christus domini*), a status which, on the repeated testimony of scripture, carried divine protection from the attacks of rivals and enemies. 'Touch not mine anointed' (*christos meos*), God warned in the Old Testament.[32] A king also emerged from the rites *a deo coronatus* (crowned by God), and indeed as the son of God by adoption (eg. Ps.2.7), with a position uniquely majestic and exalted, even in comparison with that of the leading nobles. All alike were his subjects (*subjecti, subditi*). All this was naturally welcome to rulers, and so were the more or less magical consequences they looked for from their anointing and crowning – enhanced fertility, for example,[33] the ability to heal certain diseases[34] and the promise of *felicitas* and good luck for them and their subjects.[35] Since the coronation service made clear that a responsible performance of his duties would enhance the ruler's own prospects of salvation,[36] a motive was provided for him to attend seriously to the bishops' admonitions.

As in most societies, rule was exercised primarily through law. The king was held to be the source of all human law, though in his royal, and not simply his personal, capacity; as we have seen, the office and the office-holder were increasingly distinguished.[37] It was recognized that in a fallen world the law would often need to be repressive and punitive, but that was tolerable because of the belief that the function of the laws was to fulfil and complement divine law and to maintain the conditions necessary for human salvation. Given the king's status, the law, as the expression of his will, was to be accepted without question, and so were his interpretations of the Bible which underlay it.

Since the law expressed the will of God in this way, it possessed a majesty and a moral character such that anyone who failed to obey it was not a Christian. That being so, it was vital that the law should be known and clear, and in the later ninth century Hincmar, himself a lawyer, repeatedly stressed the importance of its proper codification and promulgation.

As we have seen, Frankish society in the ninth century was taken to consist of three orders, Religious, clerks and laity; although the king belonged to the last, he was dominant over all, but that did not mean that the people (*populus*) belonged to him. They were *God's* people, the *populus christianus*. Did that give them any independent power over against him? What if the king proved a *rex iniustus*, whose rule and law were tyrannous? Although the king was expected – and admonished by the bishops – himself to keep the laws, once they were made, the problem of the unjust king could hardly be ignored in the conditions of the ninth and tenth centuries; and in many passages the logic of Hincmar's thought brought him to the verge of declaring that if the bishops, on behalf of the whole people, adjudged a king unjust, they had a right to depose him. Yet neither Hincmar nor anyone else ever quite brought himself to say as much. Partly, no doubt, the fear of complete breakdown of government lurked at the back of people's minds, and it is also true that the kings mostly followed the old Germanic custom of taking counsel before enacting laws. Whether or not the *consensus omnium* or *consensus fidelium* had any constitutive force in the enactment of legislation, such consultation had Old Testament overtones, and kings seem generally to have gained such consent as they could from those (of the upper order) who would be affected by the laws they passed. Perhaps more significant for the bishops' hesitation was the teaching of the New Testament, as then interpreted: 'The powers that be are ordained of God ... every soul must be submissive to the authorities in power. Anyone who opposes authority is a rebel against the ordinance of God, and rebels bring damnation on themselves.'[38] Even if it was true that a tyrannous king in some sense forfeited his kingship by his failure to fulfil its aims, it was still possible to argue that he should be endured, on the grounds that God sent such tyrants to punish the people's sin.[39] So, although kings were sometimes made away with, and the bishops reserved the right to judge the royal conduct, no machinery for deposing rulers existed or was proposed. The issue of resistance to sovereigns lay in the future, and at this period the existing – and continually evolving – system of government worked well enough for most of the parties involved to be content with it, or at any rate to be content to work together to improve it.

The confused objectives of the coronation rites, and the inconsistencies and loose ends in our other sources, make generalization hazardous. Yet beyond any doubt the theory of government in tenth-century Francia was one dominated by religion. Frankish society was co-terminous with the Frankish church. There was no independent secular policy and no secular state, only a secular power within the church, designed to be the agency through which the church's aims were given practical effect. Janet Nelson goes so far as to say that 'the bishops saw the royal office as an executive post, themselves as the directors of the corporation'.[40] The aims rulers were to pursue, the ways in which they were to pursue them, and the kinds of life and faith they were to secure by their legislative activity, were all laid down by church leaders on the basis of their interpretation of the Bible and the Christian tradition. The very purpose of government was taken to be the maintenance of the conditions in which the church could most effectively help people to save their souls. Bishops decided what qualities a ruler needed and how far a particular leader was exhibiting them, remonstrating with him if he fell short. It was only through a rite which centred on a sacrament in the exclusive competence of bishops to administer that a king could become a king, and that alone gave the bishops great leverage over monarchs. The principle that 'the one who anoints is greater than the one who is anointed' was often invoked, and many arguments were produced to prove the superiority of the episcopal to the royal order; for example, that whereas sacerdotal authority is universal, that of a king is confined to one people.[41] Yet once a king, a man was a figure of godlike stature, conspiracy against whom amounted to sacrilege. *Cor regis in manu dei.*[42]

Such was the theory, and it should not too readily be assumed that it was imposed by an all-powerful church on reluctant monarchs. As we have seen, the system had much to offer to rulers, and it did much to facilitate the government of a still very unruly people. There were occasions when kings resisted the bishops' policy, especially with respect to church property, but in general there is no reason to doubt that the kings accepted it sincerely. That, however, is not to say that they always lived by it. Greed, naked aggrandisement and self-regarding power politics often lay behind their policies and wars; and they often appropriated church property to get the wherewithal to keep their followers loyal: in many cases they had no alternative.

In our period, when thirteen rulers, some Carolingian, others Capetian, were raised to the throne by various factions in the course of little over a century, and the real influence of the monarchs was rapidly passing to the local nobility, it must have been hard to associate the monarchy, which Boussard describes as now 'no more than the memory of a splendid dream, a necessary fiction to unite the realm', with all the royal splendour the theory suggested;[43] and we naturally ask ourselves how much impact the monarchy, or the theory of it, had on the majority of people. Certainly an anointed king continued to be separate from all his subjects, even his most powerful magnates. Sovereignty was distinct from suzerainty, or feudal lordship, which many of the nobles enjoyed on a greater scale than the sovereign. As the king travelled round, there would be 'crown wearings', solemn occasions involving much pageantry, when the royal dignity would be displayed in its full grandeur for all to see.[44] Kings also ordered that special prayers should be offered on all royal anniversaries, and the royal *Laudes* were sung in most Frankish cathedrals on the major festivals of the church. These and other propaganda measures must have helped to keep the monarchy before many people's minds. Yet people were probably not conscious of the extent to which the laws by which they were governed, and the way of life to which these laws gave rise, were the result of the system. Ullmann pointed out that the increasing insistence on the overriding influence of God in the appointment of kings meant that the people had no part to play in government, and led to their increasing alienation from their rulers, whose policies they were in no position to understand; most people had no means of informing themselves about the issues at stake.[45] Especially in the conditions of the tenth century, it would be a mistake to suppose that what kings did affected or involved most of their subjects. In any case, as James says, 'kings did not necessarily want to have complete control over events in their kingdom ... a Frankish king did not govern or administer – he reigned'.[46]

In practice, authority for most people meant the authority of the local lord or his immediate superior; and it is difficult to tell how far the ecclesiastical understanding of government affected the policy and behaviour of these lords. Alongside the 'mirrors of princes', churchmen composed 'mirrors' for the lords in which they were urged to exhibit the same truthfulness, moderation, generosity, approachability and evenhandedness in judgment as their sovereign, and to use their power to secure the peace and order that God required.[47] The response was patchy, to say the least. Young landless nobles in particular were easily moved to savage fighting, with little regard for the damage and suffering this caused; and in the absence of effective royal control, it was left to the church to attempt to restrict such fighting and the barbaric methods often employed in it, through the movements known as the Peace of God and the Truce of God.[48] At a later stage the church would try to divert this militaristic proclivity, and direct it into what was regarded as the worthy cause of conquering God's enemies the Saracens.

Meanwhile, whatever pre-eminence might be accorded to the pope, the spirit of Charlemagne largely lived on. Kings, and indeed their leading subjects, believed they had the right to appoint bishops and to dispose of other ecclesiastical posts and properties in their territories; they sometimes became lay abbots of well-endowed monasteries themselves. The question of the respective responsibilities of the ecclesiastical hierarchy and lay rulers in respect of the government of the church was to become a major subject of controversy in the following century. Once again, we must be careful not to judge the situation of the tenth century with hindsight, if we want to get the flavour of what it felt like at the time.

18

Conclusion

The aim of this book has been to present the Christianity of northern Francia in the tenth century in such a way that readers may be able to judge for themselves how far and in what ways it differs from the Christianity of any other periods with which they may be familiar, and to get some idea of the extent to which historical, cultural and economic factors affect the form Christianity takes in a particular situation. What follows is offered in the hope that it may facilitate the answering of such questions.

First, a point of clarification. In an important book published some thirty years ago Wilfred Cantwell Smith proposed a distinction which he suggested might be useful in religious studies of this sort, namely a distinction between 'cumulative tradition' and 'faith'.[1] The cumulative tradition of a religion is the body of authoritative texts, doctrines, rites, moral behaviour, tabus and the like, which distinguish it. These Cantwell Smith calls 'observables' because they can form an object of empirical study about which there need not in principle be any dispute between scholars of different religious persuasions, or none. However, he insists that the tradition is far from being all there is to a religion. Central to every religion is the faith of its adherents, that is, the relation to the transcendent – or what they take to be the transcendent – they practise and enjoy within the categories the tradition provides. Clearly such faith is not observable in the sense suggested. Where other people's faith is concerned – even that of contemporaries close to us – knowledge of it has to be a matter of inference.

In the foregoing chapters we have quite deliberately concentrated primarily on the former of the two, attempting to describe the Christian tradition in the form it had taken in Francia by the tenth century. A cumulative tradition is so-called because it grows and develops as the members of each generation modify and augment it in the light of the influences and circumstances of their particular time. Personal insights also play their part, and some individuals modify the tradition as it has reached them, in significant ways. In that case they make their mark and are usually remembered subsequently; for example, the name of Gottschalk of Orbais is still known because of his vigorous, if ultimately unsuccessful, attempt to modify the current form of the tradition in an Augustinian direction in the ninth century. Yet even those who leave no memorial all make at least some contribution to the process, however minute, as they appropriate the tradition, each in his or her own way, and hand it on to their children in the form in which it has made sense to them.

The question then becomes: what did the Franks of the tenth century make of the Christian tradition in the form in which they inherited it? Since faith is not an 'observable', that might seem an unanswerable question, and certainly it is idle to suppose that we can stand in their *calceamentis* and 'think their thoughts after them' in their full particularity.[2] Anyone who wishes even to approximate to such a goal would need to study not only the general religious situation of the time but the personal views of someone who had left sufficient evidence about them.[3] Our concern is more general, and in dealing with a society so conservative and conformist, and so deeply suspicious of the idiosyncratic, it is safe to assume that the faith of the overwhelming majority will have remained well within the confines of the tradition. So, provided we do not expect too much, it makes sense to ask what sort of faith the tradition outlined in this book is likely to have generated.

We can do so the more confidently because the age exhibited a well-defined mentality. This mentality has been investigated from the side of cognitive psychology, and one characteristic of it was an incapacity to plumb other minds, or outlooks different from one's own. Strange though it may seem to us, no attempt was made to understand what people of other views were trying to say, or to consider whether there might be any truth in it. All was black and white. As far as thinkers of other cultures were concerned, no such attempt was really possible. As we have seen, sheer ignorance prevented the age from understanding the real drift of ancient classical authors, or having its beliefs challenged by them. In the same way scholars knew too little about contemporary intellectual movements outside Christendom for their outlook to be affected or stimulated by them.

In some ways early mediaeval people were like children who have reached the stage where they are aware that their elders possess important truth, but can assimilate it only in a simplified and partly misunderstood form, adapted to their level of comprehension. This applies not only to tenth-century study of ancient classical writings, but also to the study of the Christian Fathers.

Also like children at this stage of development, tenth-century people seldom, if ever, attempted to work out the truth for themselves by a process of investigation, argument and dialogue. In the case of lawsuits, for example, there was little understanding that the truth probably lay somewhere between the protestations being made by the opposing parties, and might be worked out by a process of cross-examination and the weighing of conflicting evidence. The truth of the matter was assumed to lie with one side or the other and to be capable of discovery only by recourse to some such procedure as the ordeal, through which it could be authoritatively declared by God. In the same way, those in power did not attempt to work out what would be in the people's interest through discussion with the parties concerned, but assumed that there was an objectively right policy which could be discovered by consulting the church authorities and seeking out the appropriate precedents.

This essentially authority-seeking outlook had a good deal to do with the emphasis on God as an authority figure, who, as such, was inevitably conceived along the lines of the authority figures of the time, the autocratic kings and feudal nobility.[4]

Had you been a tenth-century Frank, religion would have penetrated and permeated your existence at almost every point, even if you were not particularly pious. Neither you nor anyone else would have entertained the slightest doubt about the truth of the Christian faith and the accuracy of the world-picture it presented. You would have accepted the Christian account, without reservation or further thought, as conveying the way things were; no alternative would have been known or conceivable in the society to which you belonged.

The way you behaved, or believed you ought to behave, would have been controlled by church directives, or laws based on them, at innumerable points. Your very membership of society would have depended on your having been baptized, and you would have been required under sanction to go to confession and to put in regular attendances at church services. The way you spent the rest of your time would have been considerably affected by church law, which would have required you, for example, to keep all the prescribed fasts and to abstain from work on the many feast days, even when it was inconvenient from a practical, agricultural, point of view. Your diet too would have been affected; what you might and might not eat and drink would have been limited by the food laws and fasting regulations of the church, and also, in many cases, by the terms of some penance. Your social status and the extent of your civic rights – or if you were a woman or a slave, the total lack of them – would have been controlled by a system which claimed a religious basis, and so would your degree of marital choice and your behaviour within marriage. If you had occasion to go to law, you would have found that the necessary oaths had to be taken on a sacred object, and often the procedure employed, for example the ordeal or compurgation, would have been in effect a way of committing the issue to divine decision.

The payment of tithes and other church dues for which you would have been liable would have been enforced by law, and in general even the secular laws which governed your conduct would have been drawn up with the approval of the church authorities, usually with the aim of ensuring that you and all members of the society remained Catholic

Christians in good standing. The very contents of your mind would have been controlled by the unchallenged tradition of the church, the holding of unorthodox views being an offence. All this you would have accepted without question or complaint, simply as part of the way things were.

Then there would have been the almost continual consciousness of the presence of the supernatural – not just the presence of God himself but of the innumerable other supernatural beings, the saints, angels and demons, by which you would have been comforted or terrified. A journey through an unfamiliar forest, for example, might well have turned out to be a nightmare experience, during which you needed to be constantly on the watch for the emergence of the terrifying beings whom you would have believed to be lurking in the undergrowth; and you would have had to be ready with the appropriate rites, sacred formulas and invocations of saints to defend yourself against them. Moreover there would always have been the background fear that some evil power might take you over altogether and turn you into a monster or a madman.

If tenth-century people were thus vividly conscious of the supernatural in the present, they also expected it to have decisive influence in the future. None of them doubted that they would continue to exist for ever, either in heaven or hell, and that the decision as to which it would be rested exclusively with God. This naturally influenced their decisions in many areas. Just as people today modify their behaviour for fear of contracting AIDS or smoking-related diseases, so tenth-century people modified their behaviour in the hope of gaining God's favour and attaining heaven, even if in practice a bird in the hand of this world often seemed worth two in the bush of the world to come.

Another route by which the supernatural impinged was through the need to find supernatural ways of dealing with situations which are dealt with today by technological, scientific and other this-worldly means. Since means of this sort were largely lacking, the only recourse was to supernatural power in order to cure or ward off illness, get rid of deformities, promote the fertility of oneself, one's crops and herds, fight famine and floods, repel invasions, achieve success in war or litigation, secure happiness in marriage and meet a whole host of other human needs, both personal and communal.

With this in mind, prayer and sacramental activity were organized in a systematic way and on a large scale, and the community was happy to support an army of men and women to engage in them. They were, so to speak, the backroom boys of the age. Just as a modern country houses hospitals and factories producing such things as medicines, fertilizers, guns, ambulances, flood barriers and rescue equipment, so the tenth-century landscape was dotted with relatively large buildings – monasteries and cathedral complexes – dedicated to the prayer and other activities needed to maintain the survival and prosperity of the realm and its inhabitants. All this undoubtedly gave a certain utilitarian character to a good deal of tenth-century religious practice.

Yet another way in which the the supernatural penetrated the consciousness was through events of various sorts which were taken to be divine punishments, or indications that such punishments would ensue if people did not mend their ways. Eclipses, thunderstorms, abnormally high winds, excessive rain or drought, sheep-scab, blight in the crops and a large number of other phenomena were regularly understood in this way. The hand of God seemed ever present.

Life was thus lived out against a strongly supernatural backdrop. Yet that hardly does justice to the situation: it was not just that people believed, in the abstract, in the existence of supernatural forces and factors which could affect things: events were actually experienced as the work of these beings; they were directly felt intertwining themselves with all that went on, encircling all sorts of persons, places and activities with their protective or destructive presence. We may cast our minds back to the representations on the *trumeau* at Souillac and similar sculptures (see plate 2).

If we ask about the response to this all-pervasive supernatural presence, many of the beings in question were regarded as wholly malevolent, and that is bound to have had some effect on the picture of God who allowed them to plague his creatures. To most people, as we have seen, God himself appeared a formidable, remote and inscrutable lord, intensely concerned about his honour, and unwilling to show favour until it had been fully satisfied. He was implacable to his foes, a God who had no hesitation in visiting eternal torture on the great majority of his human creatures, including many who had had no opportunity of knowing about him, and all those who had died unbaptized in infancy. Not only baptism but complete acceptance of the Christian creed, particularly at the moment of death, was an absolute condition of enjoying his favour.

Since God was God, all this, it was felt, must in some mysterious way be just, and indeed benevolent, but inevitably fear was a strong component in people's attitude towards such a God; and, as we have seen, such fear was encouraged by the church authorities. It was calculated to lead those who felt it to make their peace with God, but this was not simply a matter of a private approach in prayer. There was, it is true, a firmly established doctrine of grace, which sought to do justice to the work of the Holy Spirit in helping people's search for union with God. Yet whatever God in his mercy had done in the past to make salvation possible – and hymns and prayers reveal deep gratitude for it – no one could hope for his favour now without earning it. It is impossible to read the sermons and treatises of the time without concluding that the overall attitude they engendered must in practice have been Pelagian in the sense of assuming that God's favour had to be won through merit.

This merit did not have to be one's own; it could be the merit of Christ, invoked through the mass, but this needed to be supplemented by the merits of the saints or one's monastic patrons, or anyone else who possessed merit and was prepared to plead it on one's behalf. Whether it was one's own, or that of others, such merit was not just a matter of inward disposition; it was gained through the performance of specific acts of penance, reparation and charity. Appropriate acts of the required kind were prescribed by the church, which recommended as particularly effective, generous almsgiving, the enriching of shrines and the founding of churches and monasteries, or going on pilgrimage – activities, incidentally, possible only for the affluent. Given the low estimate of the natural world, neglect of it and denial of bodily satisfactions ranked high among the behaviour recommended. Such denial of the self and the world was institutionalized, and, as we have seen, monastic withdrawal was regarded as much the surest path to salvation.

Such an outlook could hardly fail to lead to a habit of quantification, and a contractual view of relations with God: so many good works, or so much suffering endured, it mattered not by whom, would make satisfaction for so many sins. The approach to the supernatural had to be through the proper channels. One sought forgiveness through the priest and the penances he prescribed or through the rites he performed. Good harvests were sought through the prescribed Rogationtide rites, recovery from illness through the prescribed prayers and the taking of medicines prepared in accordance with the church's directives; there were rites and formulas laid down for warding off evil of every kind.

In whatever connexion one sought to approach the divine, one worked through ecclesiastically-provided means, which tended, at least, to be thought of as effective *ex opere operato*, and in most cases required the intermediacy of the clergy. In such a transactional atmosphere, personal relationship with God was apt to fade into the background. Just as the king was too remote a figure for immediate contact, and had to be approached through one of his courtiers, so for most people God was an infinitely remote and formidable figure, only to be approached through friends at court, the angels, or, more commonly, the saints. It was only with the saints that any personal relationship, not to say intimacy, was to be expected; only from them that any real warmth or loving-kindness was to be experienced in the religious sphere. Even Jesus was not the object of devotion he was to become later. It was undoubtedly the saints who were the real object of a great deal of early mediaeval piety, and, as we have seen, they were taken in practice for virtually independent powers who answered prayer and worked wonders in their own right. In the matter of forgiveness and acceptance with God, one's only real hope lay in them and their willingness to plead on one's behalf.

However, as we saw in the Introduction, religions are never wholly coherent and self-consistent systems, and there were those in the tenth century whose approach to God was very different from that just described. Starting with the idea of God as *summum bonum*, they found in him the perfection of all the excellence they knew in this world, including such qualities as loving-kindness, sympathy, warm acceptance and even maternal love.[5] Christ was often spoken of in terms of the bridegroom imagery of the Song of Songs, and nuns especially saw themselves as his brides, and were to all intents and purposes in love with him. There is no mistaking the ardour and devotion of all these souls, though we may find difficulty in reconciling the perfect goodness they found in God with some of the attitudes and characteristics we have seen attributed to him above. People in the tenth century did not see it in the same way. They did not feel that the unaided moral judgment of fallen and fallible creatures could give any ground for criticizing God as infallible revelation presented him, or for suggesting that some of the behaviour attributed to him by the tradition fell short of the perfection these worshippers found in him. Since God was God, nothing he did *could* be inconsistent with his goodness. If they could not reconcile all the aspects of his behaviour theoretically, that was a problem of the kind we discussed on pp. 28–9. The solution must lie in the limitations and inadequacy of finite minds. 'The love of God is broader than the measures of man's mind,' and it was therefore possible to contine to hold that 'the heart of the Eternal is most wonderfully kind' without denying any of the rest of the church's teaching about him. As we have seen, those whose spirituality was built on this approach were a minority, even in the monasteries, and they, like everyone else, had to follow the institutional path to salvation, and command the necessary merits as the price of it.

Finally we return to the questions raised in the Introduction about whether religions do and should change. The contents of the book have made clear that to be a Christian in tenth-century Francia was in many ways different from what being a Christian can mean for anyone in the West today. Is that a matter for concern, and if so, why?

The extent of the differences between the religion of the tenth century and the religion of our own day can easily be masked by the obvious continuities and identities between them. We still use the same churches, or churches built on the the same pattern, and it is not uncommon to find a notice in an old parish church to the effect that 'Christian worship has been carried on continuously in this building for eight or nine or ten centuries', as the case may be. In the course of that worship the same Bible has been read (give or take the Apocrypha, and allowing for more accurate versions of the original), the same creeds have been recited and, until quite recently, in the Roman Catholic Church the same Latin liturgy has been celebrated.

What is more, we still confess the same fundamental doctrines, notably the distinctive Christian doctrines of the Trinity and the Incarnation.

These and similar points of agreement and contact are clearly very significant, especially when we add our common devotion to the figure of Jesus and our common reliance on the work of the Holy Spirit. At the very least, all this means that tenth-century religion and our own both stand in the common Christian tradition.

However, it would be a mistake to take it as meaning that tenth-century Christianity was fundamentally the same religion as ours, with only relatively minor and peripheral features separating them. It would be a mistake because the living religion people actually practise at any time is not to be defined simply by formal features of the sort I have been describing, still less by the elements it shares with the Christianity of earlier and later periods. In fact the features which give the Christianity of a period its real character may well be precisely those it does *not* share with the Christianity of any or all other periods. For example, among the most influential elements in the religion of tenth-century Frankish Christians were their belief in the existence of a whole army of evil powers intent on wreaking evil, and their devotion to the saints who were believed capable of providing defence against such evil, warding off illness, famine and other natural disasters, and also of winning from God a forgiveness he would not have granted without their intervention. Also central to their faith was the transgression of the first woman Eve, seen not only as revealing the inherent inferiority of the female sex, but as infecting all her descendants with a guilt so heinous that it fully merited their eternal damnation, quite apart from any sins they might have committed as individuals. As for the world, not only did they believe it to be a relatively small and recent creation produced *ex nihilo* in a single burst of creative activity, but they believed that it had been designed in every part solely with a view to human well-being, that nevertheless it had partaken in the results of the Fall and was therefore to be shunned whenever possible, and that it was now declining towards its imminent end in accordance with a predetermined and irreversible, divine decree. Readers will be able to supply other characteristic tenth-century ideas, equally foreign to anyone in the modern West, which loomed large in the religion of the time; and it was in the light of these that other elements of the faith were interpreted. The Bible, for example, understood and used in the ways described earlier, was a different book from the Bible as we read and use it. Likewise with the Creeds: the 'God the Father Almighty' of whom they speak was seen as a stern, aloof and formidable lord, and 'Jesus Christ his Son our Lord' was taken to be almost identical with him, equally formidable and remote. Jesus during his earthly life was believed to have been God the Son in person, in the full panoply of his divine attributes, whose assumption of humanity had involved no loss of omniscience and omnipotence and who was overseeing the universe at the very moment when he was sucking his mother's milk or uttering his parables in Galilee.

It was this tenth-century world of ideas in its full compass, and the Bible, liturgy and doctrinal corpus interpreted in the light of it, that engendered tenth-century faith (in Cantwell Smith's sense of the word) and determined the nature of it. The result was a piety directed primarily towards the saints, and to God almost exclusively through the saints, a strenuous and seemingly somewhat gloomy faith dominated by the fear of God and anxious concern about the salvation of one's soul. It involved a continual struggle to placate an angry God by humble self-abasement before him, by unquestioning and uncomplaining acceptance of his will, and by an unremitting effort to amass sufficient merit to qualify for one of the limited number of places in heaven.

At the same time the circumstances of the period dictated that a great deal of religious activity should be directed to the production of practical results. Religion then was a kind of alternative technology. That may serve to remind us that the peculiar features which distinguished the Christianity of that time were not the result of arbitrary choices or conscious decisions on the part of tenth-century believers, or indeed of their religious leaders. This book will have failed in its purpose unless it has made clear that tenth-century Christianity was what it was largely because of the context in which it was practised. The terms in which the lordship of God was envisaged, for example, were the terms then available, those of vassaldom and liege-lordship. The categories in terms of which the Trinity and the Incarnation were understood were the best philosophical categories then available, those of late Platonic thought. On the other hand, the technology, methodology and attitudes to history which make possible our interpretation of the Bible and the creeds, and our approach to the historical Jesus, were simply not available in the early Middle Ages.

What is more, the cultural situation not only dictated the terms in which doctrines were understood, it sometimes created doctrines. For example, we have seen that a threefold, hierarchical ordering of society under monarchical rule was believed to mirror the state of affairs in heaven and to be the clear will of God for the community, as revealed in biblical teaching and precedent. Yet the evidence of various non-Christian societies at a similar stage of development suggests that some such organization, with the great majority living only just, if at all, above subsistence level, and subjected to continual labour-intensive agricultural toil, was the only way such economies could survive; in which case the religious backing for the arrangement will have been very largely what we might call a theological rationalization of an inescapable situation.

Similarly the attitudes to space and time, and many of the other beliefs which could be derived from the Christian doctrine of creation, as we saw in Chapter 3, are to be found in other cultures at the same 'primitive' stage of development, as a book such as Hallpike's *Foundations of Primitive Thought* will make clear. Once again extra-theological forces must have been at work.

> The word 'rationalization' perhaps needs some explanation. Its use might suggest the theory, so beloved of Enlightenment thinkers, that the rulers, and especially the religious leaders, consciously produced an ideology designed to conceal the truth and so preserve their privileged style of existence. No doubt there is an element of truth in that, but it needs to be complemented by a recognition of the extent to which *theoria* arises out of *praxis*, and the outlook of an age reflects the means of production. In all probability the opinion-makers of the tenth century were to a large extent doing their honest best to make theological sense of a practical situation over which they had only very limited control and which they could do little to change.

This sort of point is widely understood nowadays, though the fact is not always so clearly recognized that it applies as much to twentieth-century Western versions of Christianity as to any others. They too must owe a good deal to the contemporary cultural milieu. When that is realized, the problem behind the relation of one manifestation of Christianity and another is revealed in its full complexity. Various ways have been suggested for dealing with the problem, and of exhibiting all the various manifestations of Christianity at different periods as capable of being brought under a single head, most often in terms either of development (one form of Christianity being seen as a development of earlier ones) or in terms of essence (different forms of Christianity being seen as so many manifestations of the essence of the religion, however that may be defined). Some of the difficulties entailed in both approaches were hinted at in the Introduction and the question cannot be further discussed here.[6]

It hardly needs emphasizing that the matter is one of great practical importance, in view of the age-old Christian belief that the Christian past is normative for the present, so that Christianity at any one period should not deviate significantly from the Christianity of earlier periods. In Catholic circles particularly, it is often urged that we should do and believe certain things – for example, believe in a personal devil or refuse to ordain women to the priesthood – on the grounds that otherwise we should be breaking with the unbroken tradition of the church. Such an argument requires clear-sighted analysis. It clearly involves, for example, that we should not break with the belief and practice of tenth-century Christians so far as they were part of the unbroken tradition: yet when we set their belief in a personal devil, and their failure even to consider ordaining women, against their total set of beliefs in both areas, is it plausible to single out one aspect of their attitude to either of these matters, and present it as normative for us in our widely different cultural situation? If, for example, we do not share their belief that the female sex is fundamentally inferior, and that woman is responsible for rendering the human race inherently worthy of damnation, why should we cling to this one outworking of it? Clearly the argument could be broadened to take in many other areas.

Protestants usually lay less stress on tradition, but they bring the past to weigh on our shoulders by their tendency to insist that modern faith and practice must conform to those of the New Testament period. The questions that raises cannot be debated here, but one point may be made: there is every reason to think that if we knew as much about first-century Christianity as we do about that of the tenth century, we should find it at least equally foreign to us. Centuries of selectivity with regard to the New Testament text, and innumerable attempts over the centuries to 'apply' it to our situation, have given many people a false sense of being at home in the world of New Testament Christianity. In fact it was a world very far removed from our own. To cite just one example, New Testament expectations of the end of the world were even more vivid than any entertained in the tenth century. Almost without exception, the early Christians seem to have expected that the end would come within their own lifetime or, at the very latest, within that of the immediately following generation, and a great deal of the rest of their religion, as they perceived it, stemmed from that.[7] Once again, if we can no longer accept such elements of their world-view, is it reasonable to suggest that our faith should be bound by ideas and teachings which were part and parcel of them, and conditioned by them?

The object of this book has been to show, through one case-study, that Christianity at any given period is part and parcel of an unrepeatable combination of cultural elements which affect it in a thousand ways, and condition, though they may not determine, its form and character. The process goes largely unnoticed at the time. Especially in periods of little cultural change, the fundamental presuppositions of their culture seem so unquestionable to those brought up in it that they are unaware how much their outlook is conditioned by them. The time has come for all this to be recognized and unreservedly accepted. Only then will it be possible for the resultant questions to be faced in a systematic and creative way.

The book is also intended to illustrate the sorts of ways and areas in which the cultural conditioning of Christianity takes place and to point to some aspects of traditional faith and practice which most need scrutiny in this connexion.

Appendix

The following extract from an essay by Dr Robin Horton is of interest in connexion with several sections of Chapter 9, and particularly with the way many people in the early Middle Ages treated the saints as effectively so many independent deities, while not surrendering their faith in one God.

It is typical of traditional African religious systems that they include, on the one hand, ideas about a multiplicity of spirits, and on the other hand, ideas about a single supreme being. Though the spirits are thought of as independent beings, they are also considered as so many manifestations of dependents of the supreme being. This conjunction of the many and the one has given rise to much discussion among students of comparative religion, and has evoked many ingenious theories. Most of these have boggled at the idea that polytheism and monotheism could coexist stably in a single system of thought. They have therefore tried to resolve the problem by supposing that the belief-systems in question are in transition from one type to the other. It is only recently, with the Nilotic studies of Evans-Pritchard and Lienhardt, that the discussion has got anywhere near the point – which is that the many spirits and the one God play complementary roles in people's thinking. As Evans-Pritchard says: 'A theistic religion need be neither monotheistic nor polytheistic. It may be both. It is the question of the level, or situation, of thought, rather than of exclusive types of thought.'

On the basis of material from the Nilotic, and on that of material from [various] West African societies, ... one can make a tentative suggestion about the respective roles of the many and the one in traditional African thought generally. In such thought, I suggest, the spirits provide the means of setting an event within a relatively limited causal context. They are the basis of a theoretical scheme which typically covers the thinker's own community and immediate environment. The supreme being, on the other hand, provides the means of setting an event within the widest possible context. For it is the basis of a theory of the origin and life course of the world seen as a whole.

In many (though by no means all) traditional African belief-systems, ideas about the spirits and actions based on such ideas are far more richly developed than ideas about the supreme being and actions based on them. In these cases, the idea of God seems more the pointer to a potential theory than the core of a seriously operative one. This perhaps is because social life in the communities involved is so parochial that their members seldom have to place events in the wider context that the idea of the supreme being purports to deal with.

(from Bryan Wilson, ed., *Rationality*, published 1970 by Blackwell Publishers, Oxford, reprinted by kind permission)

Bibliography

On the limited scope of this bibliography, see the Preface, p. x. Where more than one work by an author is listed, the titles are given in order of publication. Where an English translation of a foreign book exists the work is referred to in the English version, unless there was some special point in preferring the original, or translating directly from it.

(a) Books

Achéry, J.L.d', *Spicilegium*, nova editio, Paris 1723

Adams, H., *Mont-St-Michel and Chartres*, Mentor Book edition, New York 1961

Addleshaw, G.W.O,. *The Development of the Parochial System from Charlemagne to Urban II*, London 1954

Aelfric, *The Homilies of the Anglo-Saxon Church* (two vols), ed. B. Thorpe, London 1844, 1846

Allen, P.S., *The Romanesque Lyric*, Chapel Hill 1928

Anderson, Perry, *Passages from Antiquity to Feudalism*, London 1978

Aries, P., *The Hour of Our Death*, London 1981

Bainton, R.H., *The Medieval Church*, Princeton 1962

Bark, W.C., *Origins of the Medieval World*, Stamford 1958

Barraclough, G., *The Medieval Papacy*, London 1968

—, *The Crucible of Europe*, London 1976

Barstow, A.L., *Married Priests and the Reforming Papacy*, New York 1982

Beer, M., *Social Struggles of the Middle Ages*, London 1924

Benedict, St, *The Rule* (of the many editions perhaps the best for most purposes is that edited by Timothy Fry, which includes the Latin text, an English translation and notes – see under Fry)

Binns, L.Elliott, *The Decline and Fall of the Medieval Papacy*, London 1934

Bishop, E., *Liturgica Historica*, Oxford 1918

Bloch, M., *Feudal Society* (two vols), reissued London 1965

Blumenthal, U.-R. (ed.), *Carolingian Essays*, Washington, DC 1983

Boas, G., *Essays on Primitivism and Related Ideas in the Middle Ages*, Baltimore 1948

Bonifazi, C., *The Soul of the World*, Washington, DC 1978

Boswell, J., *Christianity, Tolerance and Homosexuality*, Chicago 1980

Boussard, J., *The Civilisation of Charlemagne*, London 1968

Brandt, W.J., *The Shape of Medieval History*, New Haven 1966

Brehaut, E., *An Encyclopedist of the Dark Ages*, New York 1912
Bridenthal, R., and Koonz, C. (eds.), *Becoming Visible*, Boston 1977
Brooke, Christopher, *The Structure of Mediaeval Society*, London 1971
Brooke, C.N.L. (with W.Swaan), *The Monastic World, 1000–1300*, London 1974
Brooke, Rosalind and Christopher, *Popular Religion in the Middle Ages*, London 1984
Brown, P., *The Cult of the Saints*, Chicago and London 1981
—, *Society and the Holy in Late Antiquity*, London 1982
Bugge, J., *Virginitas*, The Hague 1975
Bullough, D., *The Age of Charlemagne*, London ²1973
Burke, P., *Popular Culture in Early Modern Europe*, London 1978
Burnaby, J., *Amor Dei*, London 1938
Burns, C.Delisle, *The First Europe*, London 1947
Butler, C., *Western Mysticism*, London 1922
—, *Benedictine Monachism*, London 1924

Cambridge Mediaeval History, esp. Vols II, III, V and VI, Cambridge 1913–36
Cantor, N.F., *Medieval History*, New York 1969
Chélini, J., *Histoire Religieuse de l'Occident Médiéval*, Paris 1968
—, *La Vie Religieuse des Laïcs dans l'Europe Carolingienne* (Thèse pour le doctorat d'état ès lettres et sciences humaines, présentée devant l'université de Paris X, Nanterre, four vols, unpublished)
Cheyette, F.L., *Lordship and Community in Medieval Europe*, New York 1968
Cipolla, C.M. (ed.), *The Fontana Economic History of Europe*, Vol.1, London 1972
Clebsch, W.A. *Christianity in European History*, New York 1979
A.Cluny, *Travaux du Congrès*, Société des Amis de Cluny, Dijon 1950
Cohn, N., *The Pursuit of the Millennium*, London 1957
—, *Europe's Inner Demons*, London 1975
Congar, Y., *L'Ecclésiologie du Haut Moyen Age*, Paris 1968
Cook, W.R. and Herzmann, R.B., *The Medieval World View*, New York 1983
Coulton, G.G., *Five Centuries of Religion*, Vol.1, Cambridge 1923
—, *Art and the Reformation*, Oxford 1928
—, *The Medieval Village*, Cambridge 1925
—, *Life in the Middle Ages* (four vols), Cambridge 1928
—, *The Medieval Scene*, Cambridge 1930
—, *Ten Medieval Studies*, Cambridge ³1930
—, *Medieval Panorama*, Cambridge 1938
Cousin, P., *Abbon de Fleury-sur-Loire*, Paris 1954
Cutts, E.L., *Parish Priests and their People in the Middle Ages in England*, London 1898

Daniel-Rops, H., *L'Église des Temps Barbares*, Paris 1950 (ET *The Church in the Dark Ages*, London 1959)
Davidson, H.R.Ellis, *Gods and Myths of Northern Europe*, Harmondsworth 1964
Dawson, C., *The Making of Europe*, London 1932
—, *Mediaeval Religion*, London 1934

—, *Religion and the Rise of Western Culture*, London 1950

Decarreaux, J., *Monks and Civilisation*, London 1964

Delaruelle, E.E.H., *La Piété Populaire au Moyen Age*, Turin 1975

Delehaye, H., *Sanctus*, Paris 1927

—, *Les Légendes Hagiographiques*, Brussels 1955 (ET *The Legends of the Saints*, London 1962)

Devisse, J., *Hincmar. Archévêque de Reims* (three vols), Geneva 1975–6

Dhuoda, *Manuel Pour Mon Fils*, ed. P.Riché, Paris 1975

Didron, M., *Christian Iconography* (two vols), London 1851

Dixon, P., *Barbarian Europe*, Oxford 1976

Dubois, M.-M., *Aelfric, Sermonnaire, Docteur et Grammarien*, Paris 1943

Duby, G., *Rural Economy and Country Life in the Mediaeval West*, London 1968

—, *Hommes et Structures du Moyen Age*, Paris 1973

—, *The Early Growth of the European Economy*, London 1974

—, *The Chivalrous Society*, London 1977

—, *Medieval Marriage*, Baltimore 1978

—, *The Three Orders*, Chicago 1980

—, *The Knight, the Lady and the Priest*, London 1984

—(ed.), *A History of Private Life*, Vol.2, Cambridge, Mass.1988

— with R.Mandrou, *A History of French Civilization*, London 1965

Duchesne, L., *Le Liber Pontificalis*, Paris 1886, etc.

—, *The Beginnings of the Temporal Sovereignty of the Popes*, London 1908

—, *Christian Worship*, London ⁵1931

Duckett, E.S., *Alcuin. Friend of Charlemagne*, New York 1951

—, *St Dunstan of Canterbury*, London 1955

—, *The Gateway to the Middle Ages*, Ann Arbor 1951

—, *Carolingian Portraits*, Ann Arbor 1962

—, *Death and Life in the Tenth Century*, Ann Arbor 1967

Dunbabin, J., *France in the Making*, Oxford 1985

Eicken, H.von, *Geschichte und System der Mittelalterlichen Weltanschauung*, Stuttgart 1887

Einhardt, *Life of Charlemagne*, ed. H.W.Garrod and R.B.Mowat, Oxford 1915

Ellard, G., *Master Alcuin: Liturgist*, Chicago 1956

Erickson, C., *The Medieval Vision*, New York 1976

Evans, J., *Life in Medieval France*, London 1925

Fichtenau, H., *The Carolingian Empire*, Oxford 1957

Fisher, J.D.C., *Christian Initiation*, London 1965

Fliche, A., *La Réforme Grégorienne*, Vol.1, Louvain and Paris 1924

—, and Martin V., *Histoire de l'Église*, Vol.VII, Paris 1940

Focillon, H., *L'An Mil*, Paris 1952 (ET *The Year 1000*, New York 1971)

Freeman, E.A., *Historical Essays*, London ²1875

Fry, T. (ed.), *The Rule of St Benedict*, Collegeville, Minnesota 1981

Gibbon, E., *The Decline and Fall of the Roman Empire*, ed. J.B.Bury (seven vols), London 1909–1914

Gibson, M., and Nelson, J., *Charles the Bald: Court and Kingdom*, Oxford 1981

Grabar, A., and Nordenfalk, C., *Early Medieval Painting*, Lausanne 1957
Green, D.H., *The Carolingian Lord*, Cambridge 1965
Green, V.H.H., *Medieval Civilization in Western Europe*, London 1971
Gregorovius, F.A., *History of the City of Rome*, London 1894–1902
Gurevich, A.J., *Categories of Medieval Culture*, London 1985

Hamilton, B.H., *Religion in the Medieval West*, London 1986
Hardison, O.B., *Christian Rite and Christian Drama*, Baltimore 1965
Harrison, F., *Medieval Man and His Notions*, London 1947
Harrison, J.F.C., *The Common People*, London 1984
Harnack, A.von, *Lehrbuch der Dogmengeschichte*, Tübingen ⁴1909–1920 (ET of
    third edition *History of Dogma*, esp. Vols 5 and 6, London 1896)
—, *Monasticism*, London ²1913
Hauck, A., *Kirchengeschichte Deutschlands*, Berlin ⁷1952
Heer, F., *Charlemagne and His World*, London 1975
Hefele, C.J. von, and Le Clercq, H., *Histoire des Conciles* (eleven vols), Paris
    1907–1952
Heliand, The, translated M.Scott, Chapel Hill 1966
Henderson, G., *Early Medieval*, Harmondsworth 1972
Herrin, J., *The Formation of Christendom*, Oxford 1987
Hillgarth, J.N., *The Conversion of Western Europe*, Englewood Cliffs, NJ 1969
Holmes, U.T., *Daily Living in the Twelfth Century*, Madison, NJ 1952
Hoyt, R.S. (ed.), *Life and Thought in the Early Middle Ages*, Minneapolis 1967
Hubert, J., Porcher, J., and Volback, W.F., *Carolingian Art*, London 1970
Hunt, J.E., *English and Welsh Crucifixes*, London 1956

Imbart de la Tour, P., *Les Paroisses Rurales dans l'Ancienne France du 4ᵉ au 11ᵉ*
    Siècle, Paris 1900

James, E., *The Origins of France*, London 1982
Jedin, H., and Dolan, J. (eds.), *History of the Church*, Vol.3 by F.Kempf, H.-
    G.Beck, E.Ewig and J.A.Jungmann, London 1980
Jungmann, J.A., *The Mass of the Roman Rite* (one volume edition), London 1959
—, *Pastoral Liturgy*, Tenbury Wells 1962

Kantorowitcz, E.H., *Laudes Regiae*, Berkeley, Ca 1946
—, *The King's Two Bodies*, Princeton 1957
Ker, W.P., *The Dark Ages*, Mentor Books edition, New York 1958
Kern, F., *Kingship and Law in the Middle Ages*, Oxford 1939
Knowles, D., *The Monastic Order in England*, Cambridge ²1950
—, *The Religious Orders in England* (three vols), Cambridge ²1955–1959
—, *Christian Monasticism*, London 1969
—, *The Evolution of Medieval Thought*, new edition, London 1988
— and Obolensky, D., *The Middle Ages*, London 1969

I Laici nella 'Societas Cristiana' dei Secoli XI & XII, Atti della terza Settimana
    internazionale di studio Mendola (21–27 agosto 1965), Pubblicazioni dell'
    Università Cattolica del Sacro Cruore, Milan 1968

Landon, E.H., *A Manual of Councils* (two vols), Edinburgh 1901
Latourette, K.S., *A History of the Expansion of Christianity*, London 1947, esp. vol. 2
Lawrence, C.H. *Medieval Monasticism*, London 1984
Le Bras, G., *Études de Sociologie Religieuse*, Paris 1955
Leclercq, J., *Aux sources de la Spiritualité Occidentale*, Paris 1964
—, *Témoins de la Spiritualité Occidentale*, Paris 1965
—, *Chances de la Spiritualité Occidentale*, Paris 1966
—, *Love of Learning and the Desire for God*, London 1978
—, Vandenbroucke, F., and Bouyer, L., *The Spirituality of the Middle Ages*, London 1968
Le Goff, J., *La Civilisation de l'Occident Médiéval*, Paris 1977 (ET *Medieval Civilisation*, Oxford 1988)
—, *Time, Work and Culture in the Middle Ages*, Chicago 1980
—, *The Birth of Purgatory*, London 1984
Lewis, C.S., *The Discarded Image*, Cambridge 1964
Leyser, K., *Rule and Conflict in an Early Medieval Society*, London 1979
Longère, J., *La Prédication Médiévale*, Paris 1983
Lot, F., Pfister, C., and Ganshof, F.L., *Histoire du Moyen Age* I. 1 and 2, Paris 1940–1
— and Fawtier, R., *Histoire des Institutions Françaises au Moyen Age*, Vol.3, Paris 1962
Luchaire, A., *Social France at the Time of Philip Augustus*, London 1912
Lyon, B.D., *The Origins of the Middle Ages*, New York 1972

MacCulloch, J.A., *Medieval Faith and Fable*, London 1932
Macdonald, A.J.M., *Authority and Reason*, Oxford 1933
McDannel, C. and Lang, B., *Heaven. A History*, New Haven 1988
McGiffert, A.C., *A History of Christian Thought*, Vol.II, New York 1933
McGinn, B., Meyerdorff, J., and Leclercq, J (eds.), *Christian Spirituality* I, New York and London 1989
MacKinney, L.C., *Early Medieval Medicine*, Baltimore 1937
McKitterick, R., *The Frankish Church and the Carolingian Reforms*, London 1977
—, *The Frankish Kingdoms under the Carolingians*, London 1983
—, *The Carolingians and the Written Word*, Cambridge 1989
McNally, R.E., *The Bible in the Early Middle Ages*, Westminster, Maryland 1959
McNeill, J.T., and Gamer, H.M., *Medieval Handbooks of Penance*, New York 1938
McNeill, W.H., *The Rise of the West*, Chicago 1963
Maitland, S.R., *The Dark Ages*, new ed. by F.Stokes, London 1889
Manning, B.L., *The People's Faith in the Time of Wyclif*, Cambridge 1919
Manselli, R., *La Religion Populaire au Moyen Age*, Paris 1975
Mansi, J.D., *Sacrorum Conciliorum Nova et Amplissima Collectio* (thirty-one vols to 1440), Florence, then Venice 1759–1798
Mecklin, J.M., *The Passing of the Saint*, Chicago 1941
Mellone, S.H., *Western Christian Thought in the Middle Ages*, London 1935
Mercier, P. (ed.), *XIV Homélies du IX Siècle*, Paris 1970

Miegge, G., *The Virgin Mary*, London 1955
Milman, H.H., *History of Latin Christianity* (nine vols), esp. vol.3, London 1872
Morris, C., *The Discovery of the Individual*, London 1972
Morrison. J.C., *St Bernard*, London 1884

Neill, S.C., and Weber, H.-R., *The Layman in Christian History*, London 1963
Ntedka, J., *L'Évocation de l'au-delà dans la Prière pour les Morts*, Louvain 1971

Obelkevich, J. (ed.), *Religion and the People, 800–1700*, Chapel Hill, NC 1979
Ozanam, A.F., *Les Germains avant le Christianisme*, Paris 1855

Parker R., *The Common Stream*, St Albans 1976
Parsons, D. (ed.), *Tenth-Century Studies*, London 1975
Patch, H.R., *The Other World*, Cambridge, Mass. 1950
Pelikan, J., *Historical Theology*, New York 1971
—, *The Growth of Medieval Theology*, Chicago 1978
Peters, E.M. (ed.), *Monks, Bishops and Pagans*, Philadelphia 1975
Pognon, E., *L'An Mille*, Paris 1947
Poole, R.Lane, *Studies in Chronology and History*, Oxford 1934
Powicke, F.M., *The Christian Life in the Middle Ages*, Oxford 1935

Radding, C.M., *A World Made by Men*, Chapel Hill, NC 1985
Rambaud, A.N., *Histoire de la Civilisation Française* I, Paris 1893
Redfield, R., *Peasant Society and Culture*, Chicago 1956
Reviron, J., *Jonas d'Orléans*, Paris 1930
Riché, P., *Daily Life in the World of Charlemagne*, Liverpool 1978
Ritschl, A., *A Critical History of the Christian Doctrine of Justification and Reconciliation*, Edinburgh 1872
Ritzer, K., *Le Mariage dans les Églises Chrétiennes*, Paris 1970 (later edition of the German original of 1962)
Roswitha, *The Plays of Roswitha*, translated H.J.W.Tillyard, London 1923
Russell, J.B., *A History of Medieval Christianity*, New York 1968
—, *Medieval Civilisation*, New York 1968

Salin, E., *La Civilisation Mérovingienne* (four vols.), Paris 1949–59
Salmon, P., *The Breviary through the Ages*, Collegeville, Minnesota 1962
Sawyer, P.H. and Wood, I.N., *Early Mediaeval Kingship*, Leeds 1977
Schillebeeckx, E., *Marriage: Secular Reality and Sacred Mystery*, London 1965
—, *Celibacy*, New York 1965 = *Clerical Celibacy under Fire*, London 1965
Schmitz, H.J., *Die Bussbücher und die Bussdisciplin der Kirche*, I, Mainz 1883; II, Düsseldorf 1898
Schnürer, G., *Church and Culture in the Middle Ages*, Vol.1, Paterson, NJ 1956
Schulte, A., *Der Adel und die Deutsche Kirche im Mittelalter*, Stuttgart [2]1922
Seeberg, R., *The History of Doctrines* (two vols), Grand Rapids 1961
Sitwell, G., *St Odo of Cluny*, London 1958
Smalley, B. (ed.), *Trends in Mediaeval Political Thought*, Oxford 1965
—, *Historians in the Middle Ages*, London 1974
—, *The Study of the Bible in the Middle Ages*, Oxford [3]1983

Smith, W.Cantwell, *The Meaning and End of Religion*, New York 1962 and London 1963
Southern, R.W., *The Making of the Middle Ages* (1953), London 1959
—, *Western Society and the Church in the Middle Ages*, Harmondsworth 1970
Stark, W., *The Sociology of Religion*, London 1966
Stevenson, K.W., *Nuptial Blessing*, Alcuin Club Coll. 64, London 1982
Strayer, J.R., *Feudalism*, Princeton 1965
Sumption, J., *Pilgrimage*, London 1975
Symons, T., *Regularis Concordia*, Oxford 1953

Tavard, G.H., *Woman in Christian Tradition*, Notre Dame 1973
Tellenbach, G., *Church, State and Christian Society*, Oxford 1936
Thomas, K., *Man and the Natural World*, London 1983
Thrupp, S.L. (ed.), *Early Medieval Society*, New York 1967
Tixeront, J., *History of Dogmas*, Vol.3, St Louis, Mo 1916
Traill, D.A., *Walafrid Strabo's Visio Wettini*, Frankfurt am Main 1974
Troeltsch, E. *The Social Teaching of the Christian Churches*, Vol.1, London 1931
Twining, G.L., *Symbols and Emblems of Early and Mediaeval Christian Art*, London 1852

Ullmann, W., *The Growth of Papal Government in the Middle Ages*, London 1955
—, *The Individual and Society in the Middle Ages*, London 1967
—, *The Carolingian Renaissance and the Idea of Kingship*, London 1969
—, *A Short History of the Papacy in the Middle Ages*, London 1972

Vauchez, A., *La Spiritualité du Moyen Age Occidentale*, Paris 1975
Verdon, J. (ed.), *La Chronique de St Maixent*, Paris 1979
Veyne, P. (ed.), *A History of Private Life*, Vol.1, Cambridge, Mass. 1987
Vielhaber, K., *Gottschalk der Sachse*, Bonn 1956
Vogel, C., *Le Pécheur et la Pénitence au Moyen Age*, Paris 1969

Wallace-Hadrill, J.M., *The Long-Haired Kings*, London 1962
—, *Early Germanic Kingship in England and on the Continent*, Oxford 1971
—, *Early Medieval History*, Oxford 1975
—, *The Barbarian West*, London ³1977
—, *The Frankish Church*, Oxford 1983
— and McManners, J., *France, Government and Society*, London ²1970
Ward, B., *Miracles and the Medieval Mind*, revised ed., Aldershot 1987
Wasserschleben, F.W.H. (ed.), *Die Bussordnungen der Abendländischen Kirche*, Halle 1851
Watkin-Jones, H., *The Holy Spirit in the Mediaeval Church*, London 1922
Weinstein, F., and Bell, R.M., *Saints and Society*, Chicago 1982
Wemple, S.F., *Women in Frankish Society*, Philadelphia 1981
White, Lynn T., *Medieval Technology and Social Change*, Oxford 1962
—, *Machina ex Deo*, Cambridge, Mass 1968
White, T.H., *The Book of Beasts*, London 1954
Whitley, W.T. (ed.), *The Doctrine of Grace*, London 1932
Wilmart, A., *Auteurs Spirituels et Textes Dévots du Moyen Age Latin*, Paris 1932

Wilson, B. (ed.), *Rationality*, Oxford 1970
Wood, M., *In Search of the Dark Ages*, London 1981
Workman, H.B., *The Evolution of the Monastic Ideal*, London ²1927
Wormald, P. (ed.), *Ideal and Reality in Frankish and Anglo-Saxon Society*, Oxford 1983

Zarnecki, G., *The Monastic Achievement*, London 1972

(b) Articles and individual chapters

Carozzi, C., 'Rhétorique et idéologie: la tripartition sociale au XI siècle', *Annales* 33.4, July-August 1978, 683–701
Contreni, J.J., 'Carolingian Biblical Studies', in Blumenthal, *Carolingian Essays*, 71–98
Darlington, O.G., 'Gerbert the Teacher', *American Historical Review* 52.3, April 1947, 456–76
De Clercq, C., '*Ordines unctionis infirmi* des IX et X siècles', *Ephemerides Liturgicae* 44, 1930, 101ff.
Katzenellenbogen, A., 'The Image of Christ in the Early Middle Ages', in Hoyt, *Life and Thought*, 66–84
Le Goff, J., 'Les Trois Fonctions Indo-Européens: l'Histoire et l'Europe Féodale', *Annales* 34.6, 1187–215
Leyser, K., 'The German Aristocracy from the Ninth to the Early Twelfth Century', *Past and Present* 41, December 1968, 25–53
MacKinney, L.C., 'Tenth-Century Medicine as seen in the *Historia* of Richer of Rheims', *Bulletin of the Institute of the History of Medicine, Johns Hopkins University, Baltimore*, 2, 1934, 347–75
—, 'Bishop Fulbert and Education at the School of Chartres', *Texts and Studies in the History of Medieval Education*, Medieval Institute of the University of Notre Dame, Indiana, VI, 1957, 13ff.
McKitterick, R., 'Charles the Bald and His Library: The Patronage of Learning', *EHR* XCV, 1980, 28–47
Morris, C., 'A Critique of Popular Religion: Guibert of Nogent on *The Relics of the Saints*', *SCH* 8, 1972, 55–60
Nelson, J., 'Royal Saints and Early Medieval Kingship', *SCH* 7, 1971, 41–59
—, 'Kingship, Law and Liturgy in the Political Thought of Hincmar of Rheims', *EHR* 92, 1977, 241–79
—, 'Sanctity and Secularity', *SCH* 10, 1974, 39–44
—, 'Inauguration Rituals', in Sawyer and Wood, *Early Mediaeval Kingship*, 50–71
Russell, J.C., 'Late Ancient and Medieval Population', *Transactions of the American Philosophical Society* 48.3, 1958, 5–148
Schmitt, J.C., 'Religion populaire et culture folklorique', *Annales* 31.5, 1976, 941ff.
Singer, S., *Germanische-romanische Monatschrift* XIII, 1925, 187–201 and 243–58
Southern, R.W., 'The Church of the Dark Ages, 600–1000', in Neill and Weber, *Layman in Christian History*, 88–110

Toubert, P., 'La théorie du mariage chez les moralistes carolingiens', *Settimane di studio del centro Italiano di studi sull' alto medioevo XXIV, Il matrimonio nella società altomedievale, Tomo primo*, Spoleto 1977, 233–82

Turmel, J., 'Histoire d'angélologie des temps apostoliques à la fin du Ve siècle', *Revue d'Histoire et de Littérature Religieuses* 3, 1898, 289ff., 407ff., 533ff.

Vogel, C., 'Les rites de la célébration du mariage', *Settimane di studio del centro Italiano di studi sull' alto medioevo XXIV, Il matrimonio nella società altomedievale, Tomo primo*, Spoleto 1977, 397–465

Notes on Illustrations

Jacket: Tenth-century statue-reliquary of St Foy at Conques. It illustrates the great importance attached to relics, and the wealth of materials and workmanship that were lavished on them (Photo Giraudon).

1. This crucifix dates from *c.* 1050–1100 and illustrates how, even after the tenth century, the crucified Christ was seen as essentially a royal conqueror, with crown, colobium and arms outstretched in victory. This was clearly not a kindly figure with whom close personal relations would have seemed possible or appropriate (Aaby crucifix, Copenhagen National Museum, II no. D629).
2. This trumeau from Souillac in the Dordogne (*c.* 1125) illustrates both the inventive pattern-making and high artistic achievement of the period, and also 'that dark undercurrent of vehemence and tension' which flowed deep in the early mediaeval mind (Bildarchiv Foto Marburg and photo Edwin Smith).
3. Charlemagne's throne at Aachen. A 'high throne' both in the sense of being placed at the top of a number of steps and in the sense of being 'exalted' by being put on the first floor, though remaining visible from below (Bildarchiv Foto Marburg).
4. Ivory of *c.* 980. The Holy Roman Emperor Otto II and his wife and son do obeisance to the ultimate *imperator* exactly as their subjects were expected to do to them. The relation between Christ and his people is understood in the same terms as that of an earthly sovereign to his subjects (Museo Archeologico, Milan. Foto Scala, Florence).
5. Late eighth century. Illustrated the 'Carolingian minuscule' script which replaced the Anglo-Saxon style and ultimately became the prototype of modern Western printed documents. Although a lot clearer than earlier styles, it was obviously not easy to ready quickly, especially as a system of – recognized – abbreviations was regularly used. Being a version of the Bible, this example is a great deal clearer than many.
6. This picture of the eighth-century church at Mistail in Switzerland suggests how modest in size most churches of the period were. There are many parish churches of comparable size, eg. at Bradford-on-Avon and Escombe in England. It should be remembered that all these have survived because they were built of stone. The majority of parish churches were extremely modest wooden structure (T. and H. Seeger).
7. Otto II enthroned (*c..* 975). The four figures holding the band of material symbolize the Evangelists. Below are representatives of the *bellatores* and the *oratores* (Mrs Bredof-Lepper).

8. A late tenth-century crown. Although intended for the head of a statue, it gives a good idea of the sort of crown worn at the time (E. Bohn, Mainz).

9. Early eleventh century. The picture illustrates the vivid realism with which people looked forward to life after death. The four angels are blowing their horns to announce the Last Judgment, and the beseeching gestures of those rising from their graves speak for themselves (Munich, Bayerische Staatsbibliothek. Photo Sächsische Landesbibliothek, Deutsche Fototek).

10. The translation of the relics of St Alban. Although this picture comes from a fourteenth-century manuscript, it illustrates clearly the pomp which surrounded such events, the richness of the feretory and the way cripples and others attempted to get access to the healing properties of the relics. The figure at the front is asperging with holy water (British Library, London).

11. The monastery of St Martin du Canigou in Roussillon, founded in 1007. Its site, 3,495 feet above sea-level, was no doubt chosen partly in the interests of inaccessibility and withdrawal, but, as many commentators have argued, it is difficult to doubt that considerations of natural beauty also played a part (Wim Swaan).

12. Frescoes at Müstair in Switzerland. Even such a small photograph is enough to show how inaccessible to view much of the painting was. When the confusion in the iconography is borne in mind, it will be seen that even such quite exceptional church decoration conveyed less information about the biblical story than might appear at first sight (Arts of Mankind Photo).

13. A *mappa mundi* (map of the world). This one is Spanish and dates from the thirteenth century, but all maps of this kind appear to be based on the work of Isidore of Seville. They were intended to teach about 'the compass of the world and them that dwell therein' (Psalm 24.1) and to give information about religion and natural history as well as geography and history.

   East is at the top, and Rome is the centre of the world which is surrounded by Ocean. The picture of Adam and Eve shows where paradise was located, and the strip of land on the extreme right represents 'a fourth party of the world unknown to us on account of the heat of the sun', where 'the Antipodaeans are fabulously said to dwell' (Isidore) (Bibliothèque nationale, Paris).

   The schematic and inaccurate character of such maps, which was because they were based on religious data as much as on observation, made impossible any clear idea of locations and relative distances, or of the geographical factors in human affairs.

14. Carving from the twelfth-century church of St Pierre de Chauvigny near Poitiers. It reveals the realism with which the demonic forces, and the possibility of being destroyed by them, were taken (Photo Caisse Nationale des Monuments Historiques et des Sites, © J. Feuillie).

15. A reliquary of *c.* 980–990. It is only 12¼" high and an example of the portable reliquaries in which nobles and churchmen carried round their relics with them for protection on their journeyings. Some had fastenings for chains or belts by which they could be attached to the person (N. Haas, Trier).

Notes

Preface

1. Dame Felicitas Corrigan, *The Nun, The Infidel and The Superman*, London 1985, 30 (italics, etc., as in the original).

1. Introduction

1. L. von Ranke, *Über die Epochen der neueren Geschichte*, Leipzig 1888, Erste Vortrag, 25 September 1854, 4–5.
2. See B. Malinowski, *The Argonauts of the Western Pacific*, London 1922, xvi.
3. *Protagoras*, 329A.

2. The Franks

1. Focillon, *L'An Mil*, 13.
2. At any rate in *Christian* Frankish society, compurgation amounted to much more than the giving of a character witness. Compurgators were required to swear fearful oaths, which had to be repeated faultlessly for the witness to succeed. The oath, which laid the maker open to God's judgment, was the heart of the matter, and compurgation was thus a form of ordeal in the sense that the result of it was to reveal God's mind on the matter at issue. See Radding, *World Made by Men*, 4–5, and the references to other literature given there.
3. See Wallace-Hadrill, *Frankish Church*, 18, for the dangers of using later evidence from Scandinavia in this connexion.
4. Gregory of Tours, *HF* II, 30.
5. In 911, for example, Rolf, or Rollo, consented, even if only half-seriously, to do homage to Charles the Simple in return for the districts of Rouen, Lisieux and Évreux, which he already held in fact, thus inaugurating Normandy, the land of the Northmen, or Norsemen.
6. R.H. Tawney seems to have exaggerated when he described this as 'an age ... when most men have never seen more than a hundred separate individuals in the course of their whole lives' (*The Agrarian Problem in the Sixteenth Century*, London 1912, 64). After changing his mind more than once, Coulton was inclined to put the number at 'two or three hundred' (e.g. *Medieval Village*, 65), while Duby has argued that there was a comparatively high degree of mobility, when travelling ecclesiastics, fighters, penitents, pilgrims, pedlars and so on are taken into account (e.g. in *The Fontana Economic History of*

Europe, ed. C. M. Cipolla, I, 182). The fact remains that among the lower ranks of society the majority will scarcely ever have been further afield than the nearest town, and many will not have been even so far.

7. For contemporary evidence see e.g. the proceedings of the Synod of Trosley in 909 (Mansi, XVIII, 263ff., esp. cap. III) or the contemporary Irish writer who claimed that 'if there were a hundred tongues in each head', it would not be possible 'to recount or narrate or enumerate all the hardships, injury and oppression suffered in every house from those valiant, wrathful, purely pagan people'. For differing views on the part of modern writers see e.g. Charles Wilson in the Introduction to Wood, *In Search of the Dark Ages*, and on the other side E. Joranson, *The Danegeld in France* (1923), and MacKinney, *Early Mediaeval Medicine*, esp. 107–8.

8. Wood, *In Search of the Dark Ages*, 152.

9. Ibid., 179 (Wulfstan) and 189. See the *Anglo-Saxon Chronicle* for 1005 CE. See also F. Ogg, *A Source Book of Mediaeval History* (1909), 228.

10. See his *Daily Life in the World of Charlemagne*, Ch. 7 and esp. p.300, where references are given to the original sources.

11. For the surprisingly controversial question of the relation between malnutrition and mortality rates see J. McManners, *Death and The Enlightenment*, 1981, Ch. 1.

12. Thomas Hobbes, *Leviathan*, Ch. 13.

3. The Cultural Background

1. A striking example is the fact that, although the emperor Justinian produced a major new codification of Roman law in the middle of the sixth century, by the beginning of the eleventh century Fulbert of Chartres, one of the most learned men of his day in the West, knew nothing of Roman civil law at all. See L. C. MacKinney, *Texts and Studies in the History of Mediaeval Education* VI, 1957, 34.

2. See Brehaut, *Encyclopedist of the Dark Ages*, 73–4.

3. According to Plato God, being perfect, could change only for the worse, and would obviously not do that (*Republic*, 381C). Formally, at least, the Fathers mostly maintained the doctrine of God's impassibility, that is, complete immunity to change of every sort. Whatever their lip-service to such a view, the early mediaeval writers, under the influence of the Bible, and being much less influenced by Greek philosophy than the Fathers, tended to envisage God in more personalist and anthropomorphic terms.

4. For an early mediaeval expression of this distinction between *scientia* and *opinatio* see Isidore, *Etym.*, PL 82, 141.

5. Ed. Eyssenhardt, IV, 13.

6. W. Durant, *The Age of Faith*, London 1950, 984; cf. also Brehaut, *Encyclopedist*, 76.

7. PL 61, 232. Many similar texts could be cited. Cf. e.g. the extended analogy in Augustine, *De doctr. Christ.* I. 4, PL 34, 20–1.

8. Isidore, PL 83, 963–4 and 978–9; 82, 174 and 141; 83, 985.

9. Cf. also e.g. II Cor.4.18, 'Our eyes are fixed not on the things which are seen,

but on the things which are not seen', and Gal.5.17; Heb.13.14; also Augustine, *Confessions* 11.2, 12.26.

10. It is indicative of mediaeval failure to appreciate the real drift of Paul's thought in this matter that the Vulgate substitutes 'flesh' for 'body' in Rom.8.13. This strand of thought naturally reinforced hostility to the natural world, of which the body is a part.

11. Isidore, *Differ.* II. 17, 48, 67. For the analogous affinities involved see p.21.

12. MacKinney, *Early Medieval Medicine*, 35.

13. These examples are taken from an English herbarium quoted in Harrison, *Medieval Man and His Notions*, 68ff.; there are many more examples in MacKinney, *Early Medieval Medicine*, 30ff.

14. For a purely magical formula cf. the following from an English herbal: 'When you have toothache, say *argidam mergidam sturgidam*, spit in the mouth of a frog and ask the frog to make off with the toothache' (Harrison, *Medieval Man*, 68ff.).

15. Isidore, *Sent.* III, 3, 5, PL 70, 81–4.

16. Such anthropocentrism was easier to embrace with reference to a universe so limited both temporally and spatially.

17. Augustine, PL 34, 20–1.

18. Isidore, *Etym.*, PL 82, 259.

19. The fact that in *Etym.* 10.68 Isidore derived *decorus* from *decem* (ten, implying perfection) occasioned no difficulty: relations between things were multiple.

20. Isidore, *Etym.* III, 50, 2 and V, 31, 3.

21. *Etym.* XVI, 26, 10.

22. The root fault of Adam and Eve had been their unwillingness to accept the limits imposed on the range of human activity and knowledge.

23. See Ch. 13 (i) for the extent to which peasants were included in this notion of vocation. The mediaeval cleric or knight was not just a human being behaving as a cleric or knight; he *was* a cleric or knight.

24. Cf. the case of the saint described in Radding, *World Made by Men*, 68–9, and the author's comment: 'the orientation is ... to the divine rules obeyed by the saint, not to his actual attitudes'.

25. Boethius, PL 64, 1343.

26. Radding, *World Made by Men*, 24, likens what he calls their 'passive' attitude to that of what Piaget called the egocentric stage in a child's development.

27. Gurevich, *Categories of Medieval Culture*, 98.

28. It has been pointed out that the abstract notion of space in general is not found before the time of Gassendi and Newton.

29. For the repeated use of the metaphor of dwarfs sitting on the shoulders of giants see R. Klibansky, *Isis* 26, 1936, 147–9. Jonas of Orléans, for example, depreciated his own writings as 'of little value', whereas 'in the Fathers one could discover as if in a mirror what one ought to do and to avoid' (Reviron, *Jonas d'Orléans*, 113).

30. The elementary level attained is illustrated by the fact that even Fulbert of Chartres, one of the most learned teachers of our period, had no idea what was meant by 'the interior angles of a triangle', an expression found by some of his pupils in Boethius (P. Tannery and A. Clercal, *Notices et extraits des manuscrits de la Bibliothèque Nationale et autres bibliothèques* XXXVI, ii, 1901,

497f.). Behrends's warning in his edition of the Letters of Lupus of Ferrières (p.xxxii) against taking this incident too seriously is not very convincing.

31. According to this text, an Israelite could marry a captive foreign slave girl provided she shaved her hair, cut her nails and threw away the clothes in which she had been captured. In the same way, said Jerome, having removed all wantonness and idolatry from pagan texts, he could use them to 'beget sons unto the Lord of Hosts' (PL 22, 665–6).
32. E. Dümmler, *Epist. Ermeric ad Grim.*, 29.
33. Some examples will be found in Helen Waddell's *Mediaeval Latin Lyrics*, London 1929, or in *The Penguin Book of Latin Verse*, Harmondsworth 1962.
34. See further Gurevich, *Categories of Medieval Culture*, 63.
35. For bibliography see ibid., 322 nn. 32–4, 36.
36. In England, for which the best statistics are available, over 5,000 watermills are recorded in Doomsday Book.

4. The Impact of Religion

1. This was not just a matter of what is often called the notion of corporate personality. The point is well put by Gurevich: 'All people in all generations bear responsibility for the original sin committed by Adam and Eve, just as all Jews are guilty of the crucifixion of Christ; for these events – the Fall and the Passion – are not simply events in the past, but persist eternally and are eternally present. The Crusaders at the end of the eleventh century were convinced that they were punishing, not the descendants of Christ's executioners, but the executioners themselves. The centuries that had elapsed meant nothing to them' (*Categories of Medieval Culture*, 130). See also p. 49 above.
2. Southern, *Making of the Middle Ages*, 252.
3. H. Adams, *Mont Saint-Michel and Chartres*, 246.
4. Cf. e.g. the tenth-century grammarian Viligardius who, according to Ralph Glaber, was misled on certain points through reading the classical poets; or Probus, a ninth-century monk of Fulda, whose classical studies led him to doubt parts of the church's teaching on damnation (Glaber II, xii, 23, ed. France et al., p.92, and Lupus of Ferrières, *Ep.*20). The case of Othloh of St Emmeram in the early eleventh century was more serious, for he tells us: 'I doubted completely whether there was any truth or profit in Scripture, and whether Almighty God existed' (PL 146, 32–3). However, Othloh was a disturbed and neurotic man, and he himself recognized that his doubts were quite exceptional, and in any case no more than a temporary aberration caused by the devil. It is significant that he has no language in which to describe and explain them other than that of current orthodoxy.

It *may* be significant that when the saintly Peter the Venerable had a visionary encounter with William, the recently deceased prior of Cluny, he felt moved to ask: 'Is it certainly true, what we believe about God, and is the faith we hold the true faith, without any doubt?' (PL 189, 939). However, we may suspect that the question was largely rhetorical, and the point of recording it simply to introduce the emphatically positive reply.

5. Cf. in the same vein, Morris, *Discovery of the Individual*, 62, or Coulton, *Medieval Scene*, 159.
6. Ibid.
7. T.E. Hulme, *Speculations*, London 1924, 50–1.
8. Gurevich, after speaking of 'the defining categories of human consciousness' in a culture, goes on to say: 'The point is that in any culture these universal concepts are mutually interrelated to form a "world model" *sui generis*, a "network of co-ordinates" through which the bearers of this culture perceive reality and construct their mental image of the world' (*Categories of Medieval Culture*, 13).
9. For the New Testament see e.g. E.P. Sanders, *Paul*, London 1991, 34ff. For a similar outlook in comparable cultures see C.R. Hallpike, *Foundations of Primitive Thought*, London 1980, e.g. 457–62. See also the quotation from Robin Horton in the Appendix, 238–9 below.
10. Southern, in Neill and Weber, *Layman in Christian History*, 89.
11. See e.g. Aelfric's *Homilies* 1, 20–1 and cf. Gregory the Great, PL 75, 1092; speaking of the sinner, he says: 'He is not consumed in death, because if his life after his death were consumed, his punishment likewise would be brought to an end together with his life, but in order that he may be tormented (*crucietur*) without end, he is forced to live on without end in punishment, that he whose life here was dead in sin, may have his death there living in punishment (*ut cuius vita hic mortua fuit in culpa, illic eius mors vivat in poena*). And see Burchard Cap. 100 in PL 140, 1055.

5. The Christian Story

1. PL 75, 517 and 121, 137. 'It would,' said Ratramnus in the ninth century, 'be madness to contradict what the Bible says' (PL 121, 137). For similar views, cf. the Caroline Books, Paschasius Radbert, Hrabanus Maurus and Haymo of Halberstadt (PL 98, 1105; 116, 874; 117, 899; and 120, 126). Characteristically, Agobard, at any rate in some moods, took his own line. He rebuked Fredegisus for holding that the actual words of the Bible were dictated by God. Its sense, he said, is no doubt divine, but its form is human (*Lib. contra objects. Fredeg.*, PL 104, 166). A lot of what he wrote in this treatise has a very modern ring. The way the exponent of literal inspiration views the biblical writers, he says, puts them on the same level as Balaam's ass, whose words were directly formed in his mouth by the ministry of angels (ibid., 166; cf. Num. 22. 28ff.). He asks why, if the Holy Spirit gave all the biblical writers a uniformly beautiful style, St Paul was more eloquent in Hebrews than he was elsewhere. It is the divine mysteries and doctrines which matter, not the beauty of the language or the grandeur of the philosophy.
2. Cf. e.g. *Anglo-Saxon Homilies*, ed. Thorpe, I, p.100.
3. The story of the tree of forbidden knowledge in Gen. 2.17ff. played its part here.
4. PL 100, 169.
5. MGH, *Leg II Capit. reg. Franc.* I, p.54. For formal Frankish claims to be the new Israel see *Libri Carolini*, Pref. pp.2, 3, 7; I, 17, 19 (MGH, *Conc.* 2).

Although this New-Israel mystique lost some of its force as the balance of power shifted towards the bishops, from the time of Louis the Pious, it by no means lost all its impact, and is a good example of the influence of biblical precedent on Frankish public life.

6. Delaruelle, for example, cites as part of the evidence the observance of the sabbath and of various Jewish regulations about food, drink and sex, as well as the overwhelming emphasis on sacramental activity. Chélini, however, enters a word of caution.

7. In the course of 138 short (modern) pages, she cites the Old Testament more than 600 times, as compared with a figure of under 200 times for the New Testament.

8. Cf. e.g. the statement of Gregory the Great that sometimes 'the plain words ... cannot be understood literally, because when the obvious meaning is taken, they convey no sort of instruction to the reader, but only engender error' (PL 75, 514; cf. Jerome, *Ad Damasum* in the same sense).

9. E.g. Gal. 4.24 or I Cor. 5.6–8.

10. The growth of a whole saga about the Virgin Mary, to whom little reference is made in the New Testament is instructive. See D. Cupitt, *The World to Come*, London 1982, 105f.

11. See, for example, the wholly unbiblical accounts of St Bartholomew and St Matthew in I, 454ff. and II, 472ff., or the detailed account in I, 58–77 of the later life of St John the Evangelist – which is wholly without biblical support.

12. See Tobit 6.18–22 and 8.4f. in the Vulgate, and J.N.D. Kelly, *Jerome*, 285 n.10, where he remarks that 'these texts have had a considerable influence on the advice given to the newly married in the Roman Catholic Church till quite recently ...' See also p. 210 below.

13. McNally, *Bible in the Early Middle Ages*, 11.

14. Ratherius of Verona (*c.* 887–974), for example, claimed that not only the Fathers, but canons of church councils, and even the Decretals of Isidore (in fact largely forgeries) were as much part of the *disciplina dei* as the Bible, while Paschasius Radbert said that to contradict Augustine 'was simply not on' (*fas non est*).

15. PL 63, 444.

16. See e.g. R.L.S. Bruce-Mitford, *The Art of The Codex Amiatinus*, 1967, p.2 – a reference I owe to Dr M.B. Parkes.

17. On the possession and distribution of Bibles see Maitland, *Dark Ages*, nos. xii and xiii. Even in the twelfth century a list of the equipment necessary for a church does not include a Bible. See Alexander Neckham, ed. T. Wright, 172. For the bishop – Fréculf of Lisieux – see MGH *Epp. V (Karol. Aev. III)*, p.392. Bibles were so valuable that the gift of one to a monastery or large church was felt deserving of mention in the Chronicle. See e.g. *Anglo-Saxon Chronicle* I, 470, and *Chronic. Fontan.*, apud d'Achéry, *Spicil.* II, 280b.

18. Nor, for that matter, did many of the higher clergy. It was, for example, at least plausible for Liutprand (*c.*922–c.972) to claim that Manasses, the Archbishop of Milan, had never read the Acts of the Apostles; and if the passages Liutprand quoted from him are to be trusted, he certainly had a wildly inaccurate notion of its contents (*Ant. IV*, vii).

19. Gregory PL 77, 1128 (the whole section is worth consulting); Paulinus, PL 61,

648ff., a passage interestingly discussed by Coulton in *Art and the Reformation*, 247–8, though under the misapprehension that it comes from Venantius Fortunatus; John Dam. *Contra imag. calumn.* I. 17, 5–7, ed. B. Kotter, 1975, p.93; Synod of Arras, d'Achéry, *Spicil.* I, 622a.
20. PL 112, 1608; and see plate 12.
21. For good brief discussions of this question, see Coulton, *Art and the Reformation*, 242ff., and the Brookes, *Popular Religion in the Middle Ages*, 132. On Müstair see, e.g., J. Hubert, J. Porcher and W.F. Volbach, *Carolingian Art*, London 1970, 24ff.

6. God the Lord

1. See further on this Russell, *History of Medieval Christianity*, 54ff.
2. There is a magisterial study of some of the questions involved here in Green, *Carolingian Lord*.
3. *Colla submittentia*, edd. R.H. Bautier and G. Lebory, 82.
4. Cf. also Isidore, PL 82, 261: *solus totius mundi habet imperium*.
5. MGH, *Poet.* I, 395, vv.10ff.
6. MGH, *Epp.* V, 189.
7. MGH, *Epp.* IV, 329, 198, 386, 240, 233f., 18.
8. Dhuoda, *Manuel*, p.76, 74–6 and Helgaldus, *Life of King Robert*. See also Wasserschleben, *Bussordnungen*, 362, for God as *dominator*.
9. Boswell's *Life*, ed. G.B. Hill, rev. L.F. Powell, II, 35.
10. Pope Leo, for example, insisted that even in the throes of his passion he did not 'cease to exercise his divine functions' (PL 54, 315).
11. Mansi XI, 978–9.
12. Southern, *Making of the Middle Ages*, 246; cf. how J.E. Hunt describes even a crucifix produced well after our period as 'a very early example of realism. Its painful details are not found again ... for at least two centuries' (*English and Welsh Crucifixes*, 30).
13. *Regnavit a ligno Deus*, from *Vexilla Regis Prodeunt*, verse 4; ET in EH 94 v.3.
14. Hrabanus Maurus, MGH, *Poet.* II, 249. There is a good example here of the way in which the orthodox story often built a considerable edifice on very scanty biblical evidence, in this case the brief and obscure references in I Peter 3.18ff and 4.6.
15. Significantly, it is interchangeably the Father and the Son who is thus portrayed in the domes and apses of churches.
16. E.g. Hrabanus Maurus, MGH, *Poet.* II, 253.
17. It is significant that, as Riché points out, 'for Dhuoda the Holy Spirit plays a much larger part than Christ in helping man in his fight against evil' (*Manuel*, Introd. 29).
18. PL 104, 281.
19. PL 75, 635 and 659.
20. Schmitt, III, 11ff.
21. Admittedly, a small number of people who had lived before the Incarnation made baptism available, were believed to have been saved. This was explained, by Gregory the Great, for example, as follows: 'What the water of baptism

effects for us was brought about in earlier times either by faith alone, on behalf of infants (he is thinking of the Holy Innocents), or for those of riper years by the virtue of sacrifice, or, for all who came from the stock of Abraham, by the mystery of circumcision.' After the Incarnation, no such dispensation was envisaged (PL 75, 635).

22. Gregory, PL 75, 889.
23. E.g. ibid.
24. Burchard, PL140, 964; Ratramnus, PL 121, 129.
25. Ibid., 134.
26. The adoptianism referred to on p.47 above was largely confined to Spain, and in any case died out by about 800 CE.
27. Some readers will be reminded of Browning's 'Soliloquy of the Spanish Cloister'.
28. *Christus te habet perditum*, MGH, *SS Rerum Germanicarum*, Vol.55, 38–9.
29. See e.g. Gregory of Tours, *Hist.Franc.*, PL 71, 339–40.
30. *nihil in terra sine causa fit*, PL 137, 698.
31. Wallace-Hadrill, *Frankish Church*, 41.

7. The Lesser Inhabitants of the Supernatural Realm

1. PL 24, 407.
2. PL 49, 740, see the whole chapter; cf. in the same sense Isidore, PL 82, 273.
3. PL 83, 556.
4. When the cult of St James at Compostella was established, the devil often appeared to pilgrims in the guise of the saint.
5. *Hist.*, Vol.2, ed. France et al., 218. The last trait is unusual; when on a terrorizing mission, a devil generally appeared naked. For a similar description see Aelfric, I, 466–7.
6. Le Goff, *Medieval Civilization*, 161.
7. Henderson, *Early Medieval*, 92.
8. Ibid., 95; pp.82–95 are worth consulting in the present connexion, and see plate 2. Notice, too, the tenth-century Jelling Stone, reproduced ibid., 84.
9. For an example, see the Life of Adelard of Corbie (PL 120, 1512–3), where the devil caused a quarrel between the people of Benevento and the people of Spoleto.
10. John Myrc's *Liber Festialis* of *c*.1400 CE. That the same sort of belief was shared in our period is shown by the different but equally fearsome list which can be collected from Isidore: 'They unsettle the senses, stir lost passions, disorder life, cause alarms in sleep, bring diseases, fill the mind with terror, distort the limbs, control the way lots are cast, make a pretence at oracles by their tricks, arouse the passion of love, create the heat of cupidity, lurk in consecrated images ... tell lies that resemble the truth, take on different forms and sometimes appear in the likeness of angels' (PL 83, 660ff.).
11. PL 83, 556.
12. PL 83, 667.
13. Some readers may recall the words of the Book of Common Prayer (1662), 'Suffer us not, at our last hour, for any pains of death, to fall from thee.'

14. For 'wanhope' see e.g. Manning, *The People's Faith in the Time of Wyclif*, 91 and 157.
15. PL 76, 1290.
16. *sollicitus cum Deo gradiebatur*, PL 120, 1522.
17. PL 104, 324.
18. For the military terminology see below, p. 59.
19. Cf. Gregory, PL 76, 1249: 'almost every page of scripture attests the existence of angels and archangels'. There are some 185 references to angels in the New Testament alone.
20. PL 76, 1249ff. and PL 82, 272.
21. See Henderson, *Early Medieval*, 29–30 and plate 12.
22. A widely disseminated story told how a destructive plague in Rome at the beginning of Gregory I's papacy came to an end when the pope saw Michael sheathe his flaming sword as he stood on the dome of Hadrian's mausoleum, henceforth known as the Castel S. Angelo. The story is not evidenced in writing until the thirteenth century, but is known to go back at least to the tenth century. See Homes Dudden, *Gregory the Great*, London 1905, I, 219–20 and 220 n.2; the scene was frequently represented in mediaeval art.
23. PL 83, 76, an interesting example, incidentally, of the extent to which detailed knowledge of the invisible world was believed possible.
24. PL 82, 273.
25. See O. Guillot, *Mémoires de la Société archéologique de Touraine*, 9, 1975, as cited in G. Duby, *Three Orders*, 366 n.19.
26. See *Scarapsus* 12 in *Der Heilige Pirmin und sein Missionsbüchlein*, ed. U. Engelmann, p.44. They are also referred to, for example, by Isidore (PL 101, 591–2), by Dhuoda (*Manuel*, III, 11. 144–5, p.194) and in the Leofric Missal of c.900 (ed. F.E. Warren 1883, 209).

8. Sin and Forgiveness: The Work of Christ

1. Cf. e.g. the canons of the Council of Chalons, 25, 32 and 37, Hefele and Leclercq, *Histoire des conciles* III, 2, p.1144.
2. *Eccles. Discip.* II, 5, qu.65, PL 132, 285.
3. PL 140, 949–50.
4. *Synod. Strigonens*, II, in Batthyani, *Legg. Eccl. Hung* II, 120.
5. For full details see H.C. Lea, *Auricular Confession and Indulgences* I, London 1896, 191ff.
6. The list in Gregory, PL 79, 238–9, simply combines the first two.
7. Cf. e.g. Gregory, PL 76, 1200, on the grace of compunction.
8. Gregory, PL76, 1070f.; 77, 300; and 76, 14.
9. *De vera et falsa penitentia*, wrongly attributed to Augustine; it probably dates from about 900: *dolorem cum vita finiat*, i.e., in effect, let it finish only with life itself, PL 40, 1124.
10. For that cf. e.g. Peter the Chanter (died 1197), *Verb. abbrev.*, PL 205, 342ff. Long before this, however, it was accepted that if a penitent who was genuinely trying to perform a penance was prevented by death or some other unavoidable cause, God would be satisfied.

11. PL 76, 231–2 and 1200–1.

12. Cf. Alcuin, PL 101, 498, and Regino of Prüm, PL 132, 233, also Burchard, PL 140, 978.

13. Vogel,*Pécheur et Pénitence*, 10 and cf. 19, 'la taxation précise des fautes'.

14. McNeill and Gamer, *Medieval Handbooks of Penitence*, contains the texts of the principal penitentials in an English translation, with useful introductory and commentary material. The originals will be found in Wasserschleben, *Bussordnungen*, and in Schmitz, *Bussbücher und Bussdisciplin*.

15. McNeill and Gamer, *Medieval Handbooks of Penitence*, 227; Schmitz, *Bussbücher und Bussdisciplin* II, 658–9.

16. See *Der Heilige Pirmin und sein Missionsbüchlein*, ed. U. Englemann, 1968, 14ff., where incidentally Pirminius says 'hate the vices and sins, not the sinner'. See also the Penitential of Bede, which gives a very similar list of sins and demands penance from anyone who 'is greedy or covetous ... or proud or envious or grasping or long angry or abusive or has like faults' (Schmitz, *Bussbücher und Bussdisziplin* II, 658–9).

17. Harnack, *History of Dogma*, V, 324.

18. M.W. Baldwin, *Christianity Through the Thirteenth Century*, London 1970 134.

19. J.T. McNeill is an authority on the penitentials, so his partial corrective to this deserves to be quoted *in extenso*, even if it perhaps involves some exaggeration. 'The confessor was taught to regard himself as a minister of supernatural grace; but not less prominent is the thought of the process of penance as constituting a treatment in itself effective towards the recovery of the health that has been lost through sin. Lacking the sensitive humanitarianism generally professed and sometimes practised today, the authors of these handbooks nevertheless had a sympathetic knowledge of human nature and a desire to deliver men and women from the mental obsessions and social maladjustments caused by their misdeeds. While in general the documents have the appearance of exact schedules of equivalents between crime and punishment, frequently the confessor is reminded that penalties are to be not so much equated with offences as adjusted to personalities. Not all are to be weighed in the same balance, but there must be discrimination according to cases' (McNeill and Gamer, *Medieval Books of Penitence*, 45–6).

20. Cf. e.g. the *Corrector* of Burchard, PL 140, 982ff.; Bede, *Penit*. 10, 229f.; and Egbert, *Penit*. 15f., p.246. Thus 100 Psalms said at night, to the accompaniment of 300 strokes of the lash, were the equivalent of three days' fast.

21. Pelikan, *Growth of Medieval Theology*, 148.

22. E.g. Tertullian, PL 1, 1235.

23. This was often attempted by way of flagellation; a man who constantly flagellated himself with both hands while repeating psalms, redeemed a thousand years of fasting in a single Lent, and earned the approbation of St Peter Damian (1007–1076). Flagellation, though sometimes prescribed in earlier penitentials, did not yet enjoy the almost fanatical esteem it came to have in some circles later.

24. Gregory, *Epp.*. V, 25.

25. Harnack, *History of Dogma* V, 271; cf. Gregory's repeated remark *Deus terrores incutit*, 'God instils terrors'.

26. Ibid., 268.
27. Bede, *Homil.*, PL 94, 223.
28. PL 39, 2216.
29. In the same text he writes: 'God, being by nature merciful, is prepared to save by mercy (*per misericordiam*) those whom he can find no way of saving by justice (*per iustititiam*). He wills that all men should be saved and that none should perish' (I Tim.2.4 is cited). Similar sentiments could be quoted from other writers of the period. Yet if they suggest universalism and a doctrine of justification by faith, we need to remember that similar words can be found in the later Augustine, and he was certainly no universalist. Everything depends on the way such statements are contextualized, and the meaning and weight their context gives them.
30. PL 38, 1012 and 910. Examples could be multiplied.
31. PL 54, 211.
32. See PL 54, 323 and cf. also 54, 329.
33. Cf. *magis uteretur justitia rationis quam potestate virtutis*, Leo, *Serm.*, PL 54, 358.
34. See p.49 above, and cf. Greg, PL 76,32: 'the devil lawfully lost him whom he had, as it were, lawfully held'.
35. PL 76, 179, and cf. the preceding passage.
36. It will be obvious how largely this view depends on the metaphysical account described above.
37. For the evidence see e.g. Tixeront, *History of Dogmas*, III, 343ff.
38. Isidore, PL 83, 567, and Bede, *Homil.* 54, 138; cf. also Leo, *Serm.*, PL 54, 313ff.
39. *Deo in se opera quibus erga homines placaretur ostendit*, PL 75, 893–4. The uncertainties of translation, of which there are even more than those indicated, do not affect the general sense of the passage.
40. Gregory, PL 76, 32.
41. E.g. Bede, PL 92, 671.
42. Gregory, PL 76, 289, and cf. PL 76, 32–3: 'Because there was no one by whose merits (*meritis*) the Lord would have been bound to be reconciled with us, the only-begotten appeared as the only righteous one.' Note the contractual language 'would have been bound to …'.
43. Harnack, *History of Dogma*, V, 330 n.1.
44. PL 75, 452.
45. Cf. e.g. Maximus of Turin in the fifth century, *Sermones*, PL 57, 689–90, or Germanus of Paris and Gregory the Great in the sixth. Martène, *Thes.* v.95, and PL 76, 1127 and 1178.
46. PL 76, 1279, and 72, 425.
47. PL 94, 75.
48. On purgatory see pp.134ff. below; the sacrifice of the mass could not avail for those among the dead who were irrevocably destined for hell.
49. PL 77, 416–7.
50. PL 77, 224, 424.
51. Translation from EH 613; see also the last verse.
52. PL 77, 428.
53. Harnack, *History of Dogma* V, 271.

54. Gregory, *Dial.*, PL 77, 425.

55. As Chélini, *Thèse* III, 19, has shown, the mass was not at this period anything like as central in popular religion as it later became.

56. Particularly the *communicatio idiomatum* (sharing of characteristics), according to which whatever could be said literally of either nature could, in virtue of the union, also be said of the other.

57. *sine nobis*, Gregory, PL 75, 1135.

58. PL 146, 200 and 136, 206.

59. To cite an extreme example, Aelfric (e.g. II, 112–3) presents a view which more or less completely contradicts Augustine's. 'God predestined the elect for eternal life,' he says, 'because he knew they would be such ... he would not predestine the wicked to his kingdom because he knew they would be such.'

60. See *Journal of Ecclesiastical History* 40.1, January 1989, 11.

61. *velim nolim*, PL 137, 702.

62. Ildefonsus of Toledo, PL 96, 144; cf. e.g. Gregory, PL 75, 876–7, and Isidore, PL 38, 588.

63. Cf. e.g. Gregory: 'God's judgments are hidden; and they ought to be revered with a humility as great as the obscurity which hides them' (PL 76, 402). This is a good example of the point by Alasdair MacIntyre discussed on pp.28–9.

64. PL 83, 33, cf. PL 83, 606.

65. On all this see Isidore, PL 83, 556 and Gregory, PL 76, 333.

66. PL 45, 1029ff., though see also 1025 and 1017–18.

67. Gregory, PL 75, 589–90 and 77, 317–20, where the part of the Holy Spirit is emphasized.

68. For example, sinners are moved to loving behaviour by 'the grace of the Spirit poured into them', and our virtues are 'his gifts poured into us'. Gregory, PL 76, 535–6 and 525, also 73–4.

69. Schmitt, II, 263–4.

70. It makes no difference if *subsequente* is taken verbally: 'our own free-will following it up'.

71. Ratherii Veronensis, *Opera Minora*, ed. P.L.D. Reid, CCcm 46, 1976, 50.

72. Cf. e.g. Gregory, PL 75, 1092 and 76, 379–80.

73. For explicit recognition see Anselm, *de Concordia* III. 1, Schmitt, II, 263.

74. See e.g. the *Homilies* of Aelfric, which are especially relevant as having been intended for ordinary people, ignorant of Latin; cf. for instance I, 54–5 and 112–13; II, 316–17, 330–1, 374–7.

75. E.g. ibid., I, 144–5.

9. The Saints

* My debt to Jonathan Sumption, *Pilgrimage*, and Benedicta Ward, *Miracles and the Medieval Mind* will be evident in this chapter.

1. Luchaire, *Social France*, 28.

2. Gregory's book contains forty-six miracles, about one a page.

3. See Wallace-Hadrill, *Frankish Church*, 78–9.

4. This is almost a quotation from Wallace-Hadrill, *Frankish Church*, 79; those who know his book will see how heavily these paragraphs depend on it.

5. To quote examples only from Gregory's *Dialogues* II, cf. §5, water produced from a rock (Exod. 17.1–7); §6, an iron tool rescued from water (II Kings 6.4–7); §7, walking on water (Matt. 14.28–29); §8, an obedient raven (I Kings 17.6) and grief at the death of an enemy (II Sam. 1.11–12); §21, five loaves made into food for a multitude (Mark 6.34–44); §32, raising a child from the dead (II Kings 4.32ff.; Mark 5.22ff.; Luke 7.11ff.). In §8, Peter, Gregory's dialogue partner, explicitly recognizes some of these parallels.

6. Ward, *Miracles and the Medieval Mind*, 38.

7. MGH, SRM II, p.662.

8. Ward, *Miracles and the Medieval Mind*, 38.

9. Although the proportion of female saints increased, only one saint in twelve was a woman even in the eleventh century, according to the calculations of Weinstein and Bell, *Saints and Society*, 220.

10. PL 133, 643; *Vie de St Germain d'Auxerre*, ed. R.Borius, 122–4; and PL 118, 961.

11. See Wallace-Hadrill, *Frankish Church*, 93.

12. Ibid.

13. See the instructive remarks in Mecklin, *Passing of the Saint*, 51.

14. The earliest known canonization by a pope occurred in 993, and it was not till about 1170 that a pope (Alexander III) claimed the exclusive right to decide in the matter.

15. St Martin, when Bishop of Tours, had to suppress a popular cult of a 'saint' who had in fact been a brigand executed for his crime (Delehaye, *Sanctus*, 180).

16. Hefele and Leclercq, *Histoire des Conciles*, III, ii, 1059, and cf. the *Admonitio Generalis* of Charlemagne in MGH, *Capit.reg.Franc.* I, 54–5, can.3.

17. The figures are given and the matter discussed by Weinstein and Bell, *Saints and Society*, esp.194ff. According to their estimate, of the saints recognized in the eleventh century only 2.3% were peasants and only 3.9% came from the urban poor, a class likely to have been even less well represented in the tenth century.

18. Dawson, *Religion and the Rise of Western Culture*, 152.

19. See Delehaye's chapter 'Les saints qui n'ont jamais existé', in *Sanctus*, 20ff.

20. The work known as the *Miracles of St Benedict* (ed. E. de Certain, 1858), will give a very good idea of the range of miracles with which a saint could be credited – in this case St Benedict working at the monastery at Fleury where his remains are alleged to be buried (see p.89 and n.47).

21. MGH, I.2, 632.

22. Cf. the peasant in the Miracles of St Benedict (p.353) who prayed, 'O holy Benedict … I confess myself thy serf and I confess thee for my rightful lord.' Odo's Life of Burchard, for example, describes the saints by exactly the terms (*patronus, advocatus*, etc.) that were used to describe feudal lords. Henri Pirenne described the saints as 'the great vassals of God, as it were, under whose protection one put oneself'.

23. PL 120, 1550; Helgaldus, ed. R.H. Bautier and G. Labory, Paris 1965, 14, p.82, and 14, p.84; PL 142, 688.

24. PL 676, 1238; cf. PL 75, 1151.

25. *in futuro examine cum domino iudicabunt*, PL 135, 116.

26. MGH, *Epist.* IV, *Ep.* 193, p.321.
27. Ed. de Certain, 114–15, PL 141, 925.
28. B.Pez, *Thesaurus* IV, Part iii, p.5.
29. MGH, SS XV, 1, pp.8–9.
30. MGH, *Epist.* V 52, p.135; PL 141, 931.
31. Helgaldus, ed. Bautier and Labory, p.14; *Hist.* V. ii., PL 142, 694.
32. *Poem to Louis the Pious*, 2576ff, ed. E.Faral, Paris 1932, 196.
33. MGH, *Epist.* IV, 290, p.448.
34. PG 94, 1352–1354.
35. D.Branche, *L'Auvergne au moyen age*, Clermont 1842, 460.
36. Daniel-Rops, *Église des Temps Barbares*, 653.
37. Cf. e.g. *Légendes Hagiographiques*, 158ff.; *Sanctus*, 259.
38. Cf. also Gregory, *Dial.* IV, 49. Incorruption was not claimed for all saints' bodies; for example, Paul the Deacon says that the body of St Benedict had gone to dust, and adds that only Christ's body and those of some others preserved by miracle knew no corruption.
39. Cf. e.g. the story of Benedict's vision in Gregory, *Dial.* II, 35: his head, so to speak, was in heaven even while his body was alive on earth.
40. Belief in the resurrection of the body played a part in this. Anyone buried near a saint would rise on the Last Day in the saint's company and be taken under his wing, so to speak.
41. PL 142, 679.
42. Strictly speaking, a feretory was a container for carrying a saint's relic (see plate 10), a reliquary a container for housing it (see plate 15), but usage was not exact or uniform. In our period reliquaries were usually engraved and ornamented caskets, but from the middle of the tenth century it became increasingly common to keep relics in what were in effect gilded statues of the saint (see jacket). The first known example dates from about 950, and the famous tenth-century Golden Majesty of St Faith can still be seen at Conques.
43. There is a full description of such a translation in the Chronicle of Adhémar of Chabannes, for example, including a description of the rich gifts offered to the saint by the king (PL 141, 68).
44. See plate 10. Such behaviour shows the (quasi-) impersonal way in which holy power was supposed to be transmitted. The body of the saint affected everything in contact with it. There was even a claim that an object which had been exposed to it in a shrine weighed more than it had done before. A relic was like a light sending out beams, and obviously it could easily come to be seen as an independent vehicle of magical power.
45. AA SS OSB, Vol.V, 613.
46. Cf. e.g. Compostella in north-western Spain. When what were believed to be the remains of St James the Apostle (Santiago) were brought there in the ninth century, not only did the town itself become a highly prosperous pilgrimage centre, but monasteries and hostels to provide accommodation for pilgrims were built along all the main routes leading to the city from the principal European countries. By the later eleventh century the ancient see of Iria was transferred to Compostella, and the magnificent cathedral begun as a fitting shrine for the saint. Such were the worldly implications of saints' relics.
47. The monks at St Benoit-sur-Loire still claim and exhibit the remains, though

their claim was rejected by the monks of Monte Cassino when they rebuilt
their abbey; they maintained that the remains had never been removed. The
story is a confused one, as Adrevald, a ninth-century monk of Fleury,
considerably embellished the eighth-century tradition as reported by Paul the
Deacon (MGH, SS XV, 474–7; P.J. Geary, *Furta Sacra*, Princeton 1978, 146–
9). It was in the ninth century that Le Mans claimed to have been involved
and, incidentally, to have kept the remains of St Scholastica!
48. F. Ughelli, *Italia Sacra* IV, Venice 1717, 589.
49. *AnalBoll* IV, pp.169–92.
50. For instances of this, cf. how the bodies of Sts Marcellinus and Peter refused to
remain in the church at Michelstadt, but made plain by visions and warnings
that they wished to be in the village of Mülinheim. Or there is the story that
when the remains of St Mary Magdalene were discovered in a crypt at
Vézelay, the abbot planned to move them to a shrine in the choir; but the saint
filled the church with darkness, meaning, it was thought, that she wished to
remain in the darkness of the crypt. The story about Mary Magdalene is in J.P.
Migne, *Monuments inédits sur L'Apostolat de Sainte Marie Madéleine en
Provence*, Paris 1848. Having no access to this book, I have taken the story,
without being able to verify it, from Sumption, *Pilgrimage*.
51. See *AnalBoll* IV, 175.
52. This was especially claimed in relation to the True Cross; see e.g. Paulinus,
Ep.31, PL 61, 329–30; Aquinas accepted this belief.
53. PL 156, 695.
54. MGH, SS XV, I, p.176.
55. Cf. Gregory of Tours, PL 71, 1065.
56. For vivid descriptions of dishonest relic-dealers see e.g. *Historia Translationis
Beatorum Marcellini et Petri*, PL 104, 537ff.
57. Flodoard, PL 135, 315.
58. *Detectio corporis S.Dinoysii*, II–IX, pp.166–9; see M.Félibien, *Histoire de
l'abbaye royale de Saint-Denys*, Paris 1706, 165ff.
59. Even Aquinas approved of this; see ST II, ii, quaest. 96, art.4.
60. Cf. Bede in *Vita S.Cuth*., in B.Colgrave, *Two Lives of St Cuthbert*, 23, 232.
61. Old Testament ideas of purification had been revived in the Carolingian
empire; the feast of the Assumption was much less widely observed.
62. By A.Bressolles in *St Agobard Évêque de Lyons*, 1949.
63. Traill, *Walafrid Strabo's Visio*, lines 626–7, p.200; Abbo, PL 132, 732.
64. Guibert, *De laude sanctae Mariae*, c.9, PL 156, 564; Bernard, *Sermo in
nat.B.Mariae*, c.7, PL 183, 441.
65. Mecklin, *Passing of the Saint*, 15.
66. Ed. Grant, Vielliard and Clemencet, 92.
67. A famous relic was the shift, or tunic, of the Virgin at Chartres, which was said
to have turned the tide in the siege of 911; but although it was said to have
been a gift from Charles the Bald (840–877), it may not in fact have been there
till after 1112, an indication of the relatively slow development of the cult.
68. From Herman, *de Miraculis*, PL 156, 969; see Ward, *Miracles and the
Medieval Mind*, 141.
69. *Mirac.S.Mariae Carbiotensis* XVIII, ed. A. Thomas, Bibliothèque de l'École
des Chartes, xlii, 1881, 537–8.

70. John of Coutances, *Mirac.Eccl.Constantiensis* VI, pp.370–2. See Sumption, *Pilgrimage*, 50–1. Further examples in e.g. E.A. Pigeon, *Histoire de la Cathedrale de Coutances*, 1876. It will be noticed that the woman in the first example was cured away from the shrine; most of the miracles attributed to Our Lady of Rocamadour occurred at a distance from the church.

71. C.Neuhaus, *Adgars Marienlegenden*, Heilbronn 1886, 79–115.

72. E.Albe, *Miracles de Notre Dame de Rocamadour*, Paris 1907, 70–1.

73. Ward, *Miracles and the Medieval Mind*, 149.

74. Sumption, *Pilgrimage*, 275.

75. For examples see Ward, *Miracles and the Medieval Mind*, 162 and Coulton, *Five Centuries of Religion*, passim.

76. Ward, *Miracles and the Medieval Mind*, 38–9.

77. Syrus, *Vita S. Majoli* II, 15, 17, AA SS OSB, Vol. VII, 797–8.

78. Cf. the examples quoted in Sumption, *Pilgrimage*, 159; it shows how realistically such ideas were held that Alcuin regarded the books in the library of his monastery as the personal property of the saint to whom it was dedicated (MGH, *Epp.* IV, 193).

79. See, e.g. Reginald of Durham's *Libellus de Admirandis Beati Cuthberti Virtutibus*, London 1835, in which Cuthbert's miracles are claimed as superior to those worked by St Nicholas, St Brendan, St Benedict and others.

80. AA SS *saec.* IV., ii, 376 and v, 463–4.

81. *Mirac. S. Ben.* VIII, 30, p.328.

82. J. Mabillon, AA SS OB, *saec.* V, p.530, who refers to another similar incident.

83. PL 142, 637–8.

84. *Mirac. S. Ben.* 59 and 149.

85. The last one is from *Archiv. Franc. Monast.* III, 155; for some of the others see *Mirac. S. Ben*, pp.130, 180, 184, 283, 328, 353; or Flodoard, *Hist Eccl Rem* II, iii, PL 135, 100.

86. Mecklin, *Passing of the Saint*, 27.

87. Cf. *De Virt. St Julian*, c.16, MGH, SRM, ii, p.571.

88. John of Salerno, *Life of St Odo*, PL 133, 80. In this case the dishonour involved some immoral conduct.

89. MGH, *Poet.* I, p.26. On p.121 there is a closely similar poem from the end of the century, referring to Verona. A large city such as Milan would have had more than one patron saint.

90. MGH, SS XV, i, pp.42–3.

91. Ibid., 31ff.

92. For examples see the Annals of Fulda or Xanten or St Bertin more or less *passim*.

93. Once again, such interventions were *ad hoc* or *ad hominem*, and did not interfere with the system as a whole.

94. See e.g. MGH, SS XV, i, p.172.

95. Everyman edition, p.102.

96. Frodoard, PL 135, 28, and Abbo, PL 132, 742. It should perhaps be added that the saint had foreknowledge of the 'rebellious and seditious disposition' of the descendants in question, and that Abbo, who recounts the second miracle, describes it as 'one without parallel'.

97. Frodoard, PL 135, 119 and 327 and T. Wright, *Essays on the Literature, Superstitions and History of England in the Middle Ages*, London 1846, I, 256.

98. Wallace-Hadrill, *Frankish Church*, 39, refers to an occasion when King Chilperic I wrote a letter to St Martin to which he expected a reply.

99. As we have seen, there was a well known story that St Bernard of Clairvaux had travelled all day along the shore of Lake Leman, so preoccupied with the other world that he could not remember having seen any lake at all (*Vita Prima*, III, ii, 4; *Vita Secunda* XVI, 45). The story may not be wholly representative of the early mediaeval attitude to this world, but its enthusiastic repetition shows how well it reflected contemporary ideas of sanctity in wide circles.

100. See his Life by Odo of Cluny in PL 133, 639ff. Although this life is no doubt a highly unrealistic idealization, it shows how sanctity was understood at Cluny in the early tenth century.

101. *Vita Anscharii, Praefatio*, PL 118, 960–1; Bernard, Sermon on St Martin, *PL* 183, 490ff.

102. Mansi XVII.2, 269, 40: they wanted veneration only of such as 'merited a cult because of authentic martyrdom or good lives'.

103. PL 142, 673–4.

104. PL 156, 614ff.

105. Ibid., where several similar cases are quoted.

106. See M. Deanesley, *History of Early Mediaeval Europe*, London 1956, 510.

107. *Chron*. III, 56, ed. J. Chavanon, Paris 1897, 179ff. The same can be said of much of Guibert's discussion of the milk-tooth of Christ claimed by the monks at Soissons, in his *de Pignoribus*, PL 156, 607ff.

108. Sumption, *Pilgrimage* 27.

109. PL 104, 199ff.

110. IV, 2594–5, ed. Faral, 196.

111. MGH, *Epp. Karol. Aev.* III, p.147.

112. PL 156, 620.

113. Sumption, *Pilgrimage*, 27.

114. Mecklin, *Passing of the Saint*, 16

115. The remarks of Dr Robert Horton quoted in the Appendix, pp.238–9 below, will be found interesting in this connection.

116. Luchaire, *Social France*, 28.

117. Harnack, *History of Dogma* V, 262f., brings out the extent to which the influence of Gregory the Great lay behind all this.

118. In Neill and Weber, *Layman*, 89.

119. It is just as well that he did, for he attempted to defend the authenticity of some very unlikely relics in the collection of his own abbey (*de Pignoribus*, PL I, 3–4, PL 156, 17ff.; *De Vita sua* II, i, PL 156, 896–7). 'That which is connected with the divine is itself divine,' he wrote, 'and nothing can be more closely connected with the divine than God's saints who are of one body with him.'

120. See C. Morris in *SCH* 8, 55ff.

121. *noxa delicti, Poem on Louis the Pious*, IV, 2596ff., ed. E. Faral, Paris 1932, 196.

10. The Past

1. E.g. Isidore, PL 82, 122.
2. See Ch. 9.
3. E.g. PL 188, 229 and 451.
4. Brandt, *Shape of Medieval History*, 79, with reference to the English chronicle *Gesta Stephani*.
5. Ibid., 74.
6. Burke, *Popular Culture*, 13.
7. Gurevich, *Categories of Medieval Culture*, 126.
8. Brandt, *Shape of Medieval History*, 74.
9. See e.g. the letters of Gerbert, ed. Havet, 41, 55, 72, or Liutprand, PL 136, 881 and 895 (fortune's wheel).
10. Brandt, *Shape of Medieval History*, 79; the whole of the above section owes a lot to Brandt's discussion.
11. Monasteries and other comparable institutions naturally kept some records to enable them to enforce their legal rights, but forgery was common in such documents. Chronicles were increasingly produced in monasteries and cathedral schools.
12. PL 188, 303.
13. Taking myth to mean fiction passing as fact. For the various ways in which these myths may have arisen see Burke, *Popular Culture*, 7–8.
14. E.g. PL 135, 27.
15. PL 82, 122, and 124: 'History belongs to the times which we see; annals belong to years which our age does not know.'
16. From Ralph Higden's translation of the *Polychronicon*, RS I, 19. The original is PL 82, 527.
17. He felt obliged to cite illustrious precedents in order to justify such attempts. Cf. his Life of Wigbert, Preface, PL 9, 681, or MGH, *Epp*. VI, pp.107–8.
18. See pp.92 and 101–2.
19. From Higden (n.16 above); the editor seems unable to identify the quotation.
20. On all this see Lewis, *The Discarded Image*, and Burke, *Popular Culture*, ch.1. As Burke points out, the importance placed on authoritative testimony was so high that Gregory of Tours actually put it above the evidence of his own senses (ibid., 7).
21. Cassian, PL 49, 1094ff.
22. E.g. Egbert of Wessex was credited with an ancestor born in the ark (*Anglo-Saxon Chronicle*, ed. D. Whitelock and D.C. Douglas, p.44).
23. Evidence in Sumption, *Pilgrimage*, 39.
24. For some examples see Leclercq, *Love of Learning*, 198.
25. Southern, *Western Society and the Church*, 92–3; his whole discussion of the matter is well worth consulting.
26. Erickson, *Medieval Vision*, 171.
27. Smalley, *Historians in the Middle Ages*, 10.
28. Burke, *Popular Culture*, 13; cf. also Southern, *Western Society and the Church*.
29. On all this see Burke, *Popular Culture*, ch.1, and his quotation from Jack Goody on p.18.

30. Giotto's frescoes in the Arena Chapel at Padua (*c.* 1305) are said to be the earliest example of figures from antiquity not portrayed in mediaeval guise.
31. Smalley, *Historians in the Middle Ages*, 192.
32. Ibid., 95ff.
33. Cf. the illuminating remarks of Carolly Erickson, *Medieval Vision*, 90, e.g. the 'fear of unknown yet powerful incorporeal beings and the theology of evil ... underscored the sense of arbitrary tragedy that loomed so large in the medieval period ... It was the unsettling property of divine justice to be both inexorable and unpredictable in human terms. Even the most unselfish human acts might offend God's justice.' Cf. also Coulton, *Five Centuries of Religion*, Vol.1, 165: 'divine justice was often practically indistinguishable from human caprice'.
34. *superstitiosa otia*, PL 119, 433.
35. PL 160, 421.
36. E.g. PL 188, 716.
37. MGH, *Epp.* VI, 109. On the alleged excommunication, however, see Duby, *Medieval Marriage*, 52–3.
38. PL 137, 784; nevertheless the context reinforces the point made earlier about the difficulty mediaeval historians had in finding well-based criteria. What *were* the 'less probable' things?
39. A Latin version, of uncertain date, is to be found in AA SS July, IV, 254ff., but this translation is from the early French version of *c.* 1040, given, for example, in the edition by C. Storey, *La Vie de Saint Alexis*, Oxford 1968, 1.
40. E.K. Rand, *Founders of the Middle Ages*, Cambridge, Mass. [2]1929.
41. R. Meagher, *Augustine: An Introduction*, New York 1979, 204.
42. Daniel-Rops, *Église des Temps Barbares*, 97 (my translation).
43. PL 116, 92.
44. So, explicitly, Robert of Torigny in PL 160, 421.

11. The Influence of the Non-Christian, Germanic Past

1. PL 132, 187ff.; 140, 537ff. The most important part of Burchard's work consists of Books X and XIX, the latter generally known as the *Corrector*.
2. Cf. for example MGH *Leg. Sectio* II, cc.44–45, 49, 345, 873; *Epp.* V, 461–2; Schmitz, *Bussbücher* I, 308ff.; PL 185, 584, the *Homilia de Sacrilegiis*, ed. C.P. Caspari; and see below for details based on Agobard of Lyon, Rhabanus Maurus, Hincmar of Reims, the Life of Wala and other sources. Cf. also Hauck, *Kirchengeschichte Deutschlands*, I, 488.
3. E.g. Alcuin in MGH, *Epp.* IV, 426.
4. Ibid., 267, 290, 291.
5. E.g. Agobard in PL 104, 147ff.
6. E.g. Hrabanus Maurus in PL 110, Hom.42.
7. E.g. Schmitz, *Bussbücher* II, 322, 34.
8. E.g. PL 132, 282; 125, 717.
9. PL 104, 179ff.
10. E.g. MGH, *Capit.* I, p.68.
11. Cf. Regino, PL 132, 296, and Burchard in Schmitz, *Bussbücher* II, 403ff., e.g. 96–7, 180–1, 185.

12. E.g. Life of Wala, PL 120, 1620, which makes clear that even the reading of entrails was practised at court.
13. See further pp.122–3 and 125.
14. For a full discussion of the belief-background to the ordeal see Radding, *World Made by Men.*
15. E.g. Alcuin in MGH, *Epp.* IV, p.448; and cf. the complaint of a monk in about 1050: 'O hard-hearted race of peasants, men who look with half-pagan (*semipaganus*) mind upon the cult of the spiritual law, and whose vain, frivolous and sluggish intention makes light of the solemn institutes (*sancita et instituta*) of the holy Fathers' (*Miracles de St Benoît*, ed. E. de Certain, Paris 1858, 210).
16. E.g. in the *De Divortio Lotharii et Tetbergae.*
17. PL 136, 847 apparently does.
18. Cf. F.N. Robinson on the *Deae Matres* in *ERE* IV, 410.
19. Coulton, *Medieval Panorama*, 131.
20. MGH, *Epp.* IV, 426, cf. R. Glaber, PL 142, 673ff. for a somewhat similar view.
21. It is significant, for example, that a night lamp was normally kept alight to ward off evil powers. E.g. Guibert of Nogent did this (*de Vita Sua* I, 15, p.56); and Burchard, PL 140, 971, adds that 'he cannot sleep alone ... because of his nocturnal terrors' (*Ep.* 70, Levillain II, p.6).
22. Cf. Schmitz, *Bussbücher* II, 423 § 61.
23. Sumption, *Pilgrimage*, 53.
24. Cf. e.g. Schmitz, *Bussbücher* I, p.479 § 32; II, 320; MGH, *Leg. Sectio* II, p.96.
25. Cf. Burchard, PL140, 961.
26. MGH, *Leg. Sectio* II, p.96; Schmitz, *Bussbücher* II, §§423 and 446; PL 140, 971.
27. E.g. Alcuin, MGH, *Epp.* IV, pp.185, 231, 249ff., 278ff.; Dungal, PL 105, 447–58; Einhard, MGH, *Epp.* V, pp.129f. and *Vita Karoli* 31.
28. E.g. Nithard, III 5, ed. P. Lauer, p.109.
29. Ep. 20, ed. P. Marshall, p.28.
30. Schmitz, *Bussbücher* I, 581 §1 and II, 321 §28; McNeill and Gamer, *Medieval Handbooks of Penance*, the only readily available source for the Penitential of Silos. All these documents are from the eighth or early ninth centuries.
31. PL 33, 222.
32. See Luchaire, *Social France*, 20–1.
33. Cf. e.g. MGH, *Leg. Sectio* II, p.49, 10.
34. PL 125, 688–9.
35. E.g. MGH, *Leg.* V, 658 and Burchard, in Schmitz, *Bussbücher* II, 445 §167.
36. Cf. Daniel-Rops, *Église des Temps Barbares*, 239 n. 14: 'C'était une religion naturiste ... Les dieux Germains ne sont jamais representés comme des puissances appliquées a gouverner le monde, ni comme des juges qui recompensent des humains. Au dessus des dieux, il y a toujours le destin.'
37. Cf. E.Tonnelat, 'La religion des Germains', in *Mana*, 1948; 'Ce que les Germains apprécient le plus dans une divinité, c'est son efficacité.'
38. Bede, H.E. I, 30, Plummer I, 65.
39. *Vita Eligii* II, 20, MGH, SRM IV, p.712. The bishop had been preaching against 'diabolical games, wicked dancing and other superstitions'.
40. *La Sorcière*, p.35 in the ET by L.Trotter, 52. He cites interesting evidence from

Burchard and others of the old customs the women preserved in the teeth of ecclesiastical discipline. What he says applies to the tenth century, however, not to the twelfth, to which, most surprisingly, he misdates Burchard.

41. According to Agilan, in Gregory of Tours, PL 71, 360, there was a traditional saying to this effect: *sic enim vulgato sermone dicimus: non esse noxium si inter gentilium aras et Dei ecclesiam quis transiens, utraque veneretur.*

42. Indeed the majority of people would have had at best only the haziest notion what the Christian system was, or even what the teaching of the Gospels and the characteristics of Christ were (see Duby, *Chivalrous Society*, 171, and cf. Ferdinand Lot's famous characterization of the religion of the period as 'plus pratiqué que connu'). Also relevant is the quotation from Robin Horton in the Appendix, pp.238–9.

43. James, *Origins of France*, 95–6.

44. Mecklin, *The Passing of the Saint*, 16, and cf. Latourette, *History of the Expansion of Christianity* II, 412–13.

45. Mecklin, *The Passing of the Saint*, 27.

46. E.g. Peter the Venerable, PL 189, 851–2, and Burchard, PL 140, 961. See also Hauck, *Kirchengeschichte Deutschlands*, II, 408.

47. See H.Rydh in *Bulletin* no.3 of the Museum of Far Eastern Antiquities.

48. Mecklin, *The Passing of the Saint*, 27.

49. A.Friedberg, *Corpus Juris Canonici* II, causa ii, q.5, 23.

50. PL 95 and PL 137, 799.

51. *Dial.* IV, 59; II, 3; III, 7; III, 15. An example from another source is the way the two portions of the chain which had bound Peter joined themselves together inseparably when put into the hands of a pope. For that see F.Gregorovius, *History of the City of Rome* i, 215.

52. Vauchez, *Spiritualité du Moyen Age*, 26.

53. *Annales* 31, 1976, 946.

54. Vauchez, *Spiritualité du Moyen Age*, 32. He wisely adds: 'To see in this process, as has often happened, only a degradation of the religious spirit, is an attitude with which the historian cannot be satisfied. Rather than passing a value judgment he should that a new form of relationship with the divine was born out of the impact of Christianity on uncultivated and down-to-earth minds.'

12. The Future

1. Hervé, archdeacon of Ste Croix d'Orléans, wrote in 1033: 'The life of the world is uncertain and fragile. No one knows when his passage on earth will end, for does not the whole world rush rapidly to its destruction?' (*Bibliothèque de l'École de Chartres*, II, 1890, 204–6).

2. *Mundi terminum ruinis crescentibus appropinquantem indicia certa manifestant*, quoted without reference in Focillon, *L'An Mil*, 50.

3. For the abbeys of Lézat (944) and St Germain de Muret (948) and other examples see J. Roy, *L'An mille*, Paris 1885, 188ff.

4. PL 139, 471 and 397.

5. PL 139, 461ff.

6. PL 139, 471.

7. PL 101, 1291–8. For similar views in e.g. the *Tiburtine Sybil* and the *Revelation* of pseudo-Methodius see W. Bousset in *ERE* 1, 581.

8. MGH, SS III, 790.

9. Lines 789–90, ed. Traill, 203–4.

10. Mansi 18, 263ff.; though see also Hefele and Leclercq, *Histoire des Conciles* IV, 723 n.1.

11. See e.g *The Oxford Book of Medieval Latin Verse*, ed. F.J.E. Raby, London 1959, 223, and cf. Otto of Freising: 'We behold the world ... already failing, and, as it were, drawing the last breath of extreme old age' (*Deeds of Frederick Barbarossa*, translated C.C. Mieron, New York 1953, 323).

12. According to a slightly later account, this would be at the site of his burial in Jerusalem; cf. *Descriptio*, in *Gesta Francorum*, etc., ed. Rosalind Hill, London 1962, 99.

13. The sharp dichotomy between the loving mercy of God and Christ in the present and their implacable objectivity on the Day of Judgment is a difficulty with which mainline Christianity has never succeeded in dealing satisfactorily.

14. Reproduced, with commentary, by W.R. Cook and R.B. Herzmann, for example, in *The Medieval World View*, 248–9. What the future was thought to be for those who would not have completed their purgation when the end came, or for those then still alive who deserved a period of purgatory, I have not been able to discover.

15. The principal texts were: Mark 13 and parallels in Matt. and Luke; II Thess. 2, esp. 3ff.; and Revelation, esp. 9.1–11 and 15–19; 11.7ff., 13; 16.12–17; 17.14; 19.19–21; 20.1–10.

16. E.g. PL 41, 657ff.; see *Civ.Dei* XX, XXI and *In Ev.Ioann.Tract.*, 36, 124.

17. When Norbert (1080–1134) told Bernard of Clairvaux why he believed that Antichrist would certainly come in the lifetime of the current generation, Bernard commented that 'his answer was not of a kind to make me feel I ought to adopt his view as undoubted truth' (*pro certo credere debere*, PL 182, 162).

18. As appears to have happened to some extent in New Testament times; cf. e.g. II Thess.3, in the light of an up-to-date commentary.

19. Ed. France et al., *Hist.* IV, 14ff., pp.194ff.

20. Cf. Vauchez, *Spiritualité du Moyen Age*, 44.

21. PL 133, 69–70.

22. Burns, *First Europe*, 372.

23. MGH, *Epp.* IV, p.176; cf. also pp. 61, 173, 288, 237.

24. E.g. 'I tremble all over in terror at God's judgment', *Epp.* 216 and 239, and cf. Fichtenau, *Carolingian Empire*, 96ff.

25. Cf. e.g. the poems referred to on p.251 n.33 above.

26. Le Goff, *Medieval Civilization*, 167.

27. Admittedly, the necessary technology was in any case unavailable. To what extent that fact lay at the root of the attitudes we are now describing is too big a question to be discussed at this point, involving, as it does, one's general view of the relation of *theoria* to *praxis*.

28. MGH, *Epp.* IV, 23, p.61.

29. *Ep.* 213, pp.356–7.

30. PL 110, 498.

31. MGH, *Conc.* II, 779f.
32. Souls were frequently represented in art in bodily form, as small children or miniature adults.
33. For the belief that a revered character had been deemed worthy of heaven immediately upon death see the case of Anskar (PL 118, 1000 and 1010).
34. See Augustine, PL 41, 736ff.
35. See Le Goff, *Birth of Purgatory*, for the perhaps slightly overstated case that it did not emerge until the twelfth century.
36. *De corona*, PL 2, 78ff.
37. Something mediaeval writers did not recognize, partly because they included what we call the Apocrypha, and partly because they interpreted a number of texts in Job, and the Psalms and elsewhere, in a sense other than that of the original Hebrew, as the Authorized Version also does.
38. Among the chief of these were Job, esp. 13–14; II Macc.12.41–6; Mark 13.31–2; and I Cor.3.11ff. For a sense of their (apparent) incompatibility see Augustine, PL 40, 263–5.
39. PL 41, 745.
40. PL 75, 993.
41. Ed. de Vogüé III, 146.
42. PL 77, 397ff.
43. PL 112, 35, 9.
44. Paschasius Radbert, PL 120, 165.
45. Eventually some volcanoes, especially Etna, were seen as mouths of purgatory, but although Gregory the Great tells of a volcano which was an opening of *hell* (*Dial.* IV, 31), there was no comparable localizing of purgatorial suffering in the early period.
46. PL 136, 701–2.
47. Brookes, *Popular Religion*, 149.
48. *Dialogus Miraculorum*, ed.J.Strange, I, 330.
49. For a discussion of this and an account of the documents, with copious quotations in translation, see Patch, *The Other World*.
50. For Theodoric see Gregory, *Dialogues* iv, 31 above; for Charlemagne see e.g. *Visio Wett.* lines 446ff, ed. Traill, p.197, and for the others William of Malmesbury in MGH, SS X, 458.
51. Gregory, *Dial.* IV, 37, ed. de Vogüé III, 130. Other accounts, e.g. that in Gregory of Tours, PL 71, 416–8, contain more traits directly from the Bible, e.g. no sun or moon.
52. E.g. Gregory of Tours, PL 71, 418, or the Vision of Alberic, ed. M. Inguanez. in *Miscellanea Cassinese* 11, 1932, 83–103.
53. In strict logic, that last would rule out the activities we have seen associated with the saints.
54. In his *de sacramentis*, 25–31, ed. R.M. Martin, Louvain 1937.
55. PL 172, 1237f., and cf. 40, 1029.
56. Gregory, *Dial.* IV, 31, ed. de Vogüé III, 104.
57. PL 122, 436.
58. *Lettres de Gerbert*, ed. J. Havel, Paris 1889, *Ep.* 180.
59. PL 94, 739.
60. PL 94, 743–4.

61. PL 2, 656–7.
62. In the later Middle Ages effigies on tombs, e.g. that of the Duchess of Suffolk in Ewelme church in Oxfordshire, were often carved so as to represent the subject at this age.
63. *Civitas Dei*, XXII, 30.
64. Wasserschleben, *Bussordnungen*, 108ff.
65. See e.g. Augustine, PL 41, 736ff., and Gregory, *Dial.* IV, 46, de Vogüé III, 160ff., who argues as well that God maintains the torments of hell so that the blessed, seeing what they have escaped, may enjoy the pleasures of heaven the more.
66. Cf. e.g. Bernard of Clairvaux, PL 183, 96, 'few, very few, will be saved', and Berthold of Regensburg, *Predigten*, ed. F. Pfeiffer, Vienna 1862–80, i, p. 382: 'only three out of many hundred thousand souls …' (PL 133, 59). He says that for anyone to achieve the bliss of heaven is 'one of the greatest miracles God performs. That is why we sing *mirabilis deus in sanctis suis.*'
67. See e.g. Odo of Cluny's *Occupation of the Mind*. In PL 133, 66 he even says that it would be difficult for a monk, however pure-minded, to be admitted to heaven in any garb but that of St Benedict.
68. PL 133, 59.
69. Quoted from Mabillon in Coulton, *Five Centuries of Religion*, Vol. 1, 477. The reference is to AA SS OSB *saec.* iv, *pars* ii, 191ff.
70. Dhuoda, *Manuel pour mon Fils*, 110.
71. PL 45, 1027ff.
72. Coulton, *Five Centuries of Religion*, Vol. 1, 27.
73. Id., *The Medieval Village*, 240.
74. Southern, *Making of the Middle Ages*, 90.
75. Cf. the remarks in *CMH* III, 125–7, and Southern, *Making of the Middle Ages*, 87ff.
76. For his tumultuous, but fascinating, life see *Chroniques des Comtes d'Anjou et des Seigneurs d'Amboise*, ed. L. Halphen and R. Poupardin, Paris 1913, and *Recueil d'Annales Angévines et Vendômoises*, ed. L. Halphen, Paris 1903, in both cases s.v. Foulque III Nerra in the index.
77. Alcuin, asking for prayer as he faced death, wrote, 'the time draws near that this hostel must be left behind and I go out to face things unknown' (*tempus appropinquat, quo hoc hospitium deserendum est et ignota appetenda*), MGH, *Epp.* IV 226; PL 100, *Ep.* LXV.
78. Loss of hope in the possibility of salvation was also a sin to be avoided. See pp.56–7 on *wanhope*. On the importance of holding the orthodox faith at the moment of death see p. 52.
79. For the evidence see Chélini, *Thèse* IV, ca. 15ff.
80. *Annal. St Bertin* 868, p. 144.

13. The Church and the Divisions of Society

1. The extent of my debt in this chapter to Duby's work, especially to his *Three Orders*, will be obvious to all who are familiar with it.
2. The status of the king, which was unique, will be discussed later, see pp.216ff.

3. Walahfrid Strabo describes them as *laborum toleratores*, those who put up with the toils of work.

4. Duby, *Three Orders*, 99.

5. The attitude of most members of the other classes towards these people is revealed by the author of the Life of St Bernard, Abbot of Tiron (died 1117); he thinks it remarkable that his hero turned none of them away, 'however mean or contemptible or poor' (PL 172, 1441). In the early twelfth century Hugh of St Victor described the activities of this group as stained with 'adultery ... as if the spirit engaging in them were soiled by an immoral contact with something degrading' (PL 176, 752).

6. MGH, SS II, p. 600.

7. Quoted in K. Beyerle (ed.), *Die Kultur der Abtei Reichenau*, Munich 1925, I, 64.

8. So far as historical precedent went, we have already noticed the threefold division of early Frankish society; on the Gallo-Roman side we may note that the late Roman emperors had been compelled for economic reasons to make certain professions hereditary and to encourage the landed proprietors to bind their *coloni* (farm servants) to the soil as replacements for the decreasing number of slaves. One of the last of these emperors, Majorian (457–61), deplored 'the tricks employed by these men who are unwilling to remain in the state in which they were born'. From early mediaeval times any attempt to escape from one's lot was regarded as a major sin. As Le Goff says, 'it was a stratified society, boxed off horizontally' (*Medieval Civilization*, 26).

9. Cf. e.g. Christ's resurrection on the third day; I John 5.7 (the three witnesses); Ex.25.32 (the three branches of the sacred candlestick); Hos.6.2 (Vulg 3, the third day); Isa.6.3 (the *Trisagion*), etc.

10. In particular the *Celestial Hierarchy* and the *Ecclesiastical Hierarchy*. These works were apparently written about 500 CE in Syria, but as a result of their false attribution to Paul's convert mentioned in Acts 17.34, they exercised a great influence in the Middle Ages. They were translated into Latin, first by Hilduin, Abbot of St Denis, and then, more accurately, by Eriugena. The very first chapter of the *Celestial Hierarchy* lays down that 'the division of every hierarchy is ternary'.

11. Wallace-Hadrill, *Frankish Church*, 268–9.

12. PL 75, 677.

13. PL 197, 338.

14. PL 36, 436.

15. PL 76, 203.

16. PL 83, 717.

17. PL 83, 717.

18. *Miracles de St Benoit*, V, iiff., pp.194ff. Note also the outrage occasioned at the flight of nobles in the face of humble country people.

19. Two groups stood right outside this threefold classification, namely women, whose position will be discussed separately, and slaves, of whom there were still a fair number in this period. The latter were regarded as directly under the control of their masters, and as not therefore entering into any consideration of the social order. They were simply chattels, and had no rights, or control of their own lives or destinies.

20. MGH, *Leg.Sectio* II.1, no. 33 (92).
21. Cf. Rom. 12. 4–5 and I Cor 12.14ff., though the former, for somewhat obscure reasons, was not a text much used at the time.
22. MGH, *Capit.II*, 516; note that already in the middle of the ninth century he is beginning to attribute a specific function to each group.
23. See Gregory's *Pastoral Rule*, especially books 1 and 2, where the essential equality of humankind is emphasized, and rulers are urged to bear it in mind at all times, though, when faced with wickedness, they must 'acknowledge at once the power of their pre-eminence' which they exercise vicariously on God's behalf (2.6). Although Gregory had clerical leaders in mind, he was referring to their participation in government (*praeesse* or *praeferri ceteris*), and would certainly have seen these remarks as applying to lay rulers as well.
24. MGH, SS VII, 485.
25. Quoted from *Recherches de Théologie ancienne et médiéval* XIII, 1946, 206, in Southern, *Making of the Middle Ages*, 109.
26. Southern, *Making of the Middle Ages*, 111.
27. *de principis instructione*, RS VIII, p. 258.
28. *Aucassin and Nicolette*, ed. P. Matarasso, Harmondsworth 1971, 45.
29. Luchaire, *Social France*, 385.
30. PL 158, 1081.
31. Irminon's *polytique* shows in what great detail the monastery of St Germain des Prés knew about the affairs and obligations of its dependents in the later years of Charlemagne's reign (*Polyptique de l'abbaye de St Germain des Prés*, I, ed. A. Lognon, Paris 1886).
32. Luchaire, *Social France*, 393.
33. It must not be thought that there were no good and sympathetic landlords. Naomi Mitchison, in her well-researched novel *The Oath Takers*, Nairn 1991, paints a convincing picture of one such.
33. According to Riché, *Daily Life*, 241, at Corbie in 822 manual work was forbidden on thirty-six days in the year, in addition to Sundays, i.e. on one day out of every four – a high proportion when the seasonal character of farmwork and the farmworker's need to take advantage of suitable weather are taken into account.
34. For the 'puritanism' and sabbatarianism – which went back to Augustine (e.g. *De decem chordis*, ser. ix, §3) – involved in the official reaction, see e.g. Coulton, *Medieval Village*, 272ff.; *Five Centuries*, appendix, 28.
35. For example, *c.* 1020 Dudo wrote that all three orders 'marched toward heaven at the same pace' (on the views of Dudo and Martin of Jumièges see Duby, *Three Orders* 83ff.). Burchard of Worms was another writer who insisted that the Religious had no essential advantage over the secular clergy or the laity in this matter.
36. Augustine, *De sanct. virg.* 27.
37. Dudo, PL 141, 201.
38. Although so many saints were recognized in this period, there was no peasant among them before the twelfth, or even the thirteenth, century.
39. Fichtenau, *Carolingian Empire*, 48, who refers to Hrabanus Maurus, MGH, *Poet.* II, 166 and *Epp.* V, 233ff.; and Ntedka, *Evocation de l'au-delà*, 220ff. It is worth pointing out that in this as in so many other matters, Agobard of Lyon

was an exception. He was against social distinctions, present and future, and wrote of *Apostolus ... interiorem hominem ab omni sexus diversitate, ab omni conditoris et generis distantia liberum esse demonstrans* (PL 104, 177, cf. also 114–159).

40. Quoted by Le Goff, *Medieval Civilization*, 301, without reference.
41. Sitwell, *Odo of Cluny*, x.
42. Translated from his Introduction to *Dhuoda*, 13–14.
43. PL 99, 240.
44. William of Jumièges and Wace in *Roman de Rou*, ed. A.J. Holden, Paris 1970, Tom i, pp, 191ff., lines 819ff.
45. Wallace-Hadrill, *Early Medieval History*, 2–3.
46. PL 117, 790–1, quoted by Wemple, *Women in Frankish Society*, 125.
47. A good deal of early mediaeval thinking on this subject is summed up in Aquinas, ST I, 92.
48. Tacitus, *Germania* 8.
49. Diogenes Laertius, *Emin.Philos.* i, Thales, 33, ed. R.D. Hicks, I, 34–5, and S.Singer, *Authorized Daily Prayer Book*, London 1962, 6(–8).
50. 'Woman is not equal in honour with man', *Questions and Answers in Gen.* 1.27.
51. For example Eccles. 7.26–28; Ecclus. 9.1–13 (Vulg., esp.8); 25.13–26 (esp.24: Vulg. 17–36, esp.33); 42.13–14 (Vulg.12–14).
52. E.g. Gal. 3.28.
53. For example I Cor.14.34–35; 11.5, 8–10; Eph.5.22–24; Col.3.18; I Tim. 2.11–15; Titus 2.4–5; I Peter 3.1–6.
54. PL 1, 1305.
55. Cf. e.g. PL 41, 424ff.
56. See Duby, *Medieval Marriage*, 51–2, and pp.208–9 above.
57. PL 71, 1036.
58. *Civitas Dei* XIV, 18.
59. Levillain, *Epp.* cvii, p. 125.
60. Some Fathers, e.g. Gregory of Nyssa, claimed that sex was instituted only after the Fall, and in response to it; Augustine (e.g. *de Gen.ad Lit.* vi, 5), and the West after him, would not go as far as that.
61. PL 144, 232.
62. See *I Laici*, 390ff.
63. Eriugena, PL 122, 806.
64. Women's beauty was a puzzling theme, especially to monastic writers. Odo of Cluny, for example, wrote that 'beauty is a deceiving grace because it is often the cause of lust and pride'; and in a well-known passage in his *Collationes* he sought to offset the impression made by woman's outward beauty by directing attention to the revolting presence of entrails and faeces within. A woman's outward form should be viewed simply as the container of disgusting tripes (PL 133, 650, 556).
65. PL 34, 1250.
66. E.g. Aquinas, ST I, qu.99, art 2.
67. *De Gen. ad Lit.* VI, 5.
68. Pseudo-Augustine, CSEL 50, 83.
69. One obscure incident even seems to suggest a doubt whether women were

spiritually equal to men, or even whether they were capable of salvation. See Gregory of Tours, HF 8, 20, and with it M.C.Ragut, *Additio ad Concilium Matisconense*, Macon 1864, cclv. There is a full account of views on the matter up to 1909 in Hefele and Leclercq, *Histoire des Conciles* III, 211ff., and see Schnürer, *Church and Culture* I, 265; P.Riché in *Histoire Mondiale de la Femme*, Paris 1965, 36. Such doubts were speedily put to rest, but the very fact of their existence, if that is what the story implies, would be significant.

70. PL 94, 450.

71. E.g. MGH, SS *rer.mer.* 6,86; *Acta. SS Belgii Selecta*, 3,581.

72. Laeuchli, *Power and Sexuality*, Philadelphia 1972, 97.

73. Duby, *Three Orders*, 209.

74. For all this see the *Decretum* of Burchard of Worms, an influential collection of canon law which appeared in about 1010, and reveals a good deal about the activities of women, and attitudes towards them, both at the time and earlier. Book XIX is especially relevant.

75. Mansi, 18, 171–2.

76. PL 34, 450.

77. Hincmar, for examples, speaks of wives being butchered like animals (PL 125, 657, see also 1023).

78. III, 13; MGH, *Conc.* II, Supplement, 127. Charlemagne's irritation with the pretensions (as he saw them) of the Eastern empress Irene no doubt finds an echo here.

79. CSEL 50, 83.

80. CCL 148A, 269–70.

81. Hefele and Leclercq, *Histoire des Conciles* IV, 414, §§36, 37, 42.

82. Bede, HE, ed. Plummer, I, p.54.

83. PL 105, 193–4.

84. The case of Dhuoda, a well-educated lay woman of the noble class in the ninth century, who could quote readily, not only from the Bible but from Gregory, Prudentius, Donatus and many other authors, reminds us of the patchiness of the evidence and the dangers of over-hasty generalization.

85. Kari Elisabeth Borresen as quoted in Tavard, *Woman in Christian Tradition*, 125.

86. E.g. PL 140, 961.

87. Boswell, *Christianity, Tolerance and Homosexuality*, 109.

88. Quoted by R. Bultot in *I Laici*, 391 – see also his remarks in the surrounding pages.

89. Aquinas, ST I, 92, 1, *Respon.*

90. For details see Wemple, *Women in Frankish Society*, 103.

91. E.g. PL 125, 656 and 106, 176–7.

92. *Cur Deus-homo?* II, viii, Schmitt II, p.104.

14. The People of God

1. Sons often in fact succeeded their fathers, both in dioceses and parishes, but this was never an officially recognized practice.

2. Exact figures are impossible to discover. Russell, 'Late Ancient and Mediaeval

Population', 137, speaks of the clerics in major orders as numbering 'only a tiny fraction of the population'; if those in minor orders are included, some historians think the number may have been of the order of three per cent of the *adult* population.

3. MGH, *Leg.II Capit.*, Vol.2, p.2, 184.

4. In its full ideological rigour this division was a feature of the eleventh century. At the end of the tenth century Francia was still to some extent under the influence of the earlier Carolingian outlook which had ascribed to lay rulers a spiritual awareness and authority similar to those conveyed by holy orders (see p.163).

5. See Carozzi, *Annales* 33, no.4, January–April 1978, around p.685.

6. The question whether the quality, or 'character', conferred by ordination was indelible was not definitely settled in favour of indelibility until later; but the presumption was already in that direction.

7. As we shall see when parish priests are discussed, by no means all clerics were economically unproductive.

8. Gerbert described the church as *sanctissima societas humani generis* (*Epp.* LXXIX); it was to be the realization of the divine *respublica* on earth. See Elliott Binns, *Decline and Fall of the Medieval Papacy*, 2.

9. In fact virtually any educated man, if he was in any sense in the church's service, could be described as a cleric. The number of orders later stabilized at seven, but in our period the matter was one of some uncertainty. Those in minor orders carried less of the sacred aura and they were allowed to be married. Yet even they partook of the clerical superiority, and the higher clergy made extremely high claims for themselves. Theodulph of Orléans, for example, called them 'the salt of the earth ... because if the faithful people is God's food, we are the spice of his food ... the bishops hold the rank of the chief priest Aaron, the priests the rank of his sons' (PL 105, 192). Some clerical writers, such as Hincmar, for example, even spoke of the church itself as comprising essentially the priesthood, and lay believers only by extension. By the same token, however, God would hold the clergy responsible for the salvation and spiritual well-being of those committed to their care.

10. Cf. e.g. Amalarius, in J.M. Hanssens (ed.) *Amalarii Episcopi: Opera Liturgica Omnia*, II, Studi e Testi 139, Vatican City 1948, 205, 234f., 275, etc., for the bishops as vicars of the apostles, and indeed of Christ himself, prefigured by Aaron in the Old Testament.

11. This rite, often deferred or neglected by the ordinary people, was not considered absolutely necessary to salvation, but those who died unconfirmed (something over ten per cent of the population) could expect poorer recompense in the hereafter. The number is derived from Henry of Tournai, who preserves the numbers for his area in the eleventh century. For details and references see Coulton, *Life in the Middle Ages* II, 17 n.1.

12. For the innumerable references see e.g. Congar, *Ecclésiologie*, 142 and 149.

13. In our period there were no general, or ecumenical, councils of the whole church, and few international councils of any sort. In this connexion a 'provincial' council means one attended by the bishops of a single ecclesiastical province, i.e. an area under the jurisdiction of a metropolitan.

14. PL 135, 295.

15. For the attitude of one pope at least see 174 below.
16. Cf. Ratherius, *Praeloquia* and *Dialogus confessionalis* in PL 136, 145ff. and 393ff. who quotes John 11.51; and had not even Peter obeyed Caiaphas in his capacity as high priest?
17. *Exauctoratio*, PL 97, 661.
18. PL 125, 1071.
19. Hincmar, for example, cited Gregory I as showing that in the Bible ecclesiastics were sometimes referred to as 'gods' and 'angels' and claimed that Constantine had described them as 'gods established by the true God' (MGH, *Epp.* I, 318ff., and Hincmar, PL 126, 232–3). The quotation from Constantine occurs in a spurious document.
20. MGH, *Epp.* IV, 116.
21. PL 125, 1087ff.
22. E.g. MGH, *Leg.* II, i, pp.533ff.
23. For the number see e.g. Pirminius, MGH, SS XV, pt 1, pp.27–8; the Life of Bishop Hugh of Lincoln (*c.* 1140–1200, ed. D.L. Douie and H. Farmer, I, 127–8) counts it a great virtue in him that he dismounted to confirm.
24. Chélini, *Thèse*, IV, 39.
25. MGH SS *in usum scholarum*, pp.9–10.
26. Details in Congar, *Ecclésiologie*, 79 and n.93.
27. On that see p.99 above. The saints could be relied on to secure forgiveness for what was done on their behalf. Anselm, in the eleventh century, felt this obligation to the patron saints with special intensity; he would not dare, he said, 'to appear before the judgment seat of God with the rights of his see diminished' (quoted by Southern, *Western Society and the Church*, 186).
28. Clarius, *Chronic. St Petri vivi Semonensis* for an.877, ed. L.M. Durun, *Bibliothèque historique de l'Yonne* II, Auxerre etc. 1850–64, 486–7n. Even allowing for the chronicler's bias, it is a damning indictment.
29. Ibid., an.877, p.488: here we must no doubt allow for some favourable bias.
30. Ibid., an. 999.
31. Southern, *Western Society and the Church*, 187.
32. PL 139, 479.
33. From the fifth century, papal decretals took on a style and tone similar to those of imperial rescripts.
34. *prima sedes a nemine iudicatur*; cf. *Lib.Pontif.*, Mansi II, 623, and MGH *Epp.* IV, 296.
35. See J.N.D. Kelly, *The Oxford Dictionary of Popes*, London 1986, 90–1, for whether he should be regarded as Stephen II or Stephen III.
36. The popes, for their part, refused to be admonished in this way: e.g. MGH, *Leg.*, sectio 3, Vol.2, part 2, 522, 25–7.
37. MGH, *Epp.* IV, 137–8.
38. Though see p.221 above.
39. Ibid., 288.
40. Jaffé-Wattenbach, *Regesta Pontificum Romanorum*. Leipzig [2]1885–8, 3564; PL 136, 806.
41. E.g. *Ant.* II, xlviii.
42. PL 139, 479.
43. Duchesne, *Liber Pontificalis*, II, 98–9.

44. MGH SS III, 717.
45. Liutprand, III, 346.
46. R. Glaber, ed. France et al., pp. 198–9, 252–3.
47. For once a well-known gibe by Gibbon seems scarcely an exaggeration. Of John XII he wrote: 'His rapes of virgins and widows had deterred the female pilgrims from visiting the tomb of St Peter, lest, in the devout act, they should be violated by his successor' (ch.49, ed. J.B. Bury, 1898, V, 298; the remark is derived from Liutprand, *Otto*, ch.4).
48. The word 'pope' is the Greek *papas*, Latin *papa*, meaning 'father'. In early times it was used in the West of any bishop, but in the East mainly confined to the Bishop of Alexandria. The restriction of the title to the Bishop of Rome came only very slowly. As late as 998 the Archbishop of Milan was (rebuked for) claiming it, and it was not till 1073 that the use of it was formally restricted to the holders of the Roman see.
49. PL 106, 376.
50. Mansi XIV, 463: *in superstitionis praecipitium omnino labi potuisset.*
51. Letter now lost, but reconstructed on the basis of MGH, *Epp.* V, no.17, pp.228ff.; see Ullmann, *Growth of Papal Government*, 168–9.
52. PL 124, 881–2.
53. In Cheyette, *Lordship and Community*, 114.
54. Mansi, XIX, 423–4.
55. PL 141, 208: *Ep.* 16.
56. MGH, SS III, pp.658ff.; PL 139, 289ff.
57. Ibid., 320.
58. E.g. *Ep.* 192.
59. Or 994 or 995 – the date is uncertain.
60. Richer, *Hist Lib* IV, iv, 89, ed. R. Latouche, pp.290–2.
61. R. and C. Brooke, *Popular Religion in the Middle Ages*, 53.
62. For evidence and details see Ullmann, *Carolingian Renaissance*, 76–7.
63. Theodulph of Orléans forbids even a mother or sister, though he admits that they are allowed by the canons (PL 105, 195).
64. Ullmann, *Carolingian Renaissance*, 35ff., and McKitterick, *Frankish Church*, 81.
65. For references and details see McKitterick, *Frankish Church*, Ch.3.
66. Cf. the title of the twelfth sermon by Atto of Vercelli: 'The same sermon abbreviated, lest the common people should be bored (or disgusted)' – *ne vulgares fastidiarentur*, PL 134, 849.
67. See Ratherius of Verona, PL 136, 563, quoting a traditional document.
68. It is significant that when Alcuin gives a list like this, he insists that the life to come and its rewards and punishments should be presented first (MGH *Epp.* III, p.110).
69. John 8.59 or 10.31.
70. E.g. Mercier, XIV *Homélies*, 200.
71. Ibid., 162, 164; for alternative equivalents in Hrabanus Maurus see Neale, *Mediaeval Preachers and Mediaeval Preaching*, London 1856, 43.
72. As we have seen (p. 38), a good deal of apocryphal material was used as the basis for sermons, often without any indication of its not being biblical, or

even from the so-called Apocrypha. See e.g. Aelfric I, Sermon IV, 'The Assumption of St John the Apostle', or XXXI, 'The Passion of St Bartholomew', or XXXVIII, 'The Nativity of St Andrew'.

73. Cf. e.g. Charlemagne's *Admonitio Generalis* 82: 'You [the bishops] are not to allow [the priests] to invent and preach to the people new and unlawful things according to their own judgment' (MGH *Leg.* II *Capit.Reg.Franc.* I).

74. Aelfric I, 138, cf. 142: 'He could have spoken, had he willed; he was as wise when he was one day old as he was when he was thirty years.'

75. Aelfric II, 328.

76. Ibid., Sermon XXI.

77. E.g. Hrabanus Maurus, in Neale, *Mediaeval Preachers* (n.71), 32 and 38.

78. Cf. e.g. MGH, *Cap.* I, p. 174, 813, and MGH, *Epp.* IV, 182–5; also Theodore of Orléans, PL 105, 200, XXVIII, and C. de Clercq, *La Législation religieuse Franque*, Appendix IX, 369, xiii, where it is stated that priests incapable of preaching should just adjure the faithful: 'Do penitence, do not commit adultery, do not kill, do not covet your neighbour's possessions, love your neighbour as yourself.' See also Ratherius of Verona: 'If he knows how, let him in his preaching carefully give instruction to the people entrusted to him about the Creed and the Lord's Prayer. If not, let him at least hold to it and believe it [sc. the Lord's Prayer and the Creed 'according to the orthodox tradition']' (PL 136, 563).

79. Imbart de la Tour suggests areas of from one and a half to seven square miles, with populations of between 150 and 600 souls (*Revue Historique* LXIII, 1897, 12, etc.). A parish might sometimes include two or three villages or hamlets, and occasionally a priest be responsible for more than one parish.

80. Where the distance was very great, priests might meet to collect the oils at some suitably placed monastery or large church.

81. E.g. *Manuel* II, 11, pp. 184ff., 189ff.

82. Most, but not all; Imbart de la Tour probably overestimated the proportion.

83. The contemptuous attitude a landowner might adopt in the matter is shown by the following words one of them addressed to the bishop: 'I have a fellow here, a sort of clerk, whom I have brought up and who used to be a serf of mine; maybe I bought him from someone. I want you to ordain him as a priest for me' (quoted by U. Stutz, *Geschichte der kirchlichen Benefizialwesens*, 1895, 238 n. 7). The contemptuous *clericio* is hard to render adequately.

84. E.g. the Canons of Edgar (959–975) suggest that some priests were working as professional entertainers and singers in taverns. The shady business dealings on the part of some priests, to which many capitularies bear witness, were no doubt motivated by a desire to make money and so rise in society (cf. e.g. MGH, *Cap.* I, p. 237, c.2, and p. 244, c.26).

85. Since serfdom was regarded as a source of impurity, and therefore as incompatible with priesthood, serfs were supposed to be given their freedom before they were ordained. Even when this was done, however (which was by no means always), it did not stop the lord's continuing to treat the ordained man as a serf. Cf. what was said earlier about the impossibility of a peasant's ever becoming noble.

86. See Agobard in PL 104, 138–9, as cited and discussed in Stutz, *Geschichte* (n. 83 above), 238; cf. also 277.

87. See the astonishing story of priestly ignorance of Latin in RS, Vol. I, 304. This suggests that gross clerical ignorance was still a serious matter in 1222, and abundant evidence from bishops' and archdeacons' reports makes clear that it was a grave problem from one end of the Middle Ages to the other.

88. See Vauchez, p.126 above.

89. This is the more understandable since they were expected to perform many rites, e.g. the exorcizing of cattle, the ringing of church bells against approaching storms, or the solemn cursing of plagues of caterpillars or locusts, to the accompaniment of the sprinkling of holy water, which cannot have been altogether easy to distinguish from entirely non-Christian practices.

90. In particular they were expected to recite the (monastic) offices daily in church, and even to recite them privately when away from their parish churches.

    Chrodegang, Bishop of Metz from 742 to 766, had reformed his cathedral clergy and imposed a quasi-monastic discipline upon them, including the recitation of the offices, and his example was widely followed. In a capitulary (probably of 802), Charlemagne sought to extend the recitation of the office to all the clergy (MGH *Leg. Capit. Reg. Fran.* I, p. 106), and at a council in Aix this requirement was explicitly formalized (MGH, Leg. Sect. iii Conc. II. i, p. 408, and cf. 406). Subsequent councils (e.g. Mainz, 813; Tours, 813; Rome, 826) insisted on the 'canonical' life for all priests, and the Roman synod actually forbade the existence of churches without a priest to say the office. Later councils added the obligation of making up the office in private where that was necessary. Alcuin had already deplored failure to say the office on the part of the clergy (if PL 101, 499 is by him), and Hincmar threw his weight behind the relevant enactments, his teaching being frequently attributed by later writers to a non-existent Council of Nantes (see further PL 89, 1069 and the discussion in Salmon, *Breviary*, 9ff., though readers are warned that his citation of sources there is decidedly erratic).

91. Cf. the Council of Avignon of 1209 on the subject.

92. E.g. PL 96, 1377.

93. E.g. PL 96, 1365–6.

94. See the discussion of the matter in Coulton, *Village*, 260 n. 3.

95. Cf. Liutprand's description of a priest: 'Of short stature and swarthy complexion, boorish, hairy, intractable, rough, shaggy, wild, uncouth, fond of mad strife, and with ... no regard for right' (*Antapod.* V, xxxii). Even allowing for Liutprand's lofty attitudes, it is significant that such a description, which recalls the typical picture of the peasant given on pp.149–50 above, was not implausible.

96. Cf. e.g. Agobard, PL 104, 134, or Hincmar, PL 125, 1049.

97. Vauchez, *Spiritualité du Moyen Age*, 13.

98. McKitterick, *Frankish Church*, 81, describes as 'vacuous' the judgment which she admits is often passed to the effect that 'the chief shortcoming of the Carolingian reform was its failure to penetrate the mass of the population'. In the light of research by her and others, the judgment may need to be modified, but in the light of the evidence as a whole, was preaching quite as effective an instrument, at any rate in the case of ordinary people, as she suggests?

99. Fichtenau, *Carolingian Empire*, 170.

100. As explained on p. x, the word Religious (with a capital R) is used in this book, as it was in the Middle Ages, to differentiate all those, male or female, who lived under monastic vows, from other men and women, whether secular or clerical. Men in monasteries, for example, were known as *viri religiosi*; the significance of this terminology is discussed on p.283 below.

101. The historical existence of St Benedict has been doubted, even by some quite conservative scholars. However, the Rule appears to belong to roughly the traditional date, and the author of it will be referred to here as Benedict, without prejudice to the historical question.

102. Rule II. 2.

103. One of the things which had driven the original ascetics out into the wilds was their eagerness to fight the Devil, who was believed especially inclined to inhabit desert places.

104. Cf. the term *abbacomes* or *abbicomes*, e.g in Gerbert's *Letters* (ed. Havet 17), and see H.P. Lattin's edition, 64 n.4.

105. Abbacies and other senior monastic positions were used by ruling families as means of providing for their members.

106. Other important reform movements began at Brogne (probably in 913/4), Gorze (933) and Camaldoli (1012). Cluny itself owed a great deal to reform movements at Beaune and St Martin of Autun.

107. As we have seen, the relationship between the bishops and the monasteries in their dioceses was a sensitive and delicate issue at this period.

108. By 994, as a result of the great reputation of Cluny, some thirty-five monasteries formed an ill-defined confederation under its guidance, but it is only later, when this confederation had become an organized body, that one can speak of a religous order in the modern sense.

109. *laus perennis*: the words mean 'perpetual praise', and in some religious houses they were interpreted literally, the community being organized into three or more choirs which worked a shift system to ensure that 'the sound of praise was never silent'.

110. A. Schulte, *Der Adel und die deutsche Kirche im Mittelalter*, Freiburg im Breisgau [2]1922, 3.

111. MGH., SS III, p.54.

112. E.g. Odo, PL 133, 554 and see p.195 above.

113. Southern, *Western Society and the Church*, 227.

114. In Knowles and Obolensky, *The Middle Ages*, 120.

115. *conversi* or *monachi laici*; they seldom became priests, sat apart from the clerics in choir, wore beards and often performed tasks as altar-servers or candle-bearers which were later undertaken by lay brothers; lay brothers as a category, however, were unknown at this date.

116. Cf. Bernard, PL 183, 333ff.

117. Holmes, *Daily Living*, 125, speaks of their seeking privacy, but the word needs careful definition in this context. As we have seen, mediaeval life offered almost no privacy, and the cloister was hardly an exception. The Religious ate together, slept together in dormitories, worshipped and did the household work together; and had little opportunity for personal privacy in the modern sense, even when engaged in private prayer or study.

118. Whatever the situation had been earlier, by this time monks did no agri-

cultural work except in times of exceptional crisis. As a rather later commentary on the Rule put it: 'it amounts to nothing more than shelling the new beans, or rooting out weeds that choke the good plants in the garden; sometimes making loaves in the bakery' (PL 149, 676). The really hard work was done by serfs, and it says a lot about contemporary attitudes that they could be described as *contemptibiles personae* (*Life of Oswald*, ed. J.Raine, *The Historians of the Church of York and Its Archbishops*, I, RS, 1879, 424).

119. The *horarium* varied according to the season and the liturgical calendar, but monks rose between 1.30 and 2.30 a.m. and, apart from a siesta in summer, were busy until bedtime at sundown, 6.30 – 8.30 p.m. By our period sleep was suspect in many monastic circles. Cf. the statement in the Life of Wala: 'The longer we slumber the less we are alive; for while we are slaves of sleep we are dead though we live.'

120. E.g. Ps.119(118).164, 'Seven times a day I have given praise to thee', or Ps.91(92).2–3, 'It is good … to show forth thy mercy in the morning, and thy truth in the night.' For the biblical basis see Alcuin, MGH, *Epp.* IV, 304.

121. The feast of All Souls gained currency through Abbot Odilo of Cluny, who commanded its observance in all the houses of his congregation in 998.

122. At this period it was common for priests to say mass several times in a day.

123. Most of the monks had to have the texts by heart on account of the scarcity of books and the poor lighting.

124. The *horarium* still allowed some four or five hours daily for private study and prayer, in all houses, but in many cases that must have been an optimum, rather than an actual, figure.

125. How large, it is difficult to say, in view of the chroniclers' chronic tendency to exaggerate grossly where their own houses were concerned. Before 850 many houses seem to have had in excess of a hundred professed monks, in addition to the servants. If the numbers went down in the century or so which followed, they no doubt picked up again as the result of the reform movement. In the tenth century monasteries were quite numerous, but still relatively few by later standards.

126. Knowles, *Monastic Order*, 14, points out that the Rule will have been the only book that many Religious really knew.

127. Such friendships were often entirely innocent and were highly thought of, cf. e.g. Adhémar of Chabannes, PL 141, 73. For homosexuality as such, see e.g. Alcuin, MGH *Epp.* IV.294, and cf.Pognon, *L'An Mille*, 201–2. Heer, *Charlemagne and His World*, quotes a revealing passage from a letter of Alcuin to a male correspondent: 'If only, like Habakkuk, I could be translated to your presence! How swiftly I would sink into your arms, how my eagerly pursed lips would kiss not only your eyes, ears and mouth but also every single finger and toe, not once but over and over again.' Were these, Heer asks, some of the 'pigs of unchastity' about which Alcuin confessed to the pope in his retirement?

128. See e.g. Alcuin, MGH, *Epp.* IV, 294; Odo, PL 133, 568; Richer, MGH, SS XXV, 265; and cf. VIII, 532. Also MGH, SS XI, 535, and Odo's *Life of Burchard*, PL 143, 849. However, this aspect of things should not be exaggerated for the period of monastic reform from around the middle of the tenth century.

129. The remarks of Mecklin, *Passing of the Saint*, 59, on this matter are worth looking at even if he exaggerates somewhat.
130. For example, a monastery might be given an estate which was under obligation to provide troops or specified services to a lay lord; and since Religious, like bishops, felt an obligation to preserve and extend the patrimony of their patron saint(s), they too pressed their rights, and often became involved in litigation. They were great, and not always very scrupulous, litigators. However, contact with the outside world arising from teaching lay children disappeared in the ninth century, when the reforming statutes of Benedict of Aniane forbade monasteries to educate any but their own novices.
131. Hauck, *Kirchengeschichte*, III, 343–4.
132. Kenneth Clark, *Civilisation*, London 1969, 17.
133. Morris, *Discovery of the Individual*, 32. Cf. Dom Ursmer Berlière: 'The Benedictine abbey was a little state which could serve as a model to the new Christian society which was arising from the fusion of conquered and conquering races, a state which had religion for its foundation, work restored to honour as its support, and a new intellectual and aristocratic culture as its crown' (*L'Ordre Monastique*, Paris [2]1924, 41).
134. PL 144, 990.
135. Although the words *religio* and *conversio* were used in more than one sense, by far the commonest meaning of them in the monastic writers was 'the monastic condition' and 'taking monastic vows'. Such a restriction of the terms speaks for itself. In accordance with Jerome's teaching, *conversio* was believed to be a second baptism which washed away all previous sin (see Odo, PL 133, 554, etc.). An unhistorical age believed monasticism to be an apostolic ordinance, coeval with, and essential to, the church, the apostles themselves having been the first monks.
136. AA SS, Oct. VI, 277ff. He so abhors violence that he refuses to fight with weapons; if attackers force him to respond, he twirls his sword round and pretends to fight, but takes care not to wound anyone. Fortunately, miracles always seem to come to his rescue. Cf. Vauchez, *Spiritualité*, 56: 'Mais qu'on ne s'y trompe pas: on ne trouve chez Saint Géraud aucun idéal de sainteté laïque.' As a result of illness at one time, which prevented more active pursuits, Gerald had been more than usually given to reading and study, and is thus in any case untypical.
137. This was known as dying *sub cucullo* (under the cowl, cf. e.g. Life of Burchard, PL 143, 859); a sizeable gift or legacy to the monastery was normally involved, and those who did not in fact die sometimes demanded it back.
138. As we have seen, many of the penances imposed on individuals were so burdensome as to be impossible to fulfil; and when heavy corporate penances were imposed, as in 923, the situation could not have been coped with had it not been possible to off-load a large part of the burden on to the Religous. See Southern, *Western Society and the Church*, 225–6, and cf. Peter Damian in PL 144, 323.
139. PL 182, 889.
140. Cf. Bernard's quotation of Phil.3.20 in PL 183, 1045.

141. Cf. e.g. the description of Cluny by Peter Damian, beginning 'I saw a paradise ...' (PL 144, 374).
142. In connection with all this, it is important to remember how imminent the end of this world seemed at the time.
143. See the remarks of Vauchez, *Spiritualité*, 44–5.

15. The Higher Spirituality

1. Augustine, *Confessions* I, 1.
2. See *Thes Ling Lat* III s.v. and Leclerq, *Love of Learning*, 37f.
3. For these and similar terms see e.g. Gregory's *Moralia*, the source of most early mediaeval teaching on the matter, especially 27, 42; 6,40ff. and 32,1.
4. Bernard of Clairvaux, PL 182, 942. For the two kinds of compunction, see e.g. Grimlaic, PL 103, 617–18.
5. The habit was not as uniform at this time as it later became, but it was always extremely sober and often somewhat threadbare.
6. Such teaching derived from Evagrius; and through Cassian, who was constantly read aloud to the Religious, it was influential in the early Middle Ages. See especially Evagrius, *On The Eight Evil Thoughts*, PG 40, 1271ff., and cf. Clebsch, *Christianity in European History*, 75ff.
7. Cf. e.g. Rule 3, 4, 5, 7 (steps 1 and 2) or 33: 'It is not lawful for monks to have either their bodies or their wills at their own disposal.'
8. Luke 14.26; cf. Matt.10.37.
9. Acts 4.32ff.
10. Cf., out of many texts, Matt.19.12, 21, 23–24; Mark 8.34ff.; 10.21, 28ff.; Luke 6.20; 9.57ff.; II Cor.6.4ff.
11. We have already seen (p.250 n.10) that the Middle Ages did not fully appreciate Paul's highly nuanced use of the word *flesh*.
12. PL 103, 356f.
13. Cf. E.Vacandard, *La Vie de St Bernard* I, Paris 1927, 19, 45f., 76f.
14. Gen.1.31.
15. §73, *recto cursu perveniamus ad creatorem deum*.
16. Cf. the well known description of Benedict as *scienter nescius et sapienter indoctus*, Gregory, PL 66,126.
17. E.g. Matt.5.8, and note the comment of the Jewish scholar C.G. Montefiore on it: 'The meaning of seeing God would be no less and no more than what the Psalmist meant by the phrase (Pss.11.7 and 24.4): the highest bliss. To see God is to be near him, and to know him and to rejoice in him, in one' (*The Synoptic Gospels*, London 1927, II, 38).
18. Fathers of unimpeachable orthodoxy had frequently spoken of 'God's having become human (in the Incarnation) in order that we might become divine'.
19. Abbot Butler, *Benedictine Monachism*, 287, reckoned four hours' reading and three and a half hours for the *opus dei* in the summer *horarium*.
20. The monastic day began at or before 2 a.m., so even in summer-time a good deal of the liturgy must have been conducted against a background of impressive architecture dimly picked out by candlelight.
21. The attitude often taken toward the traditional liturgy could almost be

described as 'fundamentalist'; no more than the Bible was it thought a suitable subject for critical analysis. From a slightly later period cf. e.g. Rupert of Deutz, PL 170, 11–12.

22. PL 49, 959ff.; the whole section deserves to be consulted.
23. PL 139, 463ff.
24. MGH SS VIII, 384; similar references could be multiplied.
25. For this cf. e.g. MGH, SS VII, 193ff., for Anselm on Bishop Baldrich.
26. For a brief discussion, with bibliography, see *Rule of Benedict*, 410–12.

16. The Secular World and Lay Life

1. Cf. the reservations of Alcuin in such passages as MGH, *Epp.* IV, 242, 245, 289, 293, 309, or 344.
2. A carved capital at Civaux, in Poitou, vividly portrays what happened to lay people who believed they could remain celibate in the world. Sirens dragged them into the sea (see *I Laici*, 491–2).
3. Eriugena, for example, held that there would have been no need for marriage apart from the Fall. As late as 1662, marriage is said in the Book of Common Prayer to be only 'for such persons as have not the gift of continency' (Introduction to the Marriage Service).
4. For some qualifications to this general picture, see N. Huyghebaert in *I Laici*, 346–89, though notice also the more sombre picture given in the same volume by R. Bultot, who suggests that many theologians were almost Manichaean in their attitude to sex, and regarded the sexual appetite as itself sinful. See also the very important article by Père Toubert listed in the Bibliography. Many of the points he makes in connexion with lay spirituality are not without justice, though it remains doubtful whether they substantially modify the picture given here. Ths issue largely depends on one's definition of spirituality.
5. See Andrew of Fleury, *Vita Gauzlini* c. 56. ed. R.H. Bautier, Paris 1969, 101, and cf. Duby, *Medieval Marriage*, 51f.
6. Especially in his *Adversus Jovinianum* and *Contra Helvidium*, in both of which he uses quite unbridled language.
7. Toubert, 'Théorie du mariage', 252.
8. Though cf. eg. Odo of Cluny, PL 133, 568–9 and Guibert of Nogent, PL 156, 589–90.
9. Nevertheless, there was something of a revival of *Friedelehe* known as marriage *more danico* in the ninth and tenth centuries. While opposed to it, the church in many cases tolerated it as being the lesser of two evils; Ralph Glaber, for example, declined to judge it too harshly on the ground that something like it was practised by Old Testament figures such as Jacob. From Augustine to Aquinas a similar argument was used to defend the continued existence of prostitution (PL 32, 1000 and S.T II IIae qu.10, art.11); Pope Leo I could be quoted as recognizing the existence of concubinage (PL 54, 1204).
10. The number seven was problematic, and despite a number of rather desperate guesses, theologians were hard put to it to provide any biblical or other grounds for it.
11. The teaching of the Isidorean Decretals, particularly that of Benedictus Levita,

played a considerable part here; and the role of the clergy in checking proposed marriages for possible incest, and registering marriages when concluded, made the transition easier.

12. Cf. e.g. Charlemagne's *Capitulare Missorum* of 802 (MGH, *Capit.* I. p. 98) and Burchard (PL 140, 958). At one time the blessing of the marriage bed or bed chamber (*thalamus*) when the couple were ready to enter it was a common practice, but for obvious reasons it gradually fell into desuetude.

13. Cf. e.g. Pope Nicholas I, PL 119, 980.

14. Burchard's citation of Pope Hormisdas in PL 140, 816 is false.

15. E.g. by Hincmar, who also claimed that without the *nuptiale mysterium* a marriage was not valid in the eyes of God. It is not clear, however, that such *mysterium* depended on a nuptial blessing.

16. MGH, *Capit Reg, Franc.* II, 425.

17. Cp. Wasserschleben, *Bussordnungen*, 582, and Schmitz, *Bussbücher*, 284. At this stage the church had not succeeded in reconciling its teaching on the absolute indissolubility of marriage with its recognition that certain circumstances might justify *discidium*, solemn and official rupture. Burchard, for example, recognizes the right of a bishop to dissolve marriages on a number of grounds, besides incest which made such rupture compulsory.

18. PL 89, 1289–90.

19. A.Friedberg, *Corpus Juris Canonici* I, Leipzig 1879, xii qu i, vii.

20. PL 105, 198.

21. In Charlemagne's time there had been rather more, for example his minister Einhard.

22. As Liutprand makes clear, for example, in his account of a speech by Duke Otto (*Antap* I, xxvi). On the other hand, since we get such rare opportunities to penetrate the minds of lay people of the time, it is right to mention two cases of a different sort. In 895 when Odo, the king of France, recaptured the fortified monastery of St Vedast of Arras, he made straight for the chapel and prostrated himself before the saint's tomb; and when the French king was at Tours on the eve of St Martin, Fulk II of Anjou (942–960) braved mockery from his peers by absenting himself to join in chanting the offices, clad in a monk's habit (*Ann. Vedastini*, ann. 895, and P.Lauer, *Louis IV d'Outremer*, 235 n.4).

23. For contemporary recognition of their minority-status see Ullmann, *Carolingian Renaissance*, 186.

24. *vulgus oberrans*, PL 156, 685.

25. MGH *Epp.* IV, *Ep.* 305, p.465.

26. Cf. e.g. Delaruelle in *I Laici*, 559.

27. Cf. the words in the canon *memento, Domine … omnium circumstantium*.

28. Secondary certainly to fasting and almsgiving. See his *Thèse* III, 19, and also his remarks in *Revue d'Histoire de l'Église de France* XLII, 1956, esp. 173. There are similar remarks by Riché in the Introduction to *Dhuoda*, 30.

29. In Carolingian times there had been quite a high level of devotion in some aristocratic families, but the circumstances which led to a decline in lay literacy also led to decline in devotion (cf. Southern in Neill and Weber, *Layman.* 108).

30. Cf. J. Trénel, *L'Ancien Testament et la Langue Française du Moyen Age*, Paris 1904.

31. Gregory, PL 76, 657, has a slightly different classification.

32. See e.g. Congar in *I Laici*, 83ff., and F.Chatillon in *Revue du Moyen Age Latin* 10, 1954, 169ff.
33. Cf. McKitterick, *Carolingians and the Written Word*.
34. Sumption, *Pilgrimage*, 267–8.

17. Kingship, Government and Religion

1. See p.221 above.
2. He and his predecessors back to 639 are known as the *rois fainéants* (do-nothing kings). The office of Mayor of the Palace (*maior domus*) was one peculiar to the Merovingian court. The holder of the office was primarily the administrator of the royal estates, which, with the decline of the Roman system, had become the chief source of revenue. He was thus responsible for the maintenance of the royal household and army, with the powers to command which that required. He often presided over the tribunal and commanded the army, and was in fact the head of the government. The office became hereditary in the house of Arnulf and Pepin.
3. MGH, SS I, 312.
4. For example, there appears to have been no ecclesiastical rite when Charlemagne's son Charles became king of Neustria in 790, or when Louis the Pious or his son Charles the Bald became sub-kings; and no one, not even Hincmar, challenged the legitimacy of their kingship. The Frankish bishops allowed the practice of royal anointing to fall into abeyance after 751. See further J. Nelson in *SCH* VII, 58.
5. On that see Nelson in Sawyer and Wood, *Early Mediaeval Kingship*, 58ff.
6. See Wallace-Hadrill, in *Trends*, 26, where he writes that the Old Testament 'was the biblical background to Carolingian kingship'. He adds: 'Perhaps if we knew the Old Testament as well as the Carolingians did, we should find their royal activity less confusing.' The example he cites from Hincmar (PL 126, 22) shows in what detail the Old Testament model could be pressed.
7. Just as you could not be an Israelite without being a worshipper of Yahweh, you could not be a Frank without being a Christian.
8. Charlemagne was referred to as *vicarius Christi* and as *vicarius dei*. Lupus of Ferrières wrote to Charles the Bald: 'Who does not know that you stand in the place (*vicem gerere*) of God?'
9. Wallace-Hadrill, in Smalley, *Trends*, 31.
10. Cf. PL 96, 1363–6.
11. See Kantorowicz, *Laudes Regiae*.
12. PL 101, 919ff.
13. For an extended tenth-century account of the conduct expected see Abbo, PL 139, 477, and MGH, *Epp*. IV, p. 503.
14. He bore children by at least eleven women, to some of whom he was not formally married in any sense. He dismissed his first wife and married another. He kept a number of concubines, by whom he had a series of children, and in his reluctance to see his beautiful daughters leave him for marriage, and no doubt for political reasons too (for these see Duby, *Knight, Lady and Priest*, 42). He colluded with numerous illlicit love affairs on their part, finding advan-

tageous positions for their illegitimate children. It would be interesting to know how conscious he was of the extent to which all this fell short of Christian standards and how seriously the Christian tradition took such matters. Einhardt, his friend and first biographer, mentions the concubines and their children without remark, though he makes clear that the king recognized the immorality of his daughters' conduct, and the unfortunate experiences to which it led (if indeed the relevant two sentences are from Einhardt's hand. For a discussion of the manuscript evidence see the Life, ed.H.W.Garrod and R.B.Mowat, viii and 23).

15. Cf. his title *'rector* of the Christian people', and Cathwulf's words to him, 'you are the vice-gerent of God (*in vice dei*) and the bishop is in the second place only, the vice-gerent of Christ' (*Lib. Carolini*, Preface, and MGH, *Epp.* IV, 503. See also pp.221ff. above).

16. *episcopalis unanimitas*, Hincmar, PL 125, 757.

17. *Rer.Gest.Saxon. Libri Tres*, ed. H.E. Lohmann, revised P. Hirsch, Hanover 1935, 64–5.

18. *Annales de St Bertin*, ed. F. Grât, J. Vielliard and S. Clémencet, Paris 1964, p.221.

19. See e.g. Alcuin, *Epistles*, ed. Jaffé, 78, or the comment of Adhémar of Chabannes in connexion with the accession of Hugh Capet in 987: 'His uncle Charles wanted to get the kingdom, but was unable to do so because God chose a better ruler' (*Receuil des Histoires des Gaules et de la France*, X, 1440).

20. When, exceptionally, Henry I of east Francia refused consecration, he was referred to as 'a sword without a hilt'. The ninefold form of anointing (head, chest, on and between both shoulders, both elbows and palms of both hands) was certainly current in the mid-eleventh century, but it is not altogether clear when it reached that form.

21. *Libellus contra Wenilonem*, ch.3, MGH, *Capit.* II, p.451.

22. See the careful article by Janet Nelson in *EHR* 92, 1977, 241–79, and the literature referred to in it.

23. The earliest of them were composed by Hincmar, the Archbishop of Reims. The crowning of the west Frankish kings came to be a prerogative of that see.

24. See Nelson in Sawyer and Wood, *Early Mediaeval Kingship*, 50ff.

25. See Ullmann, *Growth of Papal Government*, 154–5.

26. See e.g. Neill and Weber, *Layman*, 95, and for the subject in general Kantorowicz, and Leyser ch.7; for representations of Charles the Bald and others see Hubert, Porcher and Volbach, Part 2.

27. See p.220 above. Although Hincmar, for example, stressed the constitutive character of the anointment of Charles the Bald in 848, he did not cast doubt on his royal title before that date, or on the titles of other unanointed kings – an example, perhaps, of the inconsistencies and loose ends referred to above.

28. *alius vir*, cf. I Sam.10.6.

29. PL 120, 1609.

30. Mansi XVIII, Appendix septima, 172.

31. Wallace-Hadrill, *Trends*, 28.

32. Ps.105 (104).15 and I Chron.16.22; and see e.g. II Sam.1.14, 16; 19.21; Ps.18.50 (17.51); 2.2ff.; 20.6 (19.7), noting the fate that was said to await those who disobeyed the command.

33. When Charles the Bald had his queen Irmintrud anointed and crowned in 866, there was no secret about the fact that part of the purpose was to enable her to bear him more, and more satisfactory, sons (MGH, *Capit.* II, p.455). The crowning and anointing of queens became a regular practice; apart from childbearing, there were often important functions for which they needed to be made ready, in connexion with the control of the treasury, for example, and various political activities.

34. English monarchs 'touched' for scrofula down to the time of Queen Anne in the early eighteenth century. Samuel Johnson was touched in 1712 on the advice of the distinguished physician Sir John Floyer.

35. It is unclear whether such supposed royal powers were a hangover from the sacrality which may have hedged Frankish kings in pre-Christian days. In any case they were credited by such a highly orthodox figure as Alcuin: 'We read that the king's goodness equals (*est*) the welfare of the whole people, victory of the host, mild climate, fertility, male offspring [note the implication] and health' (MGH, *Epp.Kar.Aev.* II, 51). Cf. the similar list in Jonas of Orléans, *Instit.Reg* III, Reviron, p.141. It even includes calm seas. Such claims seem particularly to have impressed the rural population.

36. And cf. e.g. Cathwulf, PL 96, 1363ff.

37. Cf. already Augustine, *Ep.* 185: '*aliter ... quia homo est, aliter quia etiam rex est*'.

38. Rom.13.1–2; see also Titus 3.1; I Peter 2.13.

39. So e.g. Abbo, PL 139, 178, and Liutprand, PL 136, 821.

40. Nelson, *SCH* VII, 53.

41. E.g. Ratherius of Verona, PL 136, 224ff.

42. 'The heart of the king is in the hand of God' (Prov.21.1). Yet even if, as may have been the case, the sacring of a king was held to convey an indelible character, that did not guarantee his throne for life, any more than the indelible character of episcopacy guaranteed a bishop against deposition (see Nelson, *EHR* 92, 1977, 243).

43. Boussard, *Civilization of Charlemagne*, 117. Their lack of hereditary legitimacy to some extent undermined the position of the Capetians, despite the efforts of their propagandists, which included the claim that they could cure leprosy, and also the claim that the ampulla from which they and their predecessors had been anointed was brought to earth by the Holy Spirit. For this see Abbo and Helgaldus.

44. The enthronement, sometimes repeated at crown-wearings, was meant to present the king as high above the people, in a sublimity shared by no one else. It was always the grand finale of a coronation ceremony, and the directions laid down that there must be a *thronus excelsus* 'so that the king may be clearly beholden of the people' (see plate 3).

45. Ullmann, *Carolingian Renaissance*, 13. The word 'alienation', however, should not be taken as necessarily implying that people felt oppressed or suppressed by the monarchs.

46. James, *Origins of France*, 123. This reflects the fact that the isolation of communities, and the poor and slow means of communication, made the modern detailed type of supervision and detection impossible. Detailed regulation of life by governments was simply not an option.

47. Cf. e.g. Alcuin: the nobles 'must lead the people in justice and piety, be as fathers to widows, orphans and the poor ... defenders and guardians of the churches of Christ, for "a people is uplifted by their fairness" '.
48. The former of these movements belongs to the very end of our period, the latter to the eleventh century. The details are obscure. In the Midi, where the process of political decomposition was particularly marked, the bishops and the common people, with the support of the crown, held large and enthusiastic assemblies, in the presence of powerful relics, designed to persuade the nobility to undertake to refrain from attacks on the goods of the church and the poor. Despite opposition from the middling nobility, the movement spread north, and in the early eleventh century there developed the Truce of God movement, which sought, among other things, to ban fighting on certain days of the week and at certain periods of the church's year. While they represented a genuine desire for peace on the part of many churchmen, these movements were the product of complicated political motives and manoeuvring (on which see e.g. Duby, *Three Orders*, and Jedin and Dolan, *History*) and in the end met with little success.

18. Conclusion

1. Cantwell Smith, *Meaning and End of Religion*.
2. The phrase is one coined by R.G. Collingwood to describe the ultimate object of the historian as he understood it. It is now generally agreed that his programme was over-optimistic.
3. It would need to be a voluminous writer; cf. e.g. J. Devisse's great three-volume study of Hincmar. Perhaps, as Herbert Butterfield suggested, the historical novel is the best vehicle for such attempts. See his book *The Historical Novel*, Cambridge 1924.
4. On this question see especially C.M. Radding. I am grateful to Prof. Karen Fuson of North-Western University, Evanston, herself a Piagetian developmental psychologist, for illuminating discussions on this matter.
5. Cf. the later part of Anselm's Prayer to St Paul, e.g.: 'And you, Jesus, are you not also a mother? ... Truly Lord, you are a mother' (Schmitt, III, 33ff., esp. 40–1).
6. See e.g. S.W. Sykes, *The Identity of Christianity*, London 1984, and Sarah Coakley, *Christ without Absolutes*, London 1988. A brief discussion will be found in *A New Dictionary of Christian Theology*, ed. Alan Richardson and John Bowden, London 1983, s.v. 'Continuity'.
7. For example, Paul's argument against the desirability of marriage in I Cor. 7 springs from it; cf. v. 31b, 'the world as we know it is passing away'.

Index of Subjects

Index of Names

It proved impracticable to provide an entry for every name referred to in the text. In the case of figures mentioned very frequently, such as Charlemagne, Augustine or Alcuin, only the most significant references to them are listed here.